Research in
Religious Education

The publication of this work has been supported by grants from Westhill College and the Book Publishing Committee of Trinity College, Carmarthen.

Research in Religious Education

edited by
Leslie J. Francis
William K. Kay
and
William S. Campbell

Gracewing.

SMYTH & HELWYS
PUBLISHING, INC.

First published in 1996
jointly by

Gracewing	Smyth & Helwys Publishing, Inc
Fowler Wright Books	6316 Peake Rd
2 Southern Ave,	Macon
Leominster	Georgia 31210-3960
Herefordshire HR6 0QF	USA

UK ISBN   0 85244 342 0   US ISBN   1 57312 053 7

Typesetting by Reesprint
Radley, Oxfordshire, OX14 3AJ

Printed by Redwood Books
Trowbridge, Wiltshire, BA14 8RN

Contents

Foreword

Research in Religious Education celebrates the considerable achievements which have been made in empirical studies in religious education since the early 1960s. Key researchers in the field from England, Scotland, Wales, Ireland, Germany, Finland, Switzerland and Israel have come together to provide an up-to-date map of the field, to illustrate the variety of ways in which different research perspectives can illuminate the practice of religious education, and to shape future research.

The essayists offer their work as a *Festschrift* to acknowledge the significant contribution and stimulus given to research in religious education by the pioneering work of the Revd Dr John E. Greer. This *Festschrift* marks the retirement of Dr Greer from the post of Reader in Religious Education in the University of Ulster at Coleraine.

Research in Religious Education also signals the collaboration between two new centres designed to promote research in this field. The editorial work has taken place in these centres. The Centre for Theology and Education was established at Trinity College, Carmarthen, Wales, in 1992. The Centre for Beliefs and Values was established at Westhill College, Selly Oak, Birmingham, England, in 1995.

The editors gratefully acknowledge the vision of the Principals and Governors of Trinity College Carmarthen and Westhill College, Birmingham, in facilitating this book. They also gratefully acknowledge the assistance of Diane Drayson, Teleri James and Anne Rees in shaping the manuscript, Jo Ratcliffe in maintaining the publishing schedule, and Robin Rees in setting the text.

As well as celebrating considerable achievements, *Research in Religious Education* also draws attention to the considerable work which yet remains to be undertaken. It is the editors' sincere hope that these essays will challenge a new generation of scholars to see the possibilities for further research and to grasp the initiative.

After all, good research in religious education leads to good practice in the classroom, and in turn to improved pupil attitudes toward the subject.

Leslie J. Francis
William K. Kay
Trinity College, Carmarthen

William S. Campbell
Westhill College, Birmingham

September, 1995

Overview

Leslie J. Francis

Research in Religious Education brings together the work of thirty-three scholars in twenty-seven distinct chapters. Each chapter earns its place in the volume by being the work of an individual who has undertaken his or her own empirical research in religious education and who knows the strengths and weaknesses in the field. Many of the contributors are veteran scholars who have an established international reputation for excellence in research in religious education. Most of the contributors are already well known through their publications in journals like *British Journal of Religious Education*. Others are younger scholars whose work, as yet less well known, is already beginning to make a significant impact on the field. The fact that so many of the chapters have been co-authored both points to the complexity of the field and demonstrates the clear advantages of collaborative work. At last research in religious education is coming of age and generating a momentum of its own. John Greer, in whose honour the chapters have been assembled, stands tall among that small band of pioneers upon whose initiative and careful scholarship the up and coming generation of researchers in religious education is building.

Taken together, the twenty-seven chapters in *Research in Religious Education* provide a thorough map to contemporary initiatives in the field, together with a unique introduction to the scholars in whose hands these initiatives rest. The original invitation to the contributors invited them to provide either an *overview* of one specific aspect of research in religious education or an *example* of their own research perspective at work. Many of the contributors have achieved both objectives by providing an authoritative and concise review of previous work before demonstrating how a new empirical study builds on that work and extends knowledge beyond

1

what was previously known. In this way many of the chapters present new empirical data published for the first time. Each in its own way is an exemplary model of how research in religious education should be conducted and presented. In their turn these data will stimulate and shape new initiatives both in empirical research and in educational practice. Such studies are both original and archival.

Each chapter has been crafted as an autonomous contribution to knowledge in its own right. In this sense, it matters little in which order the chapters are read. Some readers may choose their own path through the volume, following their own particular interests and concerns. At the same time, the chapters have been presented in a coherent sequence, clustering topics which go naturally hand in hand and allowing new ideas to build on those presented in earlier chapters. The aim of this overview is to provide a brief introduction to each chapter, and to draw attention to the links between the chapters.

Chapter 1 by Leslie J. Francis fulfils two basic functions. It reviews John Greer's major contribution to research in religious education by summarising his extensive series of publications within the context of the main themes he has addressed, including concern with issues like readiness for religion, sixth form religion, moral values, attitude toward religion, rejection of Christianity, religious thinking, Belfast pupils, the divided community of Northern Ireland, religious experience, and qualitative as well as quantitative methods of research. At the same time, this chapter provides a succinct introduction to many of the key topics which have occupied researchers in religious education since the 1960s, since John Greer has systematically engaged with new movements in research as they came into prominence. In turn, John Greer built on, criticised and developed the work of pioneers in the field like Ronald Goldman, Edwin Cox and John Peatling.

In chapter 2 William K. Kay takes the story back behind John Greer's work in order to examine in greater detail the contribution of the five scholars who pioneered the foundations for modern research in religious education in Britain during the 1960s. He reviews Harold Louke's study, *Teenage Religion* (published in 1961), Ronald Goldman's two major books, *Religious Thinking from Childhood to Adolescence* and *Readiness for Religion* (published in 1964 and 1965), Kenneth Hyde's monograph, *Religious Learning in Adolescence* (published in 1965), Edwin Cox's study, *Sixth Form Religion* (published in 1967) and Colin Alves' study, *Religion and the Secondary School* (published in 1968). While each of these studies established patterns for further research, it was Goldman's work which was to prove to be most influential in shaping the future practice of religious education. Goldman's work drew much of its credibility from roots in Piagetian psychology. For this reason chapter 2 also provides an introduction to the issues at stake in this wider field of enquiry.

In chapter 3 David Hay, Rebecca Nye and Roger Murphy draw attention to one of the major areas eclipsed by Ronald Goldman's emphasis on the development of *religious thinking* during childhood and adolescence, namely the development of childhood *spirituality* in a wider sense. This chapter both criticises developmental stage theories for their narrowness and offers a fresh basis for research into childhood spirituality by drawing on established research traditions concerned with religious experience.

In chapter 4 Nicola M. Slee provides a succinct and authoritative overview of research stimulated by James Fowler's theory of faith development. In some senses James Fowler built on Ronald Goldman's research tradition and extended it greatly. Since most of the post-Fowler research has been conducted in the United States of America and remains within unpublished dissertations, Nicola Slee's chapter brings much new material to a wider audience for the first time. Five broad categories of research influenced by Fowler are identified in this chapter. First, there are replication studies which have sought to test or refine Fowler's hypothesised stage development theory. Second, there is a small group of literary studies which have applied Fowler's theory to documentary evidence. Third, there are correlation studies which have examined the relationship between faith development and other variables. Fourth, there are cross-cultural studies which have tested Fowler's hypothesis of cultural invariance. Fifth, there are studies which have examined women's religious development in the light of Fowler's theory.

In chapter 5 Andrew G. McGrady reviews Goldman's research from another perspective. In the first part of the chapter he discusses the two main techniques which have been developed for measuring religious thinking in Piagetian operational terms, namely the semi-clinical interview technique refined by Goldman himself and the pencil and paper multi-choice test, *Thinking about the Bible*, devised subsequently by John Peatling. In the second part of the chapter, Andrew McGrady reports the results of a replication study which used part of Goldman's semi-clinical interview

methodology with Irish Roman Catholic secondary school pupils
and which examined the concurrent validity of a modified version
of the multiple-choice test, *Thinking about the Bible*.

In chapter 6 Karl Ernst Nipkow, Friedrich Schweitzer, Gabriele
Faust-Siehl and Bernd Krupka examine the practical usefulness of
developmental research for promoting religious education in the
classroom. They describe and discuss a classroom research project
conducted between 1988 and 1993 at the Department of Religious
Education, University of Tübingen. Altogether twenty-four lessons of Protestant and Roman Catholic religious education, in
different types of schools and at different age levels, were each
observed by two people, taped, transcribed and subjected to interaction analysis. The aim was to discover how the developmental
status of students is addressed in the praxis of religious education.
As a second strand of the research, the teachers were interviewed.
The aim was to discover how the developmental views of the
teachers affect the ways in which they interact with students.

In chapter 7 K. Helmut Reich introduces the concept of Relational and Contextual Reasoning (RCR) in religious education,
building on his earlier discussion of 'thinking in terms of complementarity'. He argues that relational and contextual reasoning
promotes a better understanding of Christian doctrines and world
views and that it is helpful for developing religious life. He discusses the main characteristics of relational and contextual reasoning and its development in childhood, adolescence and adulthood.
Then he describes initial attempts to introduce relational and
contextual reasoning in the religious education classroom.

In chapter 8 Robert Jackson introduces a different research
tradition and illustrates the strength of ethnographic studies in
religious education. The chapter reports the preliminary results of
a three year series of ethnographic studies conducted by the
Religious Education and Community Project at the University of
Warwick among four religious communities (Christian, Jewish,
Sikh and Muslim), together with related, ongoing curriculum
development work which is being published as the Warwick RE
Project.

In chapter 9 Kalevi Tamminen draws on the rich data assembled
by a series of studies in Finland over two decades from 1974 among
children and adolescents from the age of four to the age of twenty
years. Kalevi Tamminen demonstrates how this rich source of data
can be reanalysed to explore gender differences in religiosity. The
first part of this chapter illustrates the different responses of boys

and girls to religion in both qualitative and quantitative ways. The second part of this chapter employs these data to discuss the different factors and theories which have been advanced to account for observed gender differences in religiosity during childhood and adolescence.

In chapter 10 Susan H. Jones demonstrates a quantitative perspective in the psychology of religious development by exploring the theoretical and empirical relationship between religiosity and self-esteem. She reports on data derived from three samples, comprising 166 pupils between the ages of eight and eleven years, 755 pupils between the ages of thirteen and fourteen years, and 642 pupils between the ages of fifteen and sixteen years. In all three samples, after controlling for sex differences, the data demonstrate a positive correlation between high self-esteem and a favourable attitude toward Christianity.

In chapter 11 Mandy Robbins explores the relationship between religiosity and happiness, employing the Francis Scale of Attitude Toward Christianity and the Oxford Happiness Inventory among a sample of 360 first year undergraduates. The data demonstrate a positive correlation between a favourable attitude toward Christianity and happiness, even after taking into account individual differences in personality. The study provides, therefore, some further evidence on the positive psychological correlates of religiosity during young adulthood.

In chapter 12 Christopher A. Lewis examines the relationship between religiosity and obsessionality, employing the short form of the Francis Scale of Attitude Toward Christianity alongside three measures of obsessional personality traits among a sample of Northern Irish adults. The data demonstrate a positive correlation between a favourable attitude toward Christianity and scores on each of the three measures of obsessional personality traits in the male sample, and two of the obsessional measures in the female sample. The data provide further evidence that a more positive religious attitude is associated with higher scores on measures of obsessional personality traits.

In chapter 13 John M. Lewis builds on a considerable body of recent research concerned with exploring the relationship between personality and individual differences in religiosity. The personality theory employed in this chapter is the three-dimensional model of personality developed by Hans Eysenck and his associates which argues that individual differences can be most adequately and economically described in terms of the three orthogonal dimensions of extraversion, neuroticism and psychoticism. The model also contains a lie scale. Drawing on data from a sample of 12,557 adolescents between the ages of thirteen and fifteen years, John Lewis demonstrates that a more positive attitude toward religious education is associated with lower scores on the psychoticism scale, higher scales on the lie scale and higher scores on the neuroticism scale. There is no significant relationship between extraversion scores and attitude toward religious education.

In chapter 14 Jeff Astley also draws on Eysenck's dimensional model of personality, this time to explore the relationship between A level gospel study and adolescents' images of Jesus among a sample of 279 sixth form students attending a study day at the North of England Institute for Christian Education. The students undertaking A level gospel study located Jesus higher on the extraversion scale, higher on the neuroticism scale and lower on the psychoticism scale than those not taking A level gospel study. These findings are interpreted as indicating that A level gospel study promotes a more human image of Jesus and a lower Christology.

In chapter 15 Harry M. Gibson discusses the issue of Christian fundamentalist belief among adolescents in Scotland and proposes a twelve item scale to measure this construct. A study conducted among 866 adolescents between the ages of eleven and fifteen years supports the reliability and construct validity of the instrument. The results demonstrate that girls record significantly higher scores of Christian fundamentalist belief than boys and that pupils in year nine and year ten record significantly lower scores of Christian fundamentalist belief than pupils in year seven and year eight.

In chapter 16 Peter Fulljames builds on and develops a series of recent studies concerned with science and religion in the world view of adolescents. Using data provided by a sample of 3,427 pupils between the ages of eleven and fifteen years, Peter Fulljames explores the relationship between attitude toward Christianity, conflict between science and religion, creationist belief, and the view that Christianity necessarily involves creationism. The data demonstrate that the view that Christianity necessarily involves creationism has a detrimental influence on attitude toward Christianity among this age group, after taking personal belief in creationism into account. The implications of this finding for religious education are discussed.

In chapter 17 William K. Kay demonstrates the value of reanalysing data from two previously published studies to generate fresh insights into the changes which take place in pupils' attitudes toward religious education and assemblies between the final years of the primary school and the middle years of the secondary school. The data are derived from nearly 5,000 pupils in year six at primary school, reported in *Religion in the Primary School* by Leslie J. Francis, and from over 13,000 pupils in year nine and year ten at secondary school, reported in *Teenage Religion and Values* by Leslie J. Francis and William K. Kay. The reanalysis indicates that, while at primary school pupils prefer school assembly to religious education, at secondary school pupils prefer religious education to assemblies. It is suggested that the reversal is caused by the removal, at secondary level, of those features of assemblies which younger pupils most enjoy and by the tendency for older pupils to evaluate more positively those aspects of school which are related to public examinations and the job market.

In chapter 18 Thomas E. Evans argues that psychometric research in religious education needs to take seriously the situation of minority language communities. He illustrates this point by providing a Welsh language translation of the Francis Scale of Attitude Toward Christianity. The reliability and validity of this instrument is supported by a study conducted among 258 year nine and year ten pupils attending Welsh medium secondary schools in Dyfed.

In chapter 19 Bernadette O'Keeffe moves the debate to the issue of religious schools and discusses the development of the independent Christian schools movement in Britain. Drawing on her own recent survey of fifteen primary and secondary schools in this sector, she provides an introduction to the main characteristics of the Christian school. Then more detailed information is presented on the religious attitudes, beliefs and practices of the children and young people who attend these schools, based on a questionnaire survey of 439 pupils between the ages of eight and seventeen years.

In chapter 20 Carolyn Wilcox turns attention away from pupils to those who teach them. Her aim is to assess the contribution of Church of England schools by examining the attitudes of those who teach in church schools toward the church school system, toward the distinctiveness of church schools, and toward traditional teaching methods. Data provided by 145 teachers indicate that age and personal commitment to the church are significant predictors of

the individual teacher's attitude toward church schools. Older
teachers and teachers who attend church hold a more positive
attitude toward church schools and are more likely to wish to
emphasise the distinctiveness of church schools. These findings
have implications both for the claims that the Church of England
makes regarding the contemporary distinctiveness of church
schools and for future changes in the character of church schools.

In chapter 21 James Arthur and Simon Gaine focus attention on
the Roman Catholic sector of schools within the state maintained
system in England. The first part of the chapter traces the history
of the distinction between catechesis and religious education, with
particular reference to its more recent applications, through the
publication of the programmes of the National Project, *Weaving the
Web* and *Here I Am*. The second part of the chapter reports provisional findings from a research project designed to ascertain how
far a distinction between catechesis and religious education has
been appropriated by primary school teachers themselves. Data
provided by 47 primary school teachers in Kent indicated that a
strong separation between catechesis and religious education has
not been greatly influential at primary level.

In chapter 22 Linda Burton provides a profile of what it means
to young people to be growing up as Catholics in England today.
The religious identity of young people who claim affiliation to the
Roman Catholic Church is constructed from a database provided
by 673 twelve to sixteen year olds, and this identity is compared
with the religious profile of 2,112 young people who have no
religious affiliation. A further distinction is made between three
groups of young Catholics: regular Catholics who attend church
most weeks; occasional Catholics who attend church from time to
time; and lapsed Catholics who never attend church.

In chapter 23 Michael Curran takes a closer look at what is
involved in pupils' own assessment of Catholic identity. He employs statistical techniques of item analysis to identify twelve
features which best cohere to produce a unidimensional scale of
Catholic identity. The data demonstrate that the pivotal factor
concerns the importance and helpfulness of attendance at mass.
Young people who are baptised Catholic, whose parents are baptised Catholic, and who attend a Catholic primary school hold a
more positive view of Catholic identity than young people who are
not characterised by these features.

In chapter 24 Alice Montgomery and William K. Kay explore
attitudes toward assembly and religious education among a sample

of 588 girls attending a Roman Catholic secondary school, alongside their attitudes toward other aspects of school life, using an Osgood semantic differential questionnaire. The areas compared were attitudes toward games, English lessons, maths lessons, music/singing lessons, religious education/lessons about religion, school assemblies, and school itself. The data demonstrate how attitudes toward all these areas, except English lessons, decline in an age-related way. However, attitude toward assemblies declines non-linearly, while attitude toward religious education declines linearly. The theoretical implications of these findings are discussed both with regard to attitude toward Christianity and with regard to Piagetian psychology.

In chapter 25 Yaacov J. Katz examines the roles of religiosity and personality in shaping tertiary educational choices in a sample of 176 female Jewish students. His aim was to contrast entrants to the University of Bar-Ilan School of Education and the Jerusalem College for Women. Both are religious institutions, but whereas the university is open to secular students, the college only accepts students who are religious in their outlook and observance. As in three earlier chapters in the book, the model of personality adopted by Yaacov Katz was that proposed by Hans Eysenck and his associates. He also employed Glen Wilson's model of conservatism. The data indicated that, despite similarity between the two groups of students in their religious practices and principles, the college students were characterised by significantly higher levels of religion-puritanism, anti-hedonism, anti-feminism, anti-artism, and neuroticism, and by lower levels of democracy, thus supporting a more conservative personality disposition.

In chapter 26 Avraham Leslau and Mordechai Bar-Lev explore the values of two samples of pupils in their final year of schooling in Israel, one from state religious schools and the other from state non-religious schools. All students completed Schwartz' values questionnaire, rating fifty-six specific values on a nine point scale. After controlling for individual differences in the students' self-reported levels of religiosity, the data demonstrated that students educated in religious schools placed a greater emphasis on the values of tradition and universalism, while students educated in non-religious schools placed a greater emphasis on values of hedonism, achievement, self-direction and security.

Finally, in chapter 27 Mordechai Bar-Lev and Avraham Leslau discuss reasons for leaving religion and the religious way of life, basing their findings on two surveys conducted in 1990 and 1991.

One survey involved 5,345 grade twelve pupils from state religious schools in Israel. The other survey involved 1,344 thirty year old adults who had studied in state religious schools in Israel. The authors conclude that there are two main factors for leaving religion in both samples, which they define in the study as the social factor and the convenience factor.

1

John E. Greer: research pioneer in religious education

Leslie J. Francis

Summary

This chapter reviews John Greer's contribution to research in religious education by summarising his extensive series of publications and setting them within the context of the main themes he has addressed. These include Greer's concern with readiness for religion, sixth form religion, moral values, attitude toward religion, rejection of Christianity, religious thinking, Belfast pupils, the divided community of Northern Ireland, religious experience and qualitative as well as quantitative methods of research.

Introduction

John Greer's professional career has combined and integrated three well developed areas of expertise: as priest and pastor, as educator and curriculum developer, and as educational researcher. This paper focuses exclusively on Greer the researcher.

In the 1960s John Greer brought to research in religious education a unique blend of three well honed commitments. Greer was committed to understanding and promoting the role of religious education as a professional subject within the school curriculum. Greer was committed to understanding and clarifying the role of Christianity in Irish society. Greer was committed to applying the highest standards of *scientific* enquiry to educational research. Having trained first in a scientific discipline and completed his doctoral research in biological sciences, Greer was determined to accept no lower standards in empirical research in religious education. This clear stance has continued to inform both the research he has initiated himself and his critical scrutiny of the research conducted by others. In the course of his research career Greer has engaged in debate with the work of all the major innovators in research in religious education.

Readiness for religion

The first major research in religious education with which Greer engaged was the movement initiated by Ronald Goldman through his two influential books, *Religious Thinking from Childhood to Adolescence* (Goldman, 1964) and *Readiness for Religion* (Goldman, 1965). Goldman's revolution in religious education was based on empirical research conducted among 200 children, using three bible stories and theory derived from Piagetian developmental psychology.

First, Greer was obviously intrigued by Goldman's *method* of research and set out to test the method for himself. The results are reported in a paper entitled, 'The child's understanding of creation' (Greer, 1972a). This early paper reveals important characteristics of Greer's approach to research. It shows respect for the model on which it builds, coupled with critical awareness of the limitations. It tackles a central and difficult issue by focusing on the creation narrative. It displays awareness of current biblical scholarship against which the child's thinking is to be assessed. It listens to the child with care and perception. It recognises its own limitations (in this case the sample size of 46 pupils) and avoids overclaiming for the findings. While Goldman's work would have benefitted from a number of careful extensions of this nature, Greer's study stands almost alone in the field.

Second, Greer was obviously intrigued by Goldman's influence on syllabuses of religious education. Goldman himself claimed that the new approach toward religious education would inhibit the general decline in pupil attitude toward religious education, but had produced no evidence to support this claim. Greer looked for the evidence. In June 1970 a study was made of the attitudes and opinions of two matched samples of primary school pupils: 305 taught according to the Northern Ireland Agreed Syllabus, which promoted a traditional bible-based approach, and 273 taught according to the West Riding Agreed Syllabus, which promoted a thematic approach. The results are reported in a paper entitled, 'The effects of new approaches to religious education in the primary school' (Greer and Brown, 1973). The data demonstrate that pupils taught according to the new syllabus hold a more positive attitude toward religious education, but achieve less well in tests of biblical knowledge. Again Greer cautions that 'it is dangerous to make generalisations from the results of such a limited study'. Greer remained alone, however, in attempting to test this issue.

Third, while aware of the limitations of Goldman's original research, Greer became impatient with what he saw to be extravagant and insecurely grounded criticisms of Goldman's pioneering work. In particular, in a paper entitled 'Stages in the development of religious thinking', Greer (1980b) took Roger Murphy to task for his series of studies criticising Goldman (Murphy, 1977a, 1977b, 1978a, 1978b). There are, Greer maintains, serious inconsistencies and contradictions in Murphy's writings. Greer's balanced evaluation of the situation is as follows.

> It would be most unfortunate if educators were either to reject the insights already achieved by Goldman and his school or to maintain the infallibility of his theory despite all subsequent research.

Elsewhere, Greer (1984b) provides a helpful overview of the contribution of Goldman's school of research to the psychology of religious education.

Sixth form religion

The second researcher to influence Greer's own programme of research was Edwin Cox, through the publication of his influential book, *Sixth form religion* (Cox, 1967). Cox's study had been conducted in 1963 to profile the religious and moral attitudes of sixth form pupils, using a self completion questionnaire. Additional findings from the study had been reported by Wright and Cox (1967a, 1967b).

Greer saw the advantages of replicating this study in Northern Ireland and approached 47 grammar schools and twenty secondary (intermediate) schools. He did not include Roman Catholic schools. Of those approached, 35 grammar schools and seven secondary (intermediate) schools participated. Questionnaires were completed by 980 boys, 640 girls and eleven pupils who did not declare their sex, representing 87% of the total second year sixth form population in the participating schools. In addition, pupils were asked to take home to their parents an envelope containing a letter of explanation, a short questionnaire and a stamped addressed envelope for reply. From 832 parental replies received, 803 were matched with a corresponding pupil's reply.

These data led to four important publications. The first paper, 'The attitudes of parents and pupils to religion in school' (Greer, 1970), set out the views of parents and pupils regarding religious instruction and religious worship in schools. Both received more support from parents than from pupils. In the second paper, Greer (1971) investigated the relationship between the religious belief and church attendance of sixth form pupils and their parents. The data confirm the importance of parental influence. In the third paper, 'Sixth form religion in Northern Ireland', Greer (1972b) provides much more detail regarding the findings and discusses the data in comparison with Cox's findings in England. He is at pains to emphasise that the comparison is less than straightforward because the two surveys were separated by five years. Finally, the full results were published in the book, *A Questioning Generation* (Greer, 1972c).

Cox followed up his original study in England seven years later in 1970. This enabled shifts in sixth form opinion to be assessed over that period of time (Wright and Cox, 1971a, 1971b). Greer also spotted the good sense in replication studies and invited the 42 schools involved in his original study to repeat the exercise *ten* years later in 1978. This time 35 of the 42 schools agreed to participate in the replication study. This time questionnaires were completed by 1,090 boys, 780 girls and two pupils who did not declare their sex. The findings were published in a paper entitled, 'The persistence of religion' (Greer, 1980a). In this paper, Greer employed the data to discuss both the secularisation thesis and the role of religion in Northern Ireland.

Ten years later in 1988, Greer replicated the study for a second time to produce a unique empirical insight into the change or stability in adolescent religiosity in Northern Ireland over two decades. This time the number of participating schools had dropped to 28, but the number of participating pupils had grown to 1,190 boys and 1,213 girls. Again Greer is at pains to discuss the details and possible implications of shifts in the sampling. The findings from all three studies were present in both a full and summary form (Greer, 1989a, 1990), still under the title, 'The persistence of religion in Northern Ireland'. Greer's main conclusion is that 'although there was no significant difference in the responses to a number of the questions, answers to others indicated a significant trend toward *greater* or more orthodox belief over the twenty year period'. At the same time, a small number of indices showed a significant difference in the direction of the rejection of traditional practice or moral judgement.

Clearly this is a body of research which deserves further replication in 1998.

Moral values

The questionnaire designed by Cox (1967) to inform his study of sixth form religion included a set of questions on moral issues. His questionnaire listed eleven topics: gambling, drunkenness, smoking, lying, stealing, premarital sexual intercourse, capital punishment, suicide, colour bar, war, and the use of nuclear arms. Greer (1972b, 1972c) had used the same set of questions in his study of sixth form religion in Northern Ireland. The findings from this survey had raised in his mind the possibility of repeating the enquiry into moral values over a wider age range and using an extended list of topics.

In 1981 the questionnaire was extended by six items (drinking alcohol, drug taking, abortion, artificial birth control, divorce and religious discrimination) and administered to 1,207 pupils between the ages of fourteen and sixteen years attending Roman Catholic and Protestant schools in Northern Ireland (Greer, 1984a). The data demonstrated that there was no significant difference between the responses of Roman Catholic and Protestant pupils on drinking alcohol, drunkenness, lying, stealing and drug taking. Protestants were more severe than Roman Catholics in their judgement on gambling and smoking. Roman Catholics were more severe than Protestants on the remaining ten issues, including premarital sexual intercourse, artificial birth control and divorce. Greer formulated the following conclusion based on these findings.

> While there was evidence of a common morality on some issues, there was also evidence that on other issues the conflicting views of Roman Catholics and Protestants were clearly reflected in the moral judgements of pupils attending secondary school.

The 17 items of Greer's modification of Cox's questionnaire on moral values were subsequently administered to a sample of 1,079 third, fourth and fifth year secondary pupils, attending nine Roman Catholic and ten Protestant schools in Northern Ireland (Francis and Greer, 1992a). This time the data were used to develop and to establish criteria of reliability and validity for a scale of traditional Christian moral values. Tentative scale norms indicated that pupils in Roman Catholic schools held more strongly to traditional moral values than pupils in Protestant schools, that girls held more strongly to traditional moral values than boys, and that the acceptance of traditional moral values declines between the third and fifth years of the secondary school.

Attitude toward religion

The measurement and scaling of attitude toward religion was brought into prominence during the 1970s by two researchers. In Northern Ireland, Turner (1970) developed and deployed a scale of attitude toward religion among a sample of 400 boys in Belfast. Ten years later the study was replicated among another sample of 400 boys attending the same school by Turner, Turner and Reid (1980). This study allowed changes in attitude to be monitored over a ten year time span. In England, Francis (1976, 1978) developed and deployed a scale of attitude toward Christianity among a sample of 900 pupils from the first year of junior school to the fifth year of secondary school. This study allowed changes in attitude to be monitored over a nine year age span.

Greer became intrigued both by the claims made for these instruments and by the considerable differences between them. He set out, therefore, to examine and to compare the two instruments among a sample of 2,133 secondary school pupils (Greer, 1982a). In this study, Greer found both similarities and differences between the two instruments. He concluded as follows.

> It may be speculated that Roman Catholic pupils tended to score higher on the Francis scale because of the affective nature of the scale items while Protestant pupils tended to score higher on the Turner scale because of the cognitive nature of that scale. Thus while the two attitude toward religion scales functioned in a remarkably similar way and produced results which correlated closely, they attracted a slightly different pattern of responses from Roman Catholics and Protestants and they did not measure precisely the same thing.

The Francis Scale of Attitude Toward Christianity was subsequently used in two studies to assess the influence of different approaches to religious education on pupil attitudes by Francis (1979) and Kay (1981). In a paper entitled 'Attitude to religion reconsidered', Greer (1983a) set out to scrutinise and critique the claims made by these two studies. He draws attention to four crucial areas of concern. First, he highlights ambiguities and difficulties in defining 'the religious attitude' and 'attitude toward

religion'. Second, he illustrates the disagreement in the psychological literature regarding the components of the construct of
attitude. He takes Francis to task for preferring the one component
model, emphasising affect, over the three component model, combining affective, cognitive and conative aspects. Third, he disputes
the capability of Francis' preferred mode of data analysis, path
analysis, to test causal rather than correlational hypotheses. Finally,
he argues that the school environment is ultimately too complex
and subject to too many random influences to permit confidence
to be placed in studies which attempt to model syllabus influence
on pupil attitude. This clear critique challenged Francis and Kay
(1984) to clarify their position.

Some time later, Greer collaborated with Francis to produce two
detailed and exacting examinations of the psychometric properties
of the Francis Scale of Attitude Toward Christianity. The first study
was conducted among 1,189 pupils attending Protestant secondary
schools in Northern Ireland (Francis and Greer, 1990a). The second study was conducted among 935 pupils attending Catholic
secondary schools in Northern Ireland (Greer and Francis, 1991).
Both studies conducted separate analyses among pupils in years
one, two, three, four and five of the secondary school. Both studies
supported the reliability, unidimensionality and construct validity
of scale. In a third study, Greer collaborated with Francis to produce
a seven item short form of the scale (Francis, Greer and Gibson,
1991).

Rejection of Christianity

Greer's further examination of the two attitude scales developed
by Turner (1970) and Francis (1976) led him to identify another
possible weakness with such instruments. As is consistent with the
general structure of attitude scales, both instruments are designed
so that high scores imply the more positive attitude. Moreover, as
is also generally the case with attitude scales, the two instruments
designed by Francis and Turner both contained more items which
are positive about religion than items which are negative about
religion. These scoring characteristics, Greer realised, may suggest
both an empirical and a conceptual problem in the interpretation
of mean differences in scale scores. The empirical problem is
concerned with the unmeasured influence of the tendency toward
acquiescence, which may or may not contaminate scale scores. The
conceptual problem is concerned with the characterisation of the

low scorers, whose more negative responses may reflect an atheistic rejection or a sceptical agnosticism.

In response to such suspected limitations associated with the positive valency of conventional measures of attitude toward religion, Greer set out to develop a new scale with negative valency among a sample of 875 fourth and fifth year pupils attending ten Catholic and ten Protestant secondary schools in Northern Ireland (Greer and Francis, 1992b). The resultant twenty item scale produced alpha coefficients of 0.94 among Protestant pupils and of 0.90 among Roman Catholic pupils. Tentative scale norms indicated that pupils in Protestant schools displayed more signs of rejecting Christianity than pupils in Roman Catholic schools, that male pupils displayed more signs of rejecting Christianity than female pupils, and that the sex differences are comparable within the two types of schools.

This scale was subsequently used in a study of 574 fourth, fifth and sixth form pupils attending ten Catholic secondary schools in Northern Ireland to explore the comparative strength of different influences on shaping adolescent moral values (Francis and Greer, 1990b). The data indicated that a large proportion of Catholic pupils rejected moral absolutes maintained by traditional Catholic teaching. Path analysis suggested that the formation of a positive attitude toward Christianity in general was a fundamental condition for the espousal of traditional Catholic moral value.

Religious thinking

The measurement and scaling of religious thinking by means of a pencil and paper test was brought into prominence during the 1970s by a series of studies undertaken by John Peatling and his associates (Peatling, 1973; Peatling and Laabs, 1975; Peatling, Laabs and Newton, 1975; Tamminen, 1976; Hoge and Petrillo, 1978). These studies developed, refined and applied a test known as Thinking About the Bible which set out to operationalise the constructs advanced by Goldman (1964) through the more time consuming method of clinical interview. The test provides four indices of *very concrete, concrete, abstract* and *very abstract* modes of thinking.

Once again, Greer became intrigued by the claims made for this instrument and set out to test these claims. His critical evaluation of Peatling's work is published under the title, 'A critical study of "Thinking about the Bible" ' (Greer, 1983b). First, Greer analysed the questionnaire items by counting the words and subjecting them to standardised measures of readability, including the Flesch Formula and the Fog Index. He demonstrates that the progression from very concrete to very abstract modes of thinking is confused by a parallel progression in word length and in reading difficulty. Second, Greer analysed the theological content of the questionnaire items. He demonstrates that the progression from very concrete to very abstract modes of thinking is confused by a parallel progression away from a conservative Christian perspective. Third, Greer invited twenty independent judges familiar with Piaget's work to assess the level of thinking represented by each item. On the basis of the responses of these judges, he concluded that Peatling's sets of items were generally judged to be characteristic of the levels of thinking which they purported to represent. Fourth, Greer scrutinised the validity of the instrument. To begin with he exposes the circularity in the argument whereby Peatling attempted to establish the *construct* validity of the test. Then he set up an experiment to assess the *concurrent* validity by conducting Goldman type clinical interviews and administering the Peatling test to the same 16 pupils. From this comparison, he concludes that the Peatling test is *not* a valid indicator of the level of religious thinking which is revealed in an interview situation. Finally, Greer opens up to critique Peatling's view that plateaux exist in the transition from stage to stage.

On the basis of these examinations, Greer draws the following conclusion.

> It would seem that Thinking about the Bible is an instrument of limited value for the study of the development of religious thinking. The creation of Thinking about the Bible by Peatling was a step in the right direction, since it was a serious attempt to produce a convenient instrument. . . . Its most important flaws are firstly the overlooking of the theological dimension in the response items . . . and secondly the neglect of the study of concurrent validity.

Belfast pupils

In spite of his reservations about both the Francis Scale of Attitude Toward Christianity and the Peatling measure of religious thinking, Greer decided to employ both instruments in a study of religious attitudes and thinking among a sample of 2,149 Belfast pupils during 1979. The study included both Catholic and Protestant schools and involved pupils from eight age bands, spanning the first year of the junior school to the fourth year of the secondary school.

Care had been taken to survey pupils from a stratified sample of schools.

A full account of the data from this project was published under the title, 'Growing up in Belfast: a study of religious development' (Greer, 1982b). An abbreviated and focused account was published under the title, 'Religious attitudes and thinking in Belfast pupils' (Greer, 1981a).

The data demonstrated that pupils had an increasing preference for abstract thinking and a decreasing preference for concrete thinking as they got older. Grammar school pupils were more inclined to prefer abstract thinking than secondary (intermediate) pupils, and Roman Catholic pupils were slightly more inclined to prefer abstract thinking than Protestants. Overall, pupils had fairly positive attitudes toward religion, but these deteriorated steadily from the third year of the junior school to the fourth year of the secondary school. Roman Catholics had a more favourable attitude toward religion than Protestants, and girls had a more favourable attitude toward religion than boys. Finally, there was a small, but significant, negative correlation between a positive attitude toward religion and a preference for abstract religious thinking across the whole sample. Unfortunately, Greer did not partial out the influence of age in calculating this correlation, so it remains unclear how much the reported negative relationship between attitude toward religion and preference for abstract religious thinking may be an artifact of age differences.

A divided community

Underlying much of Greer's research resides the painful awareness of the powerful divisiveness of religion in Northern Ireland. Two of his papers begin with the same opening sentence: 'Northern Ireland is one of the most deeply divided countries in the world'. Both papers bring fresh insights into the role of religion in this divide.

In the first of these papers, bearing the title 'Viewing "the other side" in Northern Ireland', Greer (1985) developed a six item Likert-type openness scale designed to measure willingness to accept people from the other religious traditions. An example item reads, 'I would be quite happy if someone of the other religion moved in next door tomorrow'. The six items cohered to produce a homogeneous scale with an alpha coefficient of 0.85.

Greer administered this scale, alongside the Francis Scale of Attitude Toward Christianity, to 1,193 pupils in ten Protestant secondary schools and 940 pupils in nine Roman Catholic secondary schools. The sample included pupils from years one, two, three, four and five of the secondary school. The data demonstrated that Roman Catholic pupils were more open than Protestant pupils and that girls were more open than boys. At the same time, openness increased significantly with age, while attitude toward Christianity decreased significantly with age. At first these opposite trends tended to suggest that openness went hand in hand with a loss of commitment to religion itself. However, when Greer explored the relationship between openness and attitude toward Christianity, controlling for age, sex and denomination, there was found to be a positive relationship between attitude toward Christianity and openness. Young people most favourably disposed toward Christianity were the most open to the other religious tradition. When the Greer openness scale was re-applied by Greer and Long (1989) among 592 fourth form pupils in Roman Catholic schools and 289 fourth form pupils in Protestant schools, their findings confirmed there to be greater openness among pupils in Roman Catholic schools than among pupils in Protestant schools.

In the second of these papers, bearing the subtitle, 'A comparative study of pupils attending Roman Catholic and Protestant secondary schools', Greer and Francis (1990) examined the distinctive religious cultures of 1,177 fourth, fifth and sixth year secondary pupils educated in the two types of schools, by means of a survey which included the Francis Scale of Attitude Toward Christianity, Greer's scale of rejection of Christianity and Greer's scale of Christian moral values, together with questions on religious practices and beliefs. The findings indicated significant and consistent differences in the religious profiles of the two denominational groups, but not complete contrast. Roman Catholics were more inclined than Protestants to attend church and to pray privately, but not to read the bible privately. Roman Catholics were more inclined than Protestants to recognise the importance of religion in their lives, to acknowledge belief in God, to claim to have experience of God, and to be more willing to describe their experiences of God. Roman Catholics were more inclined than Protestants to express favourable attitude toward religion and less inclined to display signs of rejecting religion. Protestants were inclined to be more severe than Roman Catholics on certain issues of morality, such as gambling and drinking alcohol, but less severe on other issues of morality related to traditional Christian teaching, such as premarital sexual intercourse, divorce and abortion.

The findings of this second study were also summarised by Francis and Greer (1992b) in the *Irish Christian Handbook*.

Religious experience

Greer was aware that studies concerned with religious beliefs, religious practices, religious thinking and attitude toward religion failed to do proper justice to the complex nature of religion. He was attracted, therefore, by the range of researchers who chose to focus on religious experience, including Elkind and Elkind (1962), Paffard (1973), Robinson (1977a, 1977b, 1978) and Hay (1979). In order to test the relevance of such studies to the situation among pupils in Northern Ireland, Greer began his own series of studies into aspects of religious experience.

The first study was conducted among a sample of 1,872 upper sixth form pupils at controlled or Protestant voluntary schools in Northern Ireland (Greer, 1981b). The questionnaire included the following question.

> Have you ever had an experience of God, e.g. his presence or his help or anything else?

Pupils who answered this question in the affirmative were then asked to describe this experience if they could.

The data demonstrated that 38% of the boys and 51% of the girls felt that they had experienced something of this nature. Over a quarter of the pupils also described this experience and Greer classified their descriptions under nine headings: guidance and help, examinations, depression and sickness, death, answered prayer, God's presence, conversion experiences, good experiences, and miscellaneous.

The second study was conducted in 1981 among 940 Roman Catholic and 1,193 Protestant pupils, between the ages of twelve and seventeen years, attending 19 secondary and grammar schools in different parts of Northern Ireland (Greer, 1982c). The same key question was used. This time the answer 'yes' was given to this question by 31% of the Protestant boys, 39% of the Protestant girls, 35% of the Roman Catholic boys, and 64% of the Roman Catholic girls. No significant age differences were found in the proportions of pupils who reported religious experiences. Descriptions of these experiences were provided by 625 pupils and Greer again classifies these accounts under the same nine headings. He concludes that, while there was a great deal of similarity between Roman Catholic and Protestant pupils, some religious experiences were conceptualised and interpreted in the idiom of a particular tradition. Roman Catholics did not report any conversion experiences, while the kind of experiences which they described more often related to the sacramental and liturgical life of their church.

The third study employed data from 1,177 fourth, fifth and sixth year pupils from ten Protestant and ten Roman Catholic schools in Northern Ireland (Francis and Greer, 1993). The same key question was used, but this time the study also included the Francis Scale of Attitude Toward Christianity. This time the answer 'yes' was given by 26% of the Protestant boys, 38% of the Protestant girls, 34% of the Roman Catholic boys, and 56% of the Roman Catholic girls. Direct comparisons with the earlier samples is made difficult by variations in the age composition. This study developed a multiple regression model to test whether reported religious experience had any additional impact on shaping religious attitudes, after the influence of church attendance, personal prayer and belief in God had already been taken into account. The data indicate that the acknowledgement and naming of personal religious experience is associated with the formation of a more positive attitude toward Christianity.

The fourth study set out to replicate the third study among 2,133 pupils, between the ages of twelve and seventeen years, attending Roman Catholic and Protestant schools (Greer and Francis, 1992a). This time the answer 'yes' was given by 31% of the Protestant boys, 39% of the Protestant girls, 35% of the Roman Catholic boys and 64% of the Roman Catholic girls. Multiple regression equations were calculated for the Roman Catholic and Protestant communities separately. In both cases the data indicated that reported religious experience was associated with a more positive attitude toward Christianity, even after taking into account the influences of sex, church attendance, personal prayer and belief in God.

Elsewhere, Greer (1984c) discusses the implications of research in religious experience for classroom practice.

Qualitative methods

A key characteristic of Greer's scientific approach to researching religion during childhood and adolescence, as evident from the preceding review, is his emphasis on quantitative methods. At the same time, Greer was well aware of the limitation of *exclusive* reliance on quantitative methods and set out to redress the balance by exploiting the potential of qualitative methods. His studies of religious experience provide one example of the creative use of qualitative research. A second example is provided by two analyses of qualitative data generated by a study conducted among 1,177 pupils in 1984. These two analyses are entitled, 'Hardest to accept' (Greer, 1988) and 'The importance of religion' (Greer, 1989b).

'Hardest to accept' reports responses to a sentence completion test beginning, 'What I find hardest to accept about religion is . . .'. Of the 1,177 pupils in the survey, 955 (81%) completed the sentence. Greer sorted their responses into twelve broad categories, leaving about one hundred responses unclassified. The responses were then further sorted both by sex and by denomination (Roman Catholic or Protestant). The following categories were identified for the analysis: God, creation, miracles, suffering, life after death, the church, authority, morality, conflict, Jesus, the bible, and other faiths. Sub-issues were then identified within each category. For example, 16% of the responses were assigned to the category concerned with God. Then within this category three sub-issues were identified. The first common theme in this category drew attention to the lack of proof or evidence for the existence of God. The second common theme in this category concerned doubt about traditional conceptions of God. The third common theme in this category related to origins, the origin of God, the origin of the universe, and the origin of the human race.

'The importance of religion' reports responses to a sentence completion test beginning, 'For me the most important thing about religion is . . .'. Of the 1,177 pupils in the survey, 897 (76%) completed the sentence. Greer sorted their responses into nine broad categories, leaving an unspecified number of responses unclassified. Once again the responses were further sorted by sex and denomination. The following categories were identified for the analysis: belief in God, the presence and help of God, the practice of prayer, guidance and direction in life, going to church, life after death, freedom of choice, the importance of Jesus, and Catholics and Protestants.

Greer is well aware of the limitations in this kind of analysis and is careful not to overclaim the significance of his findings. He writes as follows.

It is recognised that such a sorting process was far from precise since it depended on the subjective judgement of the researcher. Moreover, though written responses could be gathered together about, for example, belief in God, pupils expressed many diverse comments in relation to such a broad theme, and generalisations were hard to make.... Despite the limitations of this method, it was felt that it provided a valuable way of gaining insight into the minds of pupils.

Elsewhere, Greer has also made creative use of qualitative research methods for the evaluation of curriculum development in religious education in Northern Ireland (Greer and McElhinney, 1984; Greer, Harris and McElhinney, 1989).

Personal endnote

It would be inappropriate to conclude this review of John Greer's significant contribution to research in religious education without adding a personal acknowledgement of gratitude. First, I am grateful to John for his early writings in statistical research in religious education which helped to shape my own vision for and commitment to the field. Second, I am grateful to John for a chance meeting on a flight to New York in 1980, en route to the second meeting of the International Seminar on Religious Education and Values. Walking the streets of New York city we discovered a significant overlap of interests, commitments and expertise which has led both to personal friendship and to creative and critical dialogue. These discussions, begun on the streets of New York city, have been continued in Amsterdam, Dublin, Ottawa and Copenhagen, as the International Seminar on Religious Education and Values has travelled the world. Third, I am grateful to John for the opportunity of collaborating with him on a number of his projects in which he has graciously invited me to share. Currently I look forward to continuing involvement in his most recent survey concerned with the attitudes of adolescents toward religion and science in Northern Ireland.

Acknowledgement

An earlier version of this chapter was published in *Panorama: international journal of comparative religious education and values*, 1995.

References

Cox, E. (1967), *Sixth Form Religion*, London, SCM.

Elkind, D. and Elkind, S. (1962), Varieties of religious experience in young adolescents, *Journal for the Scientific Study of Religion*, 2, 102–112.

Francis, L.J. (1976), An enquiry into the concept 'readiness for religion', Unpublished Ph.D. dissertation, University of Cambridge.

Francis, L.J. (1978), Attitude and longitude: a study in measurement, *Character Potential*, 8, 119–130.

Francis, L.J. (1979), School influence and pupil attitude towards religion, *British Journal of Educational Psychology*, 49, 107–123.

Francis, L.J. and Greer, J.E. (1990a), Measuring attitudes towards Christianity among pupils in Protestant secondary schools in Northern Ireland, *Personality and Individual Differences*, 11, 853–856.

Francis, L.J. and Greer, J.E. (1990b), Catholic schools and adolescent religiosity in Northern Ireland: shaping moral values, *Irish Journal of Education*, 24, 2, 40–47.

Francis, L.J. and Greer, J.E. (1992a), Measuring Christian moral values among Catholic and Protestant adolescents in Northern Ireland, *Journal of Moral Education*, 21, 59–65.

Francis, L.J. and Greer, J.E. (1992b), The teenage voice: the religious profile of pupils attending Catholic and Protestant secondary schools in Northern Ireland, in P. Brierley (ed.), *The Irish Christian Handbook*, pp. 20–23, London, MARC Europe.

Francis, L.J. and Greer, J.E. (1993), The contribution of religious experience to Christian development: a study among fourth, fifth and sixth year pupils in Northern Ireland, *British Journal of Religious Education*, 15, 38–43.

Francis, L.J., Greer, J.E. and Gibson, H.M. (1991), Reliability and validity of a short measure of attitude towards Christianity among secondary school pupils in England, Scotland and Northern Ireland, *Collected Original Resources in Education*, 15, 3, fiche 2, G09.

Francis, L.J. and Kay, W.K. (1984), Attitude towards religion: definition, measurement and evaluation, *British Journal of Educational Studies*, 32, 45–50.

Goldman, R.J. (1964), *Religious Thinking from Childhood to Adolescence*, London, Routledge and Kegan Paul.

Goldman, R.J. (1965), *Readiness for Religion*, London, Routledge and Kegan Paul.

Greer, J.E. (1970), The attitudes of parents and pupils to religion in school, *Irish Journal of Education*, 4, 39–46.

Greer, J.E. (1971), Religious belief and church attendance of sixth form pupils and their parents, *Irish Journal of Education*, 5, 98–106.

Greer, J.E. (1972a), The child's understanding of creation, *Educational Review*, 24, 94–110.

Greer, J.E. (1972b), Sixth-form religion in Northern Ireland: religious belief, religious practice and moral judgement in a sample of Protestant boys and girls, *Social Studies*, 1, 325–340.

Greer, J.E. (1972c), *A Questioning Generation*, Belfast, Church of Ireland Board of Education.

Greer, J.E. (1980a), The persistence of religion: a study of adolescents in Northern Ireland, *Character Potential*, 9, 3, 139–149.

Greer, J.E. (1980b), Stages in the development of religious thinking, *British Journal of Religious Education*, 3, 24–28.

Greer, J.E. (1981a), Religious attitudes and thinking in Belfast pupils, *Educational Research*, 23, 177–189.

Greer, J.E. (1981b), Religious experience and religious education, *Search*, 4, 1, 23–34.

Greer, J.E. (1982a), A comparison of two attitude to religion scales, *Educational Research*, 24, 226–227.

Greer, J.E. (1982b), Growing up in Belfast: a study of religious development, *Collected Original Resources in Education*, 6, 1, fiche 1, A14.

Greer, J.E. (1982c), The religious experience of Northern Irish pupils, *The Irish Catechist*, 6, 2, 49–58.

Greer, J.E. (1983a), Attitude to religion reconsidered, *British Journal of Educational Studies*, 31, 18–28.

Greer, J.E. (1983b), A critical study of 'Thinking about the Bible', *British Journal of Religious Education*, 5, 113–125.

Greer, J.E. (1984a), Moral cultures in Northern Ireland, *Journal of Social Psychology*, 123, 63–70.

Greer, J.E. (1984b), Fifty years of the psychology of religion in religious education: part one, *British Journal of Religious Education*, 6, 93–97.

Greer, J.E. (1984c), Fifty years of the psychology of religion in religious education: part two, *British Journal of Religious Education*, 7, 23–28.

Greer, J.E. (1985), Viewing 'the other side' in Northern Ireland: openness and attitude to religion among Catholic and Protestant adolescents, *Journal for the Scientific Study of Religion*, 24, 275–292.

Greer, J.E. (1988), *Hardest to Accept*, Coleraine, University of Ulster Faculty of Education Resource Centre.

Greer, J.E. (1989a), The persistence of religion in Northern Ireland: a study of sixth form religion, 1968–1988, *Collected Original Resources in Education*, 13, 2, fiche 20, G9.

Greer, J.E. (1989b), The importance of religion: a study of adolescents in Northern Ireland, *Search*, 12, 2, 22–31.

Greer, J.E. (1990), The persistence of religion: a study of sixth-form pupils in Northern Ireland, 1968–1988, *Journal of Social Psychology*, 130, 573–581.

Greer, J.E. and Brown, G.A. (1973), The effects of new approaches to religious education in the primary school, *Journal of Curriculum Studies*, 5, 73–78.

Greer, J.E. and Francis, L.J. (1990), The religious profile of pupils in Northern Ireland: a comparative study of pupils attending Catholic and Protestant secondary schools, *Journal of Empirical Theology*, 3, 2, 35–50.

Greer, J.E. and Francis, L.J. (1991), Measuring attitudes towards Christianity among pupils in Catholic secondary schools in Northern Ireland, *Educational Research*, 33, 70–73.

Greer, J.E. and Francis, L.J. (1992a), Religious experience and attitude towards Christianity among secondary school children in Northern Ireland, *Journal of Social Psychology*, 132, 277–279.

Greer, J.E. and Francis, L.J. (1992b), Measuring 'rejection of Christianity' among 14–16 year old adolescents in Catholic and Protestant schools in Northern Ireland, *Personality and Individual Differences*, 13, 1345–1348.

Greer, J.E., Harris, J.E. and McElhinney, E.P. (1989), A study of classroom discussion in religious education, *British Journal of Religious Education*, 11, 92–102.

Greer, J.E. and Long, J. (1989), Religion in rural Ulster, *Education North*, 1, 2, 15–19.

Greer, J.E. and McElhinney, E.P. (1984), The project on religion in Ireland: an experiment in reconstruction, *Lumen Vitae*, 39, 331–342.

Hay, D. (1979), Religious experience amongst a group of postgraduate students: a qualitative study, *Journal for the Scientific Study of Religion*, 18, 164–182.

Hoge, D.R. and Petrillo, G.H. (1978), Development of religious thinking in adolescence: a test of Goldman's theories, *Journal for the Scientific Study of Religion*, 17, 139–154.

Kay, W.K. (1981), Syllabuses and attitudes to Christianity, *Irish Catechist*, 5, 2, 16–21.

Murphy, R.J.L. (1977a), Does children's understanding of parables develop in stages? *Learning for Living*, 16, 168–172.

Murphy, R.J.L. (1977b), The development of religious thinking in children in three easy stages? *Learning for Living*, 17, 16–19.

Murphy, R.J.L. (1978a), A new approach to the study of the development of religious thinking in children, *Educational Studies*, 4, 19–22.

Murphy, R.J.L. (1978b), *The Development of Religious Thinking: a review of psychological theories*, Leicester, UCCF Religious Studies Committee.

Paffard, M. (1973), *Inglorious Wordsworth*, London, Hodder and Stoughton.

Peatling, J.H. (1973), The incidence of concrete and abstract religious thinking in the interpretation of three bible stories by pupils enrolled in grades four through twelve in selected schools in the Episcopal Church in the United States of America, Unpublished Ph.D. dissertation, University of New York.

Peatling, J.H. and Laabs, C.W. (1975), Cognitive development of pupils in grades four through twelve: a comparative study of Lutheran and Episcopalian children and youth, *Character Potential*, 7, 107–117.

Peatling, J.H., Laabs, C.W. and Newton, T.B. (1975), Cognitive development: a three sample comparison of means on the Peatling scale of religious thinking, *Character Potential*, 7, 159–162.

Robinson, E. (1977a), *The Original Vision*, Oxford, Religious Experience Research Unit.

Robinson, E. (1977b), *This Time-Bound Ladder*, Oxford, Religious Experience Research Unit.

Robinson, E. (1978), *Living the Questions*, Oxford, Religious Experience Research Unit.

Tamminen, K. (1976), Research concerning the development of religious thinking in Finnish students: a report of results, *Character Potential*, 7, 206–219.

Turner, E.B. (1970), Religious understanding and religious attitudes in male urban adolescents, Unpublished Ph.D. dissertation, The Queen's University of Belfast.

Turner, E.B., Turner, I.F. and Reid, A. (1980), Religious attitudes in two types of urban secondary schools: a decade of change? *Irish Journal of Education*, 14, 43–52.

Wright, D. and Cox, E. (1967a), Religious belief and co-education in a sample of sixth form boys and girls, *British Journal of Social and Clinical Psychology*, 6, 23–31.

Wright, D. and Cox, E. (1967b), A study of the relationship between moral judgement and religious belief in a sample of English adolescents, *Journal of Social Psychology*, 72, 135–144.

Wright, D. and Cox, E. (1971a), Changes in attitudes towards religious education and the bible among sixth form boys and girls, *British Journal of Educational Psychology*, 41, 328–331.

Wright, D. and Cox, E. (1971b), Changes in moral belief among sixth form boys and girls over a seven year period in relation to religious belief, age and sex differences, *British Journal of Social and Clinical Psychology*, 10, 332–341.

2

Historical context: Loukes, Goldman, Hyde, Cox and Alves

William K. Kay

Summary

This chapter describes research in religious education in Britain between the late 1950s and early 1970s, and sets the context in which John Greer's initiative was located. It looks at the work of Loukes, Goldman, Hyde, Cox and Alves. Loukes wrote influential books dealing with the religious questions at the forefront of the minds of teenagers. Goldman was concerned to apply Piaget's theory in the realm of religious thinking. Hyde was concerned with the determinants of religious learning among normal and slow-learning children. Cox took a particular interest in sixth form religion as well as the changing nature of religious education. Alves was concerned to survey schools and to detect the influence of good religious education upon pupils' knowledge and opinion. To all these debates John Greer made significant contributions.

Loukes

In a project begun in 1958, Harold Loukes arranged for six schools to tape record discussions held by fourteen year olds in the presence of a class teacher or researcher during ordinary lessons on religious topics. In his introduction Loukes explained his intentions. He wanted to catch the authentic and spontaneous voice of the modern adolescent frankly expressing his or her own convictions, confusions and struggles. He justified his failure to use statistics by saying that such an approach would not allow pupils to express themselves freely. Yet Loukes was aware that the discussions he recorded would only contain the opinions of the most vocal members of each class. Did the silent majority agree or disagree with its more outspoken contemporaries? To find this out, he selected a further eight schools to whom snippets of the previous discussion were given for written response, and 502 further pupils participated in this way.

Reviewing extensive quotations from the live discussions and excerpts from the written responses, Loukes considers that three conclusions can be drawn: that fourteen year olds are interested in religious issues and express themselves vigorously; that this interest in religion has been present for a long time; and that pupils are sincere in their affirmations and denials. When these considerations are focused against the background of other research which shows that the peak age for religious conversion is in the mid to late teens, Loukes is able to paint a picture of bright children beginning to doubt religious teaching by about the age of ten and, a few years later, either resolving this in the direction of faith and enlarged understanding or by means of unbelief and rejection. What his picture presupposes, of course, is that children will, before the age of ten, have been sufficiently introduced to religion to have a capacity to entertain doubts about it; such a presumption is less likely to be true in the 1990s than it was in the 1950s.

Loukes was pressingly aware that pupils at fourteen (and, when he wrote, that was the school leaving age) were about to embark on a life in the outside world in the rough and tumble of the work place. He knew that a misunderstood faith or an undigested acquaintance with bible stories would not serve school leavers well in the years that lay ahead of them. He wanted to make their religious education relevant to their religious interests and applicable to the problems and circumstances they perennially faced. These problems, like those of personal relations, personal responsibility, the meaning of suffering or death, stemmed from the inevitabilities of physical and psychological growth and the passage of time. The conclusion of his enquiry, therefore, lay in an attempt to draw up a new 'life-centred' or 'problem-centred' approach to religious education, and he gave an example of this in *Teenage Religion*. To the extent that he uncovered some of the things going on in the minds of some pupils, Loukes' enquiry was a success; to the extent that his sample was unsystematically drawn and his comments unsystematically made, his enquiry failed to produce sufficient evidence on which to base large-scale educational changes.

Piaget

Before turning attention to Goldman's work, it is necessary to review the theoretical framework in which his work was set. This framework is defined by the contribution of Jean Piaget.

Piaget's voluminous researches on children extended over more than 55 years and through successive modifications and applications. Discussion of such a body of work always risks misrepresentation through over-simplification but, without an attempt to convey the central intricacies and processes which Piaget postulated, it is impossible to assess whether his framework applies satisfactorily to religion.

Piaget's analysis and description of mental development comes very close to that of Kant in the sense that both men wished to account for the reciprocal relationship between mental structures or operations and the external flux of sensation and experience. Concepts of space, time and causality were in Kantian terms *a priori*, either part of the inherent structure of human cognition or given by the structure of the universe. Piaget, also interested in epistemological questions, was not prepared to see the emergence of these universal concepts as simply the unfolding of physical maturation. He thought that mental development was dependent upon interactions with the environment such that the child *learnt* about space, time, causality and that such learning was linked with sets of physical changes during growth.

It was for this reason that Piaget considered much of the developmental sequence to be invariant, in the sense that developmental stages could not take place in a different order. Indeed, it is the word 'stage' which is most often thought to be characteristic of Piaget's framework, an apprehension which is true but inadequate. It is true because Piaget did propose a series of stages through which normal human mental development passes; it is inadequate because it fails to take account of the richness of Piaget's notion of stage, especially insofar as what was understood at a lower stage is comprehensively transformed and re-understood at a higher stage. Stages are, therefore, similar to each other in the sense that each possesses its own equilibrium and means of accommodating to the environment. They are also similar in that the main stages related to children of school age involve operations which, in Piaget's view, are internalisations, or reflections upon internalisations, of previously performed actions. Stages are different from each other in that the highest one makes use of formal, and therefore abstract, operations, especially for example those found in mathematics and algebra. The manipulation of symbols occurs in the final stage, and this ability is not available to younger children. As a consequence of the manipulation of symbols, which also allows for thinking about thinking, children are enabled to reason systematically.

This capacity for formal thought is distinct from the content of thought. One of the essentials of any account of human development, and one which is implicit in Piaget's account, is the function of memory to allow learning to take place. One basis of Piaget's account lies in the 'interaction between organism and environment'. (The use of biological terminology here is deliberate because it recalls that Piaget's initial interests were in the natural world and that his doctorate was on molluscs.) The remembrance of earlier interactions is necessary to allow for more sophisticated ones later. Memory may record images, words, sequences of events and it is these which are transmuted by ratiocination into the mental structure through which reality is mediated. Knowledge may be stored as perceptual or imaginative images, but once the operations of the mind are applied to these images by way of comparison, seriation, differentiation and so on, the images may be altered or recoded so that they belong in new contexts.

Goldman

Goldman's first book, *Religious Thinking from Childhood to Adolescence,* was published in 1964. Goldman's work, as the title suggests, was concerned with 'religious thinking' and was set within two frameworks: a Piagetian stage-developmental framework and a theological framework. Goldman was careful to explain that in his view 'religious thinking' was like any other kind of thinking except insofar as its objects were within the religious domain. His Piagetian framework ensured that the basic stages which he anticipated in the period between six and seventeen years of age were those of intuitive, concrete operational and formal operational thinking, though he did make room for intermediate sub-stages. Three bible stories, concerning Moses and the burning bush, crossing the Red Sea, and Jesus' temptations in the wilderness, were presented to 200 children in a series of interviews. Ten boys and ten girls were selected at each of the age levels between six and fifteen to seventeen (fifteen to seventeen year olds were treated as one age group) and asked questions to discover how they explained and understood the events contained within the biblical passages. Of the total of 22 questions on the biblical passages, answers on five were categorised according to the Piagetian stage developmental scheme and Goldman reported that, prior to the onset of formal operational thinking, children understood biblical materials crudely, sometimes by invoking magic and sometimes by concentrating on features peripheral to the main thrust of the account. Symbolism was beyond them.

The 200 children were also asked questions about three pictures, which depicted a family going to church, a child praying alone and a mutilated bible. Answers to questions about these pictures helped to fill out the context of children's thinking about religion, but they did not contribute to the assessment of Piagetian stage.

The theological framework adopted by Goldman was 'from a central-to-liberal position' and pupils' answers were classified along this continuum. The answers, as might be expected, showed, for instance, an enjoyment of the adventurous element in the crossing of the Red Sea, and only among older pupils was there an invocation of the concepts of love, justice or historical purpose; in other words, younger children showed theological immaturity, older ones were capable of more lofty insights. But the theological analysis was difficult to separate from answers reflecting Piagetian stages, as Goldman himself admitted (see the next section). The misunderstandings of children were, at the time, much discussed and Goldman's research was criticised (Fleming, 1966; Howkins, 1966) and defended vigorously (Goldman, 1965b, 1966). If it were replicated today, it would certainly have to be done differently (Murphy, 1978; Francis, 1979; Kay, 1981; Slee, 1992).

Goldman's second book, *Readiness for Religion* (1965a), was subtitled 'a basis for developmental religious education'. The notion of 'readiness for religion' was explained by Goldman as being analogous to readiness for the learning of reading, writing or number work. He specified three assumptions implicit in the notion of 'readiness'. First, 'there is a time in development when the maturing of a child allows skills to be learned', and here he mentions physical as well as intellectual development. The physical co-ordination associated with learning hand-writing is coupled with an ability to separate sounds and remember shapes sufficiently well to permit the formation of words. Second, 'there is a time for a child when he is most ready to begin certain skills' or, indeed, to continue them to higher levels of complexity. Third, 'a further assumption in readiness for learning is that we do not wait patiently for children to grow into readiness, but we actively assist the process of readiness by suitable preparatory learning'. In summary, 'readiness is not concerned merely with the specific time of the beginning of a skill, but also with what precedes it and what follows it. The concept involves the whole sequence of learning'.

In addition to *Readiness for Religion*, Goldman produced a series of classroom books for junior children on 'life themes'. These themes laid out graduated work for children on topics like shepherds, water or light. Younger children explored shepherds' lives or the properties of light so that, as they grew older, they might begin to see the figurative meaning of these words in biblical passages. God is like a shepherd, Jesus is like a light. At the end of the scheme, and to facilitate the transition to secondary school and formal operational thinking, children were introduced to symbols of all kinds, and finally to religious symbols.

Does the Piagetian framework fit?

When a consideration of Piaget's framework is set alongside *thinking about religion* as understood by Goldman, there is no reason to suppose that the assimilation of experiences relating to religion will be cognitively processed any differently from experiences related to any other part of life, particularly if the child has had first-hand experience of religious activity. What is evident, however, is that religion itself involves and requires a large number of activities (like praying, performing rituals or reading certain texts whose meaning may depend on circumstances) which are much wider than the simple interpretation of biblical excerpts. The whole range of religious encounter is much larger than an encounter with a text, and for this reason Goldman's research, at best, deals only with one aspect of thinking about religion.

The much more wide-ranging question of whether Piaget's framework can be used to produce a stage developmental account of thinking about religion as a whole can only be answered if religion itself can be seen as a unitary phenomenon, and seen to be such by growing children. If, as seems more probable, religion subdivides into ethical, ritual, doctrinal and other dimensions, then it is probable that the Piagetian account should deal with each of these dimensions separately, and only at a formal operational level would some sort of synthesis between them be possible. Certainly mathematics, as a closed system, and science, as the application of a set of distinct and related methods, are much more likely than religion to be understood by children as unitary fields, though research has not settled these questions. Goldman did not ask how the interpretation of biblical texts should be related to religion as a whole or even to school religion as a whole. His focus was determined by the content of agreed syllabuses and, at that time, such syllabuses were heavily biblical. He was alert, however, to the problem he faced: 'religion, of course, is so vast a topic that no test can claim to cover the entire field' (Goldman, 1964, p. 263).

The Piagetian framework may have a part to play in throwing light on *thinking religiously* in that it will be able to show how the beliefs, attitudes and values of religious people affect their cognitive processes but, since Piaget steadfastly refused to set down age norms for the performance of stage-related tasks and since he did not enquire about the religious beliefs of the children involved in his experiments, there is no extant literature which presently addresses this question. We simply do not know whether religious people make use of different mental operations from those employed by non-religious people.

In addition, by definition, a stage-developmental model of mental development presumes the existence of plateaux or stages where no perceptible advances are made. Children function at the level determined by their stage of development and then, through maturation, make a quantum leap to the next stage or plateau. By contrast, a linear model of mental development presumes a straight line relationship between age and advance. There are no sudden shifts or leaps in this model.

A factor relevant to the *evaluation of these two models* is the linguistic development of children. On the one hand, the development of understanding of metaphor or multiple word meanings may be related to a stage-developmental model (Billow, 1975). On the other hand, the development of children's vocabulary tends to improve incrementally and so shows poor correlation with Piagetian stages (Ehri, 1976; Moore and Harris, 1978; Jamison, 1989). When children are questioned about religious matters, their answers do not always allow the investigator to decide whether the child has 'verbalised a formula' or really understood a concept (Ennis, 1975; Smedslund, 1977). Children with verbal skills may appear to think in a more advanced way than children without them. It was partly for this reason that Goldman made use of the notion of 'mental age' which was calculated using intelligence tests. Goldman's findings are therefore expressed in terms of chronological and mental age. But this has theoretical implications.

First, if the findings are accepted at face value, they presume that abler children can understand the symbolic and abstract nature of biblical texts much earlier than less able children. Second, however, they assume that abler children cannot use their symbolic capabilities to understand a text on two levels at once, a symbolic and a concrete level, and that the symbolic level may help understanding of the concrete level. Conversely, in the case of less able children, understanding at a concrete level may validly function even in the case of texts which have a symbolic component: the Exodus story may function perfectly well as a story about setting people free without the encumbrance of notions of divine justice, retribution and miraculous walls of water (McGrady, 1990, 1994a, 1994b). Third, if Goldman's findings are *not* accepted at face value, a debate opens about the relationship between the concepts of mental age and stages. These two concepts come from quite different traditions within the history of psychology and are not usually treated together. Mental *age* is calculated by reference to precise chronological age. Mental *stage* is reached by reference to a combination of internal changes within the brain caused by maturation and interaction with the outside world. Consequently, mental stages and mental ages are not translatable into one another (Webb, 1974; Keating, 1975).

A method of evaluation occurred to Francis (1976) who constructed an attitude toward Christianity scale. If attitude toward Christianity and cognitive development in religion are connected, then it would be rational to expect either a stage-related or a linear relationship with age to occur in both cases. Extensive surveys showed attitude toward Christianity declined linearly between the ages of eight and sixteen years. There was no evidence in a graph of attitudes that stages had halted or accelerated this decline.

To what extent, then, can the connection between attitude toward Christianity and cognitive development be sustained? This is partly a matter of definition. If attitudes are defined as evaluations of beliefs about something, and if evaluations are dependent on mental activities, then cognitive development is relevant (Fishbein, 1963). Changes in cognitive development are bound to cause changes in evaluative outcomes, and changes in evaluative outcomes are bound to cause changes in attitudes. Yet, even when these changes are taking place, the *beliefs* which are being evaluated may *not* be influenced by changes in cognition. They may be held on emotional grounds and for subconscious reasons.

Stage-developmental theories do attempt to account for emotional development and naturally see this form of development as being stage-related also. The probability therefore is that, if religious beliefs are linked with emotional *or* with cognitive development, some sort of non-linear relationship between age and attitude toward religion ought to be discoverable, especially in the period between eight and sixteen years of age. The linear decline in attitude toward Christianity with age suggests that Goldman's concept of 'readiness for religion' is erroneous. Children are neither more nor less ready for religion at any age. Kay, Francis and Gibson (1996), utilising fresh empirical data, explore this issue in greater detail.

Goldman (1969) wrote, 'some people find it difficult to disentangle my psychological arguments from my educational and theological assumptions. I must confess I have encountered this difficulty myself'.

Hyde

Hyde's work was less well publicised but, in some respects, more extensive and equally important. Hyde (1965) developed a scale of attitude toward religion, composed of six sub-scales concerned with God, the bible, religion, the institutional church, the local church and church-going. He also developed an image of God test, a religious concept test and a religious knowledge test. He administered these tests to groups of secondary age pupils and reported that, while religious attitudes consistently fell between the ages of eleven and sixteen years, and while girls consistently showed more favourable attitudes than boys, those pupils who went to church once a month or more were far less inclined to suffer an erosion in their favourable attitudes, and such erosion as did occur was greatly retarded. Hyde went further and made use of student teachers to try out four separate classroom approaches to teaching the same syllabus. Pupils were tested both before and after the teaching in an attempt to discover what differences might result. The findings were disappointing, except in one respect. He was able to show that while 'religious attitude is not directly related to classroom attainment, indirectly it determines and influences pupil's knowledge of religious concepts and his general background of religious knowledge by which his attainment is most strongly influenced' (p. 84). Or, as Jeffreys in his foreword succinctly stated, 'religious learning depends significantly on religious attitudes, and [that] attitudes are closely connected with church-going'.

Goldman and Hyde, therefore, in their own ways contributed to a theoretical understanding of religious learning. Goldman considered he had found evidence for a stage-related progression in the acquisition of religious concepts; Hyde gave evidence to show how attitude toward religion influences the acquisition of religious concepts. Nevertheless, whether favourable attitudes promote religious learning or religious learning promotes favourable attitudes is not properly settled. Hyde's findings linked the two factors through church attendance with which both attitudes and concepts are connected, but Goldman assumed that misunderstandings of religion caused by a too early introduction of theological concepts based on the bible would lead to a later rejection of faith.

Cox

Edwin Cox wrote *Sixth Form Religion* in 1967. It was a report of research sponsored by the Christian Education Movement and elicited 2,276 completed questionnaires which had been sent to a randomly selected sample of grammar schools. In total 96 schools each contributed up to 25 pupils aged about eighteen years in the second year of the sixth form. These pupils were an academically elite group: they had been chosen to go to grammar school and then, having done well at examinations at the age of sixteen, were allowed to stay on for examinations at eighteen. Cox was concerned to find out what this highly selected group of pupils believed about God's existence, Jesus, life after death, the bible, the church, religious education, personal religious behaviour and a series of moral behaviours. His questionnaire contained fixed response items and also room for unrestrained personal expression.

In reporting his results, Cox's basic method was to present the percentages of pupils who held certain positions and then to illustrate these positions from the free responses. For example, the fixed responses allowed pupils to record their views on the existence of God on a five point scale. The responses ranged from 'I am completely confident that God exists', through uncertainty to 'I am completely confident that God does not exist'. Cox reported these percentages separately for boys and girls. The more open-ended answers were then classified into eight views of the kind of God that pupils felt was acceptable to them, and percentages were

again given. Thus, 26% thought of God as creator and 20% of God
as a father or a friend. Each of these categories was also illustrated
by examples using some of the pithy comments made by pupils
and then contrasted with the ideas about God which pupils found
unacceptable. Differences in beliefs about God were then presented, in one table, according to the degrees of certainty that God
exists and, in a different table, by church attendance. The responses of regular, occasional and non-churchgoers could be contrasted. In this way, it was possible to see that 24% of regular
churchgoers did not think of God as the creator, a statistic which
contrasted with the 43% of non-churchgoers who took the same
view.

Each of the chapters was presented in a similar way. The findings
about moral judgements included the percentages of different
types of reason given by pupils for the wrongness of certain behaviours. For example, gambling is wrong because it has a bad effect
on oneself, but more pupils think it bad because of its effect on
others. It may be thought of as wrong only if taken to excess or if
it becomes a regular habit.

All in all, the findings confirmed the general approval of religious
education by pupils, though their answers also indicated a desire
for reform. Pupils certainly preferred discussing moral topics rather
than listening to radio broadcasts or abstract philosophising.

The pungent comments of pupils and the quality of the research
design produced a piece of work with few serious weaknesses
within the limitations set for it. If there were weaknesses, they
derived from two sources: first, Cox tended occasionally to com-
ment on very small subdivisions of the whole sample. The problem
of evil worried only 7% of the sample, but there is an attempt to
suggest that it 'exercises some pressure on religious thinking' in a
much larger number of pupils. Or, again, 'the influence of the
logical positivist' is found in just under 5% of the sample of whom
we are told that 'two-thirds are boys'. Such a statistic does not
mean a great deal. Secondly, it is not clear from the presentation
of figures in the tables whether we are being offered percentages
of responses or percentages of pupils. In the figures given above,
it is not clear whether some of the pupils who thought of God as a
father also thought of God as creator or whether each pupil was
only counted once even if he or she thought of God in more than
one way.

Alves

Colin Alves undertook a survey of 520 schools for the Education Department of the British Council of Churches in 1965 and 1966. Loukes, although he was not a member of the survey committee (which, however, included Goldman), provided a list of nearly 300 schools that had previously been identified as having a particularly good standard of religious education. These schools were divided into categories based on type (comprehensive, grammar and secondary modern), pupil intake (boys', girls' and mixed), two size groupings, and regional groupings. A random sample of schools was drawn up and matched according to the categories already devised. A total of 20,000 questionnaires were sent out, that is, enough for the top fourth form (14–15 year olds) class in each school. The intention was to compare the practice of religious education in the good schools with the rest, but the project did not in the end report on this very fully. A further sample in the 'good' schools was then made of either their fourth form (15–16 year olds) or their sixth form (16–18 year olds), depending on which pupils had been at the school longest and so most exposed to the religious education programme. These pupils completed a slightly modified version of the original questionnaire.

The questionnaire(s) contained a test of pupils' knowledge of the New Testament, pupils' insight into the meaning of New Testament quotations, items relating to Jesus, the bible, the church, religious education and assembly to which pupils responded on a five point scale (from complete agreement, through uncertainty, to complete disagreement) and items relating to religious behaviour including moral behaviour, self-designation or otherwise as a Christian and church attendance. The items responded to on the five point scale were used to make up an attitude scale.

It is not clear from the report exactly how many questionnaires were returned. What is clear, however, is that the analysis was conducted using means and maxima and minima for the various types of school so that the focus of the findings was on different types of school rather than on differences between pupils.

The survey found that knowledge of the New Testament was greater in the grammar schools than in the secondary modern schools. This is not surprising considering that the grammar school pupils were chosen for their superior academic ability. In the schools specially selected for good practice there was evidence that knowledge of the New Testament deteriorated in the sixth form, but that the specially selected schools continued their concern for religious education even if this was not associated with widespread commitment to the Christian position among pupils. Girls were found to be better informed than boys on the New Testament, but the most unexpected result in the survey was that geographical factors were important in determining not only attainment in religious education but also attitude toward it. The geographical factor was only slightly less strong than the factor of gender difference. Alves concluded, 'generally speaking the nearer one gets to London the less favourable the attitude to Christianity becomes' (p. 140).

Suggestive results about the effects of staff qualifications, teaching methods and pupils' moral thinking were also given. An attempt (p. 209) was made to investigate the value of discussion in religious education lessons as a partial test of Loukes' recommendations. The results were ambiguous: in one region discussion was associated with favourable attitudes and in another it was not.

Alves' work was conducted on an ambitious scale, but suffered from an unrefined handling of the data largely due, one suspects, to the unavailability of computer facilities at that time. The attitude scale was not tested in advance of its use and no justification was presented of the inclusion or exclusion of individual items. The identification of schools with 'good' religious education practice was not made on the basis of any reported criteria and the result of pooling scores together from schools selected for 'good' religious education and those randomly selected inevitably, as Alves realised, prevented any generalisation of his findings to the country as a whole. The whole research design cried out for a multivariate analysis of statistics so that the effects of school type and size, as well as internal factors within each school and external factors relating to the home backgrounds of pupils, could have been controlled for and, where necessary, eliminated.

Conclusion

The research discussed in this chapter demonstrates how much can be achieved by a relatively small number of workers. But it also shows how much more there is to be done. The theoretical work of Goldman needs revisiting and recasting in the light of the criticisms made of it. It needs also to be applied to religious texts other than those in the Christian tradition. The surveys of Alves and Cox need to be used as the baseline for replication surveys in the 1990s. The linkage found by Hyde between religious attitude and religious learning needs to be re-investigated, and also to be reapplied in a non-Christian context. The work of Loukes, suggestive though it was, calls for a wider, more representative group of teenagers in the 1990s to speak into the microphone.

References

Alves, C. (1968), *Religion and the Secondary School*, London, SCM.

Billow, R.M. (1975), A cognitive developmental study of metaphor comprehension, *Developmental Psychology*, 11, 415–423.

Cox, E. (1967), *Sixth Form Religion*, London, SCM.

Ehri, L.C. (1976), Comprehension and production of adjectives in seriation, *Journal of Child Language*, 3, 369–384.

Ennis, R.H. (1975), Children's ability to handle Piaget's propositional logic: a conceptual critique, *Review of Educational Research*, 45, 1–41.

Fishbein, M. (1963), An investigation of the relationships between belief about an object and the attitude toward that object, *Human Relations*, 16, 233–239.

Fleming, C.M. (1966), Research evidence and Christian education, *Learning for Living*, 6, 1, 10–12.

Francis, L.J. (1976), An enquiry into the concept 'readiness for religion', Unpublished Ph.D. dissertation, University of Cambridge.

Francis, L.J. (1979), Research and the development of religious thinking, *Educational Studies*, 5, 109–115.

Goldman, R.J. (1964), *Religious Thinking from Childhood to Adolescence*, London, Routledge and Kegan Paul.

Goldman, R.J. (1965a), *Readiness for Religion*, London, Routledge and Kegan Paul.

Goldman, R.J. (1965b), Dr Goldman replies, *Learning for Living*, 5, 1, 24–26.

Goldman, R.J. (1966), Two kinds of fundamentalist, *Learning for Living*, 6, 3, 14–16.

Goldman, R.J. (1969), Dr Beeching, I presume? *Religious Education*, 64, 47–52.

Howkins, K.G. (1966), *Religious Thinking and Religious Education: a critique of the research and conclusions of Dr R. Goldman*, London, Tyndale Press.

Hyde, K.E. (1965), *Religious Learning in Adolescence* (University of Birmingham, Institute of Education, Monograph 7), London, Oliver and Boyd.

Jamison, H.E. (1989), Religious understanding in children aged seven to eleven, Unpublished Ph.D. dissertation, The Queen's University of Belfast.

Kay, W.K. (1981), Religious thinking, attitudes and personality amongst secondary pupils in England and Ireland, Unpublished Ph.D. dissertation, University of Reading.

Kay, W.K., Francis, L.J. and Gibson, H.M. (1996), Attitude toward Christianity and the transition to formal operational thinking, in press.

Keating, D. (1975), Precocious cognitive development at the level of formal operations, *Child Development*, 46, 276–280.

Loukes, H. (1961), *Teenage Religion*, London, SCM.

McGrady, A.G. (1990), The development of religious thinking: a comparison of metaphoric and operational paradigms, Unpublished Ph.D. dissertation, University of Birmingham.

McGrady, A.G. (1994a), Metaphorical and operational aspects of religious thinking: research with Irish Catholic pupils (part one), *British Journal of Religious Education*, 16, 148–163.

McGrady, A.G. (1994b), Metaphorical and operational aspects of religious thinking: research with Irish Catholic pupils (part two), *British Journal of Religious Education*, 17, 56–62.

Moore, T.E. and Harris, A.E. (1978), Language and thought in Piagetian theory, in L.S. Siegel and C.J. Brainherd (eds), *Alternatives to Piaget*, London, Academic Press.

Murphy, R.J.L. (1978), *The Development of Religious Thinking in Children: a review of psychological theories*, Leicester, UCCF.

Slee, N. (1992), Cognitive developmental studies of religious thinking: a survey and discussion with special reference to post-Goldman research in the United Kingdom, in J.W. Fowler, E.N. Nipkow and F. Schweitzer (eds), *Stages of Faith and Religious Development: implications for church, education and society*, pp. 130–146, London, SCM.

Smedslund, J. (1977), Symposium: practical and theoretical issues in Piagetian psychology — III, *British Journal of Educational Psychology*, 47, 1–6.

Webb, R. (1974), Concrete and formal operations in very bright 6 to 11 year olds, *Human Development*, 17, 292–300.

3

Thinking about childhood spirituality: review of research and current directions

David Hay, Rebecca Nye and Roger Murphy

Summary

Unlike the study of religious experience, children's spirituality is a relatively new subject of academic interest. Over the past thirty years the dominance of cognitive developmental theory in the field of religious education has led to a severe neglect of the study of the spirituality of the child and to a distortion of what goes on in the religious education classroom. In this chapter we begin by presenting evidence to support the view that there is indeed a rich spirituality of childhood. Turning to developmental theory, we offer a critique of its limitations, which at times come near to dissolving religion into reason, at the expense of an holistic understanding of what it means to be human. We suggest a more comprehensive, biological theory of spirituality, based on the work of Alister Hardy and his colleagues and review some of the implications of this approach for educational methodology and research in the field of religious education.

Introduction

The theme of children's[1] spirituality, as opposed to the religious education of children, is a relatively new subject of academic interest. It was of rather marginal concern for William James and the other New England founders of the modern psychology of religion at the end of the nineteenth century (most prominently Hall, Starbuck, Leuba, Coe). Immersed in the last great Puritan culture, they were primarily interested in the nature and authenticity of its central rite of passage, the process of religious conversion, which was typically expected to occur in mid-adolescence. Hall (1904), it is true, noted reports of the conversion of children as young as seven years of age, but interpreted them as artificially created by enthusiastic evangelists.

During the lull in the psychology of religion created by the reductionist influence of early psychoanalysis and behaviourism (Beit-Hallahmi, 1974; Hay, 1990a) the study of spiritual experience in general became temporarily discredited. It was therefore not until the threshold of the 1960s that children's spirituality first began to be taken up as an object of investigation. Coincidentally, at about the same time Ronald Goldman (1964) gave a new fillip to a longstanding theme in religious education, cognitive development as it relates to children's understanding of religious narrative. In the introduction to his study, Goldman asserted, quite wrongly, that only a small minority of the general population believes that they have ever had direct personal spiritual or religious experience. Consequently, Goldman urged that the efforts of researchers should be directed away from spirituality to topics that he perceived to be of more immediate educational significance. Goldman's view continues to have some influence, despite sustained critiques of his position by Francis (1976), Hyde (1968), Murphy (1978a, 1980), Langdon (1969) and others. In more recent times, James Fowler (1981) and Fritz Oser (Oser and Reich, 1990; Oser and Scarlett, 1991) have followed him to some degree, in laying a heavy emphasis on cognitive growth as it affects children's religion.

In this chapter we propose a more holistic view of the nature of spirituality than has typically informed the work of the cognitive tradition. We suggest that an excessive concern with intellectual development has encouraged and perhaps led to an impoverishment of the meaning of the phrase 'religious knowledge'. In addition, there has been a tendency to focus on specific kinds of religious language as indicators of spirituality and an over-easy acceptance of the idea that the content of spirituality is primarily a socially constructed set of ideas. This has led to the neglect of interpretations of spiritual awareness which would highlight the roles played by emotion and forms of experience not confined to our rational, cognitive capacities. Such alternative interpretations might include arguments for a structural or biological basis for spirituality (Hardy 1966, 1979; Hay 1987; 1990a; 1994), and accounts of spiritual or religious knowing which have explored a wider range of psychological functions than the solely intellectual contribution to spirituality (Watts and Williams, 1988; Donaldson, 1992). We believe that this neglect of broader approaches to spirituality as they might pertain to children's experience is a reason for the weakness of much that passes for religious education at the present time.

Is there a spirituality of childhood?

Against the tide of opinion, some authors (Greer, 1981, 1982; Hay 1985; Hammond, Hay, Moxon, Netto, Raban, Straugheir and Williams, 1990; Hay 1990b; Francis and Greer, 1993) have steadily insisted that it is necessary to take account of religious experience in religious education. Even as Goldman was making his assertion about the virtual absence of spiritual or religious experience from the general population, the survey work of Glock and Stark (1965) and Back and Bourque (1970) was uncovering evidence of widespread report of religious experience in the adult population of the United States of America. Repeated surveys since that period have demonstrated the probable correctness of this evidence and its generalisability to the populations of Britain and Australia (Greeley, 1975; Wuthnow, 1976; Hay and Morisy, 1985; Gallup, 1978, 1985; Morgan Poll, 1983; Hay and Heald, 1987). In-depth surveys in Britain (Hay, 1979; Lewis, 1987; Hay and Morisy, 1985) and recently in Italy (Acquaviva, 1991) suggest that something like two-thirds of the populations of these countries believe that they have had some kind of direct evidence of the reality of the spiritual dimension of human experience. The question arising from this is, at what stage in life does such experience first manifest itself?

A major difficulty in investigating children's religious understanding or spirituality is in devising a plausible methodology (Murphy, 1978b). The problem has been discussed by Hay (1988) in relation to studies of adult spirituality, but the methods used there are largely inappropriate with children. There is a further difficulty in recognising spirituality in children who have been brought up with secular presuppositions and language. This will be discussed later. First of all, we will review the methodologies of some early attempts to probe this difficult area.

Klingberg (1959) published a study of the experiences of 630 Swedish children between nine and thirteen years of age. She asked them to write compositions completing the statement, 'Once when I thought about God . . .' and found that they described four types of situations. In order of frequency, the four types of situation were defined as: times of distress, experiences in nature, moral experiences, and formal worship experiences. Prayer experiences seemed to involve the deepest emotional reactions. Elkind and Elkind (1962) copied Klingberg's study, this time with 144 American ninth grade students. Although their subjects fall outside the age range we are considering, the adaptation of Klingberg's methodology is of interest. The students were asked by their English teacher to compose two paragraphs in answer to the two following questions: 'When do you feel closest to God?' and 'Have you ever had a particular experience when you felt especially close to God?' Recurrent situations in order of frequency were: church, solitude, anxiety, fear, worry, prayer and moral action. What the Elkinds referred to as 'acute' situations were, in order of frequency: thanking God, meditation, initiation, grief and revelation. The reversal of the ranking of the church as the context for spiritual experience in the two countries is noteworthy and it might be speculated that this is either a function of the very different status of religious institutions in Sweden and the United States of America, or a reflection of changing attitude toward formal religion on entering adolescence. At any rate, these pieces of research suggested that spirituality is not absent from childhood, though perhaps its nature is different from that of adult life.

In another empirical study conducted from within developmental psychology, Murphy (1980) provided a thorough critique of Goldman's earlier work. That study illustrated the fragile nature of Goldman's findings, by linking new data from children between the ages of six and eleven years with data from the research of Margaret Donaldson (1978) and her associates, which revealed the complexities of children's responses and their dependence on the context and language that was used. Murphy's research showed that young children were capable of much more than Goldman had suggested and exposed the ideological imperatives that had driven much of the 'hype' that accompanied the launch of his ideas in the mid 1960s.

Differences in the nature of religious understanding and experience before and during adolescence were explored by Long, Elkind and Spilka (1967). They noted that before the age of between ten and twelve years, prayer tends to be formulaic and petitionary, but after that it was more likely to be understood as a private conversation with God, a sharing of intimacies and confidences in which petitionary requests are of only secondary impor-

tance. This finding might seem to imply a growing religious awareness with physical maturation, perhaps lending some support to
the developmentalists' theories of religious understanding. However, several research findings published over the past twenty
years, and more particularly since 1990, suggest another picture.

The Original Vision by Edward Robinson (1983) was a pioneering
attempt to question the educational validity of the Piagetian
developmental model which Goldman recycled in the area of
religious development. At the time, Robinson was director of the
Religious Experience Research Unit in Oxford[2] and he noticed that
a sizeable proportion of accounts of religious experience sent in to
the Unit were reminiscences of events occurring in childhood,
sometimes in very early years. The experiences had remained in
the memories of his correspondents for the rest of their lives, often
seeming to be of the greatest personal significance when they were
considering questions of meaningfulness and personal identity.
Whilst recognising the likelihood of a degree of adult elaboration
of such experience, Robinson found himself questioning the cognitive emphasis given to the development of children's religious
understanding. It made him wonder, as it had made the poets
Edwin Muir and William Wordsworth before him, whether the
original spiritual vision of childhood was perhaps locked out of
awareness as we enter the 'prison house' of adult life. We ourselves
pose the following question. Could it be the case in certain circumstances, for example in a highly secularised society, that the social
construction of reality is such that instead of permitting the
development of a mature understanding of one's spirituality, it
actually becomes suppressed or, to use a psychodynamic concept,
repressed out of consciousness?

The weakness of Robinson's approach is the fact that he depended for his data on reminiscences of childhood by adults, some
of whom were very elderly. How reliable could such long term
memories be, and what sort of elaboration and retelling of the story
of childhood had gone on? In his book *The Spiritual Life of Children*,
Robert Coles (1992) corrects this limitation by giving an account
of his conversations with children about their spiritual lives. Like
Robinson, Coles sees it as a mistake to give priority to cognition in
our attempts to understand religious development. He quotes
Pascal's *Pensées* (282) 'Those to whom God has imparted religion
by intuition are very fortunate, and justly convinced. But to those
who do not have it, we can give it only by reasoning, waiting for
God to give them insight, without which faith is only human and

useless for salvation' (and we might add, for everyday religious life).

In his dialogues, conducted over many years, Coles insisted on attending to the phenomenology of the children's experience and, as far as possible, refusing to lay his own interpretations on it. For Coles, children quite clearly have a dynamic spiritual life, as is shown by the vivid, lively interviews he records with children of many faiths and none. What he seeks to demonstrate is that religion/spirituality is a living matter of personal experience and not simply a sequence of dead cognitive stages. He begins from a psychodynamic perspective, following the ideas of Ana-Maria Rizzuto (1979), in particular her view that God constitutes a transitional object in Winnicott's (1958) sense. In the end though, he is unhappy with Rizzuto's continued use of the word 'illusion' to refer to spiritual experience, since 'illusion' and 'reality' even if, as she asserts, they are not contradictory nevertheless are not identical.

In fact Rizzuto does advert to the Winnicottian concept of 'transitional space' to resolve the tension. This psychological phenomenon describes the all important realm *between* illusion and reality, in which many of the most significant human experiences, such as creative and religious impulses, appear to find expression both in childhood and adulthood (and in which transitional objects achieve their special, quasi-sacred status). As such, the notion of the transitional space appears to offer an important potential source of spirituality which takes respectful account of both inner and outer worlds, reducing spiritual experience to neither. Nevertheless, although benevolent in her attitude toward religion, Rizzuto is in fact reductionist and avoids certain realities of religious experience, for example interpreting 'presence' as a product of the Oedipal crisis, rather than allowing the direct religious phenomenology to express itself. That is, she falls into the trap of basing her argument on prior structural assumptions about the nature of reality rather than allowing her informants (adult psychiatric patients who had been referred to her) their own supposedly less sophisticated interpretations.

We ourselves do not wish to dismiss the psychoanalytic contribution to our understanding of children's spirituality. It is clear from the work of many researchers that in the images of God developed by most children there is a strongly projective component, usually drawn from the parents. But the Finnish researcher Kalevi Tamminen (1994) has recently reminded us of the ambiguity of this evidence. If Freud is correct that God is a projected parent figure, then, if children prefer the opposite sex parent, it follows that girls should be more concerned with a deity presented as a fatherly male (Argyle and Beit-Hallahmi, 1975). According to some researchers (Vergote and Tamayo, 1981) the father figure is more dominant in the idea of God, but others (Godin and Hallez, 1965; Deconchy, 1968; Spilka, Addison and Rosensohn, 1975) find that the dominant figure is either the mother or alternatively the parent who is closer to the child. Clearly the situation is more complex than a simplistic interpretation of Freudian theory would lead us to suppose. Perhaps the apparent significance of one or other parent figure is underpinned by the contribution such a person makes to the child's experience and understanding of personal relationships, of self knowledge and of being known, both of which are recurrent themes for progress towards spiritual enlightenment in most faiths.

Two other pieces of research predate Coles in publication but have similarities to his work in that they emphasise the autonomy of childhood spirituality. In *The Children's God*, David Heller (1986) gives an account of his research into children's notions and ways of talking to God. His conversations were in the form of lengthy, one off, semi-structured interviews. Hence his relationships with the children seem to have been a good deal briefer than at least some of those set up by Coles. His perspective is overtly religious, but he is careful to ask the children to use their own terms and to relate them to other issues of personal significance. His analysis is 'interpretative', linking his findings to a broad range of psychological theories. Jo-Anne Taylor's (1989) small study, much briefer in compass than Coles' book, is in many ways as impressive. It contains a set of very sensitive individual interviews and analytic comments with a small sample of children from a range of faiths, aged between four and twelve years. Her interpretative comments are related specifically to Christian religious literature, but this is done very creatively, exploring the children's use of metaphor and also the way that their drawings amplify their verbal expression. No attempt is made to link this work to developmental theory.

Rather different methodologies to those described above have been used by two German researchers. Theophil Thun's (1959) approach almost certainly owes something to Karl Girgensohn, the major figure in the Dorpat school of religious psychology (Wulff, 1991). Girgensohn devised a systematic method for experimental introspection into religious experience, which Thun seems to have borrowed in a large-scale study of German Catholic and Protestant children in the first four grades of school. He offered the children a series of what, within the Christian cultural context, were existential questions to reflect upon, for example 'What was Jesus like?', 'What is the nature of prayer?' and 'How did they experience meeting death?' The children were asked not to respond immediately, but to sit quietly with their eyes closed whilst they contemplated the theme presented. They were then invited to discuss the questions. Thun reports a variety of observations, but in the present context he notes that from the second grade onwards the children demonstrated the capacity for wonder as well as the experience of both the *mysterium tremendum* and the *mysterium fascinans* described by Rudolf Otto (1950) in his phenomenology of religious experience.

Maria Bindl (1965) did a study of over 8,000 drawings on religious themes by Roman Catholic school pupils aged between three and eighteen years of age. Her thinking was particularly influenced by the work of Otto (1950) and also Eduard Spränger (1974). To interpret the children's drawings she used a version of the graphological procedure of Ludwig Klages (1927). She considered she had detected four developmental phases. The first extends till about the age of seven, and is labelled by her as *naive relatedness to the wholly other*. At this stage God is experienced naïvely in an I–Thou relationship. In her second stage, *decline in spontaneous experience of the numinous*, which may appear as early as the age of six, the powerful experience of the wholly other begins to fade as reason displaces fantasy. Bindl does, however, note the potential for a *consciously striven for relation to transcendence* in the later teenage years. Klages' approach has been severely criticised as invalid (Wulff, 1991), but the interpretation of drawings by more recent practitioners, for example in the identification of severe physical illness and deeper psychological issues in children (Furth, 1988; Bach, 1990), suggests that it may have possibilities as an instrument for supplying evidence supplementary to the limited verbal data children can articulate.

As mentioned earlier, these pieces of research share a Wordsworthian understanding of spirituality, seeing childhood as a period when adult secular interpretations of reality, with their typical reverence for cognitive rationality at the expense of any other kind of knowing and feeling, have not yet had a chance to smother spiritual awareness. We are reminded here of the findings of Tamminen (1991), who in a large scale Finnish study of religious development in childhood and adolescence noted both very high levels of report of religious or spiritual experience in children up to the age of about twelve or thirteen years, followed by a fairly steep decline. Similarly, Francis (1987) has charted the decline of religious interest in British children from the ages of eight to fifteen years. Speculating from a socio-historical perspective, one might note that twelve was typically the age at which children in Europe have their first serious induction into the scientific tradition of the enlightenment, with its associated religious scepticism. That children are now often receiving scientific instruction from a much younger age may have the effect of inhibiting early spiritualities at an even more sensitive, vulnerable stage, when such spirituality is even less coherent and therefore defendable, though precious or possibly vital nonetheless.

Together with the evidence of the researchers reviewed above which finds positive support for a variety of forms of childhood spirituality, Tamminen's identification of declining reports of spiritual experience with age can therefore be assimilated to an hypothesis that the 'blotting out' of spirituality is a socially constructed phenomenon. This hypothesis directly contrasts with a sceptical opinion which might argue that spirituality itself is socially constructed and therefore only gradually in evidence as children are artificially inducted into this otherwise 'unnatural' sensibility. Our stance is that the research evidence reviewed here does not support the sceptical view. The data do not run entirely counter to the currently dominant cognitive theories of religious development, but they do raise questions about the adequacy of developmental theory as the sole basis for an account of childhood religion.

Critique of developmental theory

Schweitzer (1992) has traced the idea of religious development back to the sixteenth century, detecting vague notions already present in the writings of reformers like Luther, Comenius and Francke. By the time of Rousseau and Locke this had turned into a conscious and highly rationalistic interest in genetic epistemology, leading paradoxically in the work of religious writers to an avoidance of the spiritual dimension of human experience, which as Stock (1982) shows, became increasingly relegated to the world of literature and art. Dykstra and Parks (1986) suggest that the potency of cognitive psychology as a plausible means of gaining self-understanding has meant that developmental theories of religion have tended to follow on its coat-tails. If Schweitzer is right, we have at hand an historical explanation of why religious development has come to be looked at with a very cognitive eye and why the experiential dimension of religion, though from our perspective fundamental, suffers from problems of plausibility.

From our point of view, the major problem about developmental stage theories is their narrowness, coming near to dissolving religion into reason and therefore childhood religion into a form of immaturity or inadequacy. If cognitive development is central, it also puts out of court the work of Bissonnier (1965) who writes about the profound religion of people who are mentally retarded. Similarly, it rules out Jaspard's (1994) discussion of the comprehension of religious rituals among male and female mentally handicapped adults. Jaspard hypothesises that in this human group, ritual is the major way in which the relationship with God is mediated.

When we examine the total phenomenon of religion directly, rather than theorise about its cognitive aspects, we find that central to its praxis is the use of rituals or exercises which in many cases have developed over thousands of years and are highly sophisticated. They can be seen as designed to enhance awareness through meditative or contemplative techniques. Such awareness is an extremely subtle and intricate phenomenon, and may have a biological basis, as noted by Hay (1995):

> From an evolutionary perspective this can be understood as a consequence of the need to survive within the multi-faceted intricacy of the natural environment. This has been an important theme amongst sociobiologists in recent years. In his pioneering study of the evolution of consciousness, John Crook (1980) demonstrated through comparative studies of the life of other modern primates, how living and hunting in communities as our forebears did leads to the need for a brain that can process, prioritise and make speedy decisions on the basis of the well-nigh infinite mass of data constantly entering the sensory apparatus. Such a process cannot follow the dictates of linear logic, which depends on a watertight set of arguments following sequentially and unidimensionally from a static point in time. It cannot even depend on multi-dimensional logical sequences such as could be generated by a computer, because the flow of data is far too large and dynamic to be processed in this way.

The fact that the expressive dimension of religion is marked particularly by a rich emphasis on metaphor, ritual and symbolism seems to be related to these holistic aspirations. In its preoccupation with the profoundest questions of existence, religion is the most extreme form of human ontological ambition and though in its arguments it may use linear logic, it cannot be confined by it and needs to turn to ritual and symbolism. Interestingly Winnicott argued that both these aspects occupy the transitional space between fantasy and reality, hence though they may be practically rooted in the outer world, the experience of them necessarily goes beyond the logical restraints of reality and can borrow qualities from the mysterious realm of fantasy.

In recent years there have been a number of attempts by researchers in the field of religion to reinstate the validity of these dimensions of thinking, of ritual and symbol. Hans-Günther Heimbrock (1986), for example, asks whether, in religion, symbolic thinking is truly inferior to linear logic. Elsewhere, Heimbrock (1992) questions the apparent belittling or ignoring of ritual, especially by Fritz Oser. Oser appears to accept the view that ritual is primitive, a stage which we grow out of, yet it is central to the mediation of spiritual experience in many religious groups, not least in Oser's own Roman Catholic faith. By insisting on linear logic as the most valid criterion for assessing religious understanding we are perhaps assimilating an imperialistic assumption about developmentalism which may not correspond to human reality. Margaret Donaldson's (1992) recent account of the development of the human mind is a rare example of an attempt to describe the emergence and role of alternative forms of human thinking and feeling to the logical or rational. Her argument makes clear that psychology has overlooked what she calls these value-sensing modes for far too long, and is in danger of failing to address the totality of human psychology as a result.

Our feeling is that Goldman, and to a degree James Fowler and Fritz Oser, are tempted to fall into an ontological error alluded to clearly in a recent paper by Lorelei Farmer (1992). In a study of adult reminiscences of childhood spiritual experience, following on from the work of Robinson (1983), Farmer points out that no amount of refinement and blending of the ideas of Piaget, Kohlberg or Erikson will bring us closer to understanding religious knowledge. The basic mistake committed by developmentalists in this field is false philosophical categorisation. Religious knowledge is different from knowledge about religion in that it is much more akin to sensory knowledge. Indeed, the description of this area as one of religious knowing, given by Watts and Williams (1988), is preferable since it captures the sense in which this refers to processes rather than a set content or structures of knowledge. This characterisation of the psychology of religious/spiritual experience as a process of knowing also affords consideration of the quality of 'not knowing' or unknowing[3] which can occur in the spiritual experience, in which there is a greater sense of the experience being beyond knowledge than 'about' knowledge of a particular thing.

Farmer notes that our care in distinguishing these two kinds of knowledge (religious knowing and knowledge about religion) implies that we must also be willing to permit the possibility that religious knowing may be independent of the growth of cognitive abilities and/or emotional capacities. At most we should be looking at the functioning of cognitive/emotional structures and processes which precede, accompany or even follow upon religious knowing. The point Farmer is making is that all the adults with whom she talked spoke of a process of slowly coming to understand (in some kind of quasi rational way) through being faithful to the truths they perceived (in some other way) in their early transcendent experiences. An important area for research must be to investigate the form in which such experiences are held by children at the time, before they are able to reflect on them fully, rationally or otherwise. How, if at all, do children articulate or at least store such memories which are later recalled as spiritually significant? And how many more experiences are forgotten in the absence of any context which allows their expression?

Need for a broader theory of spirituality

What is implied in the criticisms made by Farmer is the necessity to turn to a more holistic model of human spirituality, which sees it as something larger than any individual religion. Readers may have been struck so far by our partisanship for researchers who insist on taking religious and particularly Christian interpretations of reality seriously. Nevertheless, we now want to go on to say that the strong historical link in the Western world between spirituality and the Christian religion is itself a constriction of meaning which has had serious practical consequences in the school curriculum. Because of the rapid de-Christianisation of British society, it is a legacy that makes for considerable difficulties in implementing the requirements of the 1988 Education Reform Act in regard to spiritual education.

The problem is not new. A quarter of a century ago, R. A. Butler (1971) remarked in his book, *The Art of the Possible,* that the 'perfunctory and uninspired nature of religious instruction' had begun 'to imperil the Christian basis of our society'. This process has accelerated since then and what it has led to in the end is stated in Stuart Sutherland's (1994) report for OFSTED, *Religious Education and Collective Worship.* The report concludes that the major issue in religious education is widespread non-compliance with the Education Reform Act and the low status accorded to religious education in school plans.

Because of the uncertainties surrounding the term 'spirituality' the practicalities facing inspectors who are required to comply with the ordinances of the OFSTED (1994) *Handbook for Inspection of Schools* are awesome (Ungoed-Thomas, 1994). This highlights the urgent need for a plausible model of human spirituality that takes account of contemporary realities. Hence, if we are to take spirituality seriously, we have to face the fact that it has a broader meaning than is suggested by the term 'religion'. There have been a number of attempts to create a definition which recognises this fact. We have some sympathy with Kevin Mott-Thornton (1994), who in summarising the range of understanding of the term 'spirituality' links it with 'ethos':

> Spirituality is that quality of being, holistically conceived, made up of insight, beliefs, values, attitudes/emotions and behavioural dispositions, which both informs and may be informed by lived experience. The cognitive aspects of our common spirituality can be described at any particular time, as being a framework of ideals, beliefs and values about oneself, one's relations with others and reality/the world. Logically intrinsic is some notion of the good life, which informs (implicitly or explicitly) all action.

For Mott-Thornton spirituality applies to all human beings, religious or not, and is not located exclusively with cognition. That is, as implied by what we were saying earlier, it has physical and affective aspects as well as cognitive.

Since the authors of this chapter are all practising Christians, we wish to add that it is by no means necessary to abandon a religious perspective to take this view. The Jesuit theologian Karl Rahner offers a contemporary Christian perspective which takes the human end of spirituality to be a natural phenomenon, not confined to the field of formal religion. In one of his *Theological Investigations,* Rahner (1974) invites his readers to imagine a world in which all religious institutions have disappeared and the word 'God' no longer exists:

> And even if this term were ever to be forgotten, even then in the decisive moments of our lives we should still be constantly encompassed by this nameless mystery of our existence ... even supposing that those realities which we call religions . . . were totally to disappear . . . the transcendentality inherent in human life is such that [we] would still reach out towards that mystery which lies outside [our] control.

Our position is akin to that of Rahner. We conceive of an innate spiritual capacity in childhood, but recognise that this may focus in particular ways and take different and changing forms as the child's other capacities develop.

As we have said, the difficulty about many theories of spirituality is their narrow focus. In a recent paper, Helmut Reich (1992) describes the ideal theory of religious development, and his five criteria are strikingly applicable to our needs in understanding children's spirituality. First, it must refer to psychological processes in the organism, including meaning making. Second, it must explore the coordination between the psyche and the biophysical, sociocultural and perceived spiritual reality and explore their relationships. Third, it must explore social contexts and how they relate to the individual's spirituality. Fourth, it must account for universal features of spirituality as well as individual differences. Fifth, it must specify mechanisms by which change occurs, including factors favourable or unfavourable to spirituality.

On these criteria, very little research that has been done to date even begins to approach adequacy as the basis for a satisfactory understanding of the spirituality of children. However, Alister Hardy's (1966, 1979) hypothesis about the biological origin of our religious awareness does offer a broadly based, plausible and testable conjecture about spirituality. Used in conjunction with developmental and other theories, it could potentially respond to Reich's requirements, more especially the second and fourth criteria which have been almost completely neglected to date.

Hardy's idea is in fact to be found as an unexplicit presupposition in numerous precursors going back at least as far as the end of the eighteenth century. We are thinking here of Schleiermacher's (1799) natural theology and in later times the work of E.D. Starbuck (1901), William James (1902), Ernst Troeltsch (1906), Rudolf Otto (1950), Joachim Wach (1958) and probably Mircea Eliade (1960). What seems to be implied is a structural understanding of religious awareness akin in some ways to Chomsky's (1957) proposals about linguistic competence. Over the past few years such structural notions have been gaining broader currency in the field of cognitive psychology (Wellman and Gelman, 1992; Hirschfeld and Gelman, 1994). Interestingly, much the same idea has been made explicit by James Fowler himself (Fowler, Nipkow and Schweitzer, 1992):

> We are prepotentiated, as it were, to generate the capacities necessary for us as a species to fulfil our vocations as reflective-responsive members of creation. We have as part of our creatively evolved biological heritage the generative deep-structural tendencies that make possible our development as partners with one another and with God.

Hardy's hypothesis appears to stand up well in comparison with other more reductionist explanations of religious experience (Hay, 1994). There is also some independent evidence to support his supposition. Waller, Kojetin and their colleagues (Waller, Kojetin, Bouchard, Lykken, and Tellegen, 1990) used the method of studying twins reared apart and together to examine the genetic and environmental influences on religious interests, attitudes and values. They found statistically significant evidence of religious similarities in the twins reared apart to suggest a biological component of religiousness. This is in agreement with the hypothesis propounded by Michael Jackson (1992) that the capacity to have spiritual experience is a function of a biologically inherited trait of 'schizotypy' which normally has survival value for the individual but in certain extreme circumstances can engender schizophrenia.

A new direction for spirituality research?

The implication of taking Hardy's view seriously for an understanding of children's spirituality is considerable because it implies that there is in every child a spiritual potentiality no matter what the child's cultural context may be. Of course, it is likely that the specific context will come to play an important role in shaping, nurturing or stunting this innate potentiality, just as the specific language environment serves to shape the linguistic expressions made possible by our human capacity for language, the innate potential to which Chomsky (1957) refers as our language acquisition device (LAD). Rahner (1974) in discussing what, from his Christian perspective, is the experience of God today, speaks of religions as 'conceptual reflections on, and social institutionalisations of our experience of God'. He adds that conceptual reflections always fail to capture the experience, *'just as it is possible to talk about God without being spiritual'* (our italics). The difficulty with almost all research on children's spirituality up to the very recent past is that it focuses on God-talk, or, in the case of Goldman and his descendants, the Piagetian development of God-talk. Given that the religious contexts surrounding children today are typically much less explicit than in the past or even absent, in order to uncover the innate spiritual potential children may possess, research needs to take a different direction. We suggest the need for researchers to focus on the perceptions, awareness and response of children to those ordinary activities which can act as what Peter Berger (1967) calls 'signals of transcendence'.

We mentioned the lack of a research tradition that has looked at children's spirituality from a broad perspective. But very recently there are signs of a move in this direction. Elaine McCreery (1994) in her work on 'talking to children about things spiritual' is enquiring about the spiritual notions of children as young as four or five. She points out that people who gave accounts of their childhood experience to Edward Robinson (1983) were unable to articulate it at the time that it happened. From a Vygotskian (1986) perspective (see below), they did not have the language available and it is only in adult life that they were able to retrieve it as a spiritual experience. McCreery's straightforward definition of spirituality is 'an awareness that there is something other, something greater than the course of everyday events'. She has tried to identify events in the home (birth, death, love, trust, joy, sadness, special occasions, religion), school (nature studies, stories, danger, failure, reward, companionship, success; also activities such as painting, drawing, sorting, matching, play, story, singing), television (cultural difference, violence, death, social taboos, nobility, despicable behaviour, suffering, charity) which might relate to her definition.

It is notable that in her conversations with children, she is keen to give no verbal cues which might trigger off standard religious phraseology, that is, theoretical talk about spiritual experience rather than direct reference to personal spirituality. Thus the question 'What do you think happens when we die?' is too leading. McCreery feels it is better to tell a story involving the death of an animal, perhaps a pet and invite the children to give their reflections on it, for example by asking them how they would console the owner.

Erricker and Erricker (1994) stress the problem of identifying an immutable spirituality in a social context where normal spiritual or religious language is either absent or suppressed or repressed because of problems of plausibility in modern, scientific culture. In another paper, Erricker, Sullivan, Erricker, Logan and Ota (1994) pose the question 'How can we converse in an informed way about such notions as spiritual and moral, unless we have an understanding of the views, attitudes and concerns of children nurtured in a plurality of social, religious and educational environments?' In this paper they give an account of talking to two ten year old boys (one a Muslim, one a Sikh) about their interest in bangra dancing, the metaphorical power of the dancing and how it expresses the individuality and spiritual self of the boys.

The task of the Errickers' research is to access the ontological paradigms and metaphorical frameworks of the children in which the 'open ear' can search for spirituality. They are working with stage 2 children in an inner city comprehensive school in Southampton. They suggest that there are a set of 'genres', that is ideas and attitudes constituting an identifiable package, that children in today's world tend to take up. Thus they have identified four that are fairly clear and which they describe as follows: *My little pony*, a Disneyesque approach concentrating on the welfare of animals; *All American kid*, theme parks, McDonalds and consumerism; *Family centred*; and *The hard man*.

Children can switch genres and it is interesting that the Errickers have not yet identified a genre purely based on religious tradition (though surely this would be the case at least with some Muslim children). The method used is that of Grounded Theory (Glaser and Strauss, 1967) and they focus on existential themes, for example, loss and conflict and how children attempt to resolve these issues with the personal narratives available to them. From the perspective of the student of spirituality, there is a need to deconstruct the children's storytelling in the process of bringing their own spirituality to their awareness.

Nye and Hay (1995) follow a Vygotskian line (Vygotsky, 1986) on the nature of preverbal experience in a culture which has lost the necessary vocabulary to isolate and characterise spiritual experience. They discuss the aspects of human experience that might constitute the realm of spirituality for children. Awareness, mystery, value sensing and meaning making are identified as four major dimensions of experience to which attention should be paid by researchers working with children in contemporary culture. In their ongoing project to study the spirituality of six year old and ten year old children Hay and Nye are analysing conversations with the children, designed to focus on these dimensions and uncover the way that spirituality comes to expression either verbally or symbolically. They are also using a grounded theory approach which utilises the NUD.IST software package (Richards and Richards, 1994) as a means of identifying the structure and expression of the children's experience, with these four major dimensions as guides. What has emerged is the clear presence of what can be defined as a spirituality in all the transcripts so far examined. In many cases overtly religious language is absent and children are adapting other cultural idioms to give a framework to their emerging awareness of spiritually significant experiences.

The pieces of research mentioned above are still at an early stage and no firm conclusions can yet be drawn from the data. It is notable, however, that their assumptions and the validity of their findings depend much more on a structural notion of the nature of spirituality than on any of the contemporary variants of developmental theory. It seems to us that research of the kind described does not, as some of our critics claim, further attenuate or damage religious understanding. On the contrary, by drawing attention to a realm of human awareness commonly avoided in school, even in the religious education classroom, it may help children to appreciate the experiential perspective of the religious believer. Religious understanding can grow out of a recognition by individuals of the existence of such spiritual experience within themselves.

We might add that from the Christian believer's perspective,[4] Vygotsky's (1986) research on the 'zone of proximal awareness' provides a rationale for the introduction of bible stories to children *before* they are 'ready' in Goldman's terminology. Vygotsky emphasises the role of challenging concepts as powerful developmental instruments, when sensitively introduced, to help to reach the next level of understanding. Could it be that particular cultures, secular or perhaps 'over-cognitively religious', hamper the development of the expression of spirituality because of preconceptions about children's competencies, or more commonly, their lack of competence? Certainly, there has been a neglect of the educational philosophy of 'scaffolding' identified by Jerome Bruner (1974), a keen student of Vygotsky's developmental legacy. This identifies the importance of sensitively scaffolding new cognitive input onto children's existing, sometimes natural, sense of the phenomena in question.

As we have emphasised, research has tended to neglect the investigation of children's personal experiences of spirituality and concentrated on children's cognitive comprehension of religious themes. In the absence of empirically based accounts of the forms children's 'natural' spirituality can take, it must be difficult or impossible for those committed to developing children's spirituality to scaffold children's learning onto their own experiences, meanings and values. It is here that the importance of recent research on children's spirituality lies.

Notes

1. In this chapter, childhood is taken to refer to children of primary age.
2. Renamed the Alister Hardy Centre in 1985 and located at Westminster College, Oxford.
3. Zen Buddhism places much emphasis on this aspect of spirituality. However it is also found in Christianity, in the apophatic way of the Eastern Church (Lossky, 1957) or in fourteenth century mysticism in the Western tradition, for example in *The Cloud of Unknowing* (edited by J. Walsh, 1982).
4. The same of course is true in relation to sacred scripture in other faith contexts, for example Islam.

References

Acquaviva, S.S. (1991), *Eros Morte ed Esperienza Religiosa*, Bari, Laterza.

Argyle, M. and Beit-Hallahmi, B. (1975), *The Social Psychology of Religion*, London, Routledge and Kegan Paul.

Bach, S. (1990), *Life Paints its own Span: on the significance of spontaneous pictures by severely ill children*, Zurich, Daimon Verlag.

Back, K. and Bourque, L.B. (1970), Can feelings be enumerated? *Behavioral Science*, 15, 487–496.

Beit-Hallahmi, B. (1974), Psychology of religion 1880–1930: the rise and fall of a psychological movement, *Journal of the History of the Behavioral Sciences*, 10, 84–90.

Berger, P. (1967), *A Rumor of Angels*, Harmondsworth, Penguin.

Bindl, M. (1965), *Das religiöse Erleben im Spiegel der Bildgestaltung: Eine Entwicklunsgs-psychologie Untersuchung*, Freiburg, Herder.

Bissonnier, H. (1965), Religious expression and mental deficiency, in A. Godin (ed.), *From Religious Experience to Religious Attitude*, pp. 143–154, Chicago, Loyola University Press.

Bruner, J.S. (1974), *Beyond the Information Given: studies in the psychology of knowing* (selected, edited, and introduced by Jeremy M. Anglin), London, Allen and Unwin.

Butler, R.A. (1971), *The Art of the Possible: the memoirs of Lord Butler*, London, Hamish Hamilton.

Chomsky, N. (1957), *Syntactic Structures*, The Hague, Mouton Press.

Coles, R. (1992), *The Spiritual Life of Children*, London, Harper Collins.

Crook, J.H. (1980), *The Evolution of Human Consciousness*, Oxford, Clarendon Press.

Deconchy, J.P. (1968), God and parental images, in A. Godin (ed.), *From Cry to Word*, pp. 85–94, Brussels, Lumen Vitae Press.

Donaldson, M. (1978), *Children's Minds*, Harmondsworth, Penguin.

Donaldson, M. (1992), *Human Minds*, Harmondsworth, Penguin.

Dykstra, C. and Parks, S. (eds) (1986), *Faith Development and Fowler*, Birmingham, Alabama, Religious Education Press.

Eliade, M. (1960), *Myths, Dreams and Mysteries*, London, Harvill Press.

Elkind, D. and Elkind, S. (1962), Varieties of religious experience in young adolescents, *Journal for the Scientific Study of Religion*, 2, 102–112.

Erricker, C. and Erricker, J. (1994), Where angels fear to tread: discovering children's spirituality, Paper presented at the Roehampton Conference, Education, Spirituality and the Whole Child, July 15–16.

Erricker, C., Sullivan, D., Erricker, J., Logan, J. and Ota, C. (1994), The development of children's worldviews, *Journal of Beliefs and Values*, 15, 2, 3–6.

Farmer, L. (1992), Religious experience in childhood: a study of adult perspectives on early spiritual awareness, *Religious Education*, 87, 259–268.

Fowler, J.W. (1981), *Stages of Faith: the psychology of human development and the quest for meaning*, San Francisco, Harper and Row.

Fowler, J.W., Nipkow, K.E. and Schweitzer, F. (eds) (1992), *Stages of Faith and Religious Development: implications for church, education and society*, London, SCM.

Francis, L. (1976), An enquiry into the concept 'Readiness for religion', Unpublished Ph.D. dissertation, University of Cambridge.

Francis, L. (1987), The decline in attitudes towards religion among 8–15 year olds, *Educational Studies*, 13, 125–134.

Francis, L. and Greer, J. (1993), The contribution of religious experience to Christian development: a study among fourth, fifth and sixth year pupils in Northern Ireland, *British Journal of Religious Education*, 15, 38–43.

Furth, G. (1988), *The Secret World of Children's Drawings: healing through art*, Boston, Sigo Press.

Gallup Poll (1978), *Religion in America: the Gallup Opinion Index 1977–78*, Princeton, A.I.P.O.

Gallup Poll Report (1985), 4 in 10 Americans have had unusual spiritual experiences, Press release.

Glaser, B. and Strauss, A. (1967), *The Discovery of Grounded Theory*, Chicago, Aldine.

Glock, C. and Stark, R. (1965), *Religion and Society in Tension*, Chicago, Rand McNally.

Godin, A. and Hallez, M. (1965), Parental images and divine paternity, in A. Godin (ed.), *From Religious Experience to Religious Attitude*, pp. 65–96, Chicago, Loyola University Press.

Goldman, R. (1964), *Religious Thinking from Childhood to Adolescence*, London, Routledge and Kegan Paul.

Greeley, A.M. (1975), *The Sociology of the Paranormal: a reconnaissance*, Sage Research Papers in the Social Sciences (Studies in Religion and Ethnicity Series No. 90-023), Beverley Hills, Sage Publications.

Greer, J. (1981), Religious experience and religious education, *Search*, 4, 23–24.

Greer, J. (1982), The religious experience of Northern Irish pupils, *The Irish Catechist*, 6, 49–58.

Hall, G.S. (1904), *Adolescence: its psychology and its relations to physiology, anthropology, sociology, sex, crime, religion, and education*, New York, D. Appleton.

Hammond, J., Hay, D., Moxon, J., Netto, B., Raban, K., Straugheir, G. and Williams, C. (1990), *New Methods in RE Teaching: an experiential approach*, London, Oliver and Boyd / Longmans.

Hardy, A. (1966), *The Divine Flame*, London, Collins.

Hardy, A. (1979), *The Spiritual Nature of Man*, Oxford, Clarendon Press.

Hay, D. (1979), Religious experience amongst a group of postgraduate students: a qualitative study, *Journal for the Scientific Study of Religion*, 18, 164–182.

Hay, D. (1985), Suspicion of the spiritual: teaching religious education in a world of secular experience, *British Journal of Religious Education*, 7, 140–147.

Hay, D. (1987), *Exploring Inner Space: scientists and religious experience*, Oxford, Mowbrays.

Hay, D. (1988), Asking questions about religious experience, *Religion*, 18, 217–229.

Hay, D. (1990a), *Religious Experience Today: studying the facts*, London, Mowbrays.

Hay, D. (1990b), The bearing of empirical studies of religious experience on education, *Research Papers in Education*, 5, 1, 3–29.

Hay, D. (1994), 'The biology of God': what is the current status of Hardy's hypothesis? *International Journal for the Psychology of Religion*, 4, 1–23.

Hay, D. (1995), Dreams and spirituality, in D. Armstrong and B. Sievers (eds), *Discovering Social Meanings*, London, Process Press.

Hay, D. and Heald, G. (1987), Religion is good for you, *New Society*, 80, 1268, 20–22.

Hay, D. and Morisy, A. (1978), Reports of ecstatic, paranormal or religious experience in Great Britain and the United States: a comparison of trends, *Journal for the Scientific Study of Religion*, 17, 255–268.

Hay, D. and Morisy, A. (1985), Secular society/religious meanings: a contemporary paradox, *Review of Religious Research*, 26, 213–227.

Heimbrock, H-G. (1986), The development of symbols as a key to the developmental psychology of religion, *British Journal of Religious Education*, 8, 150–154.

Heimbrock, H-G. (1992), Religious development and the ritual dimension, in J.W. Fowler, K.E. Nipkow and F. Schweitzer (eds), *Stages of Faith and Religious Development: implications for church, education and society*, pp. 192–205, London, SCM.

Heller, D. (1986), *The Children's God*, Chicago, University of Chicago Press.

Hirschfeld, L.A. and Gelman, S.A. (eds) (1994), *Mapping the Mind: domain specificity in cognition and culture*, Cambridge, Cambridge University Press.

Hyde, K.E. (1968), The critique of Goldman's research, *Religious Education*, 63, 429–435.

Jackson, M. (1992), Divine Madness? A study of the relationship between psychotic and spiritual experience, Unpublished D.Phil. dissertation, University of Oxford.

James, W. (1902), *The Varieties of Religious Experience: a study in human nature* (reprinted 1960), London, Fontana.

Jaspard, J.-M. (1994), Comprehension of religious rituals among male and female mentally handicapped adults, Paper presented at the Sixth European Symposium for the Psychology of Religion, University of Lund, June 1994.

Klages, L. (1927), Die 'religiöse Kurve' in der Handschrifte, *Zeitschrifte für Menschenkunde*, 2, 1–8.

Klingberg, G. (1959), A study of religious experience in children from 9–13 years of age, *Religious Education*, 54, 211–216.

Langdon, A.A. (1969), A critical examination of Dr Goldman's research study on religious thinking from childhood to adolescence, *Journal of Christian Education*, 12, 37–63.

Lewis, D. (1987), All in good faith, *Nursing Times*, 83, 11, 40–43.

Long, D., Elkind, D. and Spilka, B. (1967), The child's conception of prayer, *Journal for the Scientific Study of Religion*, 6, 101–109.

Lossky, V. (1957), *The Mystical Tradition of the Eastern Church*, Cambridge, James Clark.

McCreery, E. (1994), Talking to young children about things spiritual, Paper presented at the Roehampton Conference, Education, Spirituality and the Whole Child, July 15–16.

Morgan Research (1983), Unpublished poll of reports of religious experience in Australia.

Mott-Thornton, K. (1994), Experience, critical realism and the schooling of spirituality, Paper presented at the Roehampton Conference, Education, Spirituality and the Whole Child, July 15–16.

Murphy, R.J.L. (1978a), *The Development of Religious Thinking in Children: a review of psychological theories*, Leicester, UCCF.

Murphy, R.J.L. (1978b), A new approach to the study of the development of religious thinking in children, *Educational Studies*, 4, 1, 19–22.

Murphy, R.J.L. (1980), An investigation into some aspects of the development of religious thinking in children aged between six and eleven years, Unpublished Ph.D. dissertation, University of St Andrews.

Nipkow, K.E. (1992), Stage theories of faith development as a challenge to religious education and practical theology, in J.W. Fowler, K.E. Nipkow and F. Schweitzer (eds), *Stages of Faith and Religious Development: implications for church, education and society*, pp. 82–101, London, SCM.

Nye, R. (1996), Childhood spirituality and contemporary developmental psychology, in R. Best and P. Lang (eds), *Education, Spirituality and the Whole Child*, London, Cassells, in press.

Nye, R. and Hay, D. (1995), Identifying children's spirituality: how do you start without a starting point?, *British Journal of Religious Education*, in press.

OFSTED (1994), *Handbook for Inspection of Schools*, London, OFSTED.

Oser, F. and Reich, K.H. (1990), Moral judgment, religious judgment, world views and logical thought: a review of their relationship, *British Journal of Religious Education*, 12, 94–101, 172–181.

Oser, F. and Scarlett, W.G. (eds) (1991), *Religious Development in Childhood and Adolescence*, San Francisco, Jossey-Bass.

Otto, R. (1950), *The Idea of the Holy*, Oxford, Oxford University Press.

Rahner, K. (1974), The experience of God today, in *Theological Investigations XI* (translated by David Bourke), pp. 149–165, London, Darton, Longman and Todd.

Reich, K.H. (1992), Religious development across the life span: conventional and cognitive developmental approaches, in D.L. Featherman, R.M. Lerner and M. Perlmutter (eds), *Life-Span Development and Behavior*, pp. 145–188, Hillsdale, New Jersey, Lawrence Erlbaum Associates.

Richards, T.J. and Richards, L. (1994), Using computers in qualitative research, in N.K. Denzin and Y.S. Lincoln (eds), *Handbook of Qualitative Research*, London, Sage Publications.

Rizzuto, A-M. (1979), *The Birth of the Living God: a psychoanalytic study*, Chicago, University of Chicago Press.

Robinson, E. (1983), *The Original Vision*, New York, Seabury Press.

Schleiermacher, F. (1799), *On Religion: speeches to its cultured despisers* (translated by John Oman, with an introduction by Rudolf Otto), New York, Harper Torchbooks.

Schweitzer, F. (1992), Developmental views of the religion of the child: historical antecedents, in J.W. Fowler, K.E. Nipkow and F. Schweitzer (eds), *Stages of Faith and Religious Development: implications for church, education and society*, pp. 67–81, London, SCM.

Spilka, B., Addison, J. and Rosensohn, M. (1975), Parents, self, and God: a test of competing theories of individual-religion relationships, *Review of Religious Research*, 6, 28–36.

Spränger, E. (1974), Gibt es eine 'religiöse Entwicklung'?, *Gesammelte Schriften*, 9, 1–14.

Starbuck, E.D. (1901), *The Psychology of Religion*, New York, Walter Scott.

Stock, R.D. (1982), *The Holy and the Daemonic from Sir Thomas Browne to William Blake*, Princeton, Princeton University Press.

Sutherland, S. (1994), *Religious Education and Collective Worship*, London, OFSTED.

Tamminen, K. (1991), *Religious Development in Childhood and Youth: an empirical study*, Helsinki, Suomalainen Tiedeakatemia.

Tamminen, K. (1994), Religious experiences in childhood and adolescence: a viewpoint of religious development between the ages of 7 and 20, *International Journal for the Psychology of Religion*, 4, 61–85.

Taylor, J. (1989), *Innocent Wisdom: children as spiritual guides*, New York, Pilgrim Press.

Thun, T. (1964), *Die Religion des Kindes* (second edition), Stuttgart, Ernst Klett.

Troeltsch, E. (1906), Das wesen der religion und der religionsgeschichte, (translated by Robert Morgan and Michael Pye), in *Ernst Troeltsch: writings on theology and religion*, Atlanta, John Knox Press, 1977.

Ungoed-Thomas, J. (1994), Inspecting spiritual, moral, social and cultural development, *Pastoral Care*, (December, 1994), 21–25.

Vergote, A. and Tamayo, A. (eds) (1981), *Parental Figures and the Representation of God: a psychological and cross-cultural study*, The Hague, Mouton.

Vygotsky, L. (1986), *Thought and Language* (revised edition), Cambridge, Massachusetts, MIT Press.

Wach, J. (1958), *The Comparative Study of Religions*, New York, Columbia University Press.

Waller, N.G., Kojetin, B.A., Bouchard, T.J. Jr., Lykken, D.T. and Tellegen, A. (1990), Genetic and environmental influences on religious interests, attitudes and values: a study of twins reared apart and together, *Psychological Science*, 1, 138–142.

Walsh, J. (ed.) (1982), *The Cloud of Unknowing*, London, SPCK.

Watts, F.N. and Williams, M. (1988), *The Psychology of Religious Knowing*, Cambridge, Cambridge University Press.

Wellman, H.M. and Gelman, S.A. (1992), Cognitive development: foundational theories of core domains, *Annual Review of Psychology*, 43, 337–375.

Winnicott, D.W. (1958), *Collected Papers: through paediatrics to psychoanalysis*, London, Tavistock Press.

Wulff, D.M. (1991), *Psychology of Religion: classic and contemporary views*, New York, John Wiley and Sons.

Wuthnow, R. (1976), *The Consciousness Reformation*, Berkeley, University of California Press.

4

Further on from Fowler: post-Fowler faith development research

Nicola M. Slee

Summary

This chapter sets out to review the considerable body of research influenced by James Fowler's theory of faith development. Five broad categories of research are identified: first, replication studies and other studies which have sought to test or refine Fowler's hypothesised stage development theory; second, a small group of literary studies which have applied Fowler's theory to documentary evidence; third, correlation studies which have been concerned to test the relationship between faith development and other variables; fourth, cross-cultural studies which have attempted to test Fowler's hypothesis of cultural invariance; and finally, a group of studies which have examined women's religious development in the light of Fowler's theory. The main findings in each category of research are identified and their significance discussed for the state of faith development research and theory.

Introduction

James Fowler's theory of faith development (Fowler, 1981, 1984, 1987, 1991) has generated a good deal of interest amongst theologians and educators world-wide, and, although scholarly interest has been slow to develop in the United Kingdom, there are recent signs that this is changing (Astley, 1991; Fowler, Nipkow and Schweitzer, 1992; Astley and Francis, 1992). A persistent criticism levelled against Fowler is his seeming lack of interest in providing detailed evidence of the empirical basis of the theory (Nelson, 1982; Webster, 1984; Broughton, 1986), preferring, instead, to develop the theological, educational and pastoral implications of the theory in his later writings (Fowler, 1984; 1987; 1991). Nevertheless, if Fowler himself has shown surprisingly little interest in ongoing empirical research, the same cannot be said of his followers. The theory has spawned a considerable body of secondary empirical research, though much of it remains unpublished and thus inaccessible to all but a scholarly elite. It is the intention of this article to review this research literature, in much the same way as earlier articles reviewed the post-Goldman literature (Slee, 1986, 1992), in order to assess the ways in which faith development research and theory have themselves been developed and refined beyond Fowler's original elaboration, and to highlight issues which still require further exploration and clarification.

To date, most of the existing research emanates from the United States of America, although there are a few European studies. Much of the research has been conducted by Fowler's students and collaborators and thus, not surprisingly, shows a high level of dependence on Fowler's theoretical framework, methodology and theological and educational concerns. A good deal of the earlier research has been concerned to refine, extend and develop Fowler's account of faith development, rather than to test it as such. Following Fowler, these studies have operationalised faith in dynamic, inclusive and implicitly religious terms as the making, maintenance and transformation of human meaning through the use of Fowler's wide-ranging semi-structured interview, and assimilated results into Fowler's broad theory of faith development. However, it is interesting to note the emergence of a range of research in the past five years or so which is more loosely and critically related to Fowler's work, and which reflects a rather broader approach to faith development insofar as it seeks to marry insights from the Fowler paradigm with those of other theological and psychological traditions, or addresses issues ignored by Fowler, such as the distinctive pattern of women's religious development. Doubtless this more creative adaptation of Fowler's work has been made possible by the critical debate on the theory which has flourished over the past decade, encouraging a more healthy critical distance from Fowler's work.

Five broad categories of research influenced by Fowler will be identified here: first, replication studies and other studies which have sought to test or refine Fowler's hypothesised stage development theory; second, a small group of literary studies which have applied Fowler's theory to documentary evidence; third, correlation studies which have been concerned to test the relationship between faith development and other variables; fourth, cross-cultural studies which have attempted to test Fowler's hypothesis of cultural invariance; and finally, a group of studies which have examined women's religious development in the light of Fowler's theory. After considering the main findings in each of these categories of research, I shall conclude by a brief discussion of their significance for the state of faith development research and theory more widely.

Replication studies

Although there is a broad range of studies based on Fowler's hypothesis of stage development which have employed his interview schedule and scoring procedures, I have been able to find only one study which has attempted to replicate Fowler's findings across the life-cycle. This is Kalaam's (1981) cross-cultural study of a large sample of Christian, Hindu and Muslim Indians, which has exceptional interest because of its rare cross-cultural evidence as well as its attempt to replicate Fowler's findings across the whole life-span. Kalaam's sample ranged from age eight to eighty, and consisted of fifty male subjects from each of the three religions chosen, each of whom was interviewed using indianised versions of Kohlberg's dilemmas and an adapted form of Fowler's interview. The main focus of Kalaam's study was the relation between moral and faith development, which will be discussed in the section on correlation studies below. However, insofar as the results provide evidence on Fowler's theory as a whole, they are relevant here. In fact, Kalaam's conclusions about the validity of Fowler's theory are largely negative. Kalaam's major finding was the lack of correlation of moral and faith stage in just under half of his subjects (49.35%), and no identifiable pattern in the relation of moral to faith stage in those cases where there was a stage difference. Kalaam concludes that neither Kohlberg nor Fowler has identified structural properties of moral and faith development in their stages but both have, in fact, confused certain content with structural stages.

Apart from Kalaam's study, no other study could be traced which attempted to replicate Fowler's findings across the whole age-range from childhood to old age. Doubtless this is because of the extreme ambitiousness and costliness of such an undertaking (although the development of a Fowler scale by Barnes, Doyle and Johnson, 1989, may provide a less costly alternative to the interview method for future studies). Rather, all the remaining studies identified here have chosen to focus, either on a particular period of the life-cycle, usually covering one or two of the Fowler stages, or a particular professional or religious constituency, or, more rarely, a particular aspect of Fowler's seven-strand theory. Thus 'replication' must be understood in a broader sense in this context to include all those studies which have attempted to test some aspect of Fowler's theory using at least a modified form of his methodology.

It will be convenient to consider these studies chronologically, starting from studies of adolescence and young adulthood, and moving to middle life and old age. Studies which focus on particular aspects of the theory will be included in this overall chronological schema. It is worth noting, in passing, that little research has been conducted investigating Fowler's account of childhood. This neglect may be accounted for by Fowler's own relative disinterest in childhood as well as the plethora of research evidence from the 1960s and 1970s, largely stimulated by Goldman's work, which has already provided an extensive account of childhood religious thinking (see Slee, 1992).

In contrast to the disinterest in childhood, considerable attention has been focused on adolescence and young adulthood, the latter in particular. A number of studies suggest several interesting refinements of Fowler's account of faith in early adulthood. Thus, Mischey (1976) interviewed thirty young adults between the ages of twenty and thirty-five years in order to investigate the process of faith formation. Mischey's findings basically confirmed Fowler's trajectory of development for this age group; thus he found that the life-styles of this age-group reflected a predominantly synthetic-conventional and individuative-reflective form of orientation. However, Mischey suggests that within these two Fowler stages, it is possible to detect a range of 'types' or 'styles' of faith, designated according to their dominant hallmark as 'disoriented', 'set', 'critical', 'idealistic', 'collapsed' and 'embraced' respectively. Mischey's findings on the relation between faith development and other developmental variables will be discussed below.

Moseley's (1978) study of conversion has further refined Fowler's account of faith development during this period of young adulthood. Employing the content/structure distinction fundamental to the theory, Moseley hypothesised two qualitatively different types of conversion which could be distinguished empirically in a sample of young adults. On the one hand, he hypothesised, one would find examples of *structural* conversion, involving 'the re-patterning of the cognitive and affective-volitional operations underlying the individual's faith perspective', whilst on the other, one would find *lateral* conversion experiences which, whilst superficially similar to 'genuine' structural conversion, would exhibit 'no such re-patterning but merely an ideational change' in which 'the structure of the faith perspective remains unchanged as new ideational content is assimilated on the same generic level as that maintained prior to the change of religious affiliation' (p. 28).

Using a modified form of Fowler's interview schedule, Moseley interviewed 25 converts to popular religious groups, in the age range between nineteen and twenty-five years. The findings confirmed Moseley's hypothesis concerning the two types of conversion and suggested that lateral conversion was particularly dominant among individuals who change religious affiliation in order to establish an affective bond with a significant other or to share the membership with the significant other. It was also common among 'stage 4 "ideological seekers" whose search for truth often spans a wide and diverse spectrum of ideological alternatives'. *Structural* conversion occurs when the subject moves from stage 3 to stage 4, 'from an affiliative mode of relating to the group . . . to the formation of a new mode of role-taking as evidenced by qualitatively different patterns of reasoning and judgement' (p. 190). According to Moseley, the level of the individual's commitment to the newly acquired religious world-view is determined by their stage of role-taking. 'Subjects at the conventional level (stage 3) are committed to their ideological system, but their commitment is highly externalised as a response to external authority and to the roles and virtues of significant and trustworthy representatives of the belief system. In contrast, the commitment demonstrated at stage 4 is centred on the internal consistency of the ideological system as tested by critical reflection and from the perspective of other ideologies and groups' (ibid.).

Whereas Moseley's study has refined Fowler's description of stage 3 and stage 4 by relating the stages to the individual's experience of conversion, Parks' (1980, 1986) study of faith development in young adulthood suggests a more radical revision of Fowler's account. She has proposed two major amendments to Fowler's theory. The first concerns Fowler's description of the move from stage 3 to stage 4. Drawing upon the work of Perry, Weyerhaeuser, Kegan and Keniston, Parks elaborates and expands upon Fowler's description and hypothesises that 'within Fowler's stage four, two separate, identifiable stages may be distinguished' (p. 122). These stages she names as 'young adult' and 'adult', following on from Fowler's stage 3 (adolescence) and leading to the eventual emergence of mature adulthood in Fowler's stage 5. The characteristic stance of young adulthood, Parks suggests, is captured by the concept of 'wary probe' (p. 124), which is indicative of a serious exploration of the adult world, different in quality from adolescent experimentation, in order to test the vulnerability, strength and integrity of society as well as the capacity of the self to withstand or use what society will make, ask and allow. Parks tested this hypothesis in a pilot study of twenty senior students in their final year of college, using a semi-structured interview which invited subjects to reflect upon their college experience. Whilst acknowledging that such limited data cannot confirm the hypothesis of the young adult stage, Parks finds in the study evidence to support her proposal.

Parks' second major amendment to Fowler's theory concerns his description of faith itself. Drawing on the work of Coleridge, Bushnell, Langer and Loder, Parks suggests that structural developmental insights into the nature of faith need to be enriched by a recognition of the composing, patterning and unifying activity of the imagination by which persons apprehend both the empirical world and the 'ideal' in images of sense. The essential connection between faith and imagination is particularly salient in the young adult era, according to Parks. 'For this is the era in which a vision of an "ideal" world that will shape all of adult faith may be most powerfully imagined, and worthy images must be available for that task' (p. 4).

Several studies provide dramatic evidence for the structuring power of institutions on the faith of adolescents. Lansdell (1980) made a study of the staff and students of a fundamentalist Christian high school in southern Ontario, using an adapted form of Kohlberg's and Fowler's interview method and a participant-observer method. The results indicated an overwhelming dependence by almost all subjects on a system of external locus of control, in other words, the dominance of Kohlberg and Fowler stage 2 and stage 3. This study clearly demonstrates Fowler's hypothesis that institutions operate at a 'modal level' of faith, and shows the impact of the institutional stage of faith on individuals' stage levels, in this case tending to depress individuals' movement out of a lower stage functioning. This is demonstrated even more clearly by Simmonds

(1986) who compared the impact of two church communities on adolescents' faith structure. Simmonds analyzed church documents and interviewed church leaders in order to determine a modal level of faith for two church communities, and then interviewed adolescents from each church in order to examine the relation between individual stage scores and the modal score of the church community. He found a clear relation. Adolescents from community A, which had a modal level of stage 4, had made significant movement into the transition between stage 3 and stage 4, while adolescents from community B (assigned a modal stage level of 3) were solidly within a stage 3 perspective. The results indicated that 'the community modal level of faith was the determinative factor in the difference between the two groups' (abstract).

Whilst many replication studies have concentrated on young and early adulthood, a number have investigated middle life and one study has concentrated on faith in old age. All of these studies are particularly concerned with identifying the factors which promote movement from the middle to the higher stages of Fowler's schema; thus they are interesting from the point of view of stage transition as well as the understanding of mid-life faith *per se*.

Bassett (1985) interviewed 42 educators and health care paraprofessionals of middle age in order to investigate how faith development was related to personality and mid-life transition. As well as discovering positive correlations with certain personality profiles (see below), Bassett found that faith development was positively correlated with awareness of and examination of mid-life issues which generally brought about coping/growing outcomes. Thus, respondents at stage 3.5, stage 4 and stage 4.5 showed significant mid-life awareness which correlated with capacity for faith development. Among the stage 3 subjects, the thirteen respondents who showed little awareness of mid-life issues seemed most equilibrated at stage 3 and least likely to develop further. Hamrick's (1988) study identified somewhat different factors promoting movement to the higher stages: in particular, positive early church experience and a strong desire for knowledge were found to be particularly significant. Howlett's (1989) study of the transition between stage 5 and stage 6 suggested a further range of potent transitional influences, including 'trigger' spiritual experiences and openness to spiritual experience, motivation to transcend, choice of a teacher and a path, and the practice of detachment and solitude.

Backlund's (1990) study of homosexual middle-aged men with the HIV virus represents a fascinating attempt to examine Fowler's hypothesis that life crisis stimulates movement from one stage to another. Backlund interviewed forty white, self-identified gay men in the San Francisco area, all of whom had been informed of their HIV status, but only half of whom were diagnosed HIV seropositive, the other half being seronegative. Backlund hypothesised that the HIV seropositive men would be more likely to be in stage transition than the seronegative men. Intensive content analysis supported this hypothesis; additionally, faith stage transition was significantly associated with the death of someone close within the preceding year, though not with the threat of the participant's own death.

Backlund's examination of faith development in the light of possible impending death has some interesting similarities with Shulik's (1979) study of faith in old age. Shulik was concerned to study the relationship between faith development and various hypothesised features of old age, in particular, the characteristic features of disengagement, life-review, philosophical development and preparation for death. Forty subjects, twenty of each sex, all bar two aged between sixty and eighty-seven years old, were interviewed using a Fowler life-map schedule to which had been added questions concerning ageing and death. The forty subjects spanned a range of three faith stages, stage 3, stage 4 and stage 5. Although there was no significant relationship between chronological age and faith stage, Shulik did find a high correlation between faith stage and what he terms 'agesense', that is, the *subjective* awareness of the full range of changes which accompany the ageing process. This led Shulik to conclude that 'subjects who have achieved a higher level of faith development are likely to be more sensitised to the internal or psychological changes which accompany the ageing process, than are subjects of lower levels of faith development' (p. 158). This finding is very much in accordance with Bassett's finding of a correlation between faith development and awareness of mid-life issues. A second major finding of the study was a relationship between level of life satisfaction and faith stage, though this finding is based on very small numbers and requires corroboration. However, the study found no significant relationship between faith development and either level of engagement/disengagement or the practice of life-review. Shulik's study suggests some interesting links between ageing and faith development and highlights the need for further research with older subjects.

These studies appear to add little to Fowler's description of faith itself in the mid-life era, but rather refine his account of the transitional process during this period. Hamrick, in particular, provides a detailed model of stage transition which extends Fowler's account. He suggests that, within the movement from one stage to another, four distinct sequential periods may be discerned. The first period, described as disengagement and disequilibrium, included systemic and personal disillusionment which caused the individual to disengage from their dominant stage. This led on to a period of expansion and exploration and typically included exposure to new cultures, the influence of key individuals, spiritual truths and personal reflection. The third period of focusing and equilibrium was most often associated with formal education, individual and group projects. This then issues in the final period of reintegration and involvement, in which risk taking and a new level of commitment based on the recently acquired structure of faith can be exercised. Hamrick's model seems worthy of further testing, particularly at different phases of the lifespan, to see if it receives wider confirmation.

Literary studies

A second category of research can be identified which has attempted to test the validity and usefulness of Fowler's theory using documentary evidence. These studies may be considered a subsection of the broader category of replication studies, but their unique method sets them apart from that broader category. Thus, following Kohlberg's application of his moral development theory to ancient literary texts, Asen (1980) used Fowler's stages to categorise the faith of the biblical prophet Amos. The study distinguishes between two basic levels of textual redaction, original Amos and later redactors, assigning original Amos to Fowler's stage 5, whilst arguing that the redactional material illustrates a less developed faith stage, namely stage 3 or stage 4. In contrast to this study of ancient literary documents, Dibble (1986) used Fowler's framework to study the literary works of a contemporary religious leader, the American Baptist, Will D. Campbell, although this was supplemented by an interview. The author argues that an analysis of literary works and the interview revealed Will Campbell to possess a consistent stage 6 universalising faith perspective.

This must be of some considerable interest, since so few examples of stage 6 structuring have been found by Fowler or his colleagues. Another study by Morgan (1990) attempted to refine a narrative method of testing faith development by using a series of autobiographical sermons to examine subjects' faith development. This methodology seems to lie half-way between the clinical interview and the purely documentary analysis, containing important features of both. These studies demonstrate that Fowler's theory can be a useful tool of literary analysis, and suggest some fruitful adaptations of his interview method which might be used with subjects where the interview method is not appropriate.

Correlation studies

It is not possible to make a sharp distinction between replication and correlation studies, since many replication studies tend to include standard correlation tests in order to examine the relation between faith stages and factors such as sex, age, socio-economic status, and so on. Some studies, however, have concentrated more specifically on the relationship between faith development and other measures. Two issues in particular have dominated attention: first, the relationship between faith development and moral development, and second, the relationship between faith development and personality. In this section, I shall first summarise the evidence relating to other factors before coming on to consider these two major relationships.

Surprisingly, there is little systematic information concerning *the relationship between stages of faith and chronological age*, either from Fowler himself or from later studies. In general, the data seem to suggest a close correlation between age and faith development in the early stages, with a much looser relationship after adolescence. In particular, stage 3 and stage 4 seem to extend fairly widely across the age spectrum from early adulthood to old age. Thus, for example, Broun (1984) found no correlation between age and faith development in his sample of adults aged between seventeen and forty-nine. Whilst this is much what might be expected from the theory, the absence of a closer correlation in the later stages might be thought to tell against the construct validity of these stages.

The evidence for *the relationship between stages of faith and gender* is mixed. The theory should lead us to expect no significant difference, and many studies support this finding, but a number of others (Bradley, 1983; Bassett, 1985; White, 1985) have found that female subjects score significantly lower than male subjects. This has led to a suspicion that the theory itself contains a measure of gender bias, and has resulted in a number of studies devoted to an examination of women's faith development (see below) and the proposal of alternative theoretical models.

Likewise, the evidence concerning the *relationship between religious affiliation and faith stage* is not altogether clear. As part of his test of the construct validity of Fowler's stages, Snarey (1991) summarised the evidence from a number of major empirical studies, comparing the mean faith stage scores of adult samples drawn from different religious and cultural groups. Overall, there was not a vast range of mean score, the lowest being 2.85 (lower and middle class Indian Muslims), and the highest 4.40 (selected American Protestant church leaders). In general, 'the lower scoring groups were typically younger adults or adults who were selected because they represented a deficit characteristic', whilst 'the higher scoring groups were generally older adults or intentionally selected elites' (p. 295). However, Snarey noted 'an apparent tendency for groups of elite Protestants to post somewhat higher mean scores than both elite and non-elite non-Protestants' (ibid.). Interestingly, a number of studies suggest that those with an atheistic stance or those who are less strongly affiliated to religious groups may demonstrate higher stage scores than those who profess strong theistic belief. For example, amongst White's (1985) sample of Roman Catholic undergraduates, those who had only a marginal affiliation to the denomination of their parents scored higher faith stages than those who were strongly affiliated, whilst Snarey's (1991) sample of non-theistic Jews scored higher than many other religious groups.

There is also evidence to suggest a significant *relationship between socio-economic status and faith stage*. A number of studies demonstrate a positive correlation between faith stage and higher levels of socio-economic status, or higher levels of education (Gorman, 1977; Shulik, 1979; Sweitzer, 1984). Although this may be accounted for by the cognitive developmental framework of the theory, which would lead one to expect some relationship with higher levels of educational ability, some critics remain profoundly concerned by the implications of this finding, suggesting that the theory has an in-built bias towards middle class patterns of reflection and lifestyle.

Other studies indicate a *relationship between the faith stage of the individual and their patterns of social interaction*. Thus, studies by Hunt

(1978) and Vanden Heuvel (1985) indicate a significant relationship between the individual's level of faith development and the communication system of the family, whilst Lansdell (1980) and Simmonds (1986) demonstrate the impact of the faith level of the church congregation on that of the individual. Green and Hoffman (1989) found a significant correlation between the individual's faith stage and the strategy of social categorisation they adopted when invited to classify candidates for a job interview. Whilst these studies employed diverse methodologies and measures of social functioning, together they do provide evidence for a close correlation between individual and group level of faith functioning.

Whilst research has begun to highlight a number of interesting relationships between faith stage and other factors, raising critical issues about the theory, two issues have dominated correlation studies. The first is the perplexing question of the *relationship between faith development and moral development*. This question arises out of the conflicting stances of Fowler and Kohlberg respectively; although both theorists are agreed that there is a close relationship between moral and faith stage, Fowler suggests that faith development is primary and prior to moral development, representing the more fundamental matrix of meaning-making out of which moral decisions are made, whilst Kohlberg asserts the opposite. As early as 1976, Fowler asserted 'every moral perspective, at whatever level of development, is anchored in a broader system of belief and loyalties. . . . There is, I believe, always a faith framework encompassing and supporting the motive to be moral and the exercise of moral logic' (p. 209). He has continued to maintain this stance. For Kohlberg, although 'it is religion which gives the ultimate reason for being moral' (Power and Kohlberg, 1980, p. 346), this does not mean that religion is the cause of morality. Rather, Kohlberg views religion and morality as fundamentally related, but logically distinct domains; developmentally, moral reasoning precedes faith development and is a necessary, though not sufficient, condition for it.

The empirical evidence to decide between these two positions is confusing and inconclusive. Whilst studies identify a significant correlation between faith and moral stage, there is no consistent finding about the direction of this relationship. Gorman (1977) and Shulik (1979) both found a high correlation between faith and moral stages in their samples of young people and old people respectively, but neither analyzed the nature of the relationship. Power, in association with Kohlberg (Power and Kohlberg, 1980), produced some modest evidence for Kohlberg's decalage thesis, insofar as 20% of subjects at higher stage levels demonstrated higher levels of moral development than faith stage score. In contrast, Mischey's (1976) study tends to support Fowler's thesis, insofar as he found far more of his subjects with higher faith stage scores than moral stages (only four subjects had moral scores exceeding their faith score). In an effort to clarify this issue, both Kalaam (1981) and Snarey (1991) have made detailed and rigorous analyses of the relationship between faith and moral stages, using far larger samples than previous studies. Their findings, however, do not resolve the issue. Just over half (50.66%) of Kalaam's 150 subjects had parallel faith and moral scores, and of the remaining 74 subjects, 55.4% showed a difference of only half a stage, whereas 44.6% demonstrated a difference of one or more stages. No particular pattern emerged in the direction of the stage differences, and they were spread across the full range of stages from stage 1 to stage 4.5, not restricted to higher stages, as Power and Kohlberg (1980) had reported. Likewise, in Snarey's subjects, the findings are mixed: 41.6% of his subjects received the same moral and faith development scores; 26.6% scored higher in moral than faith development, and 31.6% of the subjects scored higher in faith than in moral development. It is difficult to account for these findings with any certainty. It may be, as Snarey suggests, that the relationship between faith and moral development changes throughout the lifespan, though Kalaam's evidence does not support this.

The second major issue to dominate the attention of correlation studies is *the relationship between faith development and personality*. However, in contrast to studies of the relationship between moral and faith development, which have utilised consistently a Kohlbergian framework in interaction with Fowler's theory, these studies have employed a wide range of theoretical and methodological approaches, making it extremely difficult to map the findings coherently. There has been some attempt to relate Fowler's theory to a psychodynamic perspective, using Jungian or Freudian theory to investigate the relationship between faith development and personality or ego development. Thus, Thompson (1988) explored the relationship between Fowler's stages and Rizzuto's neo-Freudian analysis of the God-image, and suggests some interesting refinements and enrichments of Fowler's stage accounts by incorporating aspects of Rizzuto's theory. Raduka (1980) examined the relationship between Fowler's stages and Jung's stages of personality development, and Bradley (1983) employed the Myers-Briggs Personality

Inventory to investigate this relationship, whilst Chirban (1980) operationalised the Jungian distinction between introversion and extraversion using measures of intrinsic and extrinsic motivation. Loomis (1987) focused on the relationship between imagination and faith, drawing on a Jungian analysis of the role of imagination in religious faith. There was little evidence for a relationship between faith stages as measured by Fowler and Jungian personality types, although Chirban found some correlation between extrinsic motivation and lower faith stages and an increasing correlation between intrinsic motivation and later faith stages whilst Loomis found a strong correlation between higher faith scores and intuitive imagination, which is an interesting corroboration of Parks' (1980, 1986) thesis. Whilst using different measures, several studies provide evidence for a significant relationship between ego development and faith development. Thus, Broun (1984) found that low ego scores tended to match with low faith scores and high ego scores correlated with high faith scores. Mischey (1976) found a similar pattern, leading him to assert: 'it appears that identity achievement is the "backbone" for one's faith orientation' (p. iv). This finding is corroborated by Bassett (1985), who found that 'greater intelligence, trust, self-sufficiency / resourcefulness, tranquillity / composure, and self-assurance / security correlated positively with faith development' (p. 1). Indeed, some have suggested that Fowler's faith stages are primarily a measure of ego formation, similar to Kegan's (1982) stage schema, and do not properly distinguish an independent dimension of faith structuring.

Cross-cultural studies

One of the criticisms that is regularly made of Fowler's work is that it has an in-built cultural bias to Western liberalism, and to liberal Protestantism in particular. Empirical research evidence from a variety of religious and cultural settings is needed to test the hypothesised universalism of the theory. As yet, there is very little cross-cultural evidence. Only three relevant studies could be located. The first of these is the study by Kalaam (1981) already referred to above. The main thrust of Kalaam's study is the vexed question of the relation between moral and faith development, rather than the cross-cultural question *per se*. However, his study does have some interest from a cultural perspective. Methodologically, it is interesting to note that he had to adapt the Fowler interview considerably to be able to use it with his sample, since he found that some of the broader questions (such as 'What gives your life meaning?') proved too abstract and difficult for many people. However, in an adapted form, the interview yielded reliable data which were capable of scoring by Fowler and his associates, and demonstrated the range of stages from stage 1/2 to stage 5. Nevertheless, in a comparison by Snarey (1991) of the mean scores of subjects from a range of studies, Kalaam's subjects scored significantly lower than any others. This raises the question of whether Fowler's theory is culturally biased against non-Western populations, or whether the lower scores were due to methodological differences. Kalaam's data also reveal significant differences between the mean scores of the Christian, Hindu and Muslim subjects. While the Christian and Hindu mean scores are identical (3.07), the mean score of the Muslims is considerably lower (2.85), and no Muslim subject was scored higher than a transitional 4/5. Does this indicate that the theory is culturally prejudiced against non-Western forms of theism?

Furushima's (1983) study is relevant to this question, since it was specifically designed to test the universality of Fowler's theory by studying in depth the faith development of subjects from a non-Western culture. The study comprises a detailed analysis of interview data from twelve Hawaiian Buddhists aged between twenty-eight to fifty-nine years. Furushima concludes that Fowler's hypothesis of universality is partially substantiated by his findings, insofar as all of his subjects could be located within the stage schema and much of the data could be accounted for within the framework of the theory. However, the stage identities were not able to account exhaustively for the data, and Furushima identified a number of features which disclose other dimensions of Fowler's aspects of faith not sufficiently developed by him. The most significant of these are as follows. First, the data suggested a stronger social aspect of faith than Fowler's theory allows. Second, several of Furishima's subjects appeared to display stage 6 features and yet gave no evidence of the critical orientation of stage 4 and stage 5, thus causing Furishima to question whether this critical dimension must be deemed essential for the development of mature faith. Third, the data suggested that the symbolic aspect of faith is, in some important respects, culturally variant insofar as it is dependent on culturally distinct language and symbol systems. Fourth, the data provided strong evidence for the structuring power of content and cultural context upon faith, insofar as specific Japanese qualities, such as pride, face, self-restraint and humility, were demonstrated to frame the way in which faith was perceived and experienced by the subjects.

In order to test the claim of cross-cultural universality, Snarey (1991) obtained data from sixty Jewish non-theists who were founders of an Israeli kibbutz and compared their stage designations with the results from other studies. He hypothesised that there should be no significant difference between the mean level of faith development among the Jewish sample and that found in comparably aged theistic populations. The comparisons were made between seven religious groups (Buddhist, Catholic, Greek Orthodox, Hindu, Jewish, Muslim and Protestant) and the non-theistic Jewish group. Overall, the scores ranged through the whole stage spectrum, including stage 6, and the higher scoring groups were generally older adults or intentionally selected elites, as one might expect. The kibbutz founders compared very favourably with adult subjects in the other studies, and their mean level of faith was similar to that of somewhat older middle class and upper class Protestant, Catholic and Jewish subjects. There were only two groups with a higher mean level of faith development, and these were Fowler's original selective Protestant sample and a selected group of religious leaders. From these findings, Snarey concluded that 'Fowler's model and measure is able to capture the thinking of persons whose religious orientation and background is quite different from those of his original sample' (p. 301). In broad terms, then, the claim of universalism was supported.

These few studies provide some fascinating, but as yet inconclusive, evidence regarding the universality of Fowler's theory, as well as demonstrating some of the difficulties of translating Fowler's methodology to a non-Western milieu, and highlight the need for more systematic research using cross-cultural samples.

Gender studies

As a result of evidence that women tend to score less highly on the Fowler scale than do men, and that men advance to higher stages at younger ages than do women (Bradley, 1983; Bassett, 1985; White, 1985; Leary, 1988), and in the light of feminist critique of Fowler (Harris, 1986; Parks, 1990), some researchers have attempted to probe women's faith development in more detail than Fowler has done. Following Gilligan's (1982) critical refinement of Kohlberg's theory of moral development and his research methodology, these studies have tended to adapt Fowler's interview format

in significant ways and many do not use the Fowler stage designations to analyse their data. Using Gilligan's well-known metaphor,
these studies are concerned to articulate 'another voice' in faith
development theory: the neglected, relational voice of women's
experience and understanding of faith. Thus, Cooney (1985) interviewed twelve self-confessed 'biblical feminists' about their
understanding of faith, as well as the process of development to
their present faith stance. A number of themes emerged as characteristic of the transition into biblical feminism, the most important
of which was an overarching theme of 'holistic relationality': this is
'characterised by a commitment to connectedness with God, self
and others'.

Devor's (1989) findings echo similar themes, and confirm
Cooney's central thesis that women's faith is marked by a sense of
'holistic relationality'. She used insights from psychological work
on women's development and feminist theologies alongside
Fowler's theory to examine the understanding of faith of twelve
women ministers. An analysis of the interviews established the
essentially relational nature of faith for these women. Faith was
experienced as a relationship with God, as an experience of ongoing
connection amidst the loss or threatened loss of connection in
human relationships and amidst the uncertainties of existence,
nurtured in the community of faith, the church, and revealed in
the way life is lived with others. Conversely, absence of faith was
perceived as a disconnection from God, and sin and evil were
described as actions or tendencies which disrupted or harmed
human relationships. As a result of these findings, Devor suggests
that Fowler's understanding of faith and his account of the stages
of faith need to be adapted to include a much more prominent
relational perspective. 'The results of this study imply that our
relationships not only inform our faith, but are the context in which
faith is composed' (pp. 255–7).

Devor accordingly reworked each of Fowler's stages, suggesting
ways in which they need to be refined to take account of women's
unique relational perspective. Where Fowler describes a process of
growing separation and individuation, as well as a shift from external to internal authority and from a tacit belief system to an explicit
system of meanings, Devor proposes a very different pattern of
development through ongoing relationship and responsibility for
the women in her study. Separation was a far less important theme,
and when it did occur, it was within the context of relationship.
This suggested to Devor a need for a redescription of the transition

from stage 3 to stage 4 which can account for women's growing sense of self within the context of relationship.

Leary's (1988) study of the relationship of coping with chronic stress and faith development in women focuses on a context within which women's caring and relational faith is heightened: namely, that of caring for disabled children. Leary interviewed 21 mothers of severely disabled children, all of whom were the primary care-takers of their children and each of whom had chosen to keep her child within the family unit, at least until early adolescence. She concluded that faith development theory, whilst of some value, could not account adequately for the central aspects of these women's experience. In particular, Fowler's theory could not offer satisfactory criteria to account for the self-sacrifice chosen by the women which necessarily limited the scope of their responsibility and thus, on Fowler's criteria, implied a low level of faith. Nor could the theory hold together these women's movement from an outer to an inner locus of authority with their choice to remain embedded in a relationship of care. Because they had not made a clear cut move away from the significant other, they were scored in a lower faith stage, even though their relocation of authority within themselves led to a tested, rather than a naïve and unreflective, commitment. Leary found evidence that the women operated on an ethic of care and commitment rather than the impersonal imperatives of law, rules and standards which Fowler sees as characteristic of stage 4. Whilst all of these features tended to depress the women's scores to stage 3, Leary found a high incidence of tolerance of ambiguity amongst her subjects, that is, 'a willingness to consider the multiple dimensions of reality and a more flexible adaptation to varying circumstances' (p. 133), which, as she points out, is close to Fowler's description of stage 5.

These results led Leary, like Devor, Parks and White, to propose a redescription of Fowler's stage 4 for female subjects. She corroborates Parks' thesis of two separate, identifiable stages in the transition between stage 3 and stage 4 that have to do with relationship and commitment. The first of these phases is described by Parks as 'probing commitment', characterised by a tenuous, exploratory and divided quality of a person's initial considerations of commitment. This then leads into 'tested commitment' when the individual becomes more self-aware and centred in the process of living out their chosen commitment. 'This commitment is not a transitional point for [these] women, rather it is an indication of a faith stage beyond stage 3' (p. 137).

An interesting postscript to the conclusions drawn by these studies (i.e. that women's faith development is conducted within the framework of an essentially relational context) is provided by Mader's (1986) study of faith development in older, post-generative women. This study is a detailed case study of only three subjects, all women in their fifties who were experiencing depression, from which it is impossible to generalise, but Mader's findings are of interest insofar as they throw additional light on women's relational experience of faith. In this study, the three women came to a crisis of faith because of the loss of connectedness with self-image and with the 'God' they had known and trusted throughout their lives, which precipitated a period of acute depression or loneliness. These women experienced a growing distance and separation between themselves and others, especially men, as they discovered that their generative caring was not valued or affirmed by society, and this distance extended to their relationship with God, who had previously been the safe, dependable, life-giving source of their lives. 'Their agonising loneliness was a longing for the reappearance of God in a form that would validate what they had become, and allow them once more to feel fully related.' Nevertheless, these women were able to 'wait for God without despair because in whatever images, male or otherwise, God, as transitional object, had been constant, dependable, and available for all the transitions and crises of their lives until this one' (p. 392). Mader's findings might suggest that, contrary to some feminist theory, separation is an important aspect of women's faith development, but that it tends to feature much later in women's lives than in men's, after rather than as the precursor to the generative stage of life, and that it is held within an ultimate context of relationality which is a kind of bedrock for women. Thus Mader's findings alert us to the dangers of drawing conclusions too quickly about the pattern of women's development. Gender differences are intimately related to other variables such as age, class and race and domestic circumstances (single women, for instance, are likely to experience the balance between separation and connectedness very differently from women in committed partnerships or mothers), and will not remain constant across all these variables. There is a need for much more research in this area. Nevertheless, there does appear to be a gathering consensus that Fowler's theory and methodology require revising in some important respects.

Conclusion

Sharon Parks has suggested that the attractiveness of Fowler's theory resides in its capacity to offer 'a dynamic language for an understanding of faith and religion which provides one way of addressing the reality of change and pluralism in a secularised world, yet its concern for the quality of mature faith counters the conventional dogma of relativism to which an ideology of pluralism is all too vulnerable' (1990, p. 6). This tension at the heart of Fowler's theory between the claim to universalism on the one hand and the openness to cultural and religious diversity on the other, is both its great strength and its point of greatest vulnerability. Whether faith development theory is capable of continuing to hold this tension in creative balance is an open question. The theory is still too susceptible to the charge that it maintains this balance in favour of a Western, white, liberal and masculinist world-view, and to the disadvantage of any who stand outside this experience. What little empirical evidence we have from samples representing a wider cultural and gender diversity begins seriously to call into question Fowler's claim to universalism. Further cross-cultural and gender studies are urgently needed to test, critique and refine Fowler's account of faith development. The risk of such studies is that they will challenge Fowler's description of faith to such an extent that the delicate balance between universalism and pluralism will collapse. This is a risk that has to be taken. It may be that, out of the collapse of Fowler's grand claim to offer a universally valid account of faith, a new theoretical perspective will emerge which is capable of a more differentiated and nuanced narrative of cultural, religious and sexual pluralism which yet does not fall into total relativism. Such a possibility seems a good way off yet, and until we arrive there, Fowler's account of faith continues to offer a rich resource to educators, pastors and others concerned with the development of spirituality. In the meantime, the broadening base and range of empirical research such as I have indicated in this article offers a practical pathway towards such a future.

References

Asen, B.A. (1980), Amos' faith: a structural-developmental approach, Unpublished Ph.D. dissertation, University of St Louis.

Astley, J. (ed.) (1991), *How Faith Grows: faith development and Christian education*, London, National Society and Church House Publishing.

Astley, J. and Francis, L.J. (eds) (1992), *Christian Perspectives on Faith Development: a reader*, Leominster, Fowler Wright.

Backlund, M.A. (1990), Faith and Aids: life crisis as a stimulus to faith stage transition, Unpublished Ph.D. dissertation, Pacific Graduate School of Psychology.

Barnes, M., Doyle, D. and Johnson, J. (1989), The formulation of a Fowler scale: an empirical assessment among Catholics, *Review of Religious Research*, 30, 412–420.

Bassett, P.E. (1985), Faith development and mid-life transition: Fowler's paradigm as it relates to personality profile, Unpublished Ph.D. dissertation, University of Baylor.

Bradley, R.B. (1983), An exploration of the relationship between Fowler's theory of faith development and Myers-Briggs personality type, Unpublished Ph.D. dissertation, Ohio State University.

Broughton, J.M. (1986), The political pyschology of faith development theory, in C. Dykstra and S. Parks (eds), *Faith Development and Fowler*, pp. 90–114, Birmingham, Alabama, Religious Education Press.

Broun, S.N. (1984), An analysis of ego development and religious development, Unpublished Ph.D. dissertation, University of Texas.

Chirban, J. (1980), Intrinsic and extrinsic motivation in faith development, Unpublished Th.D. dissertation, University of Harvard.

Cooney, J.A.M. (1985), Holistic relationality: themes of transition in women's faith development, Unpublished Ed.D. dissertation, University of Boston.

Devor, N.G. (1989), Toward a relational voice of faith: contributions of James Fowler's faith development theory, psychological research on women's development, relational feminist theology and a qualitative analysis of women minister's faith descriptions, Unpublished Ph.D. dissertation, University of Boston.

Dibble, R.L. (1986), An investigative study of faith development in the adult life and works of Will D. Campbell, Unpublished Ed.D. dissertation, New Orleans Baptist Theological Seminary.

Fowler, J.W. (1976), Stages in faith: the structural-developmental approach, in T.C. Hennessy (ed.), *Values and Moral Development*, pp. 173–211, New York, Paulist Press.

Fowler, J.W. (1981), *Stages of Faith: the psychology of human development and the quest for meaning*, San Francisco, Harper and Row.

Fowler, J.W. (1984), *Becoming Adult, Becoming Christian*, San Francisco, Harper and Row.

Fowler, J.W. (1987), *Faith Development and Pastoral Care*, Philadelphia, Fortress Press.

Fowler, J.W. (1991), *Weaving the New Creation: stages of faith and the public church*, San Francisco, Harper and Row.

Fowler, J.W., Nipkow, K. and Schweitzer, F. (eds) (1992), *Stages of Faith and Religious Development: implications for church, education and society*, London, SCM.

Furushima, R.Y. (1983), Faith development theory: a cross-cultural research project in Hawaii, Unpublished D.Ed. dissertation, University of Columbia.

Gilligan, C. (1982), *In a Different Voice: psychological theory and women's development*, Cambridge, Massachusetts, Harvard University Press.

Gorman, M. (1977), Moral and faith development in 17 year-old students, *Religious Education*, 72, 491–504.

Green, C. and Hoffman, C. (1989), Stages of faith and perceptions of similar and dissimilar others, *Review of Religious Research*, 30, 246–254.

Hamrick, T.R. (1988), Transitional factors in the faith development of middle adults, Unpublished Ph.D. dissertation, University of Georgia.

Harris, M. (1986), Completion and faith development, in C. Dykstra and S. Parks (eds), *Faith Development and Fowler*, pp. 115–153, Birmingham, Alabama, Religious Education Press.

Howlett, E.W. (1989), Entering the unitive life: a study of Fowler's faith stages five and six and the intervening transition, Unpublished Ed.D. dissertation, University of Massachusetts.

Hunt, L.C. (1978), The impact of family dynamics on adult faith development, Unpublished M.A. dissertation, Whitworth College.

Kalaam, T.P. (1981), The myth of stages and sequence in moral and religious development, Unpublished Ph.D. dissertation, University of Lancaster.

Kegan, R. (1982), *The Evolving Self,* Cambridge, Massachusetts, Harvard University Press.

Lansdell, C.E. (1980), Religious convictions and interpersonal relations in a Christian community, Unpublished Ed.D. dissertation, University of Toronto.

Leary, J.P. (1988), The relationship of coping with chronic stress and faith development in women: mothers of multi-handicapped children, Unpublished Ph.D. dissertation, Boston College.

Loomis, D.J. (1987), The relationship of imagination to religious faith among Presbyterian church elders, considering the mediating influence of intuition, Unpublished Ph.D. dissertation, University of Maryland.

Mader, S.T. (1986), Depression as loneliness in post-generative women: a crisis of faith development, Unpublished Ph.D. dissertation, University of Boston.

Mischey, E.J. (1976), Faith development and its relationship to moral reasoning and identity in young adults, Unpublished Ph.D. dissertation, University of Toronto.

Morgan, E.F. (1990), 'Journeys in faith': a narrative theological study of religious autobiographical quests, Unpublished Ph.D. dissertation, University of Ohio.

Moseley, R.M.S. (1978), Religious conversion: a structural-developmental analysis, Unpublished Ph.D. dissertation, University of Harvard.

Nelson, C.E. (1982), Does faith develop? An evaluation of Fowler's position, *Living Light*, 19, 162–173.

Parks, S.D. (1980), Faith development and imagination in the context of higher education, Unpublished Th.D. dissertation, University of Harvard.

Parks, S.D. (1986), *The Critical Years: the young adult search for a faith to live by*, San Francisco, Harper and Row.

Parks, S.D. (1990), Faith development in a changing world, *The Drew Gateway*, 60, 4–21.

Power, F.C. and Kohlberg, L. (1980), Religion, morality, and ego development, in C. Brusselmans (ed.), *Toward Moral and Religious Maturity*, pp. 344–372, Morristown, New Jersey, Silver Burdett.

Raduka, G.G. (1980), An investigation of hypothesised correspondence between Fowlerian stages of faith development and Jungian stages of personality development, Unpublished Ph.D. dissertation, University of Maryland.

Shulik, R.M. (1979), Faith development, moral development and old age: an assessment of Fowler's faith development paradigm, Unpublished Ph.D. dissertation, University of Chicago.

Simmonds, R.J. (1986), Content and structure in faith development: a case study of James Fowler's theory, Unpublished Ph.D. dissertation, Southern Baptist Seminary.

Slee, N. (1986), Goldman yet again: an overview and critique of his contribution to research, *British Journal of Religious Education*, 8, 84–93.

Slee, N. (1992), Cognitive developmental studies of religious thinking: a survey and discussion with special reference to post-Goldman research in the United Kingdom, in J.W. Fowler, K. Nipkow and F. Schweitzer (eds), *Stages of Faith and Religious Development: implications for church, education and society*, pp. 130–146, London, SCM.

Snarey, J. (1991), Faith development, moral development, and nontheistic Judaism: a construct validity study, in W.M. Kurtines and J.L. Gewirtz (eds), *Handbook of Moral Behaviour and Development*, pp. 279–305, Hillsdale, New Jersey, Lawrence Erlbaum.

Sweitzer, E.K. (1984), The symbolic use of religious language among Evangelical Protestant Christians from the perspective of James Fowler's faith development theory, Unpublished Ph.D. dissertation, University of Boston.

Thompson, M. (1988), Fowler and Rizzuto: making sense of life and ourselves, Unpublished M.Ed. dissertation, University of Birmingham.

Vanden Heuvel, A. (1985), Faith development and family interaction, Unpublished Ph.D. dissertation, Union for Experimenting Colleges and Universities.

Webster, D.H. (1984), James Fowler's theory of faith development, *British Journal of Religious Education*, 7, 14–18.

White, V. (1985), Faith stages, affiliation, and gender: a study of the faith development of Catholic College undergraduates, Unpublished Ed.D. dissertation, University of Boston.

5

Measuring religious thinking using Piagetian operational paradigms

Andrew G. McGrady

Summary

The first part of this chapter discusses two techniques for the measurement of religious thinking in operational terms, the semi-clinical interview technique of Goldman (1962) and the paper and pencil multiple-choice test, Thinking about the Bible, devised subsequently by Peatling (1973). The second part of the chapter reports the results of a replication study which used part of Goldman's semi-clinical interview methodology with Irish Roman Catholic secondary school pupils and which allowed for an examination of the concurrent validity of a modified version of the multiple-choice test, Thinking about the Bible.

Introduction

Over the past thirty years there has been considerable interest in the empirical investigation of religious thinking. This can be regarded as a major component of the cognitive dimension of religious understanding, a broader category which includes affective and behavioural as well as cognitive dimensions. The classical studies of religious thinking were carried out during the 1960s and early 1970s using a Piagetian operational paradigm. In the United Kingdom Ronald Goldman (Goldman, 1962, 1964, 1965) firmly established this tradition of examining the operational aspects of religious thinking using the categories of intuitive, concrete and abstract thought. Corresponding research was carried out in the United States of America by Elkind (1961, 1962, 1963, 1965). Both researchers confirmed that religious thinking exhibits a developmental component progressing through the classical Piagetian stages.

Using three pictures and three biblical stories (Burning Bush, Crossing the Red Sea and Temptations of Jesus), Goldman (1962) examined the development of a number of key religious concepts (the bible, the identity and nature of the Divine, God's activity in the natural world, holiness, God's concern for humanity, Jesus, evil, prayer, the church). Using semi-clinical interviews Goldman interviewed 200 pupils in English state maintained schools. His results made a substantive contribution to this field of enquiry by illustrating the applicability of classical cognitive approaches, by highlighting the role of the child's immediate experience as a basis for religious thinking, and by substantiating the developmental nature of such thinking. Some important limitations of the approach have subsequently been recognised. These limitations include the restricted applicability of operational paradigms (they are particularly suited to investigating the propositional aspects of religious thinking, referred to by Hyde [1984] as 'theological thinking', especially in the context of possible conflict between biblical and scientific world views), their relative insensitivity to the affective aspects of religious thought, their tendency to deal with concepts in a non-analogical rather than metaphorical or symbolic way, and their reductionist tendencies with respect to religious narratives. A fuller discussion of these points is provided by Murphy (1977a, 1977b, 1979), Greer (1980a, 1980b, 1983, 1984a, 1984b), Hyde (1984, 1990), McGrady (1982, 1983, 1990), and Slee (1986a, 1986b). Goldman's early operational research has however remained a vital reference point around which other research has orbited.

In related areas, the research of Kohlberg (1958, 1980), Fowler (1981) and Oser (1980) has provided evidence that the development of moral judgement, religious judgement and faith development is also influenced by the stages of Piagetian operational thought. In the light of this, Oser and Reich (1990b) propose a dynamic model of the relationship between moral judgement (MJ), religious judgement (RJ), world view (WV) and logical operational thought. Based upon a research approach that compared Oser's stages of religious judgement with Kohlberg's stages of moral judgement, they noted that, while at the early stages a certain isomorphism existed, the higher the stage, the fewer the common elements, and the more autonomous the structure. With 'development the stage structures (were) qualitatively more and more independent of each other' (Oser and Reich, 1990b, p. 172). They propose a common core (CC) of general cognitive operations which are influenced by cognitive development and to which the pure Piagetian paradigm relates. Both moral judgement and religious judgement, while independent, are affected by the common core processes as well as by their mutual interaction. The links are stronger in the early stages of development and weaker towards the higher stages. The common core also influences social perspective taking (which in turn also exerts an influence on moral judgement) and world view (WV) which exerts a similar influence on religious judgement. Adopting such a stance allows a redefinition of the relationship between the development of religious thinking and Piagetian stage development. The model adopted by Goldman (1962) equating the development of religious thinking with advancement through the stages of logical operations can now be recognised as being over-stated; rather than talking of stages of religious thinking development, it is more accurate to refer to the effect of the underlying stages of operational development upon religious thinking skills.

While the research tradition pioneered by Goldman and Elkind has held up well under subsequent investigation, the problem of identifying with ease the stage of operational development of an individual's religious thinking remains. The semi-clinical interview technique used by these researchers is not suitable for use by the average teacher or with large samples. During the early 1970s Peatling sought to develop Goldman's semi-clinical interview into a standardised paper and pencil test suitable for use with large samples. The resultant test instrument, Thinking about the Bible (TAB), was based solely upon the three biblical narratives used by Goldman. Each of the three stories was followed by a series of multiple choice questions, each with four possible responses intended to be representative of each of the following scales, religious thinking very concrete (RTVC), religious thinking concrete (RTC), religious thinking abstract (RTA) and religious thinking very abstract (RTVA). Subjects were required to indicate which of the four possible response items was *most like* and which was *least like* their own view. While confirming Goldman's findings in general terms (the development of the operational component of religious thinking was found to proceed through the classical Piagetian stages), Peatling also reported that the transition between concrete and abstract religious thinking occurred through an extended intermediate period lasting up to six years and covering most of the period of secondary education.

Peatling's test, TAB, has been used in a number of large scale studies including the following: Peatling (1973) with 1,994 students in Episcopalian schools in the United States of America, Tamminen (1976) with 1,374 students in Finnish schools, and Greer (1981) with 2,149 pupils in Belfast schools. However, while a number of criticisms have been made of Goldman's original research, mainly relating to the limited selection of biblical material examined, the liberal theological hermeneutic adopted and the reductionist tendency of many of the interview questions, more sustained and substantial criticisms have been made of the reliability and validity of Peatling's instrument. Greer (1980a) for example subjected TAB to rigorous psychometric investigation and concluded that 'Goldman's model of the development of religious thinking in adolescence is to be preferred' (1980, p. 1). Using both the Flesch Reading Ease Formula and the Fog Index of readability, Greer observed that the various TAB response category items reflected different reading ages; he provided evidence that the TAB very abstract scale (RTVA) measured a dimension of belief-disbelief as well as concrete-abstract development; and concerning the extended intermediate phase, concluded that 'it seems probable that this five year period was in fact an artefact of Peatling's method' caused by his defining an intermediate period in terms of scores falling within one standard deviation on either side of the chance mean. Other criticisms have been noted by other researchers: McGrady (1983, 1990) adds to Greer's criticisms the failure of TAB to differentiate between five of the twelve Goldman questions used by Peatling which proved reliable indicators of operational development, and the remaining seven which Goldman subjected only to a theological analysis, the confusion between intuitive and concrete thinking evident in the TAB RTVC scale, the tautologous nature of the scoring system adopted by Peatling, and the problems inherited from Goldman relating to the versions of the biblical narratives used in the test. Despite these criticisms many reviewers welcome the intention behind the construction of TAB and have used it in their subsequent research, often with a modified scoring system, including for instance Greer (1981), Kay (1981) and McGrady (1990).

Method

Procedure

The study reported in this present discussion formed part of a wider research project examining the metaphorical dimension of religious thinking and comparing this to existing Piagetian operational dimensions (McGrady, 1990, 1992, 1993, 1994a, 1994b). One of the stories used in Goldman's (1962) Picture and Story Test of Religious Thinking, the story of the Temptations of Jesus, is suitable for the examination of both the operational and metaphorical aspects of religious thinking. This story was therefore examined along with a range of other metaphorical religious material from a variety of religious belief systems not examined by Goldman. Subjects initially received a modified form of Peatling's TAB (described below) and the AH4 test of general intellectual ability; these were administered on a group basis during regular lesson periods. Subjects then individually received a semi-clinical interview, the initial part of which was a replication of the relevant part of Goldman's semi-clinical interview dealing with the story of the Temptations of Jesus (the final part of the interview added questions dealing with the metaphorical aspect of the story).

Sample

The sample which was exposed to the story of the Temptations of Jesus was a sub-group of a larger sample and consisted of 59 pupils in a Dublin Roman Catholic secondary school. The school followed a five year primary cycle, the first three years of which led to the state Intermediate Certificate examination and the final two years of which led to the state Leaving Certificate examination. Subjects were randomly selected from average class groups from three of the five year grades. The sample comprised ten males and ten females from junior grade one (entrance grade) with a mean age of 13.20 years (s.d. 0.37); ten males and ten females from junior grade three (students taking the Intermediate Certificate of Education examination) with a mean age of 15.21 years (s.d. 0.59); and eleven males and eight females from senior grade two (school-leavers taking the Leaving Certificate of Education examination) with a mean age of 17.05 years (s.d. 0.32). The mean overall age for male subjects was 15.19 years (s.d. 1.56), while that for females was 15.10 years (s.d. 1.75). The slight difference in age was not significant ($t = 0.20$, d.f. $= 54$, $p = 0.84$). All subjects were Roman Catholic.

Replication using Goldman's semi-clinical interview

The initial section of the semi-clinical interview was limited simply to that part of Goldman's test which concerned subjects' operational responses to the story of the Temptation of Jesus. In the light of criticisms made of the version of the story used by Goldman, two changes were made: a recognised translation of the scriptures (*The Good News Bible*) was used to present the story, rather than Goldman's simplified version, and a slightly wider selection from the biblical text was used, the additional verses allowing for the context of the story of the Temptation of Jesus to be more clearly set, thereby eliminating the possible reductionist tendencies of the Goldman version (Howkins, 1966; McGrady, 1983). Following the presentation of the story, the relevant part of the Goldman interview schedule was followed exactly. The typed interview transcripts were scored twice. The correlation between judgements was $r = 0.87$. In the few cases in which there was disagreement, the lower score was used.

Goldman (1962, pp. 86–88) provides criteria for determining the operational religious thinking stage (ORT) from the responses to his interview schedule relating to the story of the Temptation of Jesus. Central to such scoring was the subjects' response to the question 'If Jesus was hungry why didn't he turn the stone into bread?' interpreted in the light of responses to follow up questions such as 'How would he do it?' The responses of the subjects in the present study fell into four of the possible ORT stages: concrete operational (score 3), intermediate between concrete and formal operational (score 4), formal operational (score 5) and advanced formal operational (score 6).

Each of these categories can be illustrated in turn, using responses from the Dublin subjects. Goldman (1962) classified as concrete responses those which saw the devil as an actual person, which appealed to a magical power that Jesus possessed but would not use for the devil, or which could not interrelate Jesus' refusal with his subsequent action of turning water into wine at Cana. Such a response was offered by a junior grade one female subject (13.2 years):

interviewer   What was the devil asking (Jesus) to do?

subject   To see if he had powers. . . . Like he could do anything he wanted.

interviewer   What sort of thing could Jesus do?

subject   Help people; if someone was hungry he would probably make food.

interviewer Why didn't Jesus turn the stone into bread when the devil asked him; he was hungry?

subject 'Cos he didn't want to do it for the devil.

The appeal to magical power was also evident in the response of a junior grade one male subject (12.5 years):

interviewer How would Jesus (turn the stone into bread)?

subject: He would just bless it. . . . You'd see him blessing the stone, and then it would turn into bread.

Goldman classified as intermediate between concrete and formal operations responses which, although they showed the beginning of the construction of hypotheses, were not too successful because they were still limited by a literal interpretation of the food situation. Examples provided by Goldman included the observation that Jesus went into the desert for a different reason, such as to pray or to fast, or the 'thin-end of the wedge' hypothesis, that to turn the stone into bread would put Jesus in the devil's power. Such emergent hypothetical justification limited by the persistence of a concrete perspective was evident in the transcript of a junior grade one female subject (12.7 years):

interviewer Could Jesus turn the stone into bread?

subject Yeah, 'cos he has very good powers being God's son. . . . (If) people are really in need, starving to death, he probably could turn a stone into bread.

interviewer So why doesn't he turn the stone into bread here?

subject Because he doesn't want to show the devil what he can do, and he doesn't want the devil to get him underneath his powers.

The response of a junior grade one male subject (12.9 years) illustrated the wider interpretative framework provided by the version of the story used in the replication interview. The possibilities generated were ultimately still limited by the concrete however:

interviewer (Turn the stone into bread) What is that about?

subject (Jesus) thinks that by having the Holy Spirit in him that he can do anything, or make things change. He has special power.

interviewer Could Jesus have turned the stone into bread though?

subject No. . . . He's a human being. He is just a person who felt something when the Holy Spirit came down to him, about God.

interviewer Could Jesus have survived in the desert for forty days?

subject   No. He hadn't got anything to eat. Unless he brought something with him when he was going in. Some sort of water, you know the tanks that cowboys take with them. Something like that, and he drank it very slowly.

Goldman classified as exhibiting formal operational thought any response which was an orderly systematic proposition, such as if he turned the stone into bread Jesus would be using his powers for trivial things or for his own good, or that it was a test to show if he was worthy to be the son of God, or responses which calculated the probable outcomes of the act. The first of these was exhibited by a junior grade three male subject (14.1 years):

interviewer   Why didn't Jesus turn the stone into bread?

subject   He didn't want to use the power that God had given him for himself but for others.

interviewer   He turned water into wine once. What is the difference between the two situations?

subject   The wine was for his followers, in this case the bread would have been for himself.

An orderly systematic proposition coming from a position of faith was exhibited by the response of a senior grade two female subject (17 years):

subject   I think he had the power because, do you remember the other bible story of the little girl who died, and he went in and healed her? The power of that was much greater than just turning a stone into bread. And then with the fishes, Simon Peter went fishing and there were loads of fishes.

interviewer   So he did other things that were similar or even greater than this?

subject   Yeah, and the other times he wasn't under so much pressure. He wasn't told (to do it), he just did it out of an act of love. And this wouldn't be an act of love. . . . The other things he did . . . it was for other people. This wouldn't be an act of love, it was just showing his power. . . . You don't associate love with the devil; I associate evil with the devil.

Finally Goldman classified as being at a stage of advanced formal operations, responses which exhibited abstract parabolic thinking, such as suggesting that the struggle was one within Jesus' own conscience (rather than with an external physical devil), or responses which highlighted the notion that belief in the Word of

God would provide all of Jesus' needs. Awareness of such an inner struggle was exhibited in the response of a senior grade two male subject (16.4 years):

interviewer Could (Jesus) have actually turned the stone into bread?

subject I imagine he could. That would mean displaying his glory. That would be destroying the whole purpose of (his mission), he wouldn't have actually come to earth as man, he would have come as God which would have sort of suggested he wasn't capable of being man.

interviewer So he could have turned the stone into bread?

subject The possibility was there; if he couldn't it wouldn't have been a temptation.

Replication using a modified version of TAB

Given the criticisms of TAB (some of which are reported earlier in this article) a modified version of the instrument was prepared. The modifications to the test were, the use of recognised biblical versions of the stories which included a wider selection of verses to ensure that the biblical context of each story was evident, and the requirement for the respondent simply to select one of the four possible response items which was similar to their own view (the additional requirement to identify the item *least like* their view was not used). Substantial modifications were made to the scoring of the twelve TAB questions. Scoring was based upon the stage of operational religious thinking (SORT) as indicated by analysis of only the five TAB questions which Goldman (1962) found amenable to operational analysis. The remaining seven TAB items were not scored. Scores were allocated to response items as follows: RTVC = 1, RTC = 2, RTA = 3, RTVA = 4. Final scores over five items ranged from a minimum of 5 points to a maximum of 20 points. Scores in the range of 9–11 points were regarded as indicative of concrete thinking, 12–13 points as indicative of intermediate between concrete and formal thinking, 14–16 points as indicative of formal thinking and 17–20 points as indicative of advanced formal thinking. For a fuller discussion see McGrady (1990, appendix 3).

Results and discussion

Research results relate to the estimate of religious thinking provided by the use of part of Goldman's interview schedule, the estimate provided by a modified version of TAB, and a consideration of the concurrent validity of the modified version of TAB. In the following discussion school grade level is used as a convenient metric.

Goldman semi-clinical interview

As evident from table 5.1, a clear stage related development is visible over the period of secondary schooling. In junior grade one 45% of subjects were at a stage of concrete operations, by junior

Table 5.1
Stage of operational religious thinking
as measured by replicated semi-clinical interview

	concrete	intermediate	formal
junior grade 1	9	10	1
	45%	50%	5%
			5%, 0%
junior grade 3	2	10	8
	10%	50%	40%
			(30%, 10%)
senior grade 2	0	7	12
	0%	37%	63%
			(47.4%, 15.8%)

grade three this had declined to 10%, and it was eliminated by senior grade two. The percentage of subjects within an intermediate stage declined slowly from 50% in both junior grades to 37% in senior grade two. A clear shift to formal thought is evident in both junior grade three and senior grade two. While in junior grade one only 5% of subjects exhibited formal thought, by senior grade two 63% of subjects exhibited formal (47%) or advanced formal (16%) thought. This development of operational religious thinking as indicated by the variation in ORT stage frequencies across grades was significant at beyond the 95% level of confidence (MOOD median test: Chi-square = 21.71, d.f. = 4, p<0.01).

Modified TAB

The pattern of development over the period of secondary schooling as indicated by a modified version of TAB is depicted in table 5.2.

Table 5.2
Stage of operational religious thinking
as measured by modified TAB

	concrete	intermediate	formal
junior grade 1	10 56%	3 17%	5 28% (16.7%, 11.1%)
junior grade 3	5 25%	4 20%	11 55% (50%, 5%)
senior grade 2	3 16%	3 16%	13 68% (47.4%, 21.0%)

Scores increased with successive school grade level indicating a movement towards abstract religious thinking. In junior grade one 56% of subjects were at a stage of concrete operational thought concerning religious material; only 28% were at a stage of formal or abstract operational thought, the remaining 17% were within a transitional intermediate stage. A radical shift occurring by junior grade three was clearly evident. Within the space of two years the proportion of subjects exhibiting formal operation thinking increased to 55% (including 5% at advanced formal operations) with a further 20% of subjects within an intermediate stage. The frequency of concrete operational thinking declined further into senior grade two to 16% while the continued development of formal religious thinking is evident, with 63% of subjects exhibiting formal thought (including 21% exhibiting advanced formal thought). The movement from concrete to formal operational religious thinking across grade levels did not however reach significance (MOOD median test: obtained chi-square = 8.27, d.f. = 4;

required chi-square = 9.49). Finally, it is interesting to note that the percentage of subjects indicated by the modified form of TAB as residing within an intermediate phase is considerably less than that indicated by the alternative interview methodology.

Concurrent validity of modified TAB

With the above data it is possible to compare Goldman's interview methodology and Peatling's TAB as measures of the operational aspects of religious thinking. Such a comparison represents an exercise in concurrent validity. Cronbach (1960, p. 103) argues that this is required when a new test is devised to replace an existing 'more cumbersome method' of collecting the required data. The relationship between Peatling's TAB and Goldman's Picture and Story Test of Religious Thinking is precisely such a relationship.

The only existing examination of TAB's concurrent validity was carried out by Greer (1980a) who tested eight fourteen year old pupils from both secondary and grammar schools in Northern Ireland (resulting in a sample size of 16). Subjects were administered both the standard form of TAB and an interview based upon the TAB questions. The comparison between TAB and the scored interviews was based upon the TAB *most agree* responses using a modified scoring system (also based upon RTVC = 1; RTC = 2; RTA = 3; RTVA = 4, but using all twelve TAB items). Greer reported that the correlation (Pearson product moment) between the two sets of scores was r = 0.44 (p<0.01). He further noted that the standard deviation of the scores of those who were administered TAB was considerably greater than those who were administered the alternative interview which he interpreted as indicating that the interview method gave a more consistent measure of operational development. Greer concluded that for individuals 'TAB is not a valid indicator of the level of religious thinking which is revealed in an interview situation' (1980a, p. 16), but that it provides a useful measure when used with groups. He further noted that the results obtained from the interview material 'fitted well into Goldman's account of cognitive development' rather than supporting Peatling's claim for an extended intermediate transition period between concrete and abstract thinking (1980a, p. 20).

Greer (1980a) considered that his own study was a small-scale experiment and that 'the concurrent validation of TAB deserves further serious consideration' (1980a, p. 14). The present study used a larger sample (59 compared with 16 subjects), used interviews which replicated Goldman's original semi-clinical test, and examined the five year period of secondary schooling rather than a single year grade. In one respect, however, the present investigation represents a narrower focus in that only one of the Goldman stories (the Temptation of Jesus) was examined. Table 5.3 outlines the obtained correlation matrix between the subjects' age, their school grade level, their grade on the AH4 test, their operational

Table 5.3
Correlation matrix
(Spearman's Rank Order Correlation Coefficient)

	AH4 grade	school grade	age	interview
school grade	+0.05 NS			
age	-0.09 NS	+0.93 .001		
interview	+0.14 NS	+0.58 .001	+0.57 .001	
TAB	+0.06 NS	+0.36 .01	+0.39 .01	+0.45 .001

religious thinking stage as indicated by a partial replication of Goldman's interview and their operational religious thinking stage as indicated by a modified TAB. The matrix was based upon Spearman's rank order correlation coefficient. The correlation between modified TAB and interviews based upon the story of the Temptation of Jesus used in Goldman's semi-clinical interview observed by the present researcher was $r = 0.45$ ($N = 59$, $p < 0.01$). This relationship can be considered very similar to that reported by Greer (1980a) of $r = 0.44$. This provides some support for the concurrent validity of a modified version of TAB, either in the form used by Greer (1980a) or the form used by the present investigator.

Other associations depicted in the correlation matrix are of interest. Neither instruments exhibited a strong association with general intellectual ability as measured by the AH4 test. Further, the modified version of TAB functions somewhat more independently than the replicated Goldman interview from the effects of school grade level and chronological age. While both devices indicated that, by senior grade 2, approximately two-thirds of school leavers had reached a stage of abstract religious thinking, a more rapid shift is indicated by the modified form of TAB than by the semi-clinical interviews. Finally, it should be noted that the use of an alternative scoring system (SORT) for the modified TAB effectively eliminated the five year intermediate period between concrete and formal religious thinking reported by Peatling (1973).

References

Cronbach, L.J. (1960), *Essentials of Psychological Testing*, New York, Harper and Row.

Elkind, D. (1961), The child's conception of his religious denomination: (1) the Jewish child, *Journal of Genetic Psychology*, 99, 209–225.

Elkind, D. (1962), The child's conception of his religious denomination: (2) the Catholic child, *Journal of Genetic Psychology*, 101, 185–193

Elkind, D. (1963), The child's conception of his religious denomination: (3) the Protestant child, *Journal of Genetic Psychology*, 103, 291–304.

Elkind, D. (1965), The child's conception of his religious identity, *Lumen Vitae*, 19, 635–646.

Fowler, J. (1981), *Stages of Faith: the psychology of human development and the quest for meaning*, San Francisco, Harper and Row.

Goldman, R.J. (1962), Some aspects of religious thinking in childhood and adolescence, Unpublished Ph.D. dissertation, University of Birmingham.

Goldman, R.J. (1964), *Religious Thinking from Childhood to Adolescence*, London, Routledge and Kegan Paul.

Goldman, R.J. (1965), *Readiness for Religion*, London, Routledge and Kegan Paul.

Greer, J.E. (1980a), A critical study of 'Thinking about the Bible', Unpublished paper, New University of Ulster.

Greer, J.E. (1980b), Stages in the development of religious thinking, *British Journal of Religious Education*, 3, 24–28.

Greer, J.E. (1981), Religious attitudes and thinking in Belfast pupils, *Educational Research*, 23, 177–189.

Greer, J.E. (1983), A critical study of 'Thinking about the Bible', *British Journal of Religious Education*, 5, 113–125.

Greer, J.E. (1984a), Fifty years of the psychology of religion in religious education (part one), *British Journal of Religious Education*, 6, 93–97.

Greer, J.E. (1984b), Fifty years of the psychology of religion in religious education (part two), *British Journal of Religious Education*, 7, 23–28.

Howkins, K. (1966), *Religious Thinking and Religious Education: a critique of the research and conclusions of Dr R. Goldman*, London, Tyndale Press.

Hyde, K.E. (1984), Twenty years after Goldman's research, *British Journal of Religious Education*, 7, 1, 5–7.

Hyde, K.E. (1990), *Religion in Childhood and Adolescence: a comprehensive review of the research*, Birmingham, Alabama, Religious Education Press.

Kay, W.K. (1981), Religious thinking, attitudes and personality amongst secondary pupils in England and Ireland, Unpublished Ph.D. Dissertation, University of Reading.

Kohlberg, L. (1958), The development of modes of moral thinking in the years 10–16, Unpublished Ph.D. dissertation, University of Chicago.

Kohlberg, L. (1980), Dialog: L. Kohlberg talks to L. Kuhmerker about moral development and the measurement of moral judgement, in L. Kuhmerker, M. Mentkowski and V.L. Erickson (eds), *Evaluating Moral Development*, pp. 87–99, New York, Character Research Press.

McGrady, A.G. (1982), Goldman: a Piagetian based critique, *Irish Catechist*, 6, 3, 19-29.

McGrady, A.G. (1983), Teaching the bible: research from a Piagetian perspective, *British Journal of Religious Education*, 5, 126–133.

McGrady, A.G. (1990), The development of religious thinking: a comparison of metaphoric and operational paradigms, Unpublished Ph.D. dissertation, University of Birmingham.

McGrady, A.G. (1992), Metaphorical and operational aspects of religious thinking: a discussion in the light of research with Irish Catholic pupils, Unpublished paper presented at The International Seminar on Religious Education and Values, Banff, Alberta, Canada.

McGrady, A.G. (1993), Glimpsing the divine: metaphor and religious thinking, in D.A. Lane (ed.) *Religion and Culture in Dialogue*, pp. 151–188, Dublin, The Columba Press.

McGrady, A.G. (1994a), Metaphorical and operational aspects of religious thinking: research with Irish Catholic pupils (part one), *British Journal of Religious Education*, 16, 3, 148–163.

McGrady, A.G. (1994b), Metaphorical and operational aspects of religious thinking: research with Irish Catholic pupils (part two), *British Journal of Religious Education*, 17, 1, 56–62.

Murphy, R.J.L. (1977a), Does children's understanding of parables develop in stages?, *Learning for Living*, 16, 168–172.

Murphy, R.J.L. (1977b), The development of religious thinking in children in three easy stages, *Learning for Living*, 17, 16–19.

Murphy, R.J.L. (1979), An investigation into some aspects of the development of religious thinking in children aged between 6 and 11 years, Unpublished Ph.D. dissertation, University of St Andrews.

Oser, F. (1980), Stages of religious judgement, in C. Brusselmans (ed.), *Towards Moral and Religious Maturity*, pp. 277–315, Morristown, New Jersey, Silver Burdett.

Oser, F. and Reich, H. (1990b), Moral judgment, religious judgment, world view, and logical thought: a review of their relationship (part two), *British Journal of Religious Education*, 12, 172–181.

Peatling, J.H. (1973), The incidence of concrete and abstract religious thinking in the interpretation of three bible stories by pupils enrolled in grades four through twelve in selected schools in the United States of America, Unpublished Ph.D. dissertation, University of New York.

Slee, N. (1986a), Goldman yet again, *British Journal of Religious Education*, 8, 84–93.

Slee, N. (1986b), A note on Goldman's methods of data analysis with special reference to scalogram analysis, *British Journal of Religious Education*, 8, 168–175.

Tamminen, K. (1976), Research concerning the development of religious thinking in Finnish students: a report of results, *Character Potential*, 7, 4, 206–219.

6

Developmental research in the classroom: an empirical study of teaching-learning processes

Karl Ernst Nipkow, Friedrich Schweitzer,
Gabriele Faust-Siehl and Bernd Krupka

Summary

This chapter describes and discusses a classroom research project conducted between 1988 and 1993 at the Department of Religious Education, University of Tübingen. Altogether 24 lessons of Protestant and Roman Catholic religious education, in different types of schools and at different age levels, were each observed by two people, taped, transcribed and subjected to interaction analysis. The aim was to discover how the developmental status of students is addressed in the praxis of religious education. As a second strand of the research, the teachers were interviewed. The aim was to discover how the developmental views of the teachers affect the ways in which they interact with students.

Introduction

Empirical research has to be guided by theoretical presuppositions. The following report about a classroom research project conducted between 1988 and 1993 at the Department of Religious Education, University of Tübingen (Schweitzer, Nipkow, Faust-Siehl and Krupka, 1995a), can only be understood if several theoretical factors are taken into account which are relevant to the situation in West Germany during the mid 1980s.

For centuries religious education has been taught in all state schools in Germany, either on a Protestant or Roman Catholic basis.

It is compulsory for all schools to provide religious education. The pupils, however, can accept the invitation to study religious education, but they are not required to do so. For the pupils religious education is a matter of free choice. In most regions those students who do not attend religious education classes are obliged to attend *Ethikunterricht* (classes in ethics) instead. Thus, a competitive situation has been created; for both subjects much depends on their quality to attract the young generation. This again seems to be closely connected with another point: will the pupils experience religious education as a subject which *recognises them individually*? We decided to check this question by careful analysis of the teaching-learning procedures.

Protestant religious education is open to all pupils, even to those who are not Christians; in many cases Muslim children attend Protestant religious education. Even if the majority of young people in West Germany have been baptised (in East Germany it is a very small minority only), a great number of them are sceptical towards the church. This is only one reason, however, why religious education is presented in an open-minded way. All who attend religious education know about its confessional character, but they soon come to realise that the subject is presented in a non-confessionalist way, if Protestant characteristics have any bearing at all. In the late 1960s and early 1970s a new approach called *Schülerorientierung* (pupil centred) supported the paradigm shift from Christian nurture to religious education. In combination with a so-called thematic approach, the traditional biblical content was supplemented with life themes, mostly related to current issues (referred to as problems). For this reason, the second approach was also called *thematisch-problemorientiert*, similar to the approach developed by Loukes (1961) in the United Kingdom. The 'problems' concerned religious topics, general social issues of public concern and individual interests and needs of children and young people.

It took some years to discover the shortcomings of this approach. What about the ways in which children worked through the biblical as well as the non-biblical issues? The thematic approach alone was not sufficient; it did not tell anything about the processes of how religious knowledge and understanding is acquired. By looking at what students actually say in classroom interaction, our investigation aimed at a fuller insight at this point.

To come closer to an adequate interpretation of the *Deutungsmuster* (interpretative patterns) of the pupils, hermeneutical competence is needed. Would we find it with the teachers? And by which method was our own research to be done? We soon realised that we had to use a type of research that was rather unknown to German religious educators, namely *process analysis*, the detailed analysis of a lesson as a whole, consisting of both verbal and non-verbal exchanges.

Method

The research method was shaped by two perspectives. One perspective shaping the research was the *biographical emphasis* in both religious and general education. It included accepting Piagetian and Eriksonian theoretical assumptions about *development* in childhood and adolescence. In our project, hypotheses about the dynamics of psychosocial development (Erikson) and cognitive-developmental stages (Selman, Kohlberg, Fowler, Oser) were combined. At the end of the 1970s, it was high time for the discipline of religious education in Germany to become more familiar with developmental categories which were then gradually introduced and critically discussed (Nipkow, 1979, 1982; Schmidt, 1983, 1984; Englert, 1985; Fraas and Heimbrock, 1986; Schweitzer, 1987; Nipkow, Schweitzer and Fowler, 1988; Fowler, Nipkow and Schweitzer, 1991). Extensive historical studies contributed to the understanding of the issue of the religion of the child as a basic problem of religious education (Schweitzer, 1992). However, empirical research was still lacking at the grassroots.

In order to fill this gap and to support the *hermeneutics of the classroom* from the *developmental side*, we launched our project for the benefit of the praxis and located it within the praxis. We started with a pilot phase in order to test our research instruments and develop hypotheses which were then more extensively checked in the main phase. On the one hand, the classroom interaction itself was observed. On the other hand, we interviewed the teachers. Altogether 24 lessons of Protestant and Roman Catholic religious education in different types of schools (Hauptschule, Realschule, Gymnasium) and at different age levels (between the ages of ten and twelve years in grade five and grade six and between the ages of fifteen and seventeen in grade ten) were observed (each by two persons), taped, transcribed and analysed. Then two forms of interviews were conducted with the 18 teachers involved in these lessons, a short interview of about 20 minutes after each lesson and a more extensive one (60 minutes) at a later point. The aim of the first method of classroom interaction analysis was to find out how the developmental status of students is addressed in the praxis of religious education. The aim of the second method was to find out how the developmental views of the teachers affect the ways in which they interact with students.

Since our main interest was directed towards the praxis and towards the ways in which teachers and students work with the content matter, we primarily looked at those statements which were 'structurally loaded' and could be coded according to the schemes proposed by Fowler and Oser. It was possible to assign codable statements to Fowler's stages or transitional stages (Fowler, Jarvis and Moseley, 1986), whereas the assignment to Oser's stages proved to be less easy (Oser and Gmünder, 1984). The percentage of codable statements which we called the *structural content* of a lesson varied between 5% and 47%, with an average of 24% in grade five and grade six or 28% in grade ten. As far as interpretation was directed at *psychosocial aspects*, the investigation could not be formalised, but was more in line with psychoanalytic procedures of interpretation (for more details about the methodological questions and difficulties see Schweitzer, Nipkow, Faust-Siehl and Krupka, 1995a, chapter 7; Schweitzer, Faust-Siehl, Krupka and Nipkow, 1995b).

The second perspective shaping our research was provided by the ongoing didactic discussion in the 1980s which had led to the approach of *elementarisation* (Nipkow, 1982, 1983). This concept tries to relate the traditional focus on instructional content with the insights of experiential learning. In addition to this, it includes the developmental and biographical perspective mentioned above. Four dimensions of the teaching-learning process are suggested. These dimensions can be expressed by four questions meant heuristically for the purposes of analysing and preparing the lessons. First, what are the 'elementary *structures*' of meaning on the side of the content matter? Second, what are the 'elementary *truth claims*' at stake between both poles, the objective issues and the subjective ways of understanding, rejecting, approving on the side of the students? Third, what are the 'elementary *experiences*' coming up in the interaction between the content, for example a biblical story, and the students? Fourth, what are the students' 'elementary *approaches*' when interpreting the instructional content between 'assimilation' and 'accommodation' according to their own development and life situation?

The framework of elementarisation locates the developmental dimension within the broader instructional context. The 24 lessons of our project were dealing with three fields of content: God, justice and parables. It was likely that these topics, with the questions they may raise for teachers or students, would contain elementary structures (the first question), appeal to experiences (the third question), lead to debates on what is 'true' (the second question) and give the opportunity to study the developmental preconditions (the fourth question).

A final theoretical point was taken up from the recent discussion on teaching-learning processes in general. In line with insights of *reception analysis* in linguistics, it can be assumed that in teaching situations *a three-stage process of transforming* the 'reality' of life into instructional 'reality' is taking place. A first 'reconstruction' of instructional topics by the curriculum maker (giving a piece of reality its first and more general instructionally fitting shape) is followed by a second 'reconstruction' when the teacher will prepare the topic for his or her lesson. A third 'reconstruction', now in a plural form, is done by the students themselves (Faust-Siehl, 1987). This last stage of 'reconstruction' is the most effective one, that which counts. Reception always means transformation. Thus, a lesson may be regarded as a field of many parallel and crossing paths of interpretation with considerable consequences for more flexible planning of instruction (Schweitzer, Nipkow, Faust-Siehl and Krupka, 1995a, chapter 5).

Results

The 42 interviews with the teachers (24 following the lessons, 18 longer interviews at a different time) were submitted to content analysis, following a two step procedure. In the pilot phase, eight interviews were used as a basis for formulating a number of hypotheses. These hypotheses were then tested and refined by applying them to the 34 interviews of the main phase. A brief report of some results of the interviews may serve as a background to the interaction analysis and its findings.

First, faith development, as Fowler (1981) understands it, rests upon a stage description which looks at faith as a structured whole (Fowler, Jarvis and Moseley, 1986, p. 50), characterised by seven aspects which are defined as: form of logic, social perspective taking, form of moral judgement, bounds of social awareness, locus of authority, form of world coherence and symbolic function. In our research project we added Oser's 'structure of religious judgement' as an eighth aspect. All eight aspects could be identified in our analysis of classroom interaction, and almost all of them were also addressed in the interviews. The same was true for Eriksonian viewpoints. In contrast to this result, *the teacher's explicit categories of perception and interpretation* when asked to describe the development of their students, did not yield a comprehensive or detailed picture.

The teachers' views of their students' development can be considered as *subjective* or *naïve theories*. As far as our interviews show, German religious educators are not familiar with current academic theories of religious development. The publications listed above are too recent to have had a broader influence on their training. In addition to this, most of these publications offer more or less theoretical descriptions of psychological constructs, without showing in detail their meaning for concrete classroom interaction and therefore without much chance of promoting practical skills. The teachers of religious education are aware of some general characteristics of the development from childhood to adolescence (physical maturation, separation from parents, aspects of gender, a more differentiated use of language and of critical reflection, etc.). As far as religious development is concerned, they are aware of some important characteristics, but there is no coherent and secure knowledge about it.

With respect to the three content areas of the project (God, justice and parables), the perceptions of the teachers differed in an interesting manner. Most of the teachers say in some way that understanding *metaphorical language* requires cognitive abilities which only develop in the course of secondary school. The focus here is on the figurative aspect of language and on the difficulties which can arise from this linguistic feature. Here, the teachers come close to a stage-related view of the development of symbolic understanding. Many teachers consider *justice* as a norm. When asked about their students, they tend to think about students' attitudes toward this norm or about students' behaviour. With the *issue of God*, most teachers observe that anthropomorphic images are to be found with the ten to twelve year olds. The teachers tend to consider them as deficient. With the sixteen year olds, they perceive an unclear understanding of God which sometimes is referred to as broken. As far as the relationship to God is concerned, teachers perceive a (sad) loss with the students. This loss is assumed to be due to influences of the environment. In sum, the perceptions tend to be coloured by evaluations and the criteria are conceived from an adult point of view and from a theological ideal. Such views make it difficult to take the perspective of the children and to interpret differences in language and understanding (for example, anthropomorphic, de-mythologised, spiritualised ideas of God) in terms of developmental transformation instead of religious loss or decay.

Second, a vital concern of the teachers refers to *disciplinary problems* and to *students' motivation*. More or less they want their students to follow the line they themselves have conceived as adults. They do not seem to be aware of the children's own interpretative activities in terms of cognitive structures and play of imagination. As adults they seem to have difficulties realising that children think differently. One might also say that they want to teach more effectively. Our own empirical study is primarily directed towards the ways the students learn for themselves by doing their own theologising (cf. Astley, 1995). From this point of view, teaching can be and ought to be improved by becoming open for the students' understanding.

Third, the teachers' expectations lead to a discrepancy which we observed in many lessons. In several cases the interaction in the classes was less an interaction than an acting on *two separate levels of interpretation*, one level for the teachers and another level for the students. While the teacher is hermeneutically 'moving' on a meta-level of understanding historical events, the students are 'moving' on the level of the reported events themselves. The students' attention is drawn to what had actually happened. The teacher looks at the theological meaning of the reported event. For example, while the children hoped for God's direct miraculous help, the teacher was speaking of God giving 'shelter' and 'help' in a spiritual sense. Both sides, teacher and students, seemed to think that their contributions to the conversation were interlocking, while in reality they did not fit with each other.

Fourth, if the teacher becomes aware of discrepancies of this kind, he or she can find a way out, as it were. Often teachers were simply taken by *surprise*; they either had not expected the strange religious imagery used by the student, or the answers looked very odd to them and out of place. Such moments require quick reactions.

A productive style of teaching includes patient questions which will give time to find out what is meant: 'What do you mean by it?' Or one could ask the other students: 'Do you see how what has been said relates to our topic?' Instead, we often observed rather different responses. Sometimes, no response at all was given, or only a vague 'Hm'. Sometimes, the student's contribution was rejected kindly and postponed to a later stage of discussion ('We'll come back to it'). Sometimes, the student was blocked, without giving him or her reasons why. Sometimes, to ensure adequate understanding as the teacher thinks it should be, he or she resorted to offering explanations in an abstract academic language which, contrary to his or her expectation, makes things worse. In all these cases of *blocking the conversation,* communication is not effective. We may assume that a stronger awareness of developmental factors would improve instruction.

On the one hand, it is not our intention to evaluate the teachers' views by matching them against developmental theories. Psychological theories and educational praxis follow a different logic. On the other hand, we assume that teachers' perceptions of students' development which often appear to be eclectic could profit from more coherent interpretations. On this level, developmental research may provide useful *theoretical* clarification of practical views.

Nevertheless, the relationship between *praxis* and *theory* remains difficult. Teachers have (a) to act, (b) not alone, but together with others, (c) acting in ways of their own, (d) in a process with many risks of failure (therefore the teachers' interest in implementing the lesson plan and reaching the learning objectives), (e) this all is happening during a very short time which requires quick reactions. A sober view has to recognise the fundamental *hiatus* between theory and praxis. To bridge this hiatus and to improve practical skills by theoretical means is difficult. The following report of results tries to illustrate a way which may be of more help because it is based on *case descriptions.* Its aim is to make the teachers more familiar with the actual teaching-learning processes as interactions, that is, as a successful or unsuccessful mutual exchange of *Deutungsmuster* (interpretative patterns).

Case studies of classroom interaction

Example one

Among all possible developmental phenomena, the development of the ability to understand *religious language* plays an important role. As true religious language is metaphorical and symbolic (Jüngel, 1972), the understanding of metaphors is crucial. A lesson in grade five about the parable of the Prodigal Son (Luke 15) contains a passage which shows what a teacher has to take account of in terms of structural development if he or she is interested in personally significant learning.

teacher	The great joy of the father is also expressed when he says to the servant: My son was dead and is alive again.
student	Whoever believes so [murmuring].
student	His son did not like him any more and wanted to go far away . . . this is what dead maybe is to mean, and then alive again, that he has come to live again, that he returned to his father.
student	For him, for his father he was dead. But in reality he was in fact not dead at all but he was working.
student	The father thought that his son was dead because he had not heard from him. And then when he came he thought: Yes, he has risen.
student	Perhaps he accuses himself / maybe the father accuses himself in some way because he thinks that he is guilty.

Several minor and major points are noteworthy here. First, the teacher can become aware of what Fowler means by 'symbolic function'. Second, at the age of ten to twelve, elements of transition in stage development are to be expected (here stage 2 which is one-dimensional, and literal, and stage 2/3 which is approaching metaphorical, multidimensional symbolic understanding). Third, the death of the son is understood literally, even after the first student has offered a figurative understanding. This shows how persistent structures can be; they are 'deeply' rooted schemes of assimilation (cf. Oser's term 'depth structure', 1984, p. 42). Consequently, a teacher may not simply expect that a more adequate answer given by one student will automatically influence the structures or schemes of the other students. Therefore, it would not be wise to listen only to those students whose answers correspond to the desired line of interpretation. Religious education must make time to take up patiently all the false attempts of the learners to make sense of what they hear.

Example two

The same lesson is also illustrative of the role children's *everyday experiences* play at that age level. In addition to structural analysis such experiences can be interpreted from a *psychosocial perspective*. The lesson starts with a picture held up by the teacher. It shows a young man, surrounded by pigs.

student	There are pigs [in the picture].
student	Maybe this is something like with the lost sheep or so, [only] that now a pig [is missing].

Soon the students realise that it is the parable of the Prodigal Son. The teacher reads the parable. She asks for comments:

student   The brother, he is jealous.

teacher   We will get to that in a minute.

student   But the father, he is trying to [treat them] fairly . . . how shall we say, to share.

student   And the son thought that he was no longer his real son, but he received him differently than he expected.

student   Well, at first both of them were nasty with each other, and when the son came back the father was full of regret. So both of them said they were sorry.

teacher   Yes — we will look into this later on. Now let us continue where we stopped, verse 17 . . .

What is most striking in this sequence is the assumption that both of them were nasty. This clearly refers to the father and to the son. The story is understood in such a way that father and son would have had an argument, that the son would have gone away and that now both of them would regret their former behaviour. With Piaget we may call this a clear case of *assimilation*, of making one's experience fit with one's (previous) schemes of understanding.

The same may be said about the introduction of the idea of fair treatment into the parable. The plot of the parable is reconstructed in such a manner that it advocates equal treatment for both children. In either case the parable is transformed by the students in accordance with their own world of family life, sibling rivalry and late childhood achievement orientation (Erikson's 'industry') or a morality of fair treatment (Kohlberg's and Fowler's stage 2, concrete reciprocity). The issue of fair treatment (mostly by adults) comes up in many of the transcripts. It appears to be a generic theme during early adolescence.

Example three

Expressed in categories of '*elementarisation*', the lesson is a telling example of an elementary experiential reconstruction by the students in the dimension of 'elementary approaches' which *differ* from the 'elementary structure', faith 'experience' and 'truth-claim' of the parable itself: the parable is turned into a *family scene*. For children of that age meaningful elementary learning is bound to the experiences in their every day life. A story like the one presented in Luke 15 will most probably be assimilated to the familiar relationships of family life today. The elementary theological focus of the biblical text with its relation to Jesus as the story-teller and to 'death' and 'life' (Luke 15: 24–32) in the light of 'sin' (15: 21) is replaced by the focus on family conflicts, reconciliation and fair distribution which *for the children* is of *the highest importance*.

The framework of elementarisation with its four aspects makes it possible to contrast the diverging hermeneutical alternatives from several points of view. It is obvious that although the widespread 'experiential' method in religious education remains important (see the dimension of 'elementary experiences'), it cannot sufficiently cover all interrelated factors by which the dynamic educational interplay in the classroom is built up, between the provoking elements of the 'objective' pole (content) and the ways of reception of the 'subjective' pole (students). The aspect of 'elementary structures' (of the text) and its inherent 'elementary truths' may not be dropped for the sake of experience.

The students do experience the biblical text, but their experiences differ from what the text itself intends the readers to experience. Instead of faith experience becoming 'a new experience with the (old) experience' (Jüngel, 1972, p. 8), the students rediscover their old and common experiences. Their every day experiences are more or less corroborated, not interrupted and transformed. On the one hand, seen hermeneutically, the new message of the New Testament cannot be understood without being related to the old human experiences. On the other hand, seen soteriologically, the new surpasses the old. With respect to the 'elementary structures' of the parable, the students assimilate the plot without realising the *full* dialectic tension which it includes and which contains the elementary knowledge of the new and its overwhelming truth: *God* forgives the sinner and restores life in a new totality.

How is the situation to be evaluated? The educational tasks of religious education require a theological and educational evaluation, while developmental research does not. But again this research may become useful for classroom purposes. The full meaning of the story is not grasped by the students. From a developmental perspective, it must be said that in a way this full grasp is beyond reach, since a child at that age does not yet conceive of his or her self as a totality, either totally sinful or totally redeemed, once dead, now living. Developmental research makes us aware of corresponding links between the objective and subjective structures of the world of meanings and the meaning-making child. The growing and reconstructing human mind includes corresponding structures; a structured world stimulates corresponding human responses.

Either such a *meaningful structural correspondence* takes place, or there is no meaningful learning at all. Therefore, it is of no use insisting on theoretical claims to something that practically does not or cannot exist. However, what about the 'truth' of the text? We cannot simply support an unlimited hermeneutical relativism. At the same time, it is inadequate to assume 'one' incorporated truth only in the singular. Textual traditions set free a plurality of truth experiences as the studies on *Wirkungsgeschichte* (history of effects) show (H.-G. Gadamer).

In education we also have to consider a plurality of biographically and developmentally shaped sequences of meaningful encounters, a recurrent *Wirkungsgeschichte* in a temporal sense. A developmentally informed evaluation of religious education will take this into account. We return to the parable of the Prodigal Son. Since relationships with father (and mother) or brother (and sister) are essential for students at the age of ten to twelve, the transformation of the parable into a family scene leads to a meaningful message for the students. This message is surely not fully in line with the message of this particular text, but it is in line with the Gospel's general message of reconciliation. A text has more than just one meaning, and encounters with it at different times and in different situations will set free different meanings. Thus, in our understanding, the educational evaluation has to include theological as well as developmental criteria.

Example four

The last point is to underline our general proposition that developmental research has to be linked with the complexity of educational praxis to become useful. A more detailed report on, and discussion of, this point is provided by Schweitzer, Faust-Siehl, Krupka and Nipkow (1995b). Structural development in a Piagetian sense needs proper stimulation. Kohlberg's suggestion was to stimulate development through the application of the so-called '+*1-convention*', that is, by teacher stimuli one stage above the students' stage of development.

By establishing the average stage scores for students and teachers in each lesson, we obtained a very interesting result. In grade five and grade six, the individual lessons scored between 207 and

239 for the students and between 246 and 346 for the teachers. In grade ten they varied between 257 and 331 for the students and between 317 and 380 for the teachers. Only one of the lessons did not correspond to the '+1-convention'. Four lessons showed a stage difference of more than three quarters of a stage. Three lessons fulfilled the '+1/3-convention' as it is suggested by Berkowitz, Gibbs and Broughton (1980). From these results it may also be seen that the scores of both students and teachers are higher in grade ten than in grade five. This suggests that the match between the developmental status of student and teacher statements may be due to a more or less intentional adaptation of the teachers to their students and that this adaptation is not limited to the case of younger students.

Does this result mean that the teachers sufficiently fulfil the requirements of developmentally adequate teaching? We have become more and more suspicious when we looked more closely at the lessons. As we have shown above, in many lessons mutual understanding and a clear interlock between students' and teachers' views are actually lacking. The '+1- (or +1/3-) convention' should therefore be considered as a *necessary but not as a sufficient* condition for teaching that is developmentally appropriate.

What is needed beyond following the Kohlberg convention is, according to our observations, an intense form of classroom conversation which we have named *discourse* and which is most promising if the teacher is sensitive to what we call *latent cognitive conflicts*. As long as a teacher does not perceive such conflicts with a developmentally trained eye, they will adopt a hidden role with no chance of being worked through thoroughly.

In a lesson in grade ten a teacher tries to open a path to Christian belief in God by speaking about Jesus. Here a cognitive conflict becomes plain. On the one hand, Jesus embodies a positive religious challenge for the students. On the other hand, today's reality seems to speak against Jesus.

> *student*   Well, either I am an idiot or what, if it is really true (that he did exist), or this Jesus is a little (crazy) . . . that's impossible. There are surely good people and there are bad ones, but as good as him — no way!

Another student draws a parallel to gurus of today in order to explain Jesus' influence on people.

> *student*   Well, I am still thinking that Jesus is somehow like a guru today who has his followers anywhere and then, a hundred years later, we believe him to be God. . . . And all

the others, those old gurus now, we laugh at them: 'Yeah, funny'. And in a hundred years, it is their turn.'

In the light of developmental theories, this historical scepticism is a clear example of the stage of critical hypothetical thinking (logic of formal operations). In addition to this, we know from other empirical sources why such a critical attitude must be expected; in a way, it is a necessary step in the process of coming to grips with religion during adolescence. The teacher, however, misses the opportunity to enter a serious 'discourse'. Instead, she trusts in the weight of religious tradition as such and reacts by posing a rhetorical question, with an emotionally soothing undertone.

teacher   Now I ask you, and you in particular — you need not answer, but . . . let the question reverberate within you. If it was true as you say, . . . why, tell me, was it possible for it (the Christian religion) to continue for about 2000 years?'

Conclusion

First, empirical research in general and in the field of development in particular is rather new for religious education in Germany. The research project outlined above could not follow a well documented and well established tradition, but had to examine both the research area and the instruments to explore it. With this in view, one has to consider the present application of categories of moral and religious development to classroom interaction as the beginning for necessary further research. Fowler's aspects of faith development (beside others) proved to be applicable to a field which until now, as far as developmental research is concerned, has been neglected: religious education in schools.

Second, the project makes use of three current trends in the German discussion on religious education. It mirrors the more established movement of attention towards the individual student and the more recent interest in biography and development. Moreover, it is closely linked to a didactical approach which takes these perspectives seriously, a 'developmentally oriented elementarisation'.

Third, empirical research related to processes in the classroom, our main thrust (beside the more traditional method of interviewing), requires the ability to interpret statements that are of interest from a developmental point of view in a broader living context. For this task a multi-dimensional heuristical frame of reference like the four-dimensional approach of elementarisation can be helpful.

Fourth, to work with the concrete processes and to describe them in detail is meant as a step towards bridging the gap between theory and praxis. What we would like to promote is a developmentally informed understanding of how students actively interpret the world around them and how they actively interpret what is presented to them as religion. With this we want to emphasise the perspective of children and young people, so that results from empirical research will less easily fall prey to educational technology. Our findings are not meant to strengthen the teacher's control over children and young people. Rather, they are to be acknowledged as partners in a common moral and religious search.

References

Astley, J. (1996), Theology for the untheological? in J. Astley and L.J. Francis (eds), *Christian Theology and Religious Education: connections and contradictions*, pp. 60–77, London, SPCK, in press.

Berkowitz, M.W., Gibbs, J.C. and Broughton, J.M. (1980), The relation of moral judgement stage disparity to developmental effects of peer dialogues, *Merrill-Palmer Quarterly*, 26, 341–357.

Englert, R. (1985), *Glaubensgeschichte und Bildungsprozeß. Versuch einer religions — pädagogischen Kairologie*, München, Kösel.

Faust-Siehl, G. (1987), *Themenkonstitution als Problem von Didaktik und Unterrichtsforschung*, Weinheim, Dt.Studien-Verlag.

Fowler, J.W. (1981), *Stages of Faith: the psychology of human development and the quest for meaning*, San Francisco, Harper and Row.

Fowler, J.W., Jarvis, D. and Moseley, R.M. (1986), *Manual for Faith Development Research*, Emory, Emory University, Candler School of Theology, Center for Faith Development.

Fowler, J.W., Nipkow, K.E. and Schweitzer, F. (eds) (1991), *Stages of Faith and Religious Development: implications for church, education, and society*, New York, Crossroad.

Fraas, H.-J. and Heimbrock, H.-G. (1986), *Religiöse Erziehung und Glaubensentwicklung. Zur Auseinandersetzung mit der kognitiven Entwicklungspsychologie*, Göttingen, Vandenhoeck and Ruprecht.

Jüngel, E. (1972), *Unterwegs zur Sache. Theologische Bemerkungen*, München, Kaiser.

Loukes, H. (1961), *Teenage Religion*, London, SCM.

Nipkow, K.E. (1979), Elementarisierung biblischer Inhalte. Zum Zusammenspiel theologischer, anthropologischer und entwicklungspsychologischer Perspektiven in der Religionspädagogik, in I. Baldermann et al., *Bibel und Elementarisierung*, pp. 35–73, Frankfurt am Main, Haag and Herchen.

Nipkow, K.E. (1982), *Grundfragen der Religionspädagogik*, vol. 3: *Gemeinsam leben und glauben lernen*, Gütersloher Verlagshaus.

Nipkow, K.E., Schweitzer, F. and Fowler, J.W. (eds) (1988), *Glaubenentwicklung und Erziehung*, Gütersloh, Gütersloher Verlagshaus.

Oser, F. and Gmünder, P. (1984), *Der Mensch — Stufen seiner religiösen Entwicklung. Ein strukturgenetischer Ansatz*, Zürich, Köln, Benziger.

Schmidt, H. (1983), *Didaktik des Ethikunterrichts I. Grundlagen*, Stuttgart, Kohlhammer.

Schmidt, H. (1984), *Religionsdidaktik. Ziele, Inhalte und Methoden religiöser Erziehung in Schule und Unterricht*, vol. 2: *Der Unterricht in Klasse 1–13*, Stuttgart, Kohlhammer.

Schweitzer, F. (1987), *Lebensgeschichte und Religion. Religiöse Entwicklung und Erziehung im Kindes- und Jugendalter*, München.

Schweitzer, F. (1992), *Die Religion des Kindes. Zur Problemgeschichte einer religionspädagogischen Grundfrage*, Gütersloh, Gütersloher Verlagshaus.

Schweitzer, F., Nipkow, K.E., Faust-Siehl, G. and Krupka, B. (1995a), *Religionsunterricht und Entwicklungspsychologie. Elementarisierung in der Praxis*, Gütersloh, Gütersloher Verlagshaus.

Schweitzer, F., Faust-Siehl, G., Krupka, B. and Nipkow, K.E. (1995b), Religious development and the praxis of religious education: discourse and teaching beyond the '+1-Convention', *Journal of Empirical Theology*, 8, 1, 5–23.

7

Relational and contextual reasoning in religious education: a theory-based empirical study

K. Helmut Reich

Summary

Relational and Contextual Reasoning (RCR) is a cognitively complex way of thinking and arguing, which is not limited to classical logic. The main characteristics and its development in childhood, adolescence and adulthood are discussed.

It is claimed that RCR is helpful for a better understanding of Christian doctrines and world views, and for developing religious life even in adulthood. Initial attempts to introduce RCR into the religious education classroom are described. The expected difficulties emerged, the task is arduous, but the experience was encouraging.

Introduction

Relational and Contextual Reasoning (RCR) was demonstrated to facilitate understanding Christian doctrines such as the Chalcedonian Definition or the Doctrine of the Trinity (Reich, 1994), possibly to ease cognitive dissonance regarding the Theodicy, and to further the coordination of religious and scientific world views (Reich, 1989a). Therefore, RCR was introduced in religious education in grades five, six, nine and ten of a (German) comprehensive school. Before reporting on that project, RCR needs to be explained.[1]

The term 'relational and contextual reasoning' seems fairly self-explanatory: the objective of that reasoning is to find out about

129

relationships ('Do they exist?', 'What is their nature?', 'Why is it useful to understand them?') and any context-dependency of the aspects considered. RCR is sometimes referred to as 'post-Piagetian' thought, indicating that RCR matures (if at all) *after* formal Piagetian operations have been mastered, say from late adolescence onward (Reich, 1995b).

To illustrate RCR (Oser and Reich, 1987) at work, here is an interview task on a Three Mile Island / Chernobyl type accident in a nuclear power plant followed by samples taken from such interviews (Reich, 1995a):

> The TV news reported on an accident in a nuclear power station. The main cooling pump had stopped working, and the back-up pump had not started. The emergency shutdown control unfortunately did not work either. As if this were not enough, the operating crew had become aware of the danger rather late, and in addition had underestimated it. All of a sudden the temperature rose. A steam pipe cracked and radio-active steam leaked out. What thoughts of yours are triggered by this news?

And now five rather different (partial) answers:

1. That technology was not reliable. The operating crew is not to blame — they have done their duty, day in, day out.

2. It is true that a technical breakdown has occurred for starters. But it appears that the operating crew has not been up to it either.

3. In the beginning a malfunctioning occurred. But then, such systems can't work without human control. The operating crew has simply not noticed that the instruments indicated a problem. Or perhaps they have seen it but not taken the right countermeasures. The accident involves both a technical and a human deficiency.

4. Such accidents are very rare. So one can understand that it may have taken time before the crew realised that something was amiss. But then they may well have done the wrong thing. And the situation got worse. Maybe they quarrelled about the right action to take. Maybe they even panicked when the steam came out. And they never called in a specialist who might have been able to get the situation under control. Such crews need training with a simulator under as realistic conditions as possible.

5. In this accident technical and human failure are interconnected. One has to look at the whole thing as a system, the plant and the operating crew. And one has to study the mutual interaction, the type of effects they have on each other. One really wants to

train crew members with the help of a sophisticated simulator so that they become aware of the many ways in which something can go wrong, experience their individual and collective reactions, and learn how to assess such situations as well as how to deal with them successfully. In such simulations the psychological stress must of course also be generated, not just the sequence of technical events. It is precisely such a chain reaction of technical and human malfunctioning which is so hard to foresee. By the way, I would hire only such persons who are aware of the dangers involved and are ready to face them.

These five quotations, chosen from many more comparable ones, are ordered according to the developmental level of the respondents and are typical for persons reasoning at a given level of RCR. Let us try to constitute the characteristics of each of the five levels by way of analysis and retroduction.

At level one (the first quotation) only a rather restricted part of the full story comes into view. One might say that the location of the decisive elements or phenomena within the whole of which it is part $(9)^2$ was indicated, but as yet not very effectively. Piaget and Garcia (1989) call this the 'intra' stage, meaning that in case of several possible centres of attention, the recognised focus is only on one of them. (Another person at that level could have put the full blame on the crew — thereby 'disburdening' the plant / technology — in particular if the crew was also charged with the maintenance.) In the theory of cognitive complexity (Baker-Brown, Ballard, Bluck, de Vries, Suedfeld and Tetlock, 1992) the lowest level is said to involve neither differentiation (discernment of differing categories for distinguishing and assessing various aspects) nor integration (establishment of various connections with a view to reaching a balanced overall view and assessment).

At level two the horizon is enlarged: in addition to the technical failure (A) the possible mismanagement of the situation by the crew (B) is evoked. There is a beginning of describing the whole system in functional terms (10). That involves a minimum of differentiation. Piaget and Garcia (1989) would say that the 'inter' stage is entered into, A as well as B are recognised. However, A and B are not yet firmly established, and even less interrelated. They are both put in the field of view tentatively, without, however, looking at possible relationships. Even to do that, a person must be able to handle Piagetian concrete operations (working reversibly with two variables and connecting them in various ways — Inhelder and Piaget, 1958).

Persons reasoning at level three are aware of a more adequate part of the full story. Their horizon has been enlarged further, and the process of differentiation has progressed. They even begin to assert the existence of relations and their importance (12). In the terms of Baker-Brown, Ballard, Bluck, de Fries, Suedfeld and Tetlock (1992) integration points its head. Piaget and Garcia would recognise a 'trans-intra' state, the beginning of constructing an overarching synopsis. In Piagetian ontogenetic developmental terms, level three means a transition to formal operations (recognition of a 'system' with internal structure and related functions). But there is more: at least an intuition that classical logic is not applicable (Reich, 1995b). Classical logic involves notably four features: (a) two truth values ('true' and 'false') — whereas the power plant operators may have to decide on the basis of 'undetermined'; (b) separability (or locality, meaning that the state of A is intrinsically not affected by B and vice versa) — whereas in such an accident the various processes and (re)actions may be so out of the ordinary and may be connected intrinsically in such complex fashion that they cannot justifiably be considered individually each on its own; (c) reversibility — whereas some events occurring in the plant, and possibly even in the psyche of the operators, are irreversible, at least in the short run; (d) commutativity (meaning that the result of a sequence of operations is independent of their order) — whereas in the present case it does not apply, in fact a precise post hoc simulation or reconstruction may be very difficult, if possible at all.

At level four ('trans-inter') all these developments have progressed further. A two-way reciprocal relationship between A and B is described (14) at least in a rudimentary way. Internal relations (for example, between perceptions and emotions of the operators) are affirmed (15). Contextual relativism (11) starts to point its head, that is, a context-dependency is pointed out, here in particular of the crew behaviour. Persons reasoning at this level master Piagetian formal operations, in particular they formulate hypotheses and argue abstractly. However, they transcend the underlying classical logic as already referred to in the discussion of level three.

Finally, everything falls into place at level five ('trans-trans'). The horizon is further enlarged and includes relevant aspects not mentioned in the initial event description, for example, hiring of crew members. Perspectives are multiplied to get as inclusive a view as possible (24). Both differentiation and integration are carried through fully. Notions that are foreign to classical logic such as non-separability and irreversibility are part of the reasoning without hesitation as to their 'logical' justification. Context-dependency is explicitly addressed, for instance with respect to stress generation and the ensuing behaviour.

How is RCR related to other forms of thought?

RCR may be considered as a pragmatic reasoning schema (Cheng and Holyoak, 1985). Such a scheme enables one to deal with a particular class of problems. Hence it is distinct from both a purely formal treatment independent of content such as in arithmetic and from a case by case solution based on personal considerations, for example, when looking for a job or a partner.

The RCR schema may be thought of as an amalgam of constituents as shown in figure 1. Most individual elements were already indicated above when we analysed the RCR levels, but let us discuss them more systematically. Apart from being interesting in

Figure 1
Constituents of the pragmatic mental schema
'Relational and Contextual Reasoning'

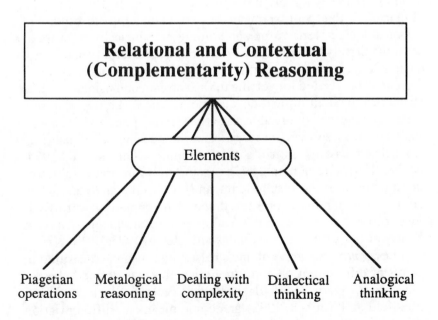

itself, the related knowledge is needed when it comes to stimulating RCR. The relation between *Piagetian operations* and RCR was studied by way of theoretical analysis and administration of relevant tasks, assessing the results and relating the two scores for each respondent (Reich, 1991, pp. 84–85). Having reached an appropriate Piagetian stage (Inhelder and Piaget, 1958) is a necessary but insufficient condition for getting to RCR level two, level three and level four. At least early concrete operations are necessary to reach level two because both forms of reasoning involve working reversibly with two 'dimensions'. Confirmed concrete operations (transition to formal operations) are necessary to reach RCR level three because both deal globally with (simple) systems. Well established formal operations are required to get to RCR level four because of the need to hypothesise, and deal with isolation and correlation of 'variables'. The empirical results supported that analysis (Reich, 1991, p. 85, table 2). The finding 'necessary but insufficient' means that a person who has reached a given Piagetian stage may well reason at a lower RCR level than indicated above (because some or all of the other elements of figure 1 are missing). However, no person at a given RCR level performed at a lower Piagetian stage than indicated.

Metalogical reasoning was illustrated by one of our respondents as follows: 'It is not logical, but it is true' (cf. Reich, 1995a, p. 17). 'Logical' in this context means 'as stipulated by the canons of classical logic'. Hence a person arguing metalogically is aware at least intuitively that there are limits to the applicability of classical logic (for example, in quantum physics), and that other types of logic may be needed for getting to the correct conclusions (such as dialectical logic in human development, where the negation of a negation may well not lead back to the starting point as in classical logic but to a new state, or fuzzy logic when dealing with qualities / quantities having multiple 'truth values' — cf. Kosko, 1994; McNeill and Freiberger, 1993). Again, an appropriate task was administered to the respondents, and the results analysed. They support the argument presented above in connection with RCR level three that reasoning in terms of non-classical logic is at least tacitly present from that level onward (Reich, 1995a).

The *cognitive complexity* of one's reasoning is usually measured in terms of differentiation and integration (both as defined above). On a seven grade scale (Baker-Brown, Ballard, Bluck, de Vries, Suedfeld and Tetlock, 1992) grade one means no differentiation and no integration, a lower middle level differentiation but no integration, a higher middle level good differentiation and some integration, and at a high level both differentiation and integration are mastered.

Dialectical reasoning enters into complementarity reasoning in the proportion 7:24, at least as far as Michael Basseches' (1989) elementary dialectical schemes are concerned. The main common issues concern relations, the main difference is that dialectical reasoning is never quite finished (dealing with change), it continues ad infinitum. In contrast, once RCR has run its course, the job is essentially done (barring small scale improvements of certain details).

Analogical reasoning contributes the elements (1) 'yoking together' two aspects that have something in common (but nevertheless differ from each other) and (2) 'searching for commonalities and differences'. This is particularly important at level three of RCR, when one has to decide whether both A and B are indeed needed to explain the phenomenon under discussion, and at level four when it is necessary to elucidate any context dependence.

How new is all this? Clearly, it has been known since antiquity that reasoning can take various forms. However, in the discussions of the 1980s, post-Piagetian development became an issue that is still not settled. To quote from one relevant book chapter (Gilligan, Murphy, and Tappan, 1990, p. 224):

> In our attempts to reconnect a cognitive stage theory of development with data on late adolescent and adult thinking about real problems and problems of choice, we have found it necessary to posit a different ideal of maturity [than Piagetian formal operations] to account for the transformations of thinking we have observed. These transformations arise out of the recognition of the paradoxical interdependence of self and relationship, which then overrides the pure logic of formal reason and replaces it with a more encompassing form of judgement, a polyphonic structure that is able to sustain the different voices of justice and care.

As may already have become clear, RCR has not much of a problem with that.

How can RCR be stimulated? Which hurdles are to be expected?

As an educator, I am interested to know how RCR can be stimulated (Reich, 1995c), because more appropriate thinking may lead to better judgments and solutions (Reich, 1989a, 1994). However, before I report on first experiences in the classroom, I would like to point out some of the challenges which may be present at each level of RCR (cf. Reich, 1991) as well as the particular interest for religious education.

At level one the viewpoint is unilateral, only one particular aspect gets attention. There is no notion that acquiring dependable knowledge means hard personal work. What happens to meet the eye is taken at its face value and as all there is to know. In such a case one may try to draw attention to the neglected aspects, even repeatedly so (gently), despite continued rejection of a viewpoint involving an enlarged horizon. It is possible, of course, that children will have to reach a certain level of cognitive development before they can consider more than one aspect.

At level two other aspects come into view. There occurs a beginning of exploration, of searching for reliable knowledge. More than one aspect is being considered. Alternatives are recognised as such. However, as already said, they are left standing side by side, without any attempt at looking into possible relationships. In case of developmental delays for getting to that level, exercises in differentiation may be helpful.

At level three comparison is made of the explanatory strength of various aspects. The drive for a genuine understanding is now fully in progress. Each aspect of the issue under study is examined both for itself, in comparison with other aspects, and as a part of the whole. Progress with respect to level two consists in the new competence to take different viewpoints and to compare the results. There occurs a beginning of integration. It becomes important not to be limited by the prescriptions of classical logic. If need be, the latter issue could be studied and exercised separately.

At level four there are internal and external connections. The acquisition of robust knowledge is now undertaken in a conscious and systematic manner. The internal links between various aspects are examined. Any context dependence starts to come into view. If there is insufficient progress, there may be a case for exercising integration.

At level five insights that previously were tacit or emergent, are now articulated. Limits of human knowledge and action are recognised. Anybody having arrived at that level is presumably sufficiently active and self-directed not to need explicit external stimulation for further progress.

RCR and religious education

Why is RCR of interest to religious education? In the first place, because certain Christian teachings go beyond classical logic — as does RCR. Thus Chalcedonian Christology declares that 'Jesus Christ . . . is truly man and truly God, . . . made known in two natures [which exist] . . . without confusion, without change, without division, without separation'. The Doctrine of the Trinity involves the three *personae* of the single God. Theoretical and empirical evidence demonstrate in those cases the helpfulness of RCR for a deeper understanding (Reich, 1989b, 1990, 1991, 1992, 1994). Theodicy needs to come to peace with a God said to be omnipotent, all knowing, and good/loving, yet facing so much misery and evil in this world. RCR cannot solve that issue completely, but helps in the following way. First, RCR admits that particular aspects need not be present simultaneously, but — depending on the context — may appear successively (such as the particle-like and the wavelike behaviour of light). Thus at one point God's goodness may be more in view, in other circumstances God's omnipotence may be more in view. Second, RCR admits that in certain cases a causal explanation involving God's action needs to be kept separate from a personal and historical description of what happened (just as in quantum physics the spacetime description has to be kept separate from a consideration of the energy balance). God's action cannot be merged point-by-point with a diachronic event description into a unified picture (Russell, 1989). As to religious development, it may well involve getting to a 'second naïveté' (Reich, 1991, pp. 86–87), which is again not foreign to RCR. Also, RCR helps to coordinate religious and scientific world views (Reich, 1989a).

Classroom experiences

The project involved team teaching with the local religious education teacher (two hours per week during four weeks — that first stage of the project continued for another one to two weeks), the themes being 'Nature and humanity' (Creation) in grades five (eleven year olds), six (twelve year olds), nine (fifteen year olds) and ten (sixteen year olds), and 'Jesus Christ' in grade ten of a German comprehensive school. The entire project, together with the questionnaires used to get to know the students and some of the teaching materials, has been written up (Reich and Schröder,

1995). Here I concentrate on the teaching of certain features of RCR and some of the results.

Differentiation (needed to get to level two of RCR, and certainly to get to level three). In grade five and grade six the co-teacher had devised the following approach, which we carried through together. First Salvador Dali's 'melting' / 'dripping' clock was projected on the screen and reactions invited. 'Somebody is trying to draw a clock who can't draw!'; 'Some figures are on twice'; 'Six, seven, nine, eight'; 'Some figures are spaced very closely, others widely'; 'Some figures follow each other counterclockwise'. In the ensuing discussion it was brought out that Dali wanted to present the subjective feeling of time, how time flows sometimes fast and sometimes slow, how we see our life passing, looking back and forward. The students thus grasped the difference between a technical 'blueprint' of a clock used for measuring standard time and an artistic symbolic message. Subsequently they successfully transferred that insight, in our case to the difference between a science book and the bible (disregarding 'creation science').

In grade nine and grade ten the corresponding exercise was done by starting from two German poems (which it is difficult for me to translate into English). Eduard Mörike's poem 'Spring' goes something like 'Spring again flies its blue ribbon in the air; sweet, familiar scents roam about full of foreboding . . .'. Rainer Maria Rilke's 'Autumn' reads 'The leaves tumble downward as if coming from far away, as if distant gardens in the skies were withering; they fall with a negating gesture . . .'. Question: 'Should we all look for blue ribbons in the Spring, and for gardens in the stratosphere in Autumn?' The discussion then led to conclusions similar to those in grade five and grade six.

Noticing the omnipresence of the stereotype 'I don't believe in God because I don't see him, I can't feel him, and anyway he can't exist, because the world is such a mess!', we asked the pupils of the class exploring the Jesus theme to respond to the following invitation: 'Suppose you were God. What would you do to make it clear that you exist and are people's friend?' Here is a sampling of the answers (Reich, 1995c): 'I do not wish to write anything, . . . because I know that God does the right thing, although at times that is hard to accept'; 'Cure people's illnesses, improve the situation in the Third World, eliminate misery and illness, establish peace and happiness, eliminate xenophobia, limit world population, let people die without fear'; 'I would do again what I did 2,000 years ago: send my son Jesus, who would heal sick people and tell everybody about me. In any event Jesus should come again and work miracles'; 'Maybe God should just talk to people and advise them, how to do things better'; 'To confront people and to express an opinion about them in no uncertain terms'; 'To mete out what they deserve to both the good and the bad people; to treat them justly'; 'I would not make myself known, because if people knew for sure, that would no longer be faith. Also, their expectations about their prayers to come true would grow, and, as I could probably not oblige in all cases, disappointment with me might follow, and people might feel treated unjustly'; 'I would only make myself known to the sceptics, but not to the believers. Otherwise I might disappoint them and destroy their "illusions" '; 'I would not do anything, because otherwise pupils would no longer have such interesting discussions in the classroom!' Clearly, we are a far cry away from the triggering stereotype: what a differentiation!

Integration (needed to get to RCR level three, and certainly level four). There are many themes one could think of (including touchy ones like abortion or fighting drug abuse). As this happened to come to pass in religious education, we concentrated on scripture. With the younger pupils we went deeper into the relation between a science book, a book on 'how to preserve the environment', and a religious book for religious education classes. Result (in adult terms): the nature preservers need to know science so as to do the right thing; they also need motivation and for that the religious book can help. The scientists can analyse the work of the preservers, and may get to new scientific insights in the process. From the religious book they may become aware of any ethical aspects of their work. Religious people may get more inspiration from God's handiwork in nature if they learn more about nature's intricacies and (internal) beauty from science, and they may learn from the book on preservation how to be better stewards of God's creation.

With older pupils we used the parable of the prodigal son (Luke 15: 11–31). First the discussion was about the character of the father and the two sons. Then the task was to find a title which brought out the gist of the parable. Soon two groups were competing for their favourite one: 'The tale of the large-hearted father' versus 'The tale of the son believed to be lost'. There was not a single attempt at integration. So we asked, 'What might have given the courage to the prodigal son to envisage a return?' After some more discussion a new proposal arose: 'The return of the son believed to be lost to his large-hearted father'. The moral was, as we attempted to make plain, that one should examine possible connections between aspects of the same state of affairs in case something is misunderstood.

Logic. For many adolescents (and maybe for some adults?) 'that is logical' means 'it goes without saying', 'it is acceptable to common sense', 'it corresponds to generally accepted views', 'it is evident to everybody'. The very notion of logic as a formal way of reasoning in order to deduce conclusions from premises may need to be acquired. The limits of classical logic need to be (recognised and) transcended to move beyond RCR level three.

In grade nine and grade ten the objective was to introduce the students to a more 'philosophical' understanding of logic. It took the following form. I emptied the breast pocket of my shirt in front of them, put my pocket calendar and pen back, and took the pen out again. Question: what is in my pocket? Answer: 'your calendar'; 'Why?'; 'Because you have put it in — no, because you did not take it out'. We could agree on that. But the discussion had to go further. What are the deeper reasons for the correctness of your logical reasoning? The discussion brought out the following three points: (a) both items are of a 'permanent' nature, at least for the duration of the demonstration; (b) they are 'separable', meaning that they can be dealt with each on their own, irrespective of the other; (c) they do not interact spontaneously. For these reasons the situation is reversible; the demonstration can be repeated ad infinitum. Similarly, mercury can be transferred from one glass vessel to the next and put back into the former. Classical logic then rightly affirms that the original situation has been re-established.

At that point the woman teacher, with whom I was team teaching, narrated in an engaging way the love story of the girl Elke and the boy Ansgar. Cutting the narrative short, I came immediately to the crucial event which occurred on one Saturday night. Ansgar did not feel well enough to go to the disco, and so Elke went with another girl. She met a boy, the two felt close, and Elke let herself be kissed. Then she noticed Ansgar, who shouted 'How can you do that to me behind my back?' Elke was not slow in answering, 'And how can you spy on me after telling me that you did not feel well? Anyway, what is this fuss about? Nothing has happened. I am still with you!' To make the point quite clear, I added, 'The mercury is back in the first vessel'. There followed a (gender-unspecific) animated discussion about who was right, Ansgar or Elke. At one point it became clear that trust had been shaken, and now it was a matter of trust versus mistrust. Standard logic did not work, because the feelings of Elke and Ansgar were not 'permanent' nor 'separable' (as was the case with the glass vessel and the mercury). If one can speak about logic, possibly a dialectic logic may underlie the future evolution of the relation between Ansgar and Elke.

Continuing with the differentiation of the notion of 'logic', the following two statements were introduced: (a) 'Where there is smoke, there is smoke', and (b) 'Where there is smoke, there is fire'. The discussion brought out that (a) is an identity, true in all possible worlds, but not very informative, whereas (b) may not be true everywhere, and in any case only statistically true, but could be more helpful. Thus the concept of the degree of strictness / hardness of a given logic was introduced.

Obviously, this single classroom period did not bring about a major change in the understanding of logic, but it seems to me that the approach outlined is a possibility for a start on the journey to master matching the logic of the reasoning to the problem structure (Reich, 1989b). Students found most of this hard going, but some felt that the exercise had been useful.

Results

In terms of the religious education themes covered, we observed notably the following progress, starting with 'creation'. In the lower grades, the large majority became clearer about the fact that Genesis is not a science book but teaches us that God has made the universe with all that it contains and that God cares about it, including about human beings. A twelve year old put it in these terms:

> I surmise this: When the Big Bang came about, God has seen to it that it all happened in the right order, and he has also prepared the basis for the life of humans, of animals and of plants, and introduced that into the various processes of the Big Bang. Thus human, animal and plant life was bound to arise with his help. Which are my hesitations? I am not quite sure about what I just said.

This may be compared with the pronouncement of Robert John Russell (1994, pp. 560, 569), the American theologian and physicist:

> The Big Bang *acts like a character witness in a trial, but not an eyewitness.* . . . God cannot be an explicit 'part of the equation', as it were, since this would introduce an entirely necessary element into what should be an entirely contingent argument. . . . Thus, since we can never gain complete knowledge of the initial conditions or the entire set of environmental factors, we can never decide, based on science [e.g. quantum physics, chaos theory], whether nature is

acting, and has been acting all along, entirely on its own or whether God is acting and has been acting all along with and immediately within nature in every event (emphasis in original).

Whereas that boy (and others of his age group) would presumably agree with Russell (although not understanding the pronouncement in its full depth), this is less certain in the case of the older pupils. There the majority was convinced that 'nature is acting, and has been acting all along, entirely on its own'. A detailed discussion of what is known scientifically about the Big Bang and the subsequent evolution (in particular the unlikelihood of certain events) as well as the discussion about logic had at least the effect that a number of pupils were less certain about their belief in an all powerful nature going it alone.

As to the theme 'Jesus Christ', it was clear beforehand that not many of the fifteen to seventeen year olds would be interested. Indeed, out of 18 pupils, only two said that Jesus meant something in their lives, a few more were interested, but the majority clearly were not. Yet, in the final questionnaire, a number of positive statements appeared, for example, 'We had good discussions'; 'For me it is important to talk about God and Jesus, because I may still get convinced to believe in Jesus'; 'The story of the prodigal son has helped me to understand God better, because he was the father'; 'I understand Jesus a little better, because the teachers tried to explain that we are not alone with our problems. If we have no friends or do not trust people, we can always pray'.

So far, the laboratory results (Reich, 1994) are more explicit than the somewhat anecdotal results in the classroom. Apart from the short time span of the work reported, this is not surprising in as much as results are usually easier to obtain in clean than in 'messy' conditions. However, improving RCR by working on differentiation, integration and logic, though arduous, seems promising for getting to an improved RCR, from which religious education, and not only religious education, should eventually benefit fully. As the local religious education teacher will continue to be in charge of religious education of most of the pupils under consideration here and will go on with our project (as I shall do whenever I get an opportunity), we should be in a position to clarify the verisimilitude of that prediction in the years to come.

Acknowledgments

My thanks go to the interview respondents and to the students in the religious education classes as well as to Anke Schröder for their collaboration, without which I would have much less to write about, and to the Hochschulrat der Universität Freiburg for providing financial support.

Notes

1. RCR was previously called 'thinking in terms of complementarity' or 'complementarity reasoning'. Although the designation 'RCR' is more to the point and less likely to induce misunderstanding, I occasionally still use the older labels.
2. These numbers refer to the respective function in Basseches' (1989) table of functions of dialectical schemata.

References

Baker-Brown, G., Ballard, E.J., Bluck, S., de Vries, B., Suedfeld, P. and Tetlock, P.E. (1992), The conceptual/integrative complexity scoring manual, in C.P. Smith (ed.) together with J. Atkinson, D. McClelland, and J. Veroff, *Motivation and Personality: handbook of thematic content analysis,* pp. 401–418, New York, Cambridge University Press.

Basseches, M.A. (1989), Dialectical thinking as organised whole: comments on Irwin and Kramer, in M.L. Commons, J.D. Sinnot, F.A. Richards and C. Armon (eds), *Adult Development (volume one): comparisons and applications of developmental models,* pp. 161–178, New York, Praeger.

Cheng, P.W. and Holyoak, K.J. (1985), Pragmatic reasoning schemas, *Cognitive Psychology,* 17, 391–416.

Gilligan, C., Murphy, J.M. and Tappan, M.B. (1990), Moral development beyond adolescence, in C.A. Alexander and E.J. Langer (eds), *Higher Stages of Human Development,* pp. 208–225, New York, Oxford University Press.

Inhelder, B. and Piaget, P. (1958), *The Growth of Logical Thinking from Childhood to Adolescence: an essay on the construction of formal operational structures* (translated by A. Parsons and S. Milgram), London, Routledge and Kegan Paul. (Original French edition: *De la Logique de l'enfant à la Logique de l'adolescent,* Paris, Presses Universitaires de France, 1955).

Kosko, B. (1994), *Fuzzy Thinking: the new science of fuzzy logic,* London, HarperCollins.

McNeill, D. and Freiberger, P. (1993), *Fuzzy Logic,* New York, Simon and Schuster.

Oser, F.K. and Reich, K.H. (1987), The challenge of competing explanations: the development of thinking in terms of complementarity of 'theories', *Human Development*, 30, 178–186.

Piaget, J. and Garcia, R. (1989), *Psychogenesis and the History of Science* (translated by Helga Feider), New York, Columbia University Press. (Original French edition: *Psychogenèse et Histoire des Sciences*, Paris, Flammarion, 1983).

Reich, K.H. (1989a), Between religion and science: complementarity in the religious thinking of young people, *British Journal of Religious Education*, 11, 62–69.

Reich, K.H. (1989b), The Chalcedonian Definition: which logic? *Scientific Contributions in Education no. 78,* Pädagogisches Institut, University of Fribourg/Switzerland.

Reich, K.H. (1990), The Chalcedonian Definition, an example of the difficulties and the usefulness of thinking in terms of complementarity? *Journal of Psychology and Theology*, 18, 148–157.

Reich, K.H. (1991), The role of complementarity reasoning in religious development, in F.K. Oser and W.G. Scarlett (eds), *Religious Development in Childhood and Adolescence: new directions for child development*, pp. 77–89, San Francisco, Jossey-Bass.

Reich, K.H. (1992), Kann Denken in Komplementarität die religiöse Entwicklung im Erwachsenenalter fördern? Überlegungen am Beispiel der Lehrformel von Chalkedon, und weiterer theologischer 'Paradoxe', in M. Böhnke, K.H. Reich and L. Ridez (eds), *Erwachsen im Glauben. Beiträge zum Verhältnis von Entwicklungspsychologie und religiöser Erwachsenenbildung*, pp. 127–154, Stuttgart, Kohlhammer.

Reich, K.H. (1994), Can one rationally understand Christian doctrines? An empirical study, *British Journal of Religious Education*, 16, 114–126.

Reich, K.H. (1995a), Komponenten von relations- und kontextkritischem (komplementärem) Denken, *Scientific Contributions in Education*, no. 107, Pädagogisches Institut, University of Fribourg / Switzerland.

Reich, K.H. (1995b), From either/or to both-and, *Thinking: the journal for the philosophy of children*, 12, 2, 12–15.

Reich, K.H. (1995c), Widersprüchlichkeit im Alltag. Zur Pädagogik eines komplementären Denkens, Unpublished typescript, Pädagogisches Institut, University of Fribourg / Switzerland.

Reich, K.H. and Schröder, A. (1996), Komplementäres Denken im Religionsunterricht. Ein Werkstattbericht über unser Unterrichtsprojekt, *Report Series* published by the Religionspädagogisches Institut (RPI — Institute for Teaching Religion), Loccum, Germany, in press.

Russell, R.J. (1989), The fruitfulness of complementarity for three theological problems, Unpublished typescript, Berkeley, California, Center for Theology and the Natural Sciences.

Russell, R.J. (1994), Cosmology from Alpha to Omega, *Zygon: journal of religion and science*, 29, 557–577.

8

Ethnographic research and curriculum development

Robert Jackson

Summary

This chapter reports the preliminary results of 'Ethnography and Religious Education', a three year series of ethnographic studies conducted by the Religious Education and Community Project at the University of Warwick among four religious communities (Christian, Jewish, Sikh and Muslim) together with related, ongoing curriculum development work which is being published as the Warwick RE Project.

Introduction

The Warwick Religions and Education Research Unit (WRERU) combines ethnographic studies of religious communities in Britain, emphasising studies of the transmission of religious culture to the young, with curriculum development, drawing on data from the research studies and on theory derived from cultural studies and the social sciences, especially social or cultural anthropology (Everington, 1993a, 1993b; Jackson, 1993, 1995). The ethnographic dimensions of the studies were funded by the Economic and Social Research Council (United Kingdom).

The Unit is particularly interested in the processes by means of which 'culture' is reproduced, especially through the informal, semi-formal and formal religious nurture of children. 'Reproduction' here does not imply a straightforward transmission of ways of life from one generation to the next. As we will see, the processes are complex and involve various blends of change and continuity.

145

Behind the research was a concern that in religious education publications, religious traditions were often presented as exotic and remote from the experience of young people growing up in Britain. When materials did reflect life in Britain, they often tended to present stereotypical pictures of the traditions or 'unitary' accounts of religions. Some curriculum materials used fictitious accounts or accounts based on superficial contacts with people from the religious communities. This concern was coupled with a second, namely the dearth of qualitative studies of children's experience of religions and the transmission and reshaping of religious culture in the religious and ethnic groups present in British society.

While maintaining an interpretive approach, our goals were broadly consistent with those of writers acknowledging 'cultures' as internally diverse, contested and changing, and we believed that the experiences of the young would be likely to reflect (or even be part of) those changes. We were also conscious of the ethnographer's influence on the representation of religious material, whether through gender, professional status, age or being an outsider (Clifford and Marcus, 1986; Jackson and Nesbitt, 1993, chapter 2).

Two of the tasks we identified were to study the processes of religious 'nurture' (see below) in four religious traditions (two studies based in each of two cities) and to use some of the data in generating religious education materials which reflected the richness and internal diversity of the data. The project proposal built on earlier research by the Project Director and Senior Research Fellow which experimented with linking ethnographic studies of the transmission of Hindu culture in Britain (Jackson and Nesbitt, 1993) with the development of curriculum materials for use with pupils in schools (Jackson, 1989a; Jackson and Nesbitt, 1990). These earlier studies were discussed in Jackson (1989b). The proposal aimed to extend the range of ethnographic studies of children and young people living in urban settings to Christian, Jewish, Sikh and Muslim traditions while developing and applying a theoretical basis for interpreting data and converting material into forms suitable for use with school students. Currently WRERU is undertaking a longitudinal study of Hindus between the ages of eight and thirteen years featured in Jackson and Nesbitt (1993) now that they are in their later teens and early twenties.

The project team included the director, two ethnographers (Eleanor Nesbitt and Peter Woodward), a co-ordinator of curriculum development (Clive Erricker from 1990-1992 and Judith Everington from 1992) and a part-time curriculum developer (Margaret Barratt) with two more joining the team in 1993 (Geoff Robson and Elizabeth Wayne). Deirdre Burke, Carri Mercier, Jo Price and Sarah Davies joined the curriculum development team in 1994. Supplementary ethnographic work on a Buddhist community was carried out by Joyce Miller who was working for a research degree at the University of Warwick (Miller, 1992). This research was drawn on in preparing one of the Key Stage one children's books.

Four studies were conducted between 1990 and 1993, with each ESRC funded researcher being responsible for two consecutive studies. Eleanor Nesbitt conducted fieldwork on Christian and Sikh children in Coventry, while Peter Woodward worked with Jewish and Muslim children in Birmingham. With regard to our approach to the interpretation of data, we found the work of Clifford Geertz to be particularly helpful (1973, 1983), while accepting some points made by his critics (Clifford and Marcus, 1986). A discussion of our use of Geertz's ideas, and a short critique of phenomenological approaches is provided by Jackson (1993).

The following summaries illustrate the range of methods and adaptations made to suit each study. Information on the Christian and Sikh studies is based on preliminary reports by Eleanor Nesbitt; material on the Jewish and Muslim studies is similarly based on preliminary reports by Peter Woodward. The studies are of particular groups of children from each tradition in the age range between eight and thirteen years. Since religious tradition (and not ethnicity or any other category) was the starting point for each piece of research, the criteria for selecting children varied to some extent across the studies. The objective was not to produce generalisable findings but to make a contribution to building a picture of the processes of religious 'nurture' in different religious communities in urban situations in Britain. 'Nurture' (adapted from Hull, 1984) was preferred as an analytic term to categories such as 'socialisation' and 'enculturation' in order to refer to the range of formal and informal influences contributing to children's religious formation. The use of the term does not imply that each child's religiosity is dependent entirely on external influences.

Method

Christian Nurture

Following a bibliographical survey of publications concerned with the religious nurture of Christian children, research took place in discrete but overlapping phases from October 1990. Research methods were decided and interview schedules were designed for use with children between the ages of eight and thirteen years and with elders especially concerned with passing on Christian belief and practice. Three key decisions were made. First, the working definition of 'Christian children' was adopted as children who regularly engaged in corporate worship or church-related activities in a church which was a member of or in sympathy with the Coventry Council of Churches. Second, criteria for selection of churches and children within this category included the statistical strength of the traditions, cultural and ethnic diversity and geographical location. It was decided to include pupils attending county, voluntary (Roman Catholic and Church of England) and independent schools. Third, the research methods would be participant observation in church communities and semi-structured interviews in school, followed by further interviews with a smaller number of children in their homes in parallel with continued participant observation. Contact was made with officers of the churches concerned, with the local education authority and with voluntary aided schools, explaining the nature and aims of the research.

The ethnographer carried out participant observation, visiting Sunday worship in churches and organised youth activities such as Sunday school and uniformed organisations. From each denominational and ethnic category an adult (for example, youth club leader) was interviewed. Through further visits a list of children between the ages of eight and thirteen years willing to be interviewed was compiled. With permission from parents, 50 children were interviewed in their day schools. Using the same criteria as for the initial selection, thirteen children, representing a range of denominational and ethnic backgrounds, were selected for interview at home. All were interviewed three times or more, including 'focused' interviews based on photographs of activities within the churches. Each child kept a 'diary'. A substantial collection of slides of children's involvement in supplementary classes, worship and other church-related activities was made and literature used in worship and in instructing young people was collected.

Certain themes and questions (based on an earlier study of Hindu religious nurture and related work at Leeds) informed the design of the interview schedules. This facilitated data analysis. Data (fieldnotes, slides, tape-recorded interviews, documents) were analysed both thematically (for example, children's experience of the sacraments, of Easter, of Sunday school) and by denomination or ethnic community (for example, the religious nurture of Ukrainian Catholic children). Processes involved in religious nurture and the evidence of continuity and change within religious groupings received particular attention. Elders' concerns with regard to the transmission of faith and culture were examined in association with children's observed and reported experience. In some cases (for example, children's views of an afterlife and perceptions of their tradition *vis à vis* other traditions) data were analysed in parallel with earlier data on Hindu children (Nesbitt and Jackson, 1992). The focus was on understanding the life world of individual children in particular membership groups rather than on reaching generalisable conclusions.

Jewish Nurture

After study of relevant literature, contacts were made with rabbis in the research area and with the headteacher of the local Jewish primary school. These helped to facilitate access to the local Jewish communities. Arrangements were made for visits to synagogue and religion school (cheder) activities and to day school events, and the names of adults and children who might be appropriate for interview were obtained. Steps were also taken to find Jewish contacts outside the immediate orbit of the observant communities to avoid paying undue attention to observant voices.

An interview schedule was compiled following a parallel approach to the Christian schedule. A separate (though related) schedule of questions was used with rabbis, teachers and community leaders. All interviews were semi-structured.

Data collection involved a combination of varied methods: participant observation during visits to maintained (county and Jewish voluntary aided) and independent schools, cheders (evening and Sunday religion schools) and places of worship; interviews with children and adults; diaries kept by the children interviewed; photography by the researcher and curriculum developers; festival participation at synagogues and schools; and attendance at rites of passage.

Ten interviews were conducted with adults in the West Midlands to gain an overview of adults' perceptions of the transmission of Jewish culture in the area, and four with Jewish community leaders in London and Liverpool, to obtain a national perspective.

Forty children aged between seven and thirteen years were interviewed in their twelve day schools and 14 were selected for case study, using a matrix designed to ensure a spread of age, gender, schooling, synagogue affiliation and religious background and commitment. Different national and traditional (Ashkenazic or Sephardic) origins were also reflected in the selection. Their parents were approached with a view to holding further interviews with the children in their homes. Ten were interviewed at home on three or four occasions each, sometimes with siblings and/or parents.

A photographic record was made of the children, their homes and the artefacts on display there, and slides were used on future occasions during 'focused interviews'. The children were invited to keep a personal diary indicating religious and secular interests, and these were subsequently analysed and their contents discussed in interviews.

Visits were made to Shabbas services and festivals at five synagogues attended by some of the children, and to three religion schools, a youth centre and the local Lubavitch Centre, as well as to school/parental celebrations at the Jewish primary school. Festival and Shabbas meals were shared in different Orthodox and Progressive homes.

Interview data were typed on to a database and organised under 42 grouped headings, to allow the material to be analysed thematically and related to comparable headings in the data acquired on the other traditions studied. Topic based searches were conducted, partly to familiarise the researcher further with the material gathered and to prepare material for writing publications.

Sikh Nurture

Planning began in January 1992. A similar research design and methodology to that used in the Christian study was employed, with a modified version of the interview schedule in order to facilitate comparative analysis. The smaller size of the Coventry Sikh population, its ethnic homogeneity and absence of 'denominations' meant that fewer criteria for fieldwork had to be considered. It was decided to represent the diversity of caste and of parental stance *vis à vis* Punjab politics and sants (living spiritual masters).

Contact was made with Coventry's five gurdwaras and questionnaires were sent out requesting information on Punjabi classes and kirtan (devotional music) to schools and Sikh organisations. Permission for interviewing in schools was obtained from parents and the local education authority.

Methods included participant observation in gurdwara worship, Punjabi classes and devotional music classes, preceded and continued alongside semi-structured interviews conducted with adults (for example, Punjabi language teachers) concerned with formal transmission of the tradition and with Sikh pupils between the ages of eight and thirteen years in local primary and secondary schools. The 45 children who were interviewed were mostly selected from those encountered during fieldwork visits. In order to include 'less observant' families the parents of all Sikh pupils of eight or above in one primary school and all in one year of a secondary school were contacted. Interviewees were selected for a balance of age and gender and to include children of different castes (though, reflecting the Coventry population, the majority were Jat) and participants in all five gurdwaras. Location was another factor in the selection of subjects.

The initial interviews took place between April and June 1992 in 15 schools (county and Church of England aided). Thirteen subjects were selected, with the same variables in mind, for interview at home. Each was interviewed on three or four occasions between June and September. They kept diaries and these as well as some of the fieldworker's collection of slides of young Sikhs' involvement in the community's religious life were cues for eliciting the subjects' experience of religious nurture.

Analysis has focused on the processes, formal (for example, kirtan classes) and informal (for example, parental influence), of religious nurture. Subjects' self-ascribed identity, the extent and role of Punjabi language in their religious nurture, their understanding of 'God' and the significance of amrit (holy water) in their experience and perception of their tradition have been examined. Nesbitt and Jackson (1994, 1995) report aspects of the research. Nesbitt (1995) examines the data in conjunction with that on Punjabi Hindus (from earlier research) and Punjabi Christians.

Muslim Nurture

After a period spent studying relevant literature, a series of initial field visits was made to mosques and madrasahs in an area of Birmingham adjacent to that used in previous research (Joly, 1987, 1995). These provided some diversity of Islamic viewpoint and a mixture of Pakistani and Bangladeshi Sunni communities, the two dominant 'ethnic' groupings of Muslims resident in Birmingham.

Arrangements were made for further visits to interview the directors of a number of these mosques, together with a selection of community leaders and teachers, and to visit their madrasahs to observe children being taught. Because of the numerical dominance of the Pakistani community among Birmingham Muslims, the majority of the mosques selected for visits represented Urdu speaking Sunni Muslims whose families originated in various areas of Pakistan, but visits to leaders and children of Bangladeshi and East African (mostly Gujarati) origin were also included. Thirteen adults were interviewed, including representatives of the Ahl-i Hadith, Jamaat-i Islami, Barelvi and Shi'ite communities.

Children selected for interview, including those who attended Muslim day schools and a centre for secular educational studies, came forward as volunteers during visits to madrasahs. Additional names were suggested by the adults interviewed or by teaching staff of Muslim private schools. Forty children were interviewed in their day schools. Most were British-born, although several had visited or lived in Pakistan, Bangladesh or India. Twenty-seven came from families whose origins were in Pakistan, five from a Bangladeshi background and two were Indian (Gujaratis by origin). Three children whose families had lived in East Africa were also of South Asian (Punjabi or Gujarati) background. Two children had Iraqi parents and one was Lebanese. Through the directors of two of the mosques visited, invitations were extended to visit two Muslim private schools, one in which Urdu and Punjabi were the community languages, and one where the majority of pupils came from a Bangladeshi background, but with English medium teaching in most subject areas. Arrangements were made for pupil interviews in each case. To avoid a total preponderance of mosque / madrasah based traditional viewpoints, contact was made with a centre where secular educational courses were provided for young Muslims.

Research methods included observation or participant observation during visits to mosques to attend prayers and festival celebrations, to madrasah lessons in Urdu and in Qur'anic and Islamic studies and to day schools. Forty children were given semi-structured interviews after permission had been obtained from parents and headteachers. In addition, three or four in-depth, semi-structured interviews were conducted in the home with the twelve children selected for case study using a matrix designed to ensure a spread of age, gender, types of school attended, mosque and madrasah affiliation and level of religious commitment and observance. Their parents were then approached to obtain permission to hold further interviews with the children in their homes. Ten of these children were interviewed at home on three or four occasions each, some-times in the company of siblings and/or parents.

In some cases the opportunity was given for girls to be accom-panied by a friend for their interviews, but in no instance was this offer accepted. All interviews took place in English, although questions were posed as to the children's ability to communicate in other languages.

Two schedules of questions, one for children and one for adults, were used based on the Christian and Jewish schedules but modi-fied for usage with Islamic communities. A separate schedule of questions was used with mosque and school directors, teachers and community leaders, interviewed to obtain a broad overview of the local communities as well as for triangulation purposes.

Photographs were taken in the field and were used to promote further discussion of relevant issues. Diaries recording their daily religious and secular activities were kept for a period of two weeks by many of the children. These were later collected and analysed. The tapes from interviews were transcribed on to a database and processed as with the Jewish data.

Results

Christian Nurture

The research found commonalities and diversity in the religious nurture of Christian children, in terms of the content, processes and style (Jackson and Nesbitt, 1992; Nesbitt, 1993; Nesbitt and Jackson, 1996). In all cases the bible and life of Jesus were central concerns, all the churches (except the Roman Catholic and Ukrain-ian Catholic) ran classes for children and all expected the partici-pation of children in congregational worship. Diversity of content and style corresponded especially to ethnic and denominational distinctions between congregations. Charismatic experience and evangelical conviction both characterised certain denominational groups (such as the Apostolic Church and the Coventry Christian Fellowship) and differentiated individuals within, for example, a Baptist congregation and congregations within the Church of England.

The subjects' understanding and expression of their Christian tradition closely resembled the understanding and expression of their parents and church leaders. However, particularly in the case of ethnic minority families, the subjects experienced a less homogeneous body of belief and practice than their parents, because of differences, for example, in ethos between home and church (in the Punjabi case) or in Catholic practice home and church school (in the Ukrainian case). For Irish Roman Catholics, attending Roman Catholic schools, the homogeneity of tradition was greater than for other ethnic minorities. Minorities, such as the Ukrainians and Greek Cypriots whose scriptures and liturgical material were in an archaic form of their mother-tongue, promoted formal language teaching whereas for the Punjabis, whose families had been converted by British missionaries, mother-tongue maintenance was a less pressing concern.

Jewish Nurture

Interviewees emphasised the support their families received from the synagogues they attended, the cheders where they studied and their day schools. It was the relationship of the individual family, whether Orthodox or Progressive, to each of these other elements that was most significant for children's nurture in the Jewish tradition, and not the quality of the particular shul, cheder, school or family. In one case, a boy's experience of the Jewish youth movement Bnei Akiva affected the whole family which became increasingly observant.

The influence exerted by the synagogue (especially in the case of Orthodox families) was more formal and impersonal in its nature than that which was evident in cheder or day school, partly since adults present did not usually take direct responsibility for the children as a group. In the cheders the effect of the teaching was limited cognitively, being provided by caring but frequently untrained adults and young people in their teens. Their influence was generally related less to their scholarship or skills than to the commitment they showed to their tradition. The staff of the Orthodox Jewish primary school were all professionally trained. They were not, however, all Jewish and much of the curriculum taught there was secular, although many activities were religiously inspired.

The use and influence of colloquial Yiddish and Hebrew terms in the transmission of Jewish culture and the upbringing of Jewish children were important, especially in the Orthodox communities where they were most frequently employed (Woodward, 1993). There was near unanimity among children in their commitment to Israel, with family, synagogue and cheder all exerting an influence.

Sikh Nurture

The research has revealed a high level of participation in gurdwara life with the same children attending usually two or more local gurdwaras, despite their differences of ethos and organisational structure. Punjabi language and kirtan (devotional music) are aspects of the Sikh tradition most actively promoted through supplementary classes. The children identified more strongly with the terms 'Sikh' and 'Punjabi' than with 'British', 'Asian' or other terms.

The impact of sants (living spiritual masters) is evident in the experience of some young Sikhs. The sant is called 'Babaji', a term which the children translated as 'God' and applied also to the scriptures and historic Gurus. Reference to aspects of a wider Hindu tradition (for example, veneration of mother goddess) differentiated the experience of subjects and their families within the Sikh community (Nesbitt and Jackson, 1995). Being 'a proper Sikh' was equated by the subjects with 'amrit chhakna' (initiation with holy water), the five Ks (outward signs of Khalsa allegiance), Punjabi dress (for women), vegetarianism and avoidance of alcohol.

The importance of amrit in the experience of Sikh children in Coventry both confirms and challenges its role and significance in normative Sikh literature. The children's references to amrit were not only to the discipline and appearance of Sikhs who have been initiated but also to amrit as holy water, which has been empowered by proximity to the Guru Granth Sahib (both scripture and Guru) or a sant. This amrit is drunk or sprinkled by children (in some cases daily) for purification, protection, healing and success in their studies. The prominence and diversity of belief and practice surrounding amrit raises issues *vis à vis* the representation of the Sikh tradition in both religious studies and religious education.

Muslim Nurture

Formal instruction at the mosques where many of the boys prayed, the daily schooling provided by adults for boys and girls in the madrasahs, the effect of day schools, and the more informal but powerful support of the family in the home, were all important influences. Where the family's observance of Islamic duties was nominal, however, neither attendance at madrasah nor day school provided sufficient compensation to ensure the child remained loyal to Muslim belief and practice.

The increasing use of English in a number of formal contexts, including certain subjects taught at the madrasahs and at the private Muslim schools, was welcomed by parents who were in many cases equally anxious that their children should retain or develop competence in the South Asian languages that were (usually) spoken in the home. Most of the young interviewees were able (in varying degrees) to speak and think in the different languages they encountered at home, school, mosque and madrasah.

The close support between family and mosque/madrasah was evident in the intense loyalty that nine case study children displayed towards their families (especially to parents, elderly relatives and siblings), madrasah teachers and to the mosques they attended.

Many children and adults emphasised the unity of Islam. Even those who were aware that many of the mosques in Birmingham belonged to minority groupings, distinguishable by sectarian or ideological viewpoints, were anxious to play this down and to keep evidence of divisions away from outsiders. Several case study children indicated ignorance of minority divisions within the Sunni tradition. The research data contained virtually no evidence of the abrasive nature of the relationships between these groups, as portrayed by Robinson (1988, p. 2). In its place there was a presentation of conformity and convergence in Islamic attitudes, especially in respect of matters relating to the nurture of children.

Many adults were anxious about being stereotyped by non-Muslims, whom they regarded as likely in many cases to portray them with hostility and prejudice. Children interviewed felt this less, although in many other respects they closely shared their parents' views, especially with regard to the moral standards of Western society (Woodward, 1994).

Theory and Curriculum Development

The curriculum co-ordinator and the curriculum developers used data and materials supplied by the ethnographers in order to devise ideas for teaching material at particular key stages. Preliminary ideas were tried out on other members of the project team, and were modified as a result of comments received. As ideas developed, contact was re-established with families from particular religious groups whose children had been suggested as case studies for the curriculum materials. The ethnographers made contact with the families to explain the potential educational uses of the field data, to ask them if they were willing to participate in the development of curriculum materials and to introduce one or more curriculum developers to them. Members of families who participated in the curriculum work commented on draft materials prepared by the curriculum developers, contributed further interview material and provided additional background and contextual material. The families were given the opportunity to approve final versions of the material, as were selected community leaders and educational consultants from inside the religious traditions being represented, and there were sometimes negotiations over the final wording of text (Everington, 1996a).

The two inter-related issues of representation and interpretation were seen to be particularly relevant to the project's ethnographic work and to the processes of curriculum development. With regard to representation, the team adopted the judicious usage of the term 'religious tradition', intended as an indication of the internal plurality of the religions and of how, in the eighteenth and nineteenth centuries, religions were defined and 'essentialised' (Smith, 1978; Said, 1978; Jackson, 1995). Our ethnographic source material was especially useful in enabling us to employ personal narratives which reflected the vigour and internal diversity of the traditions rather than abstracted, 'static' accounts.

For purposes of ethnographic and pedagogical interpretation, a model was designed that would offer a looser, more personal and organic picture of religious traditions than that presented in some versions of phenomenology and which took account of the situational character of ethnicity and of social and personal identity. Combining insights from Wilfred Cantwell Smith's work in religious studies (1978) with that of anthropologists (Geertz, 1973, 1983) and social psychologists interested in the relationship between individuals and groups (Tajfel, 1981), a matrix was constructed in which the most generalised 'whole' is the religious tradition which, although constructed differently by different insiders and outsiders, is a reference point for individuals and groups. Next there are 'membership groups' of various kinds, each evolving situationally in relation to other groups. Then there is the individual, deeply influenced through the membership of groups and identifiable as part of the wider tradition, and yet being personally unique. The interpretation of a religious 'world-view' (whether by an ethnographer or a pupil doing religious education) involves examining the relationship between individuals and groups, using the wider tradition as a general reference point. Moving back and forth from one to the other (for example, by setting up activities for teachers or pupils that demand this) increases understanding. In curriculum terms, our 'hermeneutic circle' could involve setting up an interplay between an individual and one or more membership groups (for example, denomination, sect, home, peer group) or between an individual, his or her membership group and a cumulative tradition.

The related methods of interpretation were also addressed. For all key stages, curriculum developers endeavoured to select topics from the ethnographic data which could be interpreted by pupils and to which children and young people might relate. At upper Key Stage two, for example, these are arranged into four broad categories which recurred in the data from membership groups within the various traditions, namely 'growing up', 'learning', 'preparing', 'responsibilities' and 'tradition'. These categories are intended to act as the bridge between the pupils' experience and that of the children from the religious traditions portrayed in the text. We also decided to balance our interpretations with 'statements' from different points within the tradition.

At Key Stage one, the focus of each pupil text is on one child from one religious membership group and the emphasis in the text is on learning within the family (Barratt, 1994a, 1994b, 1994c, 1994d, 1994e; Jackson, Barratt and Everington, 1994). At Key Stages two and three, pupils are encouraged themselves to engage in interpretive work, guided by activities written into the curriculum materials or through work initiated by the teacher. The focus at these stages is on several young people from different membership groups and the emphasis changes to a portrayal of learning and reflecting within the groups (for example, Christian denominations). At Key Stage two the subject matter relates especially to 'formal nurture' (children being instructed in their tradition) and the 'voice' of a commentator sometimes assists the pupil with the interpretive process. At Key Stage three the emphasis is on engaging with the comments and reflections of young people from different groups within the traditions (Robson, 1995).

A further concern was to establish a method for connecting the experience of pupils with that of insiders so that the former have a basis for interpreting the latter's concepts, feelings and attitudes. We found Richard Rorty's (1980, p. 318) metaphor of 'conversation' highly appropriate and used it to refer to the process of to-ing and fro-ing between the pupils' world and that of children operating as individuals belonging to various groups within religious traditions. In promoting 'conversation', use was made of Geertz's distinction between 'experience-near' concepts (used within a particular tradition or membership group within a tradition) and 'experience distant' concepts (usually vocabulary familiar to pupils through their experience). Finding an appropriate 'experience distant' concept is not word for word translation, but a form of provisional 'interpretation', in which the two are placed in 'illuminating connection' with each other. The curriculum developers made use of the idea of 'analogous experience', ideas and experiences likely to be familiar to pupils which would help them to interpret related ideas presented in the pupils' materials. A more detailed account of the Warwick RE Project's curriculum development is provided by Jackson (1996).

Curriculum books and materials for Key Stages one to three are being published by Heinemann in stages with the general title of *The Warwick RE Project* and under the general editorship of Judith Everington and Robert Jackson. The Key Stage one and Key Stage two materials appear under the title *Bridges to Religions*. The Key Stage one children's books, are *An Egg for Babcha*, *Lucy's Sunday*, *The Seventh Day is Shabbat*, *A Time to Share*, and *The Buddha's Birthday* (Barratt, 1994a, 1994b, 1994c, 1994d, 1994e). The Key Stage one book for teachers is Jackson, Barratt and Everington (1994). The first Key Stage two children's books are concerned with *Meeting Christians* (Barratt and Price, 1996; Everington, 1996b). The Key Stage three books appear under the title *Interpreting Religions*. The first volumes to appear in this series feature young people from four different Christian communities (Robson, 1995) and from the Muslim community (Mercier, 1996). A Key Stage three book on Hindu young people is in preparation. A feature of all the pupils' books is the original photographs taken during ethnographic research and curriculum development. In addition to those taken by ethnographers and curriculum developers, photographs were taken by Noel Barratt, Rosemary Jackson, Hilary Roberts and Peter Roberts.

The project team continues to publish academic and professional articles based on the research and a number of theoretical and ethnographic texts reporting the work of the Warwick Religions and Education Research Unit are in preparation.

Acknowledgements

An earlier version of this chapter was published in *Panorama: international journal of comparative religious education and values*, 6, 1, 115–130, 1994. The financial support of our ethnographic work by the Economic and Social Research Council (ESRC) is gratefully acknowledged. The Project's ESRC reference number is R000232489. The Warwick Religions and Education Research Unit is also grateful to the St Gabriel's Trust, the Dulverton Trust, Warwickshire Education Authority and the University of Warwick Research and Teaching Innovations Fund for their support of various aspects of the work reported in this chapter.

References

Barratt, M. (1994a), *An Egg for Babcha* (Bridges to Religions series, The Warwick RE Project), Oxford, Heinemann.

Barratt, M. (1994b), *Lucy's Sunday* (Bridges to Religions series, The Warwick RE Project), Oxford, Heinemann.

Barratt, M. (1994c), *The Seventh Day is Shabbat* (Bridges to Religions series, The Warwick RE Project), Oxford, Heinemann.

Barratt, M. (1994d), *A Time to Share* (Bridges to Religions series, The Warwick RE Project), Oxford, Heinemann.

Barratt, M. (1994e), *The Buddha's Birthday* (Bridges to Religions series, The Warwick RE Project), Oxford, Heinemann.

Barratt, M. and Price, J. (1996), *Meeting Christians: book one* (Bridges to Religions series, The Warwick RE Project), Oxford, Heinemann, in press.

Clifford, J. and Marcus, G. (eds) (1986), *Writing Culture: the poetics and politics of ethnography*, Berkeley, University of California Press.

Everington, J. (1993a), The relationship between research and teaching within teacher education: an account of recent work within the religious education and community project, *Journal of Beliefs and Values*, 14, 2, 6–8.

Everington, J. (1993b), Bridging fieldwork and classwork: the development of curriculum materials within the religious education and community project, *Resource*, 16, 1, 7–10.

Everington, J. (1996a), A question of authenticity: the relationship between educators and practitioners in the representation of religious traditions, *British Journal of Religious Education*, in press.

Everington, J. (1996b), *Meeting Christians: book two* (Bridges to Religions series, The Warwick RE Project), Oxford, Heinemann, in press.

Geertz, C. (1973), *The Interpretation of Cultures*, New York, Basic Books.

Geertz, C. (1983), *Local Knowledge*, New York, Basic Books.

Hull, J. M. (1984), *Studies in Religion and Education*, Lewes, Falmer Press.

Jackson, R. (1989a), *Religions Through Festivals: Hinduism*, London, Longman.

Jackson, R. (1989b), Hinduism: from ethnographic research to curriculum development in religious education, *Panorama: international journal of comparative religious education and values*, 1, 2, 59–77.

Jackson, R. (1993), Religious education and the arts of interpretation, in D. Starkings (ed.) *Religion and the Arts in Education: dimensions of spirituality*, London, Hodder and Stoughton.

Jackson, R. (1994), Ethnography and religious education: a research report, *Panorama: international journal of comparative religious education and values*, 6, 1, 115–130.

Jackson, R. (1995), Religious education's representation of 'religions' and 'cultures', *British Journal of Educational Studies*, 43, 272–289.

Jackson, R. (1996), The Warwick RE Project: an interpretative approach to religious education, *Religious Education*, in press.

Jackson, R., Barratt, M. and Everington, J. (1994), *Bridges to Religions: teacher's resource book*, Oxford, Heinemann.

Jackson, R. and Nesbitt, E. (1990), *Listening to Hindus*, London, Unwin Hyman.

Jackson, R. and Nesbitt, E. (1992), The diversity of experience in the religious upbringing of children from Christian families in Britain, *British Journal of Religious Education*, 15, 1, 19–28.

Jackson, R. and Nesbitt, E. (1993), *Hindu Children in Britain*, Stoke on Trent, Trentham Books.

Joly, D. (1987), Making a place for Islam in British society: Muslims in Birmingham, *Research Papers in Ethnic Relations*, No. 4, Coventry, University of Warwick, Centre for Research in Ethnic Relations.

Joly, D. (1995), *Britannia's Crescent: making a place for Muslims in British society*, Aldershot, Avebury.

Mercier, C. (1996), *Muslims* (Interpreting Religions series, The Warwick RE Project), Oxford, Heinemann, in press.

Miller, J. (1992), The forest hermitage: an ethnographic study of a Buddhist commmunity in Britain, Unpublished MA dissertation, University of Warwick.

Nesbitt, E. (1993), The transmission of Christian tradition in an ethnically diverse society, in R. Barot (ed.), *Religion and Ethnicity: minorities and social change in the metropolis*, pp. 156–169, Kampen (Netherlands), Kok Pharos.

Nesbitt, E. (1995), Punjabis in Britain: cultural history and cultural choices, *South Asia Research*, 15, 2, in press.

Nesbitt, E. and Jackson, R. (1992), Christian and Hindu children: their perceptions of their own and each other's religious traditions, *Journal of Empirical Theology*, 5, 2, 39–62.

Nesbitt, E. and Jackson, R. (1994), Aspects of cultural transmission in a Diaspora Sikh community, *Journal of Sikh Studies*, 18, 1, 49–67.

Nesbitt, E. and Jackson, R. (1995), Sikh children's use of 'God': ethnographic fieldwork and religious education, *British Journal of Religious Education*, 17, 108–120.

Nesbitt, E. and Jackson, R. (1996), *Christian Children in an Urban Setting*, in press.

Robinson, F. (1988), Varieties of South Asian Islam, *Research Papers in Ethnic Relations*, No.8, Coventry, University of Warwick, Centre for Research in Ethnic Relations.

Robson, G. (1995), *Christians* (Interpreting Religions series, The Warwick RE Project), Oxford, Heinemann.

Rorty, R. (1980), *Philosophy and the Mirror of Nature*, Oxford, Blackwells.

Said, E. (1978), *Orientalism*, London, Routledge.

Smith, W. C. (1978), *The Meaning and End of Religion*, London, SPCK.

Tajfel, H. (1981), *Human Groups and Social Categories*, Cambridge, Cambridge University Press.

Woodward, P. (1993), Empathetic guidelines for the ethnographic study of Jewish children in Britain, *Diskus* (a disk-based periodical in Religious Studies), 1, 1, 15–31.

Woodward, P. (1994), Muslim children and the abolition of stereotypes, *Resource*, 17, 1, 5–9.

9

Gender differences in religiosity in children and adolescents

Kalevi Tamminen

Summary

The first part of this chapter presents data about the quantitative and qualitative differences in the religiosity of boys and girls derived from a series of studies conducted in Finland between 1974 and the late 1980s. These data are compared with other findings from other international studies. The second part of the chapter discusses the factors and theories which may explain observed gender differences in religiosity during childhood and adolescence.

Introduction

A repeated result from both old and new studies has been that girls and women are, at least among Christians, more religious than boys and men. In general this concerns all dimensions of religiosity and all ages, perhaps with slightly divergent emphases (Argyle and Beit-Hallahmi, 1975; Batson and Ventis, 1982; Benson, Donahue and Erickson, 1989; Hyde, 1990; Aletti, 1994). Only in rather few studies has the result been the opposite. The studies have dealt more with *quantitative* differences between males and females, like church membership, participation in religious events, practice of prayer, and less with *qualitative* differences, like concepts of God, prayer or the bible, and the *reasons behind the gender differences*.

I propose to illustrate the differences in the religiosity of girls and boys mainly by drawing on the Finnish projects which I have presented earlier (Tamminen, Vianello, Jaspard and Ratcliff, 1988; Tamminen, 1991, 1993) and discuss factors which can account for these differences. The main project covered the age range between seven and twenty years, approximately the whole Finnish school age. The study was begun in 1974 and continued as a longitudinal study and replication study until the late 1980s.

In fact, this study included three different sub-studies. First, the *original study* in 1974 concerned 1,558 children and adolescents, 789 girls and 769 boys, from grade one (seven to eight years old), grade three (nine to ten years old), grade five (eleven to twelve years old), grade seven (thirteen to fourteen years old), grade nine (fifteen to sixteen years old) within Finnish comprehensive schools and grade eleven (seventeen to twenty years old), within the second grade (of three) in academic high school and vocational schools. The material was gathered in seven localities situated in different parts of Finland. Second, this original study was followed by a *longitudinal study* in 1976 and 1980 using some of the pupils from the original study. Most of these pupils (277) participated twice, in 1974 and 1976, and only sixty of them participated three times, in 1974, 1976, and 1980. By 1980 the students were already dispersed throughout many schools, which made it difficult to find them and to gather the material. In 1980, the 242 classmates of the actual test subjects were also included in the research for comparison. Third, a *replication study* was carried out in 1986 in the same localities and mainly in the same schools as in 1974 in grade three, grade four, grade five, grade six, grade seven, grade eight and grade nine (582 girls and 594 boys).

The aim of the study was to include the whole area of religious development and all the different dimensions of religiosity. Apart from religious experiences, a great deal of attention was given to religious thinking and different religious concepts (bible, God, Jesus' person and mission, prayer and death) as well as to religious beliefs and religious practice (prayer and congregational activity). Furthermore, life questions or existential questions (Tamminen, 1988) and moral values were studied, as well as the relationships between all these aspects and the background of the children and adolescents (personality, sex, home, school and hobbies). All these various issues were investigated using the same groups of children and adolescents.

The parents of pupils in grade one, grade five and grade nine in 1974 (515 mothers, 78.4% of the subjects, and 441 fathers, 75.5%) answered an extensive postal questionnaire mainly concerning the educational and religious home background of the children and their own personal religiosity. The responses and opinions of parents provide material for explaining gender differences in religiosity.

It was noticed in the preliminary studies of this project that research methods and measures have obvious effects on results. Therefore, one of the basic ideas of the study was that several research problems would be studied using measuring instruments that were as versatile as possible (Tamminen, 1990). It was impossible to interview all the subjects personally because of the size of the research area and the number of measuring instruments. The data were gathered by outside researchers (not teachers), mainly in writing, using group tests in the classrooms. The pupils in grade one were, however, also personally interviewed.

In close connection with this study, the religiosity of children aged four to six years was studied (in 1978) in the same localities. In this research project, 319 children (176 girls and 143 boys) were personally interviewed. In addition, the mothers of children (or exceptionally father or other provider) answered a questionnaire which mainly surveyed the educational home background.

The data from these studies provide an overview of the religiosity of Finnish children and adolescents. These data are limited, however, by the fact that they are derived from one particular culture and in the main from one religious group. Indeed about 95% of these children and adolescents belonged to the Lutheran Church, about 1% to the Orthodox Church and the rest to other religious communities or to none. Almost all students were participating or had previously participated (students in vocational schools) in religious instruction (mainly Lutheran) at school. Differences in religiosity between girls and boys vary to some extent in different Christian denominations, cultural milieux, and regional emphases as shown by Greer (1972a) and Nelsen and Potvin (1981).

Establishing gender differences

Religious activity and participation

To begin with I shall refer to the dimension of religiosity which is most readily measurable, namely *church attendance and other religious participation*. In relation to children and adolescents, however, its measurement is made more difficult by other contaminating factors. Religious participation by children and adolescents may depend on the environment and on the example shown by adults.

Church attendance in the Lutheran Church of Finland is minimal, with only 3–4% of church members attending church weekly. It is more common in childhood than in adolescence. In all age groups girls participate more than boys, women more than men. According to Greer (1972b) this is also the case among children and adolescents in Northern Ireland. The same kind of difference applies to participation in Sunday school, girls' and boys' clubs and youth groups. Nevertheless, in the case of Sunday school, where devotion is central, the difference is greater (in 1993 about 39% of the participants were boys) than for participation in *scouts* (boys 45%) and *clubs* (46% boys), where there is more activity attractive to boys.

The Lutheran Church in Finland has two forms of activity in which no significant difference between girls and boys is apparent. The first is day club for four to six year olds (once or twice a week), in which participation is especially widespread (in 1993 58.7% of all Finnish children in these age groups) and to which parents generally take their children. The second is confirmation school, in which about 92% of Finnish young people participate, that is to say almost all fourteen to fifteen year old adolescents belonging to the Lutheran Church. The relative participation of boys is only slightly lower than that of girls.

The motives for participation in confirmation school differ between girls and boys. For girls social expectations (pleasant company, new friends) are stronger than for boys, but also the girls have higher expectations than the boys of receiving answers to adolescent problems and religious questions. Boys more than girls come to confirmation school because of social pressure to conform, while girls come more of their own free will (Ahonen, 1981; Kiilholma, 1982; Vermasvuori and Nurmi, 1992). Confirmation school is a precondition for sponsorship at baptism and for Christian marriage.

According to Heiskanen's (1975) study of children and adolescents in Helsinki, girls between the ages of nine and eighteen years participated in divine service more because of their own interest, while boys were more likely to participate because of the wishes of others. Argyle and Beit-Hallahmi's (1975) statement that females are motivated by internalised processes, while males are motivated by external sanctions seems to be true among Finnish adolescents.

The gender differences may be more pronounced in private forms of religiosity (prayer) than in public forms (church attendance) (Argyle and Beit-Hallahmi, 1975). Among children and adolescents *prayer* may be a clearer measure of religiosity than outward participation. As tables 9.1 and 9.2 show, the practice of evening prayers increases during the first years of school apparently under the influence of school instruction, but then decreases with

Table 9.1
Percentages of girls and boys regularly engaging in evening prayer by school grade in 1974 (pre-school sample, 1978)

gender	pre-school %	grade one %	grade three %	grade five %	grade seven %	grade nine %	grade eleven %
girls	67	76	86	75	50	47	42
boys	46	48	61	46	29	19	27

Table 9.2
Percentages of girls and boys regularly engaging in evening prayer by school grade in 1986

gender	pre-school %	grade four %	grade five %	grade six %	grade seven %	grade eight %	grade nine %
girls	68	80	72	55	41	22	38
boys	51	46	37	36	29	13	21

some regularity. The 'bottom' of puberty is in Finland usually in grades seven and eight (at the age of thirteen to fifteen years). There is obviously some influence from confirmation school on prayer among adolescents in grade nine, since many adolescents attend confirmation school during the summer between the eighth and ninth grade.

The graph for frequency of engaging in evening prayers runs almost parallel for girls and boys, but at different levels. Already in early childhood there is a clear difference between girls and boys in prayer: girls are more diligent prayers than boys. In the Finnish research project among four to six year olds, only 18% of girls as compared to 41% of boys reported never performing evening prayers (Parviainen, 1987). Corresponding results were found among pre-school children by Helohonka (1973) and in the Swedish study by Hörberg (1967), but not in the Finnish study by Keskitalo (1987). It appears that girls perform their evening prayers more often alone than boys, while boys do so more with their parents or others. This may suggest that already at this stage evening prayers have become a personal habit or interiorised more among girls than among boys.

Religious experiences

It has been suggested that religiosity among girls is more personal and based more on their own experiences than the religiosity of boys (Babin, 1965; Nelsen and Potvin, 1981). Religious experiences most clearly represent the internalised side of religiosity. They were studied in our project mainly from three aspects: nearness of God; guidance of God; and answers given to prayers. In order to investigate the frequency and content of these experiences three questions were used. The first question was 'Have you at times felt that God is particularly close to you?' with the follow-up query, 'Would you like to tell about it, when and in what situation?' The second question was 'Have you at times felt that God is guiding, directing your life?' with the follow-up query, 'Can you tell about it, when and how?' The third question was 'Has God answered your prayers in some way or other?' with the follow-up query, 'If so, please write about the occasion(s)'.

There were clear differences between boys and girls, both in the quantity and quality of religious experiences. In almost all grades girls reported having experienced God's nearness, God's guidance and answers given to prayers (see table 9.3) more often than the

Table 9.3
Percentages of girls and boys reporting experiences
of God's nearness by school grade in 1986

gender	grade one %	grade three %	grade five %	grade seven %	grade nine %	grade eleven %
girls	86	81	67	50	51	42
boys	81	60	47	36	30	28

boys had. Differences in experiences of God's guidance were smaller than in experiences of God's nearness, and in 1986 in grade three and grade seven even a little contrary. This may be linked with difference in the basic nature of religiosity between girls and boys. God's guidance is more concerned with action. Regarding experiences of God's closeness, Greer (1981b) found a similar gender difference among upper sixth form pupils in Northern Ireland.

Differences in the content of religious experiences reported by girls and boys also point to gender difference of religiosity. The girls associated encounters with death, loneliness and fear, prayer and meditation, and church activities with experiencing God's nearness more often than the boys. The boys mentioned everyday and other external situations (such as escaping or avoiding danger) and quite vague situations (such as 'at home/in the evening/at night') more often than the girls did. In the content of the experiences of God's guidance there were no significant differences between girls and boys. In the experiences of God's answer to prayers the examples presented by girls were concerned with recovery from illness more often than was the case among boys. The examples given by boys were more often concerned with other concrete matters. The girls also reported more than boys about the mental and spiritual effect of prayer. The differences vary slightly in different grades (Tamminen, 1988, 1994.)

Religious beliefs

Next, I will deal with religious beliefs which were studied by using sixty statements relating to Christian faith, such as 'We can trust in God through all difficulties' or 'Other religions may be as good as Christianity'. Beliefs represent the cognitive dimension of an attitude, but they are concerned with more than just knowledge. An accepting or rejecting evaluation is always connected with them. On the basis of many factor analyses, the statements were grouped into nine dimensions: trust in God; prayer and God's help; legalistic concept of God; beliefs in Jesus as Saviour and Son of God; salvation through Jesus; veracity of the bible; uniqueness of Christianity; life after death; and religion as the basis of ethical behaviour.

As in many other studies (Kuhlen and Arnold, 1944; Hyde, 1965; Turner, 1970; Greer, 1972a; Francis, 1987, 1989; Hyde, 1990), girls' attitudes toward the Christian faith were found in this study among all grade-levels to be more positive than the boys. The changes which occur with age follow a similar pattern for girls and boys, but the girls hold a more positive attitude at each age. This is seen typically with respect to trust in God (table 9.4). There were similar trends in response to questions concerned with prayer and

Table 9.4
Mean scores of girls and boys regarding trust in God
by school grade (scale range 1–5)

gender	grade one mean	grade three mean	grade five mean	grade seven mean	grade nine mean	grade eleven mean
girls	4.6	4.5	4.1	3.8	3.5	3.6
boys	4.1	4.2	3.8	3.2	3.1	3.3

God's help, belief in Jesus as Saviour and Son of God, and in trust in the veracity of the bible. In belief in life after death and in religion as the basis of ethical behaviour, the beliefs changed to a negative direction after the age of eleven to twelve years but only among boys.

The *mothers and fathers* of the pupils in grade one, grade five and grade nine answered the same statements about religious beliefs. In regard to many belief dimensions, mothers scored the same as girls in grade five and fathers scored the same as boys in grade five or grade seven. Regarding life after death, mothers scored as the fifth grade girls, but fathers were more sceptical than boys on any grade-level. Regarding religion as the basis of ethical behaviour, mothers scored more highly than students in any grade and fathers scored at the same level as third grade pupils.

Religious thinking

In order to assess the development of religious thinking in the Finnish study, two instruments were used. First, Peatling's (1974) instrument, Thinking about the Bible, measured the development of religious thinking in the concrete–abstract dimension. This instrument uses the three biblical stories employed originally by Goldman (1964) in his study of children and young people between ages six to sixteen years. Four questions are attached to each of the stories, and each of them has four alternative answers which represent four levels of religious thinking: very concrete, concrete, abstract and very abstract. Four scales of religious thinking were formed by combining the response alternatives of the three stories. Then very abstract and abstract scales were combined to form the total abstract scale, and very concrete and concrete scales were combined to form the total concrete scale.

As was the case with Peatling's (1974) studies in the United States of America and Greer's (1981a) study in Northern Ireland using Peatling's instrument, there were in the Finnish study no differences between the results shown for girls and those for boys. The scores of abstract thinking were only slightly higher for the girls than for the boys (Tamminen, 1976, 1991). Perhaps the fact that many very abstract response alternatives included clearly critical and sceptical traits decreased the abstract choices for girls, on the grounds that believing or committed pupils would not willingly choose such response statements which were sceptical in tone. Scores on the total abstract scale had a statistically significant correlation with intelligence (measured by Raven matrices in grade seven) and in most grades with success in school. While there was no notable difference between girls and boys in intelligence, there was in many grades a clear difference in school success in favour of girls. Similarly, Goldman (1964) did not find any significant difference between girls and boys in the level of religious thinking.

Second, the difference between females and males was much clearer using Tamminen's instrument, Understanding of Parables. This instrument included two of Jesus' parables: the prodigal son and the speck and the log. Two questions were attached to both of the parables: 'What in your opinion did Jesus describe in this story?' and 'What did Jesus want to teach with this parable?' Each question had three response alternatives. They formed three levels of understanding and interpretation of parables: concrete level; human-ethical level; and religious and abstract interpretation. The understanding of parables was also studied by open interpretation of some central metaphors (concepts) in these parables.

As table 9.5 shows, the girls in all grade-levels recorded higher scores than the boys on the index preferring the religious and abstract interpretation of parables. At the same time the girls showed less preference than the boys for the concrete alternatives. The boys favoured human-ethical interpretation alternatives more than the girls did.

In the open interpretation of central concepts of parables (prodigal son, father, brother, speck and log) the girls show a better understanding than the boys. Table 9.6 shows the age trends for understanding one of these concepts (prodigal son).

The developmental process of understanding parables is complex. The gender difference in the interpretation of parables diminishes in adolescence. Although it is a well-known fact that girls advance more quickly in their mental development, the

Table 9.5
Mean scores of girls and boys on abstract interpretation
of parables by school grade (scale range 3–15)

gender	grade three mean	grade five mean	grade seven mean	grade nine mean	grade eleven mean
girls	8.8	9.9	9.8	10.1	10.3
boys	8.2	8.5	8.6	9.4	9.8

Table 9.6
Percentages of girls and boys providing correct
or almost correct interpretations of the concept
'Prodigal Son' by school grade

gender	grade three %	grade five %	grade seven %	grade nine %	grade eleven %
girls	44	73	82	85	89
boys	27	65	63	74	80

developmental tempo explains the gender difference only in little part. Many other factors affect it, such as religious attitudes and experiences, and religious education in school. The understanding of parables has rather high correlations with many religiosity variables, such as belief in God, experience of God's nearness, prayer and attitude toward religious education. On the average, girls of our study were more interested in religious education as well as in school in general, which is also reflected in their better school success ($p < .001$ in all grades). Thus, the girls' better school success and motivational factors in its background and more positive religious attitudes quite largely clarify the difference in the interpretation of parables.

Concept of bible

Regarding religious concepts, I deal with only the concept of the bible, the concept of God and the concept of prayer. Then regarding the concept of the bible, I deal with only one aspect. Peatling's instrument, Thinking about the Bible, included a scale of *literalism*. That was used to study the veracity of the bible, the literal–non-literal interpretation of the biblical stories. After each story the question was posed, 'Do you think this story really happened?' The five response alternatives varied from 'Yes . . . all of it happened' to 'No . . . none of it really happened'. As we might predict, boys were in almost every age-level slightly less literal than girls, but the difference was not great (table 9.7). The difference is chiefly due

Table 9.7
Mean scores of girls and boys on non-literal interpretation of the bible by school grade (scale range 3–15)

gender	grade three mean	grade five mean	grade seven mean	grade nine mean	grade eleven mean
girls	4.8	6.2	7.3	8.3	8.3
boys	6.0	6.5	8.7	9.0	8.6

to stronger commitment to Christian faith among girls. Literalism and many religious variables, such as belief in God, experience of God's nearness and prayer activity, correlate very highly with each other.

Image of God

The concept of God was studied using several different methods and measures. Among four to six year olds the concept of God was studied in a semi-clinical interview using photographs. Older pupils responded to a number of tests, including the question, 'What is best in what the bible tells about God?', a semantic differential of the concept 'God', a sentence completion test, 'When I think about God . . .', an essay on the topic, 'What is my God like?' and a projective photograph (a girl or a boy sitting and thinking) and an attached text: 'This girl/boy is Karin/Martin. She/he is sitting and thinking about something related to God and Jesus. She/he is now thinking . . .'.

First, among four to six year old Finnish children there were no significant differences between girls and boys in the concept of God. The image of God is at that age rather diffuse. The results among older children and adolescents gained by different measures varied in some degree according to the measures used.

The respondents evaluated four central characteristics of God. As is seen in table 9.8, boys in all grades emphasised more than

Table 9.8
Percentages of girls and boys choosing God's greatness and powerfulness for the best characteristic of God by school grade

gender	grade three %	grade five %	grade seven %	grade nine %	grade eleven %
girls	18	25	10	6	12
boys	37	29	21	12	14

girls the greatness and powerfulness of God ('God is great and powerful and rules the world'). This result confirms the findings of some other studies (Coster, 1981). Instead the girls emphasised God more as giver of security ('God gives people security'). Also God's forgiveness ('God forgives people their wrongdoings') was more important for girls whereas boys, especially in upper grades, emphasised God's ethical influence ('God influences people so that they are good to each other').

In the basic study (1974) the characteristics were compared with each other, but in the replication study (1986) this question was altered so that the respondents evaluated on a five-point scale the importance of each of the characteristics. Now girls emphasised in general each characteristic more than boys did, but also now the clearest difference is in the evaluation of God as giver of security: it is much more important for girls than for boys.

In the semantic differential examination of the word 'God', girls evaluated God as more safe, real, near, caring and forgiving than the boys. Also in the sentence completion test and essays girls had more thoughts about God's love, help, care and protection than boys. They also reported almost twice as often as boys good, secure or happy feelings when thinking about God. In all, the number of statements in essays reflecting an idea of God as gentle or loving is ten times greater than the number of those reflecting an idea of God as stern or frightening. Boys were more likely than girls to refer to God as stern or frightening. Boys were also more likely to mention God as creator, or as omnipotence and force. Anthropomorphic expressions were spread quite evenly among different grade-levels and between girls and boys.

By the age of thirteen to fourteen years and later, boys especially gave plenty of responses denying or doubting God's existence. The before-mentioned differences in the concept of God are caused not only or directly by sex, but in part by other variables. In the background there is the question of belief in God and differences in religiosity as a whole.

Concept of prayer

In the concept of prayer there are clear differences of emphasis between girls and boys. In assessing what is most important in prayer, in almost all age groups boys appreciated much more than girls the place of petitionary prayer. Boys also emphasised the external forms of prayer, like being quiet and folding one's hands. Girls emphasised in prayer conversation with God and thanksgiving more than boys did.

When the students defined prayer by completing the sentence 'I think prayer is . . .', the result was slightly dissimilar. Although girls still emphasised conversation with God and praise and worship more than boys, there was no remarkable difference between boys and girls concerning petitionary prayer. Now, especially in upper grades, boys explicitly expressed criticism of the practice and significance of prayer.

Children's and young people's conceptions of the effect of prayer and how prayer works were studied more closely by the help of two stories. I will mention only the first one, which described Mary's prayer on behalf of her sick grandmother and the sick grandmother's recovery. Four alternative answers described different opinions: God's direct answer, God's indirect influence, grandmother's recovery solely because of medical treatment, and 'cannot tell'.

Especially at the age of nine or ten years, girls believed in God's response to prayer in the form of a direct answer clearly more than boys (table 9.9). After that age girls thought mostly that God cured the grandmother but did so indirectly through medication. At the age of nine or ten years, more boys believed in the indirect effect of God, but after that age boys were less likely to believe in this than girls. In upper grades boys were clearly more sceptical than girls about God's effect. In adolescence, between the ages of

Table 9.9
Percentages of girls and boys choosing God's greatness
and powerfulness for the best characteristic of God
by school grade

effect	gender	grade three %	grade five %	grade seven %	grade nine %	grade eleven %
direct effect	girls	60	28	20	13	10
	boys	39	25	15	4	6
indirect effect	girls	31	57	54	50	57
	boys	43	50	38	28	42
no effect	girls	5	6	15	26	25
	boys	13	14	29	50	40

fifteen and twenty years, almost half of them chose the response in which the grandmother recovered solely because of the treatment she received.

Existential questions

The previous sections have explored gender differences in relation to specific institutional definitions of religiosity. We can also look at this issue from the viewpoint of a wider, functional definition of religiosity. That means questions about the most fundamental meaning of life, one's ultimate personal concern. Our research project provides material for such an examination. One of the research areas was the study of life questions, existential questions. Especially relating to children it is difficult to draw a sharp line between existential questions and other life questions. In any case the word 'existential' refers to the bases of life and existence (Hartman, 1986; Tamminen, 1988). Such existential questions already arise in small children.

Life questions were studied among children and adolescents in two ways: a questionnaire, listing 35 different experiences and problems, was used among pupils between the ages of nine and twenty years, and a projective photograph test was used among pupils between the ages of seven and sixteen years (Tamminen, 1975, 1988, 1991). Pirinen (1983) employed a similar projective photograph test concerned with life problems in his study among secondary school students (ages sixteen to eighteen years).

The first instrument consisted of a list of experiences and problems typical for young people, such as: 'I feel that nobody understands me' and 'I wonder what the purpose of my life is'. These statements were combined on the basis of factor analysis into eight groups. The second instrument consisted of eight pairs of photographs (girl/boy) and short stories and sentence completion tests. Seven of the texts were neutral in their content, while one referred to God and Jesus. The extensive database (in 1974, 10,265, and in 1986, 11,580 pupil statements) was first classified through qualitative content analysis into 162 categories, which later were combined into twelve main categories.

One issue in the *problem list* was especially interesting: *the purpose of life*. Both according to the basic study (1974) and the replication study (1986) girls had more such experiences (wondering '. . . whether life goes on after death', '. . . how life started', and '. . . what is the purpose of my life'). These experiences also correlated with religious faith and activity, in the sense that 'believers' had experienced them on the average more than others.

Life questions also show other differences between the sexes. One very clear difference is that, in connection with the projective photographs both in 1974 and 1986 and also in Pirinen's study (1983), girls expressed more joys and fewer problems concerning school than boys did. Girls also expressed more joys concerning home and parents. In general girls gave more statements concerning home. Personal relationships seem to be particularly important for girls. Girls expressed more problems of loneliness than boys did. Girls were also more conscious of environmental, social and global problems. In addition, girls were more likely to note spontaneous mention of religious questions in response to the neutral pictures than boys did, often expressing also the importance of personal relationship to God.

Pirinen (1983) stated that the boys give more weight to facts, performance, systems and cognitive factors, whereas girls give more weight to personal, aesthetic and emotional matters. In their search for personal identity, boys emphasise social issues, while girls emphasise personal issues.

Explaining gender differences

There are no unambiguous research results about what causes gender differences in religiosity. Explanations of gender differences have followed two main paths. Earlier the emphasis was on biological differences between females and males, but recently the emphasis has been more in terms of social influence or social learning (Batson and Ventis, 1982).

Psychoanalytic explanation

In their well-known book *The Social Psychology of Religion* (1975), Argyle and Beit-Hallahmi put forward a series of hypotheses for explaining sex differences in religiosity, partly based on the specific functions that religion may fulfil for women, partly on general physiological or psychological sex differences. One of them is Freud's view that God is a projected father figure. 'If children prefer the opposite-sex parent, it follows that girls should be more concerned with a deity presented as a fatherly male' (Argyle and Beit-Hallahmi, 1975, p. 77). The Freudian view has stimulated quite a lot of research and discussion, but it does not have any unambiguous empirical validity. Empirical findings concerning the relationship between the God concept of children and their picture of parents are contradictory. According to some, the father figure is more dominant in the idea of God (Vergote, Tamayo, Pasquali, Bonami, Pattyn and Custers, 1969). Some other results show that the mother's influence is more decisive (Godin and Hallez, 1965; Deconchy, 1968; Spilka, Addison and Rosensohn, 1975) or that the parent who is closer to the child has more effect on the child's image of God (Nelson, 1971; Spilka, Addison and Rosensohn, 1975). Vianello and his colleagues found that the father/God relationship was dominant for nine to ten year old Italian children, but the correlation between the idea of mother and the image of God was higher for girls than for boys (Vianello, Tamminen and Ratcliffe, 1991). Research results also vary according to cultural background of subjects (Tamayo, 1981; Vergote, 1981).

The relationship between the idea of God and the idea of parents was not illuminated by our study. The respondents, however, evaluated their relationship with mother and father in many different ways. I will return to these results later. At this point I wish simply to indicate that in all grade-levels there was a correlation between the closeness of the children's relationship with parents and their evaluations of God as being close, real, caring and forgiving. These correlations are strongest in the lowest grades. The relationship with the mother correlates with children's picture of God as real, careful, forgiving and close more clearly than the relationship with the father.

Personality traits

Gender differences in religiosity have also been explained by the different innate personality traits of females and males.

Argyle and Beit-Hallahmi (1975) point to studies which suggest that women have more *guilt feelings* than men (Wright, 1971). They state that, 'if the function of religion is to relieve guilt feelings' women on this basis should be more religious. It is thus especially in Protestantism, in which sin and salvation are emphasised. According to some researchers women are more prone to submissiveness, anxiety, worry, dependence and distress. These traits would lead both to a greater need for forgiveness and to a greater tendency for seeking help from religion (Garai, 1970; see Batson and Ventis, 1982). In addition, women would be less aggressive and more fearful (Gray, 1971) and more influenceable (McGuire, 1969) than men.

In our Finnish study we had a few questions which touched on guilt feelings. In response to the question, 'If you feel you have done something wrong does it weigh on your mind later?' 73% of girls and 56% of boys answered 'yes, very often' or 'yes, quite often'. In response to the question, 'Do you feel you need God's forgiveness?' 63% of girls and 46% of boys said they had had such feelings 'often' or 'now and then'. In the list of experiences and problems there was the item, 'I feel guilty before God'. Here also the gender differences are similar. The hypothesis that females have more guilt feelings and are therefore more religious seems to be supported by these results. The matter is, however, not this simple. It is difficult to say if guilt feelings are the cause of greater religiosity or if internalised religious faith may produce sensitiveness which in turn leads to guilt feelings. The difference may also be explained by girls' more general belief in God. Those who do not believe in God neither feel guilty before God nor in need of God's forgiveness.

In grade one, grade three, grade five and grade nine our study included a personality test (Ylinentalo, 1965, 1966). I point only to the results concerning pupils in grade three. Girls in grade three were shown to be clearly more submissive and less self-confident and hard than boys. Their attitudes toward school were much more positive than the boys. There was no difference between the sexes in fear or dependence on others.

There were significant correlations between religiosity and many dimensions assessed by the personality test. In grade three pupils who had experienced God's nearness were more anxious, submissive, altruistic, dependent and less harsh. These characteristics also clarify girls' sensitivity to religion. But we have to ask again, what affects what? These traits are not necessarily innate but are partly learned, in the sense that girls and boys are educated to behave in different ways. Batson and Ventis (1982) cite the book by Maccoby and Jacklin (1975) as supporting the view that parents and others tend to respond to little boys and little girls in different ways.

There is still one difference between sexes. According to D'Andrade's (1967) cross-cultural data, men are in most cultures less emotionally expressive and less nurturing than women (Batson and Ventis, 1982). Both in my own research (Tamminen, 1975, 1988) and in the Swedish study (Hartman, 1985, 1986) girls gave more attention to emotions in life questions than did boys. Girls are expressive in their emotional lives, which may have both biological and educational bases. Girls are allowed to express their emotions more sensitively than are boys. This difference is evident also in religiosity.

Sex roles

Recent explanations of gender differences have moved the emphasis to role expectations and learned sex roles and differences in the socialisation and education of girls and boys. According to Batson and Ventis (1982, p. 40) at least in the American society, 'the script for the role of women seems to include the expectation of more involvement of women in religion than does the script for the role of men'. Women and girls are thus directed by more social pressure to display interest and involvement in religion. It is thus expected of girls to be more religiously active and also to express their religiosity. Sex roles begin to develop in the very first months. They have a partially biological background, but they may well be chiefly acquired from the environment. Parents and other adults may treat girls and boys in different ways (Wallinga and Skeen, 1988). Different role expectations are directed to boys and girls.

Unfortunately the religious role expectations which parents directed to their children were not clarified in our project. Instead, in an adjacent area, moral values, mothers and fathers were asked how important they consider the deeds mentioned in the list for their children. The parents were informed that the questionnaire referred to the child who was included in the project. The same list was provided in the children's study.

Factor analysis of the evaluations produced six dimensions: empathy toward peers; good friendship; respecting the law; well-behaved pupil; helping a fellow human being who is far away; and unselfish behaviour at home. Girls emphasised all these values more than boys. It has been supposed that differences in moral values, norms and behaviour would be significantly influenced by the different role expectations and educational attitudes of parents (Vuorinen, 1973). Therefore, it could be assumed that parents would consider these moral values more important regarding girls than boys. This is true only to a small extent in our study, according to the responses of mothers and fathers. Good friendship and empathy toward peers was emphasised more as far as girls are concerned. Respecting the law was emphasised more as far as boys are concerned. The differences were small, and they do not give a basis for any clear conclusions (Tamminen, 1981).

Differences in socialisation and education

The relationship between mother and child is often closer than the relationship between father and child, especially during the first years of life. According to information given by mothers of pre-school aged children, children turn in difficulty for help more often to their mothers than to their fathers (Väätäinen, 1974; Massinen, 1981; Alopaeus-Karhunen, 1988). Mothers also evaluated their relationships with their children to be slightly closer than did fathers in the first, fifth and ninth school years. On the other hand, when pupils themselves evaluated their relationships with their mothers and fathers separately, the difference was not very great. In late childhood a noticeably larger proportion of boys than girls evaluated their relationship both with their mother and with their father as only satisfactory or poor. In that phase apparently peers take a decisive place in the lives of the boys. After this age the difference between boys and girls balances out and even changes a little in the other direction.

Girls, however, say that they discuss everything with their mothers (school, free time activities, comrades and also religion) more than with their fathers. The boys discuss only school more with their mothers than with their fathers. Also in the parents' evaluation, children talk to the mother more than to the father about everything in general (Tamminen, 1991).

The mother generally has the chief responsibility for the child's primary socialising and religious training. At least evening prayer is mostly learned from the mother (Helohonka, 1973; Parviainen,

1987; Keskitalo, 1987). Since mothers are more religiously active than men and more readily express their religiosity, religion more visibly relates to the mother's role. When children have evaluated the religiosity of their parents, they have generally considered the mother more religious than the father. In one project both girls and boys noted the mother's influence greater than that of the father on their concept of God and Christian faith.

Yinger (1970) noted that, because of their role in bringing up children, women are more traditional than men. These values are transferred to the following generation. But does this transfer occur more easily in the case of girls than boys? Several factors support this supposition. Presumably girls are more susceptible to such influence than boys are. They spend, according to their own evaluations, more time at home, while boys are more often outside (Tamminen, 1981). It could also be assumed that girls more readily identify to the mother and with the mother's role (Nelsen and Potvin, 1981; Francis and Gibson, 1993).

It is obvious that the religious education of boys and girls in the home differ from each other at least to some extent, but we have little information on it. Unfortunately, we had no questions about it in our questionnaire.

Although sex roles form in the home in the early years, there are of course many other contributing factors, such as children's carers and teachers at different stages, peers and peer groups, and television, all of which perhaps to some extent function in different ways for boys and girls.

Other viewpoints

Finally I draw attention to a couple of things which may have had an influence, not on the gender difference in religiosity as such, but on the differences brought out in the study. Girls are apparently more verbally adept than boys. They express themselves more readily, and for this reason their responses to life questions and their other free answers are more substantiated and nuanced. Hartman (1986) made the same observation in his study on life questions. It is possible that this may in some degree also influence the evaluation of their religiosity. In addition, there are differences in the way females and males use language (Aletti, 1994).

Girls' attitudes toward school are clearly more positive and their motivation toward religious instruction at school is stronger than boys, as was also reported by Hyde (1965). This naturally means that they are able to absorb more from what is taught, which is reflected in their better success at school.

Greer (1972b) pointed to another possibility for explaining gender differences in religiosity among sixth form students in Northern Ireland, by drawing attention to the fact that girls were less likely than boys to take scientific subjects. This reason does not seem valid in Finland, since there are no great gender differences in choices of school subjects. The study of scientific subjects is hardly a cause for the more negative religious attitudes of Finnish high school boys than those of girls.

In addition, it is apparent that the girls' attitudes toward research of this type are more positive than is the case among boys. This may also be concluded from some indifferent or slapdashed responses of boys, especially in upper grade-levels. It is, however, difficult to say to what extent the attitudes toward the research itself might influence the results in one direction or another.

Conclusion

In agreement with numerous other studies, there were in the Finnish research projects among children and adolescents between the ages of four and twenty years clear differences in the religious emphases of girls and boys. The differences are not only quantitative but also qualitative, which is demonstrated, for example, by responses to the image of God test and in the content of reported religious experiences. There is also a difference between girls and boys in the ways in which religiosity is expressed, the girls being on an average more emotionally tuned and more internal than boys. These differences came to light consistently in all age groups, in almost all the different dimensions of religiosity, and in relationship to highly varied measures.

It is, however, easier to show differences in the religiosity of girls and boys than to explain by what they are caused. From the review of the range of hypotheses advanced by earlier commentators, it is obvious that many factors together influence gender differences in religiosity. The factors discussed are still more hypothetical than based on verified empirical results. We now need more research about the upbringing and religious education of girls and boys at home, about how the role expectations of mothers and fathers as concerns girls and boys differ from each other and about the place that religiosity has in these expectations.

References

Ahonen, S. (1981), Leiririppikoululaisten asenteet Jumalaan, Raamattuun ja rukoukseen sekä niiden muuttuminen leiririppikoulun aikana (The confirmands' attitudes toward God, the bible and prayer and attitude changes during the confirmation education), Unpublished M.Th. dissertation, University of Helsinki.

Aletti, M. (1994), Religious experience, gender differences and religious language, in M. Aletti (ed.), *Religione o psicoterapia? Nuovi fenomeni e movimenti religiosi alla luce della psicologia*, pp. 381–391, Roma, LAS.

Alopaeus-Karhunen, P. (1988), Neljä-kuusivuotiaan lapsen käsitys Jeesuksesta (The concept of Jesus of a four to six year old child), Unpublished M.Th. dissertation, University of Helsinki.

Argyle, M. and Beit-Hallahmi, B. (1975), *The Social Psychology of Religion*, London, Routledge and Kegan Paul.

Babin, P. (1965), The idea of God: its evolution between the ages of 11 and 19, in A. Godin (ed.), *From Religious Experience to a Religious Attitude*, pp. 183–198, Chicago, Loyola University Press.

Batson, C.D. and Ventis, W.L. (1982), *The Religious Experience: a social-psychological perspective*, New York, Oxford University Press.

Benson, P.L., Donahue, J.D. and Erickson, A. (1989), Adolescence and religion: a review of the literature from 1970 to 1986, *Research in the Social Scientific Study of Religion*, 1, 153–181.

Coster, H. (1981), Some developmental characteristics of the parental figures and the representation of God, in A.Vergote and A.Tamayo (eds), *The Parental Figures and the Representation of God*, pp. 227–231, The Hague, Mouton.

D'Andrade, R.G. (1967), Sex differences and cultural institutions, in E.E. Maccoby (ed.), *The Development of Sex Differences*, pp. 174–204, London, Tavistock.

Deconchy, J-P. (1968), God and parental images: the masculine and feminine in religious free association, in A. Godin (ed.), *From Cry to Word*, pp. 85–94, Brussels, Lumen Vitae Press.

Francis, L.J. (1987), The decline in attitudes toward religion among 8–15 year olds, *Educational Studies*, 39, 99–108.

Francis, L.J. (1989), Drift from the churches: secondary school pupils' attitudes in England toward Christianity, *British Journal of Religious Education*, 11, 76–86.

Francis, L.J. and Gibson, H.M. (1993), Parental influence and adolescent religiosity: a study of church attendance and attitude toward Christianity among adolescents 11 to 12 and 15 to 16 years old, *The International Journal for the Psychology of Religion*, 3, 241–253.

Garai, J.E. (1970), Sex differences in mental health, *Genetic Psychology Monographs*, 81, 123–142.

Godin, A. and Hallez, M. (1965), Parental images and divinity paternity, in A. Godin (ed.), *From Religious Experience to a Religious Attitude*, pp. 65–96, Chicago, Loyola University Press.

Goldman, R. (1964), *Religious Thinking from Childhood to Adolescence*, London, Routledge and Kegan Paul.

Gray, J. A. (1971), Sex differences in emotional behavior in mammals including man: endocrine basis, *Acta Psychologica*, 35, 29–46.

Greer, J.E. (1972a), *A Questioning Generation*, Belfast, Church of Ireland Board of Education.

Greer, J.E. (1972b), Sixth form religion in Northern Ireland: religious belief, religious practice and moral judgement in a sample of Protestant boys and girls, *Social Studies*, 1, 325–340.

Greer, J.E. (1981a), Religious attitudes and thinking in Belfast pupils, *Educational Research*, 23, 177–189.

Greer, J.E. (1981b), Religious experience and religious education, *Search*, 4, 1, 23–34.

Hartman, S.G. (1985), *Children's Philosophy of Life*, Dissertation, Malmö, CWK Gleerup.

Hartman, S.G. (1986), *Barns tankar om livet* (Children's thoughts about life), Stockholm, Natur och kultur.

Heiskanen, S. (1975), 10–18 -vuotiaiden uskonnollinen kehitys (The religious development of 10- to 18-year-olds), Unpublished M.Th. dissertation, University of Helsinki.

Helohonka, S. (1973), Esikouluikäisten lasten uskonnollisuus (The religiosity of children in pre-school age), Unpublished M.Th. dissertation, University of Helsinki.

Hörberg, U. (1967), *Barn och Religion* (The child and religion), Uppsala universitet, Institutionen för pedagogik.

Hyde, K.E. (1965), *Religious Learning in Adolescence* (University of Birmingham, Institute of Education, Monograph 7), London, Oliver and Boyd.

Hyde, K.E. (1990), *Religion in Childhood and Adolescence: a comprehensive review of the research*, Birmingham, Alabama, Religious Education Press.

Jaakkola, M. (1988), Peruskoululaisten elämänkysymykset (Life questions of school children), Unpublished M.Th. dissertation, University of Helsinki.

Keskitalo, M. (1987), 4–6 vuotiaan uskonnollinen ajattelu ja jumalakuva (The religious thinking and God concept of a 4-to 6-year-old child), Unpublished M.Th. dissertation, University of Helsinki.

Kiilholma, H. (1982), Oppilaiden rippikouluodotukset ja asennemuutokset leiririppikoulun aikana (The expectations and attitude changes of students during the summer confirmation class), Unpublished M.Th. dissertation, University of Helsinki.

Kuhlen, R. and Arnold, M. (1944), Age differences in religious beliefs and problems during adolescence, *Journal of Genetic Psychology*, 65, 291–300.

Maccoby, E.E. and Jacklin, C.N. (1975), *The Psychology of Sex Differences*, Stanford, California, Stanford University Press.

McGuire, W.J. (1969), The nature of attitudes and attitude change, in G. Lindzey and E. Aronson (eds), *Handbook of Social Psychology*, pp. 136–314, Reading, Massachusetts, Addison-Wesley.

Massinen, V. (1981), Esikouluikäisten uskonnollisuus ja sen liittyminen maailmankuvaan (The religiosity of pre-school children and its connection to the world view), Unpublished MA dissertation, University of Helsinki.

Nelsen, H.M. and Potvin, R.H. (1981), Gender and regional differences in the religiosity of Protestant adolescents, *Review of Religious Research*, 22, 268–285.

Nelson, M.O. (1971), The concept of God and feelings toward parents, *Journal for Individual Psychology*, 27, 46–49.

Parviainen, K. (1987), Lasten rukouskäsitys ja rukoileminen (Children's concept of prayer and prayer practice), Unpublished M.Th. dissertation, University of Helsinki.

Peatling, J. (1974), Cognitive development in pupils in grades four through twelve: the incidence of concrete and abstract religious thinking in American children, *Character Potential*, 7, 52–61.

Pirinen, H. (1983), *Nuorten elämänkysymykset identiteetin etsimisenä*, (Life problems in adolescence: young people's search for identity), Helsinki, Suomalaisen Teologisen Kirjallisuusseuran Julkaisuja 135 (The Society of Finnish Theological Literature).

Spilka, B., Addison, J. and Rosensohn, M. (1975), Parents, self, and God: a test of competing theories of individual-religion relationships, *Review of Religious Research*, 11, 171–182.

Tamayo, A. (1981), Cultural differences in the structure and significance of parental figures, in A. Vergote and A. Tamayo (eds), *The Parental Figures and the Representation of God*, pp. 73–97, The Hague, Mouton.

Tamminen, K. (1975), *Lasten ja nuorten elämänkysymykset uskontokasvatuksessa* (Life questions of children and young people in religious education), Helsinki, Suomalaisen Teologisen Kirjallisuusseuran Julkaisuja 99.

Tamminen, K. (1976), Research concerning the development of religious thinking in Finnish students: a report of results, *Character Potential*, 7, 206–219.

Tamminen, K. (1981), Vanhempien lapsiinsa kohdistamat eettiset odotukset (The parents' ethical expectations directed to their children), in S. Seppo (ed.), *Ihmisen Kasvu ja Sosiaalistuminen*, pp. 230–243, University of Joensuu.

Tamminen, K. (1988), *Existential Questions in Early Youth and Adolescence*, Research reports on religious education C5, University of Helsinki.

Tamminen, K. (1990), *The Measurement of Religious Development in Childhood and Adolescence*, Research reports on religious education C6, University of Helsinki.

Tamminen, K. (1991), *Religious Development in Childhood and Youth: an empirical study*. Helsinki, Suomalainen Tiedeakatemia.

Tamminen, K. (1993), *Religiöse Entwicklung in Kindheit und Jugend*, Forschungen zur Praktischen Theologie 13, Frankfurt am Main, Peter Lang.

Tamminen, K. (1994), Religious experiences in childhood and adolescence: a viewpoint of religious development between the ages of 7 and 20, *The International Journal for the Psychology of Religion* 4, 61–85.

Tamminen, K., Vianello, R., Jaspard, J-M. and Ratcliff, D. (1988), The religious concepts of pre-schoolers, in D. Ratcliff (ed.), *Handbook of Pre-school Religious Education*, pp. 59–81, Birmingham, Alabama, Religious Education Press.

Turner, E.B. (1970), Religious understanding and religious attitudes in male urban adolescents, Unpublished Ph.D. dissertation, The Queen's University of Belfast.

Vergote, A. (1981), Overview and theoretical perspective, in A. Vergote and A. Tamayo (eds), *The Parental Figures and the Representation of God*, pp. 185–225, The Hague, Mouton.

Vergote, A., Tamayo, A., Pasquali, L., Bonamic M., Pattyn M-R and Custers, A. (1969), Concept of God and parental images, *Journal for the Scientific Study of Religion*, 8, 79–87.

Vermasvuori, J. and Nurmi, K.E. (1992), *Nuoret ja rippikoulu* (Young people and confirmation education), Publications in religious education B17, University of Helsinki, Department of Practical Theology.

Vianello, R., Tamminen, K. and Ratcliff, D. (1992), The religious concepts of children, in D. Ratcliff (ed.), *Handbook of Children's Religious Education*, pp. 56–81, Birmingham, Alabama, Religious Education Press.

Vuorinen, T. (1973), Koulunuorten eettiset normit ja niiden tausta (School-age ethical norms and their background), Th.D. dissertation, The Research Institute of the Lutheran Church in Finland, Serie A, Tampere.

Väätäinen, R-L. (1974), *7- ja 8 -vuotiaiden lasten uskonnolliset käsitykset* (The religious opinions of 7- and 8-year old children), Publications in religious education A10, University of Helsinki, Institute of Practical Theology.

Wallinga, C. and Skeen, P. (1988), Physical, language, and social-emotional development, in D. Ratcliff (ed.), *Handbook of Pre-school Religious Education*, pp. 30–58, Birmingham, Alabama, Religious Education Press.

Wright, D. (1971), *The Psychology of Moral Behaviour*, Harmondsworth, Penguin.

Yinger, J.M. (1970), *Religion, Society and the Individual*, New York, Macmillan.

Ylinentalo, O. (1965), *Persoonallisuusinventaario kansakoulun ala-asteelle* (A personality inventory for the common grade school pupils), Reports from Institute for Educational Research, Jyväskylä.

Ylinentalo, O. (1966), *Persoonallisuusinventaario 10–14 vuoden ikäisille* (A personality inventory for 10- to 14-year olds), Institute for Educational Research, Jyväskylä.

10

Religiosity and self-esteem during childhood and adolescence

Susan H. Jones and Leslie J. Francis

Summary

Three samples of school pupils completed the Francis Scale of Attitude Toward Christianity together with a measure of self-esteem. The three samples comprised 166 pupils between the ages of eight and eleven years, 755 pupils between the ages of thirteen and fourteen years, and 642 pupils between the ages of fifteen and sixteen years. In all three samples, after controlling for sex differences, the data demonstrate a positive correlation between high self-esteem and a favourable attitude toward Christianity.

Introduction

Theologically, the link between religion and self-concept is ambivalent, at least within the Christian tradition. One strand within the Christian tradition clearly emphasises a love of self, as well as love of God and love of neighbour. According to Mark 12: 13, Jesus said that the second most important commandment is this, 'Love your neighbour as you love yourself'. From this starting point Bahr and Martin (1983) argue that:

> those who consider themselves Christians should manifest the fruit of such love. The more religious the person, presumably, the more evident the love of self and others.

On this account, it is reasonable to hypothesise a positive correlation between being drawn to religion and self-concept.

Another strand within the Christian tradition clearly emphasises the unworthiness of self. According to Luke 18: 13, Jesus

189

commended the man who stood at a distance, not even raising his face to heaven, but beat on his breast saying, 'God, have pity on me, a sinner'. Similarly, in Mark 2: 17 Jesus proclaimed that, 'Those who are well have no need of a physician, but those who are sick: I came not to call the righteous, but sinners'. On this account, it is reasonable to hypothesise a negative correlation between being drawn to religion and self-concept.

More specifically, psychological theory concerned with self-concept suggests that individual self-evaluation is, at least partly, derived from the individual's view of how he or she is evaluated by others. If the primary emphasis in religion is thought to be a God who views individuals as unworthy and miserable sinners, it is reasonable to hypothesise a negative correlation between religion and a positive self-concept. On the other hand, if the primary emphasis in religion is thought to be a God who views individuals as unconditionally acceptable and accepted, it is reasonable to hypothesise a positive correlation between religion and a positive self-concept.

Integration of the findings from previous empirical studies concerned with the relationship between religion and self-concept is confused by three factors. These studies have used a variety of measures of self-concept. They have employed a range of indicators of religiosity. They have been conducted on diverse samples. No series of replication studies has been developed to explore the significance of these factors on shaping the reported relationship between religion and self-concept. Working within the constraints imposed by these difficulties, seven rather different pictures emerge from previous empirical studies concerned with the relationship between religion and self-concept.

The first set of studies suggests that there is no relationship between religiosity and self-esteem. For example, Strunk (1958a) administered a modified form of the Brownfain (1952) negative self-concept measure to 120 unspecified subjects together with the Allport, Vernon and Lindzey (1960) study of values. No significant difference was found on the religious value measure between high and low scorers on the negative self-concept measure.

Hanawalt (1963) administered the Social Personality Inventory for College Women developed by Maslow (1942) as a measure of self-esteem to 111 college women, equally divided between Catholics, Jews and Protestants. No differences in levels of self-esteem were found between the three groups.

Heintzelman and Fehr (1976) administered a modified form of the Coopersmith (1967) self-esteem inventory, alongside Brown's (1962) modified form of the Thouless test of religious orthodoxy to 41 male and 41 female students. They found no correlation between the two measures.

Fehr and Heintzelman (1977) administered a modified form of the Coopersmith (1967) self-esteem inventory, Brown's (1962) modified form of the Thouless test of religious orthodoxy and the Allport, Vernon, Lindzey (1960) study of values test to sixty male and sixty female students. They found no correlation between self-esteem and either religious measure.

Bahr and Martin (1983) administered a four item measure of self-esteem derived from the Rosenberg Self-Esteem Scale (Rosenberg, 1965) to a sample of high school pupils of undisclosed age. No significant correlation was found between self-esteem and church attendance (N = 471) or between self-esteem and evangelical outlook as measured by the item 'Christianity is the one true religion' (N = 453).

Aycock and Noaker (1985) employed the 37 item self-esteem scale of the Coping Resources Inventory for Stress attributed to Matheny, Curlette, Aycock, Pugh and Taylor (1981). They found no significant difference between the mean scores of two opportunity samples: 351 evangelical Christians from college and church settings and 1,115 general volunteers comprised of students, administrators and government employees.

Gill and Thornton (1989) administered the 25 item form of the Coopersmith (1967) self-esteem inventory together with their own thirteen item scale of belief to 179 high school pupils between the ages of sixteen and seventeen years. They found no significant relationship between these two variables.

Finally, Frankel and Hewitt (1994) employed the self-esteem measure developed by Pearlin and Schooler (1978) to compare the responses of 172 students affiliated to a number of Christian clubs or faith groups and 127 students recruited through first and second year psychology courses, students who were not affiliated to any campus Christian club at the time of the research. No significant differences were found between the self-esteem scores of the two groups.

The second set of studies suggests that there is a positive relationship between religiosity and self-esteem. For example, Strunk (1958b) administered a modified form of the Brownfain (1952) Self-Rating Inventory to a sample of 136 high school students, with a mean age of 16.4 years, together with a seven item religiosity index, combining questions concerned with church attendance, regular contributions of money and time to the church, the reading of some type of religious literature, regular prayer activity, a belief that the person's own religious beliefs and needs were stronger than average when compared with those of peers, and the admittance of a feeling that some sort of religious belief is necessary for a mature outlook on life. A positive correlation was found between religiosity and self-concept.

McAllister (1982) administered the Tennessee Self-Concept Scale (Fritts, 1976) to forty evangelical or fundamentalist ministers. He found that these ministers recorded a higher self-concept score than the population norms.

Krause and van Tran (1989) employed data from a national sample of 511 Black Americans aged over fifty-four to examine the relationship between a three item measure of self-esteem and two three item measures of non-organisational and organisational religiosity. They found that both indices of religiosity were positively related to self-esteem.

Finally, Forst and Healy (1990) administered the Coopersmith Self-Esteem Inventory (Coopersmith, 1967) together with Bahr and Martin's (1983) Scale of Religious Faith to 204 students. They found that the religious faith items correlated positively with aspects of self-esteem.

The third set of studies suggests that there is a negative relationship between religiosity and self-esteem. For example, Beit-Hallahmi and Nevo (1987) employed the self-concept questionnaire developed by Hofman, Beit-Hallahmi and Lazarowitz (1982) to compare the mean scores of forty Israeli men who had switched to Orthodox Judaism with a matched control group of forty Israeli men who remained secular. They found that the religious group recorded significantly lower self-esteem scores.

In a study employing the Coopersmith Self-Esteem Inventory (Coopersmith, 1967) alongside the Allport and Ross (1967) scale of extrinsic religiosity among 194 students, Watson, Hood, Morris and Hall (1985) found a negative correlation between extrinsic religiosity and self-esteem.

The fourth set of studies suggests that different indices of religiosity may lead to different relationships with the same measure of self-esteem among the same sample. For example, Cowen (1954) administered the Brownfain (1952) negative self-concept measure to 81 college undergraduates, together with a thirteen item theism scale intended to measure strength of belief in God and an eleven item ethics scale intended to measure strength of reliance on the church for one's ethical code. The comparison was made between the 26 subjects who scored high on negative self-concept and the 21 subjects who scored low on negative self-concept. While self-concept was unrelated to the theism scale, negative self-concept was significantly related to less reliance on the church for an ethical code.

Wickstrom and Fleck (1983) administered the short form of the Coopersmith Self-Esteem Inventory (Coopersmith, 1967) to 77 female and 53 male college students, all of whom had at some time lived overseas as children of missionaries, together with an unidentified measure of consensual and committed religiosity. They found that self-esteem was negatively correlated with consensual religiosity, but uncorrelated with committed religiosity.

Finally, Nelson (1990) administered the Rosenberg (1965) Self-Esteem Scale to 68 elderly persons, together with a question about church attendance and the Age Universal Religious Orientation Scale (Gorsuch and Venable, 1983). He found that self-esteem was uncorrelated with church attendance, uncorrelated with extrinsic religiosity, but significantly positively correlated with intrinsic religiosity.

The fifth set of studies suggests that different indices of self-esteem may lead to different relationships with the same measures of religiosity among the same sample. For example, Watson, Hood, Morris and Hall (1985) administered both the Rosenberg Self-Esteem Scale (Rosenberg, 1965) and the Coopersmith Self-Esteem Inventory (Coopersmith, 1967) to 98 male and 96 female students, together with the Allport and Ross (1967) measures of intrinsic and extrinsic religiosity. They found that the Coopersmith index correlated negatively with extrinsic religiosity and was unrelated to intrinsic religiosity, while the Rosenberg index was unrelated to both measures of religiosity.

In a second sample of 97 male and 130 female students, Watson, Hood, Morris and Hall (1985) administered the same two indices of self-esteem, together with the Batson and Ventis (1982) measures of internal, external and interactional religiosity. They found that the Rosenberg index was negatively correlated with external and interactional religiosity and unrelated to internal religiosity, while the Coopersmith index was unrelated to all three measures of religiosity.

Watson, Morris and Hood (1987) administered both the Rosenberg Self-Esteem Scale (Rosenberg, 1965) and the Coopersmith Self-Esteem Inventory (Coopersmith, 1967) to 75 male and 87 female students, together with the Allport and Ross (1967) measures of intrinsic and extrinsic religiosity and the Batson and Ventis (1982) measures of internal, external and interactional religiosity and doctrinal orthodoxy. They found that none of the six religious measures correlated with the Rosenberg index. The Coopersmith index was positively correlated with external religiosity, but unrelated to the other measures of religiosity.

A sixth set of studies suggest that different relationships may emerge between the same indices of self-esteem and religiosity among different groups of people. For example, Spilka and Mullin (1977) administered an abbreviated from of the Coopersmith Self-Esteem Inventory (Coopersmith, 1967) together with the Allen and Spilka (1967) measures of committed and consensual religiosity to three distinct samples: 170 students attending a Catholic college; 152 pupils attending a Catholic high school; and 99 pupils attending a Lutheran high school. Regarding committed religiosity, they found a significant positive correlation with self-esteem in one sample, but no relationship in the other two. Regarding consensual religiosity, they found a significant positive correlation with self-esteem in one sample, a significant negative correlation with self-esteem in the second sample, and no relationship with self-esteem in the third sample.

Moore and Stoner (1977) administered the Brownfain (1952) negative self-concept measure, together with Strunk's (1958b) seven item religiosity index to 46 male and 66 female high school juniors. A positive correlation was found between self-concept and religiosity for males, but not for females.

Smith, Weigert and Thomas (1979) administered a semantic differential index of self-esteem, together with a modification of the Glock and Stark (1965) measures of four dimensions of religion (practice, belief, experience and knowledge) to 1,995 adolescents from middle class Catholic high schools in six cities, representing five cultural contexts (United States of America, Puerto Rico, Yucatan, Spain and Germany). The data were analysed for males and females separately in each of the six cities. Nine of the twelve analyses demonstrated a significant positive correlation between total religiosity and self-esteem, while three of the analyses found no relationship between total religiosity and self-esteem.

Meisenhelder (1986) administered the Rosenberg Self-Esteem Scale (Rosenberg, 1965), together with an unspecified measure of the importance of religious beliefs, to 163 married women living with their husbands and children. A significant positive correlation was found between self-esteem and importance of religious beliefs among home makers. No significant relationship was found between self-esteem and importance of religious beliefs among women in employment.

Finally, Wade, Thompson, Tashakkori and Valente (1989) administered a four item index of self-esteem to students from grades seven, eight and nine in 1980. The students were also asked to assess the importance of religion to their daily life on a six point scale. The exercise was repeated in 1982. A total of 1,153 students were tested at both points in time. Eight separate analyses are reported for male and female, black and white students, in 1980 and 1982. A positive correlation was reported between religiosity and self-esteem for female white students in 1982, while the other seven analyses found no significant relationship between the two variables.

A seventh set of studies concentrated on the relationship between self-concept and God images. For example, Benson and Spilka (1973) explored the relationship between images of God and scores on a modified form of the Coopersmith Self-Esteem Inventory (Coopersmith, 1967) among 128 male students attending a Catholic high school who regarded religion as personally important. They found that self-esteem scores were positively correlated with loving God images, but negatively correlated with rejecting, impersonal, vindictive and controlling God images.

Spilka, Addison and Rosensohn (1975) administered a modified form of the Coopersmith Self-Esteem Inventory (Coopersmith, 1967) to 116 male and 82 female sixteen year olds attending three Catholic high schools, together with a semantic differential assessment of images of God producing seven measures defined as: loving God, controlling God, wrathful God, traditional Christian God, kindliness God, omni-ness God, deisticness God. They found that among male students a positive self-image was negatively related to a wrathful God. Among female students they found that a positive self-image was negatively related to a deistic God and positively related to a loving God, a traditional Christian God and a kind God.

One of the weaknesses of the existing studies dealing with the relationship between self-esteem and religion is their failure to integrate satisfactorily within a wider literature concerned with the social, personal and contextual correlates of religiosity. Against the confused and confusing background generated by these studies, the aim of the present investigation is to build on the set of eighty or so studies summarised by Kay and Francis (1995) which begin to provide a coherent account of the correlates of religiosity during childhood and adolescence. These studies are integrated by the use of a common scale of attitude toward Christianity proposed by Francis (1978a, 1978b). Previous studies in this series include the examination of age trends (Francis, 1989a); generational trends (Francis, 1989b, 1992a) and sex differences (Francis, 1989c); the influence of denominational schools (Francis, 1986), religious education syllabuses (Kay, 1981a), social class (Gibson, Francis and Pearson, 1990), parental religious example (Francis and Gibson, 1993), home stability (Kay, 1981b) and religious broadcasting (Francis and Gibson, 1992); the relationship with extraversion (Francis, Pearson, Carter and Kay, 1981), neuroticism (Francis and Pearson, 1991), psychoticism (Francis, 1992b), impulsivity (Pearson, Francis and Lightbown, 1986), empathy (Francis and Pearson, 1987), openness (Greer, 1985), moral values (Francis and Greer, 1990a), gender orientation (Francis and Wilcox, 1995) and happiness (Francis, Wilcox and Jones, 1995). No previous study in this series has examined the relationship between attitude toward Christianity and self-esteem. The present paper addresses this lacuna by reporting on three separate studies conducted among adolescents aged between fifteen and sixteen years, aged between thirteen and fourteen years and children aged between eight and eleven years.

Method

Samples

Study one involved 642 year eleven pupils, between the ages of fifteen and sixteen years, drawn from one Roman Catholic, one Church of England and two non-denominational secondary schools in England. The sample comprised 314 boys and 328 girls. Since this study involved two church schools, a higher proportion of pupils were regular churchgoers: 24% attended church weekly, while only 10% never attended church.

Study two involved 755 year nine pupils, between the ages of thirteen and fourteen years, drawn from seven non-denominational secondary schools in Wales. The sample comprised 365 boys and

390 girls. Weekly church attendance was reported by 15% of the pupils, while 36% never attended church.

Study three involved 166 pupils from years four, five and six, between the ages of eight and eleven years, drawn from two non-denominational and one Church of England primary school in England. The sample comprised 82 boys and 84 girls. Weekly church attendance was reported by 13% of the sample, while 45% never attended church.

Measures

All three groups of pupils completed the Francis Scale of Attitude Toward Christianity (Francis, 1978a). This is a 24 item instrument concerned with assessing an affective response to five key areas of the Christian tradition: God, Jesus, bible, prayer and church. Each item is assessed on a five point scale: agree strongly, agree, not certain, disagree and disagree strongly. A series of studies concerned with reliability and validity of this scale commend its use between the ages of eight and sixteen years (Francis, 1987, 1989a; Francis and Greer, 1990b; Gibson, 1989; Gibson and Francis, 1989; Greer and Francis, 1991).

In study one self-esteem was assessed by the Lipsitt Self-Concept Scale (Lipsitt, 1958). This is a 22 item instrument scored on a five point scale: agree strongly, agree, not certain, disagree and disagree strongly. While originally designed for use among children between the ages of nine and eleven years, a series of studies has demonstrated the usefulness of the instrument among older subjects (Francis, Carter and Jones, 1995). In studies two and three, self-esteem was assessed by the short form of the Coopersmith Self-Esteem Inventory (Coopersmith, 1981). This is a 25 item instrument scored on a two point scale: yes and no.

Data analysis

The data were analysed by means of the SPSS statistical package, employing the reliability, Pearson correlation and partial correlation routines (SPSS Inc., 1988).

Results

Table 10.1 examines the internal reliability of the scales of attitude toward Christianity and self-esteem in terms of the alpha coefficient (Cronbach, 1951), for the three studies separately. These data confirm the reliability of the instruments.

Table 10.1
Alpha coefficients for scales of attitude toward Christianity and self-esteem

	study 1	study 2	study 3
attitude toward Christianity	0.9655	0.9678	0.9382
self-esteem	0.8394	0.8073	0.7434

Table 10.2 presents the Pearson correlation coefficients for attitude toward Christianity with sex, self-esteem with sex, and attitude toward Christianity with self-esteem, for the three studies separately. Table 10.2 also presents the partial correlation coefficients for attitude toward Christianity with self-esteem controlling for sex. These data demonstrate that girls record a more positive attitude toward Christianity than boys in all three studies. Girls record a higher self-esteem than boys in study one, while boys record a higher self-esteem than girls in studies two and three. After controlling for sex differences, there is a positive relationship between attitude toward Christianity and self-esteem in all three studies.

Table 10.2
Correlations between attitude towards Christianity, self-esteem and sex

	study 1	study 2	study 3
attitude with sex	+0.2447	+0.0867	+0.1551
	.001	.01	.05
self-esteem with sex	+0.1238	−0.2078	−0.2291
	.01	.001	.001
attitude with self-esteem	+0.2217	+0.0595	+0.1397
	.001	NS	NS
attitude with self-esteem by sex	+0.1990	+0.0804	+0.1797
	.001	.01	.01

Discussion

Four main issues emerge from these data.

First, it is clear that measures of esteem may unintentionally discriminate in favour of one sex rather than the other. Moreover, the direction of this discrimination may vary from one measure of self-esteem to another. The data from study one demonstrate that girls recorded a higher score on the Lipsitt Self-Concept Scale than boys. This is consistent with the findings of many studies using this instrument, including Reese (1961), Bledsoe (1964), Fields (1981), Barnes and Farrier (1985) and Francis, Carter and Jones (1995). Other studies, however, have failed to find any significant differences between the scores of boys and girls on the Lipsitt Self-Concept Scale, including Lipsitt (1958) and Mayer (1966). The data from studies two and three demonstrate that boys recorded a higher score on the Coopersmith Self-Esteem Inventory than girls. This is consistent with the findings of many studies using this instrument, including Weinland, Gable and Varming (1976), Cowan, Altmann and Pysh (1978), Marron and Kayson (1984) and Joubert (1991). Other studies, however, have failed to find any significant differences between the scores of boys and girls on the Coopersmith Self-Esteem Inventory, including Craske (1988), Gill and Thornton (1989), Workman and Beer (1989) and Kelti-kangas-Järvinen (1992). Whether boys record a higher level of self-esteem than girls, or girls record a higher level of self-esteem than boys seems, at least in part, to be a function of the scale employed.

Second, there is a well established consensus in the literature that girls and women are more religious than boys and men, although there is considerably less consensus regarding why this should be the case (Kay and Francis, 1995). The data from all three studies demonstrate that the girls recorded a higher score on the Francis Scale of Attitude Toward Christianity than boys. This is consistent with a great deal of previous research using this instrument in England (Francis, 1989a), Northern Ireland (Francis and Greer, 1990b), Scotland (Gibson, 1989), Eire (Kay, 1981c) and Kenya (Fulljames and Francis, 1987).

Third, in view of the finding that there are significant sex differences in relationship to both self-esteem and attitude toward Christianity, it is necessary to take these differences into account when exploring the relationship between self-esteem and attitude toward Christianity. If girls record higher scores than boys on both self-esteem and attitude toward Christianity, these sex differences may magnify any apparent relationship between self-esteem and attitude toward Christianity. If, on the other hand, girls record higher scores than boys on the measure of attitude toward Christianity, but lower scores than boys on the measure of self-esteem, these sex differences may disguise any real relationship between self-esteem and Christianity. The data from studies two and three, which employ the Coopersmith Self-Esteem Inventory and portray girls as recording a lower level of self-esteem than boys, demonstrate that no significant relationship emerges between attitude and self-esteem according to the Pearson correlation coefficient. However, once sex differences are partialled out, the partial correlation coefficient identifies a small, but significant positive correlation between attitude toward Christianity and self-esteem.

Fourth, after taking sex differences into account, all three studies demonstrate a small but statistically significant correlation between attitude toward Christianity and self-esteem. Although not large, in each case these correlations are of comparable magnitude to the correlations reported between sex and attitude toward Christianity. This finding is consistent with the view that Christianity promotes a positive view of self during childhood and adolescence rather than detracts from a positive view of self. This finding is also consistent with a wider body of research employing the Francis Scale of Attitude Toward Christianity which suggests that during childhood and adolescence Christianity is associated with a range of positive psychological correlates, including empathy (Francis and Pearson, 1987) and happiness (Francis, Wilcox and Jones, 1995).

Further replication studies are now needed to test the security of this finding regarding the positive relationship between self-esteem and attitude toward Christianity among other age groups, in other cultural contexts, and employing other indices of self-esteem.

References

Allen, R.O. and Spilka, B. (1967), Committed and consensual religion: a specification of religion-prejudice relationships, *Journal for the Scientific Study of Religion*, 6, 191–206.

Allport, G.W. and Ross, J.M. (1967), Personal religious orientation and prejudice, *Journal of Personality and Social Psychology*, 5, 432–443.

Allport, G.W., Vernon, P. and Lindzey, G. (1960), *A Study of Values*, Boston, Houghton Mifflin.

Aycock, D.W. and Noaker, S. (1985), A comparison of the self-esteem levels in evangelical Christian and general populations, *Journal of Psychology and Theology*, 13, 199–208.

Bahr, H.M. and Martin, T.K. (1983), 'And thy neighbour as thy self': self-esteem and faith in people as correlates of religiosity and family solidarity among Middletown high school students, *Journal for the Scientific Study of Religion*, 22, 132–144.

Barnes, M.E. and Farrier, S.C. (1985), A longitudinal study of the self-concept of low income youth, *Adolescence*, 20, 199–205.

Batson, C.D. and Ventis, W.L. (1982), *The Religious Experience: a social psychological perspective*, New York, Oxford University Press.

Beit-Hallahmi, B. and Nevo, B. (1987), Jews in Israel: the dynamics of an identity change, *International Journal of Psychology*, 22, 75–81.

Benson, P.L. and Spilka, B.P. (1973), God-image as a function of self-esteem and locus of control, *Journal for the Scientific Study of Religion*, 12, 297–310.

Bledsoe, J.C. (1964), Self-concepts of children and their intelligence, achievement, interests, and anxiety, *Journal of Individual Psychology*, 20, 55–58.

Brown, L.B. (1962), A study of religious belief, *British Journal of Psychology*, 53, 259–272.

Brownfain, J.J. (1952), Stability of the self-concept as a dimension of personality, *Journal of Abnormal Social Psychology*, 47, 597–606.

Coopersmith, S. (1967), *The Antecedents of Self-Esteem*, San Francisco, Freeman.

Coopersmith, S. (1981), *Self-Esteem Inventories*, Palo Alto, California, Consulting Psychologists Press.

Cowan, R., Altmann, H. and Pysh, F. (1978), A validity study of selected self-concept instruments, *Measurement and Evaluation in Guidance*, 10, 211–221.

Cowen, E.L. (1954), The negative self-concept as a personality measure, *Journal of Consulting Psychology*, 18, 138–142.

Craske, M.L. (1988), Learned helplessness, self-worth motivation and attribution retraining for primary school children, *British Journal of Educational Psychology*, 58, 152–164.

Cronbach, L.J. (1951), Coefficient alpha and the internal structure of tests, *Psychometrika*, 16, 297–334.

Fehr, L.A. and Heintzelman, M.E. (1977), Personality and attitude correlates of religiosity: source of controversy, *Journal of Psychology*, 95, 63–66.

Fields, A.B. (1981), Perceived parent behaviour and the self-evaluations of lower class black male and female children, *Adolescence*, 16, 919–934.

Forst, E. and Healy, R.M. (1990), Relationship between self-esteem and religious faith, *Psychological Reports*, 67, 378.

Francis, L.J. (1978a), Attitude and longitude: a study in measurement, *Character Potential*, 8, 119–130.

Francis, L.J. (1978b), Measurement reapplied: research into the child's attitude towards religion, *British Journal of Religious Education*, 1, 45–51.

Francis, L.J. (1986), Denominational schools and pupil attitudes towards Christianity, *British Educational Research Journal*, 12, 145–152.

Francis, L.J. (1987), Measuring attitudes towards Christianity among 12- to 18-year-old pupils in Catholic schools, *Educational Research*, 29, 230–233.

Francis, L.J. (1989a), Measuring attitude towards Christianity during childhood and adolescence, *Personality and Individual Differences*, 10, 695–698.

Francis, L.J. (1989b), Monitoring changing attitudes towards Christianity among secondary school pupils between 1974 and 1986, *British Journal of Educational Psychology*, 59, 86–91.

Francis, L.J. (1989c), Drift from the churches: secondary school pupils' attitudes towards Christianity, *British Journal of Religious Education*, 11, 76–86.

Francis, L.J. (1992a), Monitoring attitudes towards Christianity: the 1990 study, *British Journal of Religious Education*, 14, 178–182.

Francis, L.J. (1992b), Is psychoticism really a dimension of personality fundamental to religiosity? *Personality and Individual Differences*, 13, 645–652.

Francis, L.J., Carter, M. and Jones, S.H. (1995), The properties of the Lipsitt Self-Concept Scale in relationship to sex, social desirability, neuroticism and extraversion, *Personality and Individual Differences*, in press.

Francis, L.J. and Gibson, H.M. (1992), Popular religious television and adolescent attitudes towards Christianity, in J. Astley and D.V. Day (eds), *The Contours of Christian Education*, pp. 369–381, Great Wakering, McCrimmons.

Francis, L.J. and Gibson, H.M. (1993), Parental influence and adolescent religiosity: a study of church attendance and attitude towards Christianity among 11–12 and 15–16 year olds, *International Journal for the Psychology of Religion*, 3, 241–253.

Francis, L.J. and Greer, J.E. (1990a), Catholic schools and adolescent religiosity in Northern Ireland: shaping moral values, *Irish Journal of Education*, 24, 2, 40–47.

Francis, L.J. and Greer, J.E. (1990b), Measuring attitudes towards Christianity among pupils in Protestant secondary schools in Northern Ireland, *Personality and Individual Differences*, 11, 853–856.

Francis, L.J. and Pearson, P.R. (1987), Empathic development during adolescence: religiosity the missing link? *Personality and Individual Differences*, 8, 145–148.

Francis, L.J. and Pearson, P.R. (1991), Religiosity, gender and the two faces of neuroticism, *Irish Journal of Psychology*, 12, 60–68.

Francis, L.J., Pearson, P.R., Carter, M. and Kay, W.K. (1981), Are introverts more religious? *British Journal of Social Psychology*, 20, 101–104.

Francis, L.J. and Wilcox, C. (1995), Religion and gender orientation, *Personality and Individual Differences*, in press.

Francis, L.J., Wilcox, C. and Jones, S.H. (1995), Religiosity and happiness: a study among 15–16 year olds in England, in press.

Frankel, B.G. and Hewitt, W.E. (1994), Religion and well-being among Canadian university students: the role of faith groups on campus, *Journal for the Scientific Study of Religion*, 33, 62–73.

Fritts, W.H. (1976), *Manual for the Tennessee Self-Concept Scale*, Nashville, Tennessee, Counsellor Recordings and Tests.

Fulljames, P. and Francis, L.J. (1987), The measurement of attitudes towards Christianity among Kenyan secondary school students, *Journal of Social Psychology*, 127, 407–409.

Gibson, H.M. (1989), Measuring attitudes towards Christianity among 11–16 year old pupils in non-denominational schools in Scotland, *Educational Research*, 31, 221–227.

Gibson, H.M. and Francis, L.J. (1989), Measuring attitudes towards Christianity among 11-to 16- year old pupils in Catholic schools in Scotland, *Educational Research*, 31, 65–69.

Gibson, H.M., Francis, L.J. and Pearson, P.R. (1990), The relationship between social class and attitude towards Christianity among fourteen-and fifteen-year-old adolescents, *Personality and Individual Differences*, 11, 631–635.

Gill, N.T. and Thornton, L.H. (1989), Religious orientation and self-esteem among high school students, *High School Journal*, 73, 1, 47–60.

Glock, C.Y. and Stark, R. (1965), *Religion and Society in Tension*, Chicago, Rand McNally.

Gorsuch, R.L. and Venable, G.D. (1983), Development of an 'Age Universal' I-E scale, *Journal for the Scientific Study of Religion*, 22, 181–187.

Greer, J.E. (1985), Viewing 'the other side' in Northern Ireland: openness and attitude to religion among Catholic and Protestant Adolescents, *Journal for the Scientific Study of Religion*, 24, 275–292.

Greer, J.E. and Francis, L.J. (1991), Measuring attitudes towards Christianity among pupils in Catholic secondary schools in Northern Ireland, *Educational Research*, 33, 70–73.

Hanawalt, N.G. (1963), Feelings of security and self-esteem in relation to religious belief, *Journal of Social Psychology*, 59, 347–353.

Heintzelman, M.E. and Fehr, L.A. (1976), Relationship between religious orthodoxy and three personality variables, *Psychological Reports*, 38, 756–758.

Hofman, J.E., Beit-Hallahmi, B. and Lazarowitz, R. (1982), Self-descriptors of Jewish and Arab adolescents in Israel: a factor study, *Journal of Personality and Social Psychology*, 43, 786–792.

Joubert, C.E. (1991), Relationship of liking of one's given names to self-esteem and social desirability, *Psychological Reports*, 69, 821–822.

Kay, W.K. (1981a), Syllabuses and attitudes to Christianity, *Irish Catechist*, 5, 2, 16–21.

Kay, W.K. (1981b), Marital happiness and children's attitudes to religion, *British Journal of Religious Education*, 3, 102–105.

Kay, W.K. (1981c), Religious thinking, attitudes and personality amongst secondary pupils in England and Ireland, Unpublished Ph.D. dissertation, University of Reading.

Kay, W.K. and Francis, L.J. (1995), *Drift from the Churches: attitude toward Christianity during childhood and adolescence*, Cardiff, University of Wales Press.

Keltikangas-Järvinen, L. (1992), Self-esteem as a predictor of future school achievement, *European Journal of Psychology of Education*, 7, 123–130.

Krause, N. and van Tran, T. (1989), Stress and religious involvement among older blacks, *Journal of Gerontology*, 44, S4–S13.

Lipsitt, L.P. (1958), A self-concept scale for children and its relationship to the children's form of the Manifest Anxiety Scale, *Child Development*, 29, 463–472.

McAllister, E.W.C. (1982), The self-concept structure of evangelical / fundamentalist ministry, *Journal of Psychology and Christianity*, 1, 14–20.

Marron, J.A. and Kayson, W.A. (1984), Effects of living status, gender and year in college on college students' self-esteem and life change experiences, *Psychological Reports*, 55, 811–814.

Maslow, A.H. (1942), *Social Personality Inventory for College Women*, Stanford California, Stanford University Press.

Matheny, K.B., Curlette, W., Aycock, D.W., Pugh, J.L. and Taylor, H.F. (1981), Coping Resources Inventory for Stress, Unpublished manuscript, Georgia State University, Atlanta, Department of Counselling and Psychological Services.

Mayer, C.L. (1966), The relationship of early special class placement and the self-concepts of mentally handicapped children, *Exceptional Children*, 33, 77–81.

Meisenhelder, J.B. (1986), Self-esteem in women: the influence of employment and perception of husband's appraisals, *Image Journal of Nursing Scholarship*, 18, 8–14.

Moore, K. and Stoner, S. (1977), Adolescent self-reports and religiosity, *Psychological Reports*, 41, 55–56.

Nelson, P.B. (1990), Religious orientation of the elderly: relationship to depression and self esteem, *Journal of Gerontological Nursing*, 16, 2, 29–35.

Pearlin, L.I. and Schooler, C. (1978), The structure of coping, *Journal of Health and Social Behaviour*, 19, 2–21.

Pearson, P.R., Francis, L.J. and Lightbown, T.J. (1986), Impulsivity and religiosity, *Personality and Individual Differences*, 7, 89–94.

Reese, H.W. (1961), Relationships between self-acceptance and sociometric choices, *Journal of Abnormal and Social Psychology*, 62, 472–474.

Rosenberg, M. (1965), *Society and the Adolescent Self-image*, Princeton, New Jersey, Princeton University Press.

Smith, C.B., Weigert, A.J. and Thomas, D.L. (1979), Self-esteem and religiosity: an analysis of Catholic adolescents from five cultures, *Journal for the Scientific Study of Religion*, 18, 51–60.

Spilka, B., Addison, J. and Rosensohn, M. (1975), Parents, self and God: a test of competing theories of individual-religion relationships, *Review of Religious Research*, 16, 154–165.

Spilka, B. and Mullin, M. (1977), Personal religion and psychological schemata: a research approach to a theological psychology of religion, *Character Potential*, 8, 57–66.

SPSS Inc. (1988), *SPSSX User's Guide*, New York, McGraw-Hill.

Strunk, O. (1958a), Note on self-reports and religiosity, *Psychological Reports*, 4, 29.

Strunk, O. (1958b), Relationship between self-reports and adolescent religiosity, *Psychological Reports*, 4, 683–686.

Wade, T.J., Thompson, V.I., Tashakkori, A. and Valente, E. (1989), A longitudinal analysis of sex by race differences in predictors of adolescent self-esteem, *Personality and Individual Differences*, 10, 717–779.

Watson, P.J., Hood, R.W., Morris, R.J., and Hall, J.R. (1985), Religiosity, sin and self-esteem, *Journal of Psychology and Theology*, 13, 116–128.

Watson, P.J., Morris, R.J. and Hood, R.W. (1987), Antireligious humanistic values, guilt and self-esteem, *Journal for the Scientific Study of Religion*, 26, 535–546.

Weinland, T.P., Gable, R.K. and Varming, O. (1976), Self-concept: a cross cultural study, *Perceptual and Motor Skills*, 42, 43–46.

Wickstrom, D.L. and Fleck, J.R. (1983), Missionary children: correlates of self-esteem and dependency, *Journal of Psychology and Theology*, 11, 226–235.

Workman, M. and Beer, J. (1989), Self-esteem, depression, and alcohol dependency among high school students, *Psychological Reports*, 65, 451–455.

11

Are religious people happier? a study among undergraduates

Mandy Robbins and Leslie J. Francis

Summary

A sample of 360 first year undergraduate students completed the Oxford Happiness Inventory and the Francis Scale of Attitude Toward Christianity, together with the short form Revised Eysenck Personality Questionnaire. The data demonstrate a positive correlation between happiness and religiosity.

Introduction

Conflicting traditions in the psychology of religion have advanced very different views regarding the relationship between religion and psychological wellbeing in its broadest sense (Wulff, 1991). While some strands see religion as promoting psychological wellbeing, other strands see religion as detracting from it. Psychological wellbeing itself, however, is a complex phenomenon involving both positive and negative affect (Bradburn, 1969; Strack, Argyle and Schwarz, 1991). The positive aspect of wellbeing is reflected in the recent emphasis in social psychology on the psychology of happiness as pioneered by Michael Argyle (1987).

Empirical evidence regarding the relationship between religion and happiness is scarce, due largely to the absence, until recently, of adequate instrumentation to assess happiness properly grounded in psychological theory. The recent development of the Oxford Happiness Inventory by Argyle, Martin and Crossland (1989) now provides a much more adequate theoretical discussion of the nature of happiness and an appropriate measure of this construct.

Argyle and Crossland (1987) suggest that happiness comprises three components: the frequency and degree of positive affect or joy; the average level of satisfaction over a period; and the absence of negative feelings, such as depression and anxiety. Working from this definition, they developed the Oxford Happiness Inventory by reversing the 21 items of the Beck Depression Inventory (Beck, Ward, Mendelson, Hock and Erbaugh, 1961) and adding eleven further items to cover aspects of subjective wellbeing not so far included. Three items were subsequently dropped, leading to a 29 item scale. The test constructors report an internal reliability of 0.90 and a seven week test-retest reliability of 0.78. Validity was established against happiness ratings by friends and by correlations with measures of positive affect, negative affect and life satisfaction.

A series of studies employing the Oxford Happiness Inventory in a range of different ways has confirmed the basic reliability and validity of the instrument and begun to map the correlates of this operational definition of happiness (Argyle, Martin and Lu, 1995). For example, Argyle and Lu (1990b) found that social competence was a significant predictor of happiness in a study among 63 adults. Lu and Argyle (1991) found that social skills and cooperativeness were significant predictors of happiness in a study among 114 adults. Lu and Argyle (1992) found that happiness was predicted by satisfaction with relationships with people from whom support had been received in a study among 65 adults. Lu and Argyle (1993) found an inverse relationship between happiness and the total time spent watching television, while Lu and Argyle (1994) found that happiness was positively correlated with engagement in a serious leisure activity. Other studies have reported significant relationships between happiness and self-esteem (Lu and Argyle, 1991), coping styles (Rim, 1993) and locus of control (Noor, 1993).

A set of four studies using the Oxford Happiness Inventory has begun to chart the relationship between happiness and Eysenck's model of personality which maintains that individual differences can be most economically and adequately summarised in terms of the three orthogonal dimensions of extraversion, neuroticism and psychoticism (Eysenck and Eysenck, 1985). These studies, conducted among samples of 131 undergraduates (Argyle and Lu, 1990a), 101 students (Furnham and Brewin, 1990), 114 adults (Lu and Argyle, 1991) and 95 students (Brebner, Donaldson, Kirby and Ward, 1995) have demonstrated that happiness is correlated positively with extraversion, correlated negatively with neuroticism, and uncorrelated with psychoticism. This pattern of relationships between personality and happiness stands in stark contrast with the pattern of relationships generally established between personality and religiosity. For example, a set of studies conducted among school pupils (Francis, 1992a; Francis and Montgomery, 1992) and among undergraduates (Francis, 1993; Francis, Lewis, Brown, Philipchalk and Lester, 1995) has demonstrated that, while religiosity is correlated with neither extraversion nor neuroticism, there is a significant negative correlation between psychoticism and religiosity.

The aim of the present study, therefore, was to explore the relationship between personality, religion and happiness among a sample of undergraduate students.

Method

Sample

A sample of 360 undergraduates participated in the study as part of the induction programme during their first week at college in Wales. The sample comprised 98 males and 262 females; 256 were under the age of twenty, 77 were in their twenties, and 27 were aged thirty years or over. Nearly a fifth of the respondents (18.6%) reported weekly church attendance, while 8.9% attended church at least once a month, 29.2% attended several times a year, 20.0% attended once or twice a year, and 23.3% never attend church.

Measures

The Oxford Happiness Inventory (Argyle, Martin and Crossland, 1989) is a 29 item multiple choice instrument. Each item contains four options. The respondents are asked to 'pick out the one statement in each group which best describes the way you have been feeling over the past week, including today'.

The Francis Scale of Attitude Toward Christianity (Francis and Stubbs, 1987) is a 24 item Likert type instrument, employing a five point response scale ranging from *agree strongly*, through *agree*, *not certain* and *disagree*, to *disagree strongly*, which has been shown to function reliably and validly in Britain, Ireland, the United States of America, Canada and Australia (Francis, 1992b; Maltby, 1994; Francis, Lewis, Philipchalk, Brown and Lester, 1995).

The short form Revised Eysenck Personality Questionnaire (Eysenck, Eysenck and Barrett, 1985) is a 48 item instrument, employing a dichotomous scale (yes and no) and producing four twelve item indices of extraversion, neuroticism, psychoticism and a lie scale. The instrument has been shown to function reliably and validly in England, the United States of America, Canada and Australia (Francis, Philipchalk and Brown, 1991).

Analysis

The data were analysed by means of the SPSS statistical package, using the reliability, correlation and breakdown routines (SPSS Inc., 1988).

Results

Table 11.1 presents the alpha reliability coefficients (Cronbach, 1951) for all six measures employed in the study. All scales reach a

Table 11.1
Reliability coefficients and mean scores by sex

scales	alpha	male mean	sd	female mean	sd	F	P<
Oxford Happiness Inventory	0.8903	38.7	10.9	39.7	10.2	0.7	NS
attitude toward Christianity	0.9729	76.6	24.7	84.5	18.5	10.6	.001
extraversion	0.8647	7.9	3.4	8.8	3.5	4.8	.05
neuroticism	0.7795	6.6	3.3	6.7	3.0	0.1	NS
psychoticism	0.5763	3.2	2.0	1.9	1.6	36.6	.001
lie scale	0.7437	3.1	2.7	3.9	2.6	6.7	.01

satisfactory level of internal consistency. The alpha coefficient reported by the psychoticism scale is consistent with the greater problems still associated with measuring this dimension of personality (Francis, Philipchalk and Brown, 1991). Table 11.1 also presents the mean scores for males and females separately recorded on all six measures. The major difference between the sexes in relationship to the personality variables concerns the dimension of psychoticism, which is consistent with Eysenck's underlying theoretical basis for their construct (Eysenck and Eysenck, 1976). In line with a number of other studies the females record a significantly higher score on the Francis Scale of Attitude Toward Christianity (Francis, 1989; Gibson, 1989; Greer and Francis, 1991; Francis and Wilcox, 1995). On the other hand, there are no significant sex differences in relationship to scores on the Oxford Happiness Inventory. This is consistent with previous findings reported by Argyle and Lu (1990a), Furnham and Brewin (1990) and Lu and Argyle (1991, 1992, 1993), although Argyle and Lu (1990b) reported higher scores among females in their sample.

Table 11.2 presents the Pearson product moment correlation coefficients between psychoticism, extraversion, neuroticism, the

Table 11.2
Correlation Matrix

	L	P	N	E	C
Oxford Happiness Inventory	+0.1796 .001	−0.0507 NS	−0.4443 .001	+0.5003 .001	+0.2590 .001
attitude toward Christianity	+0.1462 .01	−0.2979 .001	−0.0092 NS	+0.0743 NS	
extraversion	−0.0875 NS	+0.0045 NS	−0.3038 .001		
neuroticism	−0.1531 .01	−0.0411 NS			
psychoticism	−0.2502 .001				

lie scale, attitude toward Christianity and happiness. Three main findings emerge from these data. First, happiness is correlated positively with extraversion, correlated negatively with neuroticism, and uncorrelated with psychoticism. This is totally consistent with the pattern of relationships identified by Argyle and Lu (1990),

Furnham and Brewin (1990), Lu and Argyle (1991) and Brebner, Donaldson, Kirby and Ward (1995). Second, attitude toward Christianity is uncorrelated with extraversion, uncorrelated with neuroticism, and negatively correlated with psychoticism. This is totally consistent with the pattern of relationships identified by Francis (1992a, 1993), Francis and Montgomery (1992) and Francis, Lewis, Brown, Philipchalk and Lester (1995). Third, there is a significant positive correlation between attitude toward Christianity and happiness.

In order to confirm that the relationship between attitude toward Christianity and happiness was not contaminated by the variables of sex and personality, a multiple regression equation was calculated to take into account the influence of sex, extraversion, neuroticism, psychoticism, and the lie scale scores before examining the influence of religiosity on happiness scores. The results of this equation presented in table 11.3 confirm the significant positive

Table 11.3
Multiple regression significance test

predictor variables	R^2	change in R^2	F of change	P<	Beta	T	P<
sex	0.0021	0.0021	0.8	NS	−0.0400	−0.9	NS
extraversion	0.2430	0.2409	118.4	.001	+0.4158	+9.7	.001
neuroticism	0.3419	0.0989	55.7	.001	−0.2988	−6.7	.001
psychoticism	0.3466	0.0047	2.7	NS	+0.0157	+0.3	NS
lie scale	0.3707	0.0241	14.1	.001	+0.1532	+3.6	.001
attitude toward Christianity	0.4024	0.0318	19.6	.001	+0.1884	+4.4	.001

relationship between attitude toward Christianity and happiness, and demonstrate that this relationship is independent of individual differences in personality. The beta weights demonstrate that the happiest individuals are religious stable extraverts, while the least happy individuals are irreligious neurotic introverts.

Discussion

These new data provide clear evidence for a significant positive relationship between religiosity and happiness, among undergraduate students in Wales, using a well tested measure of happiness adequately grounded in psychological theory. This finding is consistent with the results from a number of other studies using less adequate measures of happiness. For example, in an early study, conducted among 108 men and 102 women over the age of sixty-five in the United States of America, O'Reilly (1957) assessed happiness on a three point continuum (very happy, moderately happy and less happy) alongside reported church attendance. He found that 55% of the very happy respondents were active in the practice of their religion, compared with 47% of the moderately happy and 44% of the less happy. Wilson (1965) assessed happiness on a ten point scale, from 1 (completely and utterly unhappy; terrible depression and gloom all of the time) to 10 (completely and supremely happy; tremendous joy and elation all of the time), alongside a five point index of religious commitment. He found a positive correlation of 0.33 between the two indices. In a study conducted among 225 elderly people in the United States of America, reported by Zuckerman, Kasl and Ostfeld (1984), the interviewers assess the respondents on a five point scale, which was subsequently collapsed into two categories (happy and not happy). This study reported a positive correlation between happiness and religiosity, assessed by summing three questions concerned with frequency of church attendance, self-assessed degree of religiousness and degree of comfort derived from religion.

Reanalysing data from the 1984 National Opinion Research Centre Survey, Reed (1991) explored the relationship between happiness and strength of religious affiliation among 1,473 respondents. Religious affiliation was divided into two categories (strong and weak), while happiness was assessed in three categories (very happy, pretty happy and not too happy). The data demonstrate a significant positive relationship between self-reported strength of religious affiliation and happiness. Reanalysing data from the General Social Survey in the United States of America, Ellison (1991) assessed happiness on a three point continuum (not too happy, pretty happy and very happy) alongside a range of religious variables. He reported a significant positive relationship between firm religious beliefs and happiness.

Other studies reporting a positive relationship between religiosity and a variety of measures of happiness include Graney (1975),

Cutler (1976), Balswick and Balkwell (1979) and Frankel and Hewitt (1994).

Less clear cut results, however, are reported in another set of studies, including Blazer and Palmore (1970), McNamara and St George (1978), Shaver, Lenauer and Sadd (1980), Yates, Chalmer, St James, Follansbee and McKegney (1981), Tellis-Nayak (1982), Heisel and Faulkner (1982) and Poloma and Pendleton (1989, 1990, 1991). These studies suggest that the relationship between religiosity and happiness may vary according to the measures of religiosity employed and the samples studied. It is important now, therefore, that the present study should be replicated. The Oxford Happiness Inventory now needs to be employed alongside a wider range of indices of religiosity and among samples which differ in terms of such factors as cultural context, social class and age.

References

Argyle, M. (1987), *The Psychology of Happiness*, London, Routledge.

Argyle, M. and Crossland, J. (1987), Dimensions of positive emotions, *British Journal of Social Psychology*, 26, 127–137.

Argyle, M. and Lu, L. (1990a), The happiness of extraverts, *Personality and Individual Differences*, 11, 1011–1017.

Argyle, M. and Lu, L. (1990b), Happiness and social skills, *Personality and Individual Differences*, 11, 1255–1261.

Argyle, M., Martin, M. and Crossland, J. (1989), Happiness as a function of personality and social encounters, in J.P. Forgas and J.M. Innes (eds), *Recent Advances in Social Psychology: an international perspective*, pp. 189–203, North Holland, Elsevier Science Publishers.

Argyle, M., Martin, M. and Lu, L. (1995), Testing for stress and happiness: the role of social and cognitive factors, in C.D. Spielberger and J. Brebner (eds), *Testing for Stress and Happiness: the role of social factors*, pp. 173–187, New York, Taylor and Francis.

Balswick, J.O. and Balkwell, J.W. (1978), Religious orthodoxy and emotionality, *Review of Religious Research*, 19, 308–319.

Beck, T., Ward, C.H., Mendelson, M., Hock, J. and Erbaugh, J. (1961), An inventory for measuring depression, *Archives of General Psychiatry*, 7, 158–216.

Blazer, D. and Palmore, E. (1976), Religion and aging in a longitudinal panel, *The Gerontologist*, 16, 82–85.

Bradburn, N.M. (1969), *The Structure of Psychological Well-being*, Chicago, Aldine.

Brebner, J., Donaldson, J., Kirby, N. and Ward, L. (1995), Relationships between happiness and personality, *Personality and Individual Differences*, 19, 251–258.

Cronbach, L.J. (1951), Coefficient alpha and the internal structure of tests, *Psychometrika*, 16, 297–334.

Cutler, S.J. (1976), Membership in different types of voluntary associations and psychological well-being, *The Gerontologist*, 16, 335–339.

Ellison, C.G. (1991), Religious involvement and subjective well-being, *Journal of Health and Social Behaviour*, 32, 80–99.

Eysenck, H.J. and Eysenck, M.W. (1985), *Personality and Individual Differences: a natural science approach*, New York, Plenum Press.

Eysenck, H.J. and Eysenck, S.B.G. (1976), *Psychoticism as a Dimension of Personality*, London, Hodder and Stoughton.

Eysenck, S.B.G., Eysenck, H.J. and Barrett, P. (1985), A revised version of the psychoticism scale, *Personality and Individual Differences*, 6, 21–29.

Francis, L.J. (1992a), Is psychoticism really a dimension of personality fundamental to religiosity? *Personality and Individual Differences*, 13, 645–652.

Francis, L.J. (1992b), Reliability and validity of the Francis scale of attitude towards Christianity (adult), *Panorama*, 4, 1, 17–19.

Francis, L.J. (1993), Personality and religion among college students in the UK, *Personality and Individual Differences*, 14, 619–622.

Francis, L.J., Lewis, J.M., Brown, L.B., Philipchalk, R. and Lester, D. (1995), Personality and religion among undergraduate students in the United Kingdom, United States, Australia and Canada, *Journal of Psychology and Christianity*, 14, 250–262.

Francis, L.J., Lewis, J.M., Philipchalk, R., Brown, L.B., and Lester, D. (1995), The internal consistency reliability and construct validity of the Francis scale of attitude towards Christianity (adult) among undergraduate students in the United Kingdom, United States, Australia and Canada, *Personality and Individual Differences*, 19, 949–953.

Francis, L.J. and Montgomery, A. (1992), Personality and attitudes towards Christianity among eleven to sixteen year old girls in a single sex Catholic school, *British Journal of Religious Education*, 14, 114–119.

Francis, L.J., Philipchalk, R. and Brown, L.B. (1991), The comparability of the short form EPQ-R with the EPQ among students in England, the USA, Canada and Australia, *Personality and Individual Differences*, 12, 1129–1132.

Francis, L.J., and Stubbs, M.T. (1987), Measuring attitudes towards Christianity: from childhood to adulthood, *Personality and Individual Differences*, 8, 741–743.

Francis, L.J. and Wilcox, C. (1995), Religion and gender orientation, *Personality and Individual Differences*, in press.

Frankel, B.G. and Hewitt, W.E. (1994), Religion and well-being among Canadian university students: the role of faith groups on campus, *Journal for the Scientific Study of Religion*, 33, 62–73.

Furnham, A. and Brewin, C.R. (1990), Personality and happiness, *Personality and Individual Differences*, 11, 1093–1096.

Graney, M.J. (1975), Happiness and social participation in aging, *Journal of Gerontology*, 30, 701–706.

Heisel, M.A. and Faulkner, A.O. (1982), Religiosity in an old black population, *The Gerontologist*, 22, 354–358.

Lu, L. and Argyle, M. (1991), Happiness and cooperation, *Personality and Individual Differences*, 12, 1019–1030.

Lu, L. and Argyle, M. (1992), Receiving and giving support: effects on relationships and well-being, *Counselling Psychology Quarterly*, 5, 123–133.

Lu, L. and Argyle, M. (1993), TV watching, soap opera and happiness, *Kaohsiung Journal of Medical Sciences*, 9, 501–507.

Lu, L. and Argyle, M. (1994), Leisure satisfaction and happiness: a function of leisure activity, *Kaohsiung Journal of Medical Sciences*, 10, 89–96.

McNamara, P.H., St George, A. (1978), Blessed are the downtrodden? an empirical test, *Sociological Analysis*, 29, 303–320.

Maltby, J. (1994), The reliability and validity of the Francis scale of attitude towards Christianity among Republic of Ireland adults, *Irish Journal of Psychology*, 15, 595–598.

Noor, N.M. (1993), Work and family roles in relation to women's well-being, unpublished D.Phil. dissertation, University of Oxford.

O'Reilly, C.T. (1957), Religious practice and personal adjustment of older people, *Sociology and Social Research*, 42, 119–121.

Poloma, M.M. and Pendleton, B.F. (1989), Exploring types of prayer and quality of life: a research note, *Review of Religious Research*, 31, 46–53.

Poloma, M.M. and Pendleton, B.F. (1990), Religious domains and general well-being, *Social Indicators Research*, 22, 255–276.

Poloma, M.M. and Pendleton, B.F. (1991), The effects of prayer and prayer experiences on general wellbeing, *Journal of Psychology and Theology*, 19, 71–83.

Reed, K. (1991), Strength of religious affiliation and life satisfaction, *Sociological Analysis*, 52, 205–210.

Rim, Y. (1993), Happiness and coping styles, *Personality and Individual Differences*, 14, 617–618.

Shaver, Y.P., Lenauer, M.A. and Sadd, S. (1980), Religiousness, conversion and subjective well-being: the healthy-minded religion of modern American women, *American Journal of Psychiatry*, 137, 1563–1568.

SPSS Inc. (1988), *SPSSX User's Guide*, New York, McGraw-Hill.

Strack, F., Argyle, M. and Schwarz, N. (eds) (1991), *Subjective Well-being*, Oxford, Pergamon Press.

Tellis-Nayak, V. (1982), The transcendent standard: the religious ethos of the rural elderly, *The Gerontologist*, 22, 359–363.

Wilson, W.R. (1965), Relation of sexual behaviours, values and conflicts to avowed happiness, *Psychological Reports*, 17, 371–378.

Wulff, D.M. (1991), *Psychology of Religion: classic and contemporary views*, New York, John Wiley and Sons.

Yates, J.W., Chalmer, B.J., St James, P., Follansbee, M. and McKegney, F.P. (1981), Religion in patients with advanced cancer, *Medical and Paediatric Oncology*, 9, 121–128.

Zuckerman, D.M., Kasl, S. and Ostfeld, A.M. (1984), Psychosocial predictors of mortality among the elderly poor: the role of religion, well-being and social contacts, *American Journal of Epidemiology*, 119, 410–423.

12

Religiosity and obsessionality

Christopher A. Lewis

Summary

This study extends previous work examining the relationship between religiosity and obsessionality. In order to examine the generalisability of the associations, the short form of the Francis Scale of Attitude Toward Christianity was administered alongside three previously unexamined measures of obsessional personality traits among a sample of Northern Irish adults. Higher scores on the Francis Scale of Attitude Toward Christianity were associated with higher scores on each of the three measures of obsessional personality traits in the male sample, and two of the obsessional measures in the female sample. The data provide further evidence that a more positive religious attitude is associated with higher scores on measures of obsessional personality traits.

Introduction

Within the psychology of religion there is increasing interest to test established theoretical perspectives with empirical data. One such initiative is concerned with examining theories regarding the relationship between obsessive actions and religious practices derived from Freud (1953, 1959, 1961). Freud writes of the similarities between individual obsessional neuroses and the cultural aspects of religion. Freud shows that the resemblance between obsessive actions and religious practices can be demonstrated by the rituality involved in both behaviours, the guilt invoked if these actions are neglected, and the way in which these practices are carried out to the exclusion of all other behaviours.

In recent years, a growing number of studies have explored the empirical relationship between religiosity and obsessionality. These have used different measures of both religiosity and obsessionality.

From a range of interrelated studies by the author and his colleagues there begins to emerge a coherent picture that demonstrates more positive religious attitude and greater frequency of religious practice are associated with higher scores on measures of obsessional personality traits.

Neither religiosity nor obsessionality are simple or unidimensional constructs. For example, Fontana (1980) has argued there are two forms of obsessionality. The first, the obsessional personality, is characterised by obsessional traits such as orderliness, rigidity, and overemphasis upon hygiene and self control. The second, the obsessional neurotic, is characterised by obsessional symptoms such as compulsive thoughts and impulses, indecision, guilt and ritualistic behaviour. Accordingly, researchers have employed measures of both obsessional personality traits, including the Ai3 (Kline, 1971), the Sandler-Hazari Obsessionality Inventory Trait Scale (Sandler and Hazari, 1960), the Basic Character Inventory (Torgersen, 1980) and the content scored Rorschach (Masling, Rabie and Blondheim, 1967), and a measure of obsessional symptoms, the Sandler-Hazari Obsessionality Inventory Symptom Scale (Sandler and Hazari, 1960). These different measures of obsessionality have been used alongside several different measures of religiosity, including the Francis Scale of Attitude Toward Christianity (Francis and Stubbs, 1987), the Doctrinal Orthodoxy Scale (Batson and Ventis, 1982), the Quest Scale (Batson and Ventis, 1982), the Religious Orientation Scale (Allport and Ross, 1967), as well as questions concerned with belief in God, belief in afterlife, church attendance, personal prayer and personal bible reading. The findings from these studies can be best summarised by distinguishing between perspectives concerned with religious attitudes and perspectives concerned with religious practice.

First, most research has examined the association between measures of *religious attitude* and obsessionality. Data have been largely consistent in showing that a more positive religious attitude is associated with higher scores on measures of obsessional personality traits. Lewis and Maltby (1992) found a significant association between the Francis Scale of Attitude Toward Christianity and the Ai3 (males, $r = 0.28$, $p<0.01$; females, $r = 0.35$, $p<0.01$) among United Kingdom university students. This finding was replicated by Lewis and Joseph (1994a) in Northern Irish university students ($r = 0.24$, $p<0.05$). Further, Lewis (1994) found a significant association between the Francis Scale of Attitude Toward Christianity and the Sandler-Hazari Obsessional Trait Scale (males, $r = 0.23$, p<0.01; females, r = 0.40, p<0.01) among United Kingdom university students. This finding was replicated by Lewis and Maltby (1994) in United Kingdom adults (males, r = 0.41, p<0.05; females, r = 0.26, p<0.05) and by Lewis and Maltby (1995) among English female college students and English adults (sample 1, r = 0.38, p<0.01; sample 2, r = 0.50, p<0.01). Further, Juni and Fischer (1985) found a significant association between belief in God and the Ai3 (males, r = 0.15, p<0.05; females, r = 0.19, p<0.001) and belief in afterlife and the Ai3 (females, r = 0.13, p<0.05) among United States of America university students.

However, two studies have failed to report significant associations between measures of religious attitude and obsessional personality traits. Juni and Fischer (1985) found no significant association between belief in afterlife and the Ai3 in their male sample. Similarly Kaldestad (1992, 1993, 1995) found no significant association between the obsessional scale of the Basic Character Inventory and the Quest Scale, the Doctrinal Orthodoxy Scale, the Intrinsic Scale, and the Extrinsic Scale among a sample of Norwegian adults. Research findings are also consistent in showing no significant association between religious attitude and obsessional symptoms. Lewis (1994) found no significant association between the Francis Scale of Attitude Toward Christianity and the Sandler-Hazari Obsessional Symptom Scale among United Kingdom university students. This finding was replicated by Maltby, McCollam and Millar (1994) among United Kingdom adults, and by Lewis and Maltby (1995) among English college students and English adults.

Second, several recent studies have examined the association between *religious practice* and obsessionality. Data have been largely consistent in showing that more frequent religious practices, including regularity of church attendance, personal prayer, and personal bible reading are associated with higher scores on measures of obsessional personality traits. Juni and Fischer (1985) found a significant association between church attendance and the Ai3 (males, r = 0.17, p<0.01; females, r = 0.14, p<0.01), and between church attendance and a Rorschach anal measure (males, r = 0.20, p<0.05) among United States of America university students. These findings were in part replicated and extended by Lewis and Joseph (1994b) who found a significant association between church attendance and the Ai3 (males, r = 0.48, p<0.001; females, r = 0.16, p<0.05), and between church attendance and the

Sandler-Hazari Obsessional Personality Trait Scale (males, r = 0.28, p<0.05) among Northern Irish university students. In turn, these findings were extended by Lewis and Maltby (1995) who report a significant association between the Sandler-Hazari Obsessional Personality Trait Scale and measures of religious practice (females, church attendance r = 0.28, p<0.01, personal prayer r = 0.26, p.01, and personal bible reading r = 0.29, p<0.01) among Northern Irish adults.

However, three studies have failed to report significant associations between measures of religious practice and obsessionality. Juni and Fischer (1985) found no significant association between church attendance and a Rorschach anal measure in their female sample. Lewis and Joseph (1994b) found no significant association between church attendance and the Sandler-Hazari Obsessional Personality Trait measure in their female sample. Lewis and Maltby (1995) found no significant association between the Sandler-Hazari Obsessional Personality Trait Scale and measures of religious practice in their male sample.

Due to limited data the association between religious practice and obsessional symptoms is unclear. Lewis and Joseph (1994b) found a significant association between church attendance and the Sandler-Hazari Obsessional Symptom Scale in their male sample (r = 0.32, p<0.05), but not in their female sample. Lewis and Maltby (1995) report a significant association between the Sandler-Hazari Obsessional Symptom Scale and personal prayer in their male sample (r = 0.32, p<0.05). Further they report no significant associations were found between the Sandler-Hazari Obsessional Symptom Scale and church attendance and personal bible reading. Similarly, in their female sample, no significant associations were found between the Sandler-Hazari Obsessional Symptom Scale and church attendance, personal prayer, and personal bible reading.

The aim of the present study was to extend previous work that has examined the relationship between religious attitude and obsessional personality traits. In order to examine the generalisability of these associations the short form of the Francis Scale of Attitude Toward Christianity was administered alongside three previously unexamined measures of obsessional personality traits among a sample of Northern Irish adults. It was predicted that significant associations would be found between the measures in both the male and female samples.

Method

Sample

The sample consisted of 83 Northern Irish adults (39 males and 44 females), aged between seventeen and fifty-five years (mean = 25.39, s.d. = 8.2).

Questionnaires

All subjects completed the short adult form of the Francis Scale of Attitude Toward Christianity (Francis, 1993b). This is a seven item Likert-type scale concerned with attitude toward a number of religious constructs, such as, the bible, prayer, church, God and Jesus. Each item is scored on a five point scale ranging from *agree strongly* to *disagree strongly*. Scores range from 7 to 35, with higher scores on the scale indicating a more positive attitude toward Christianity. In addition, three short measures of obsessional personality traits were administered: two 5 item scales developed by Farber (1955) and Rabinowitz (1957), and an 8 item scale developed by Centers (1969). Each item is scored on a dichotomous scale: *yes* and *no*. Scores range from 0 to 5 or 0 to 8 respectively, with higher scores on the scales indicating more obsessional personality traits.

Results

Table 12.1 presents the means and standard deviations for the male and female respondents separately on the Francis Scale of Attitude Toward Christianity and the measures of obsessional personality

Table 12.1
Mean scale scores by sex

	male		female			
	mean	sd	mean	sd	t	P<
Francis Scale	23.64	9.70	25.18	5.95	−0.86	N
Farber Scale	2.54	1.19	2.34	1.22	0.75	N
Rabinowitz Scale	1.54	1.23	1.43	1.21	0.40	N
Centers Scale	4.69	1.44	4.66	1.51	0.10	N

traits. No significant gender differences were found for any of the scales.

Table 12.2 presents the correlations between attitude toward Christianity and the three measures of obsessional personality traits for males and females separately. As predicted, higher scores on the scale of attitude toward Christianity were associated with higher scores on each of the three measures of obsessional personality traits in the male sample, and two of the obsessional measures in the female sample. This is particularly persuasive considering

Table 12.2
Partial correlations controlling for age
(males above the diagonal)

	Francis Scale	Farber Scale	Rabinowitz Scale	Centers Scale
Francis Scale		+0.4814 .001	+0.2418 .05	+0.3427 .01
Farber Scale	−0.0252 NS		+0.0832 NS	+0.6671 .001
Rabinowitz Scale	+0.2587 .05	+0.1576 NS		+0.1260 NS
Centers Scale	+0.2968 .05	+0.4611 .001	+0.3002 .05	

the wide range of associations between the three measures of obsessional personality traits (ranging between 0.67 and -0.03). Given the size of the correlations it is clear that although they have some common variance, these scales are measuring different facets of obsessional personality traits. However, despite this, a consistent pattern of associations was found between the scale of attitude toward Christianity and the measures of obsessional personality traits.

Discussion

Among a sample of Northern Irish adults, higher scores on the Francis Scale of Attitude Toward Christianity were associated with higher scores on each of the three measures of obsessional personality traits in the male sample, and two of the obsessional measures in the female sample. On the basis of these and other findings it would seem that a positive religious attitude is associated with greater obsessional personality traits.

The failure to find any sex difference on the Francis Scale of Attitude Toward Christianity is consistent with the recent findings of two student samples using the 24-item version (Francis, 1993a; Lewis and Joseph, 1994a). However, such findings do contradict those with the junior version of the Francis Scale of Attitude Toward Christianity (Francis, 1978, 1989), and with the general view of the psychology of religion (Argyle and Beit-Hallahmi, 1975).

In order to extend the body of research examining the association between religiosity and obsessionality, further research is required to test the generalisability of these findings. Future studies would be wise to employ a variety of measures of both religiosity and obsessionality, and a variety of samples, including different cultures and level of religious salience.

References

Allport, G. W. and Ross, J. M. (1967), Personal religious orientation and prejudice, *Journal of Personality and Social Psychology*, 5, 432–443.

Argyle, M. and Beit-Hallahmi, B. (1975), *The Social Psychology of Religion*, London, Routledge and Kegan Paul.

Batson, C.D. and Ventis, W.L. (1982), *The Religious Experience: a social psychological perspective*, New York, Oxford University Press.

Centers, R. (1969), The anal character and social severity in attitudes, *Journal of Projective Techniques and Personality Assessment*, 33, 501–506.

Farber, M.L. (1955), The anal character and political aggression, *Journal of Abnormal and Social Psychology*, 51, 486–489.

Fontana, D. (1980), Some standardisation data for the Sandler-Hazari Obsessionality Inventory, *British Journal of Medical Psychology*, 53, 267–275.

Francis, L.J. (1978), Attitude and longitude: a study in measurement, *Character Potential*, 8, 119–130.

Francis, L.J. (1989), Measuring attitude toward Christianity during childhood and adolescence, *Personality and Individual Differences*, 10, 695–698.

Francis, L.J. (1993a), Personality and religion among college students in the UK, *Personality and Individual Differences*, 14, 619–622.

Francis, L.J. (1993b), Reliability and validity of a short scale of attitude towards Christianity among adults, *Psychological Reports*, 72, 615–618.

Francis, L.J. and Stubbs, M.T. (1987), Measuring attitudes towards Christianity: from childhood to adulthood, *Personality and Individual Differences*, 8, 741–743.

Freud, S. (1953), Totem and taboo, in J. Strachey (editor and translator), *The Standard Edition of the Complete Psychological Works of Sigmund Freud*, vol. 13, pp. 1–161, London, Hogarth Press. (Original works published 1912–1913.)

Freud, S. (1959), Obsessive acts and religious practices, in J. Strachey (editor and translator), *The Standard Edition of the Complete Psychological Works of Sigmund Freud*, vol. 9, pp. 115–127, London, Hogarth Press. (Original works published 1907.)

Freud, S. (1961), The future of an illusion, in J. Strachey (editor and translator), *The Standard Edition of the Complete Psychological Works of Sigmund Freud*, vol. 21, pp. 1–56, London, Hogarth Press. (Original works published 1927.)

Juni, S. and Fischer, R.E. (1985), Religiosity and preoedipal fixation, *Journal of Genetic Psychology*, 146, 27–35.

Kaldestad, E. (1992), Religious orientation, personality, mental health, and religious activity, *Nordic Journal of Psychiatry*, 46, 321–328.

Kaldestad, E. (1993), Letter to the editor, *Nordic Journal of Psychiatry*, 47, 305–306.

Kaldestad, E. (1995), The empirical relationships of the religious orientations to personality, *Scandinavian Journal of Psychology*, 36, 95–108.

Kline, P. (1971), *Ai3Q: an experimental manual*, Windsor, National Foundation for Educational Research.

Lewis, C.A. (1994), Religiosity and obsessionality: the relationship between Freud's 'religious practices', *Journal of Psychology*, 128, 189–196.

Lewis, C.A. and Joseph, S. (1994a), Religiosity: psychoticism and obsessionality in Northern Irish university students, *Personality and Individual Differences*, 17, 685–687.

Lewis, C.A. and Joseph, S. (1994b), Obsessive actions and religious practices, *Journal of Psychology*, 128, 699–700.

Lewis, C.A. and Maltby, J. (1992), Religiosity and preoedipal fixation: a refinement, *Journal of Psychology*, 126, 687–688.

Lewis, C.A. and Maltby, J. (1994), Religious attitudes and obsessional personality traits among UK adults, *Psychological Reports*, 75, 353–354.

Lewis, C.A. and Maltby, J. (1995), Religious attitude and practice: the relationship with obsessionality, *Personality and Individual Differences*, 19, 105–108.

Maltby, J., McCollam, P. and Millar, D. (1994), Religiosity and obsessionality: a refinement, *Journal of Psychology*, 128, 609–611.

Masling, J., Rabie, L. and Blondheim, S.H. (1967), Obesity, level of aspiration, and Rorschach and TAT measures of oral dependence, *Journal of Consulting Psychology*, 31, 233–239.

Rabinowitz, W. (1957), Anality, aggression, and acquiescence, *Journal of Abnormal and Social Psychology*, 54, 140–142.

Sandler, J. and Hazari, A. (1960), The obsessional: on the psychological classification of obsessional character traits and symptoms, *British Journal of Medical Psychology*, 33, 113–122.

Torgersen, S. (1980), Heredity-environmental differentiation of general neurotic, obsessive and impulsive hysterical traits, *Acta Genetica Medicae et Gemellologiae*, 29, 193–207.

13

Personality and attitude toward religious education among adolescents

John M. Lewis and Leslie J. Francis

Summary

A sample of 12,557 adolescents between the ages of thirteen and fifteen years completed the abbreviated form of the Junior Eysenck Personality Questionnaire together with a Likert item to assess their attitude toward religious education. The findings demonstrate that girls hold a more positive attitude than boys, and that year ten pupils hold a less favourable attitude than year nine pupils. A more positive attitude toward religious education is associated with lower scores on the psychoticism scale, higher scores on the lie scale and higher scores on the neuroticism scale. There is no significant relationship between extraversion scores and attitude toward religious education.

Introduction

Within the state maintained system of schools in England and Wales religious education is a statutory component of the school curriculum, in accordance with the 1944 Education Act (Dent, 1947) and the 1988 Education Act (Cox and Cairns, 1989). A considerable body of research concerned with evaluating school children's attitude toward religious education alongside their attitude toward other areas of the school curriculum, however, has made it plain that the subject is generally held in low regard (Garrity, 1961; Williams and Finch, 1968; Povall, 1971; Ormerod, 1975; Keys and Ormerod, 1976; Harvey, 1984; Francis, 1987a). For example, Williams and Finch (1968) reported that, out of 14 school subjects, religious education was assigned the thirteenth rank position by boys and the eleventh rank position by girls with regard to usefulness and the thirteenth rank position by both boys and girls with regard to interest. Ormerod (1975) reported that religious education was assigned the seventeenth rank position among 17 subjects by boys and the fifteenth rank position among 16 subjects by girls. In a study which included 18 school subjects, Harvey (1984) found that religious education was assigned the sixteenth place by boys and the seventeenth place by girls.

While overall religious education is generally held in low esteem among school children, other studies make it clear that there is considerable variation in attitude toward religious education among different groups of pupils. Such studies have set out to model the influence of a range of personal, social and contextual factors on shaping the pupil's attitude toward religious education. On the basis of these studies there is general consensus that three key factors are sex, age and religious membership or practice. Girls hold a more positive attitude toward religious education than boys (Dale and Jones, 1964; Cox, 1967; Greer, 1972; Lewis, 1974). Older pupils hold a less positive attitude toward religious education than younger pupils (Francis, 1987a). Religious affiliation is a clear predictor of more positive attitude toward religious education (Lewis, 1974). Other studies have pointed to the influence of the type of school (Alves, 1968; Francis, 1987b), the method of teaching (Lewis, 1974) and the cultural context (Greer, 1972).

By way of contrast, little specific attention has been given to the influence of individual differences in personality on pupils' attitudes toward religious education, although in other areas a great deal of research has demonstrated the practical usefulness of Eysenck's dimensional model of personality in predicting a range of educational outcomes and school-related behaviours (Wakefield, 1979; Eysenck, 1983, 1990). For example, focused studies have investigated the relationship between scores on the Eysenckian personality scales and such issues as: academic achievement (Eysenck and Cookson, 1969; Wilson, 1972; Maqsud, 1980a, 1980b), art performance (Riding and Pearson, 1987), intelligence test scores (Anthony, 1973; Crookes, Pearson, Francis and Carter, 1981), learning styles and cognitive performance (Riding and Dyer, 1983), mathematical ability (McCord and Wakefield, 1981; Riding and Armstrong, 1982), number computation (Riding and Borg, 1987), physical education (Williams and Eston, 1986), reading and listening comprehension (Riding and Pugh, 1986), reading performance (Riding and Cowley, 1986), second language performance (Riding and Banner, 1986) and verbal reasoning (Pearson, 1983).

Other studies have concentrated specifically on the relationship between personality and school-related attitudes (Regan, 1967; Sharples, 1971; Whyte, 1988; Francis and Montgomery, 1993). For example, Francis and Montgomery (1993) demonstrate that more positive attitude toward school and toward a range of school subjects are associated with lower scores on the psychoticism scale and higher scores on the lie scale. They argue that the inverse relationship between psychoticism scores and more positive school-related attitudes supports Eysenck's more general theory linking personality and social attitudes. This finding is consistent with the view that positive school-related attitudes belong within the broader domain of tenderminded social attitudes, that tenderminded social attitudes are a product of socialisation and conditioning, and that low psychoticism scores are fundamental to conditioning and tendermindedness. Second, they argue that the positive relationship between school-related attitudes and lie scale scores is consistent with the view that the lie scale functions as an index of social acquiescence or conformity (Finlayson, 1972; Massey, 1980). On this account, socially conforming pupils adopt more favourable attitudes toward school and toward the school curriculum. Francis and Montgomery's study also indicates that a favourable attitude toward school itself is positively correlated with extraversion scores and negatively correlated with neuroticism scores. Outgoing children like school more; anxious children like school less.

Although the relationship between personality and attitude toward religious education is relatively uncharted, a considerable body of research has mapped the relationship between personality and attitude toward Christianity among samples of school pupils. A general consensus emerges from these studies. First, in spite of conflicting theories within the psychology of religion regarding the possible relationship between neuroticism and religiosity, the empirical evidence clearly suggests that there is no significant relationship between these variables (Francis, Pearson, Carter and Kay, 1981a; Francis, Pearson and Kay, 1983a; Francis and Pearson, 1991). Second, although Eysenck's early extraversion scales combined sociability with impulsivity (Eysenck and Eysenck, 1963), the more recent extraversion scales focus largely on sociability (Rocklin and Revelle, 1981). Repeated studies show that, once refined of the impulsivity component, there is no significant relationship between extraversion and religiosity (Francis, Pearson, Carter and Kay, 1981b; Francis, Pearson and Kay, 1983b; Francis and Pearson, 1985a). Third, repeated analyses demonstrate a significant negative relationship between psychoticism scores and religiosity (Kay, 1981; Francis and Pearson, 1985b; Francis, 1992). This finding is consistent with Eysenck's central theory relating personality and social attitudes. According to this theory, religion belongs to the domain of tenderminded social attitudes (Eysenck, 1975, 1976), tenderminded social attitudes are a functioning of conditioning (Eysenck, 1954, 1961) and individuals who score low on psychoticism have been shown by many empirical studies to condition more readily (Beyts, Frcka, Martin and Levey, 1983). Fourth, repeated analyses demonstrate a positive significant relationship between lie scale scores and religiosity (Francis, Pearson and Kay, 1983c, 1988; Pearson and Francis, 1989).

If the relationship between personality and attitude toward religious education follows the same pattern as the relationship between personality and attitude toward Christianity, more favourable attitudes toward religious education should be associated with lower psychoticism scores and higher lie scale scores, but unrelated to either neuroticism or extraversion. If, however, attitudes toward religious education are also modelled on more general attitudes toward school, more favourable attitudes toward religious education should also be associated with higher extraversion scores and lower neuroticism scores. The aim of the present study is to explore these conflicting hypotheses among a sample of adolescents between the ages of thirteen and fifteen years.

Method

A sample of 12,557 year nine and year ten pupils completed the short form of the Junior Eysenck Personality Questionnaire (Francis and Pearson, 1988). This questionnaire proposes six item scales of extraversion, neuroticism, psychoticism and the lie scale. They also responded to the question 'Religious education should be taught in school' on a five point Likert scale, ranging from 'agree strongly', through 'agree', 'not certain' and 'disagree', to 'disagree strongly'. The sample comprised 6,207 boys, 6,350 girls; 6,594 year nine pupils and 5,963 year ten pupils. The data were analysed by the SPSS statistical package, using the regression and reliability routines (SPSS Inc., 1988).

Results

The first step in the data analysis computed the alpha coefficient (Cronbach, 1951) for each of the four personality scales, using the reliability routine. The following alpha coefficients were generated: extraversion, 0.67; neuroticism, 0.68; psychoticism 0.59; lie scale 0.55. These are satisfactory levels for short scales of only six items each.

The second step in the data analysis employed the regression routine to explore the influence of the following variables on attitude toward religious education entered in this fixed order: sex, school year, psychoticism, lie scale, extraversion and neuroticism. Multiple regression was employed for two reasons. The first reason permits sex and age to be taken into account before exploring the influence of personality on attitude toward religious education. This is particularly important given the known sex differences in psychoticism and neuroticism as well as in attitude toward religion in general and religious education in particular. The second reason permits any intercorrelation between psychoticism and extraversion, due to any shared impulsivity component, to be taken into account before exploring the influence of extraversion on attitude toward religious education.

Table 13.1 presents the findings from the multiple regression significance test. From this table it is clear that the girls record a significantly more positive attitude than the boys and that year ten

Table 13.1
Multiple regression significance tests

predictor variables	R^2	change in R^2	F of change	P<	Beta	T	P<
sex	0.0271	0.0271	350.0	.001	+0.0910	+9.9	.001
school year	0.0342	0.0071	92.2	.001	−0.0586	−6.9	.001
psychoticism	0.0864	0.0521	716.4	.001	−0.1636	−16.5	.001
lie scale	0.1093	0.0229	322.9	.001	+0.1742	+18.4	.001
extraversion	0.1093	0.0000	0.1	NS	+0.0082	+0.9	NS
neuroticism	0.1107	0.0014	20.2	.001	+0.0396	+4.5	.001

pupils record a significantly less positive attitude than year nine pupils. The statistics also demonstrate that attitude toward religious education is correlated negatively with psychoticism scores, positively with lie scale scores and positively with neuroticism scales. There is no significant correlation between attitude toward religious education and extraversion scores.

Discussion

Four main conclusions emerge from these data.

First, the data confirm the findings of previous studies that girls hold a more positive attitude toward religious education than boys and that attitude toward religious education declines with age.

Second, the data demonstrate that Eysenck's dimensional model of personality is able to account for some of the variation in adolescent attitude toward religious education. Indeed, when considered cumulatively, psychoticism, neuroticism and lie scale scores are able to account for nearly three times the variance accounted for by sex differences. Personality is by no means an irrelevant factor, therefore, in explaining individual differences in attitude toward religious education.

Third, the major pattern in the relationship between personality and attitude toward religious education is closer to that in the relationship between personality and attitude toward Christianity than in the relationship between personality and attitude toward school. The strongest predictors of positive attitude toward religious education are low psychoticism scores and high lie scale scores. Previous research has demonstrated that low psychoticism scores and high lie scale scores are also the strongest predictors of positive attitude toward Christianity. On this account positive attitudes toward religious education, like positive attitude toward Christianity, are consistent with tenderminded and conformist social attitudes.

Fourth, there is one significant difference between the pattern of relationships between personality and attitude toward religious education and the pattern of relationships between personality and attitude toward Christianity. While neuroticism scores are not implicated in predicting positive attitude toward Christianity, they are implicated in predicting positive attitude toward religious education. According to the present data there is a small positive correlation between neuroticism and attitude toward religious education. This suggests that the more anxious child may have a slightly higher regard for religious education. This finding stands in the face of previous studies which suggest that the more anxious pupil may have a less positive attitude toward some school subjects, especially mathematics (Francis and Montgomery, 1993).

The major weakness with the present study concerns the relatively crude measure of attitude toward religious education employed. In view of the significance of the findings from this study, further research is now needed to replicate the findings using a more sophisticated and more widely based measure in the form of a properly constructed and validated scale of attitude toward religious education.

References

Alves, C. (1968), *Religion and the Secondary School*, London, SCM.

Anthony, W.S. (1973), The development of extraversion, of ability and of the relationship between them, *British Journal of Educational Psychology*, 43, 223–227.

Beyts, J., Frcka, G., Martin, I. and Levey, A.B. (1983), The influence of psychoticism and extraversion on classical eyelid conditioning using a paraorbital shock UCS, *Personality and Individual Differences*, 4, 275–283.

Cox, E. (1967), *Sixth Form Religion*, London, SCM.

Cox, E. and Cairns, J.M. (1989), *Reforming Religious Education: the religious clauses of the 1988 Education Reform Act*, London, Kogan Page.

Cronbach, L.J. (1951), Coefficient alpha and the internal structure of tests, *Psychometrika*, 16, 297–334.

Crookes, T.G., Pearson, P.R., Francis, L.J. and Carter, M. (1981), Extraversion and performance on raven's matrices in 15–16 year old children: an examination of Anthony's theory of the development of extraversion, *British Journal of Educational Psychology*, 51, 109–111.

Dale, R.R. and Jones, J.A. (1964), An investigation into the comparative response of boys and girls to scripture as a school subject in certain co-educational grammar schools in industrial South Wales, *British Journal of Educational Psychology*, 34, 132–142.

Dent, H.J. (1947), *The Education Act 1944: provisions, possibilities and some problems* (third edition), London, University of London Press.

Eysenck, H.J. (1954), *The Psychology of Politics*, London, Routledge and Kegan Paul.

Eysenck, H.J. (1961), Personality and social attitudes, *Journal of Social Psychology*, 53, 243–248.

Eysenck, H.J. (1975), The structure of social attitudes, *British Journal of Social and Clinical Psychology*, 14, 323–331.

Eysenck, H.J. (1976), Structure of social attitudes, *Psychological Reports*, 39, 463–466.

Eysenck, H.J. (1983), Human learning and individual differences: the genetic dimension, *Educational Psychology*, 3, 169–188.

Eysenck, H.J. (1990), Personality and school achievement, *Education Today*, 40, 2, 3–16.

Eysenck, H.J. and Cookson, D. (1969), Personality in primary school children: ability and achievement, *British Journal of Educational Psychology*, 39, 109–122.

Eysenck, S.B.G. and Eysenck, H.J. (1963), On the dual nature of extraversion, *British Journal of Social and Clinical Psychology*, 2, 46–55.

Finlayson, D.S. (1972), Towards the interpretation of children's lie scale scores, *British Journal of Educational Psychology*, 42, 290–293.

Francis, L.J. (1987a), The decline in attitudes towards religion among 8–15 year olds, *Educational Studies*, 13, 125–134.

Francis, L.J. (1987b), *Religion in the Primary School: partnership between church and state?* London, Collins Liturgical Publications.

Francis, L.J. (1992), Is psychoticism really a dimension of personality fundamental to religiosity? *Personality and Individual Differences*, 13, 645–652.

Francis, L.J. and Montgomery, A. (1993), Personality and school related attitudes among 11–16 year old girls, *Personality and Individual Differences*, 14, 647–654.

Francis, L.J. and Pearson, P.R. (1985a), Extraversion and religiosity, *Journal of Social Psychology*, 125, 269–270.

Francis, L.J. and Pearson, P.R. (1985b), Psychoticism and religiosity among 15 year olds, *Personality and Individual Differences*, 6, 397–398.

Francis, L.J. and Pearson, P.R. (1988), The development of a short form of the JEPQ (JEPQ-S): its use in measuring personality and religion, *Personality and Individual Differences*, 9, 911–916.

Francis, L.J., and Pearson, P.R. (1991), Religiosity, gender and the two faces of neuroticism, *Irish Journal of Psychology*, 12, 60–68.

Francis, L.J., Pearson, P.R., Carter, M. and Kay, W.K. (1981a), The relationship between neuroticism and religiosity among English 15- and 16-year olds, *Journal of Social Psychology*, 114, 99–102.

Francis, L.J., Pearson, P.R., Carter, M. and Kay, W.K. (1981b), Are introverts more religious? *British Journal of Social Psychology*, 20, 101–104.

Francis, L.J., Pearson, P.R. and Kay, W.K. (1983a), Neuroticism and religiosity among English school children, *Journal of Social Psychology*, 121, 149–150.

Francis, L.J., Pearson, P.R. and Kay, W.K. (1983b), Are introverts still more religious? *Personality and Individual Differences*, 4, 211–212.

Francis, L.J., Pearson, P.R. and Kay, W.K. (1983c), Are religious children bigger liars? *Psychological Reports*, 52, 551–554.

Francis, L.J., Pearson, P.R. and Kay, W.K. (1988), Religiosity and lie scores: a question of interpretation, *Social Behaviour and Personality*, 16, 91–95.

Garrity, F.D. (1961), A study of the attitude of some secondary modern school pupils towards religious education, *Religious Education*, 56, 141–143.

Greer, J.E. (1972), *A Questioning Generation*, Belfast, Church of Ireland Board of Education.

Harvey, T.J. (1984), Gender differences in subject preference and perception of subject importance among third year secondary school pupils in single-sex and mixed comprehensive schools, *Educational Studies*, 10, 243–253.

Kay, W.K. (1981), Psychoticism and attitude to religion, *Personality and Individual Differences*, 2, 249–252.

Keys, W. and Ormerod, M.B. (1976), Some factors affecting pupils' preferences, *The Durham Research Review*, 7, 1109–1115.

Lewis, J.M. (1974), An examination of the attitudes of pupils towards the content and method of teaching religious education in certain co-educational comprehensive schools in Wales, Unpublished M.Ed. dissertation, University of Wales, (Swansea).

McCord, R.R. and Wakefield, J.A. (1981), Arithmetic achievement as a function of introversion-extraversion and teacher presented reward and punishment, *Personality and Individual Differences*, 2, 145–152.

Maqsud, M. (1980a), Extraversion, neuroticism, intelligence and academic achievement in Northern Nigeria, *British Journal of Educational Psychology*, 50, 71–73.

Maqsud, M. (1980b), Personality and academic attainment of primary school children, *Psychological Reports*, 46, 1271–1275.

Massey, A. (1980), The Eysenck Personality Inventory lie scale: lack of insight or . . .? *Irish Journal of Psychology*, 4, 172–174.

Ormerod, M.B. (1975), Subject preference and choice in co-educational and single sex secondary schools, *British Journal of Educational Psychology*, 45, 257–267.

Pearson, P.R. (1983), JEPQ correlates of a verbal reasoning test, *IRCS Medical Science*, 11, 55–56.

Pearson, P.R. and Francis, L.J. (1989), The dual nature of the Eysenckian lie scales: are religious adolescents more truthful? *Personality and Individual Differences*, 10, 1041–1048.

Povall, C.H. (1971), Some factors affecting pupils' attitudes to religious education, Unpublished M.Ed. dissertation, University of Manchester.

Regan, G. (1967), Personality characteristics and attitude to school, *British Journal of Educational Psychology*, 37, 127–129.

Riding, R.J. and Armstrong, J.M. (1982), Sex and personality differences in performance on mathematics tests in 11 year old children, *Educational Studies*, 8, 217–225.

Riding, R.J. and Banner, G.E. (1986), Sex and personality differences in second language performance in secondary pupils, *British Journal of Educational Psychology*, 56, 366–370.

Riding, R.J. and Borg, M.G. (1987), Sex and personality differences in performance on number computations in 11 year old children, *Educational Review*, 39, 41–46.

Riding, R.J. and Cowley, J. (1986), Extraversion and sex differences in reading performance in eight-year-old children, *British Journal of Educational Psychology*, 56, 88–94.

Riding, R.J. and Dyer, V.A. (1983), The nature of learning styles and their relationship to cognitive performance in children, *Educational Psychology*, 3, 275–287.

Riding, R.J. and Pearson, R.D. (1987), The relationship between art performance, extraversion and field-independence in secondary age pupils, *Research in Education*, 38, 27–35.

Riding, R.J. and Pugh, J.C. (1986), Dark-interval-threshold and reading and listening comprehension in nine-year-old children, *Educational Review*, 38, 57–66.

Rocklin, T. and Revelle, W. (1981), The measurement of extraversion: a comparison of the Eysenck Personality Inventory and the Eysenck Personality Questionnaire, *British Journal of Social Psychology*, 20, 279–284.

Sharples, D. (1971), Longitudinal study of the personality and the attainments and attitudes of junior school children, Unpublished Ph.D. dissertation, University of Bath.

SPSS Inc. (1988), *SPSSX User's Guide*, New York, McGraw-Hill.

Wakefield, J.A. (1979), *Using Personality to Individualise Instruction*, San Diego, Edits Publishers.

Whyte, J. (1988), Personality variables, attitudes and attainments in boys aged 11–14, *Irish Educational Studies*, 7, 99–117.

Williams, J.G. and Eston, R.G. (1986), Does personality influence the perception of effort? The results from a study of secondary schoolboys, *Physical Education Review*, 9, 94–99.

Williams, R.M. and Finch, S. (1968), *Young School Leavers*, London, Her Majesty's Stationery Office.

Wilson, J.A. (1972), Personality and attainment in the primary school: personality structure and attainment of ten-year-olds, *Research in Education*, 7, 1–10.

14

A level gospel study and adolescents' images of Jesus

Jeff Astley and Leslie J. Francis

Summary

A sample of 279 sixth form students, attending a study day at the North of England Institute for Christian Education, completed the 'Images of Jesus Questionnaire' which utilises Eysenck's three-dimensional model of human personality. Of these subjects 66% were currently undertaking A level gospel study. The students undertaking A level gospel study located Jesus higher on the extraversion scale, higher on the neuroticism scale and lower on the psychoticism scale. These findings are consistent with the view that A level gospel study promotes a more human image of Jesus and a lower Christology.

Introduction

A survey of the current GCE A level religious studies syllabuses concerned with the New Testament gospels makes it clear that students are usually expected to be aware of the issues raised by redaction criticism and the problems associated with recovering a picture of the 'historical Jesus'. Some syllabuses make these areas of study explicit. For example, the *Origin and Foundation of the Christian Church* syllabus of the University of Cambridge Local Examinations Syndicate includes (in optional section D) reference to 'the ways in which the gospels are held by many to reflect the outlook of the evangelists and of the Christian community, as well as the attempts made to recover the facts about Jesus himself and his teaching'. Other syllabuses take such elements of gospel criticism for granted, subsuming them under heads such as 'the composition . . . of the New Testament', and then list texts for detailed

239

study. Some of these syllabuses define *illustrative passages*, including, for example, the Northern Examinations and Assessment Board (formerly the Joint Matriculation Board) which specifies the birth and infancy narratives, the Johannine prologue, a number of parables and miracles, and the passion and resurrection narratives in all four gospels. Some syllabuses specify particular gospels as *set texts*, including, for example, the Oxford and Cambridge Board which specified Matthew or John and the London Board which specified Luke or John in the year of our survey. Some syllabuses define *themes*, including, for example, the Oxford Local Examinations Biblical Studies syllabus which specified 'Son of Man and other titles' and 'resurrection and ascension'.

The picture of the historical Jesus that is likely to emerge from this study of the gospels may well be different from the view of Jesus held by those who have not undertaken such work. Despite the emphasis in many of the syllabuses on the critical analysis of the literary and oral origins of the gospel materials, and the theologies that underlie the selection and presentation of this material by the evangelists and their traditions, there is no doubt that a substantial part of gospel study at A level involves introducing students, often for the first time, to the received text of the gospels. Students are bound to construct from this evidence some sort of image of the historical Jesus, with or without the help of the reflections of scholars on the 'quest for the historical Jesus'. It is likely that this picture will in many cases conflict with their previous, often unreflective, view of Jesus, which is itself as likely to be dominated by a pious Christology (whether their own or that of other people) that images Jesus in a form appropriate to one who is worshipped within the Christian tradition. In Christian piety the 'Christ of faith' often overlays the image of the 'Jesus of history' (Astley, 1992).

It is a commonplace of Christological debate that the 'high Christology' of Christian worship and spirituality, which views Jesus 'from above' and is more concerned to stress his divinity than his humanity, sees his human nature *through* his divine nature (Turner, 1976). In an extreme form this has degenerated into the heresies entitled Docetism, Apollinarianism and Eutychianism in which Christ's humanity was, as it were, swallowed up by his divinity. Such accounts view Jesus as a thoroughgoing divine figure, without the limitations imposed on and by human knowledge, human emotions, human needs or human doubts. At the opposite end of the spectrum, a 'low Christology' will begin with a very human picture of the historical Jesus and will acknowledge the divine in Christ only through and in the context of a fully human nature. Such a 'Christology from below' may itself degenerate into a Christian heresy that sees Jesus as no more than a prophet inspired by or 'adopted by' God, as suggested by heresies entitled Ebionitism and Adoptionism, in practice denying the divinity of Christ altogether. (On the variety of Christological options available within and beyond the limits of the Christian tradition, see Cullmann, 1963; Grillmeier, 1964; Lohse, 1966; McIntyre, 1966; Kelly, 1968; Pelikan, 1971; Robinson, 1973; Lampe, 1978; Dunn, 1980; Braaten, 1984; Bowden, 1988; Macquarrie, 1990.)

It is reasonable to hypothesise that students who do A level gospel study might be more likely to put stress on the humanity of Christ, to the extent of embracing a low Christology, when compared with a control group who have not undertaken this study and whose view of Jesus is likely to be more influenced by piety than by history. The aim of the present study is to test this hypothesis against the background of the coherent theory of personality and individual differences proposed by Hans Eysenck and his associates (Eysenck and Eysenck, 1985).

Eysenck's model of human personality argues that individual differences can be most economically and adequately summarised in terms of three higher order factors defined as extraversion, neuroticism and psychoticism. These factors are operationalised in the Eysenck Personality Questionnaire (Eysenck and Eysenck, 1975) and the Revised Eysenck Personality Questionnaire (Eysenck, Eysenck and Barrett, 1985). Each of these factors defines a normal range of human behaviour and suggests a direction in which an image of Jesus influenced by piety or by a high Christology would be distinguished from an image of normal humanity.

Eysenck's neuroticism scales measure emotional lability and over-reactivity. Neurotic disorders are conceptualised as the extreme pole of a continuum of normal personality. The high scorer on the neuroticism scale is characterised by the test manual as an anxious, worrying individual, who is moody and frequently depressed, likely to sleep badly and to suffer from various psychosomatic disorders. The opposite of neuroticism is emotional stability. The majority of *normal* individuals score on the middle range of this dimension of personality. It is likely that a high Christology would minimise Jesus' normal range of human and emotional experience. On this account, adolescents pursuing A level gospel study would give more emphasis to Jesus' human and emotional experience and attribute to him a higher score on the neuroticism scale.

Eysenck's extraversion scales measure sociability and impulsivity. The high scorer on the extraversion scale is characterised by the test manual as a sociable individual, who likes parties, has many friends, needs to have people to talk to and prefers social to solitary activities. The typical extravert craves excitement, is carefree, easygoing, optimistic, and likes to 'laugh and be merry'. The opposite of extraversion is introversion. Both introversion and extraversion define *normal* ranges of human personality, although individuals characterised by the two extremes of this dimension differ greatly from each other. It is likely that a high Christology would emphasise Jesus' aloofness from the business and bustle of human activity in preference for the image of social detachment which characterises many aspects of classic Christian spirituality. On this account, adolescents pursuing A level gospel study would give more emphasis to Jesus' social engagement and attribute to him a higher score on the extraversion scale.

Eysenck's psychoticism scales measure toughmindedness. Psychotic disorders are conceptualised as the extreme pole of a continuum of normal personality. The high scorer on the psychoticism scale is characterised by Eysenck and Eysenck (1976) as being 'cold, impersonal, hostile, lacking in sympathy, unfriendly, untrustful, odd, unemotional, unhelpful, lacking in insight, strange, with paranoid ideas that people were against him'. While an undue concentration of such characteristics predicts psychotic disorders, toughmindedness itself defines a perfectly proper tone within the range of normal personality. The opposite of psychoticism is tendermindedness. It is likely that a high Christology would emphasise Jesus' transcendence over many of the normal constraints of human life. The transcendendent Jesus is indifferent to the conventions of social rules and to the social consequences of his actions. The transcendent Jesus takes a toughminded attitude toward the feelings of others and to his own destiny. The transcendent Jesus embraces the victory of death with triumph. On this account, adolescents pursuing A level gospel study would give more emphasis to Jesus' tenderminded attitudes and social conformity and attribute to him a lower score on the psychoticism scale.

Method

Subjects

A sample of 279 students attending a sixth form study day at the North of England Institute for Christian Education completed the 'Images of Jesus Questionnaire'. Of these subjects, 183 (66%) were currently undertaking A level gospel study. The remaining 34% constitute the control group of students who were not undertaking A level gospel study. The majority of the subjects, 230 (82%) were females. Nearly three-quarters of the students claimed affiliation with a Christian denomination, including 95 Anglicans (34%), 60 Catholics (22%), 21 Methodists (8%), ten United Reformed Church (4%), five Pentecostal (2%) and four Baptist (1%). Other denominations were represented by just one student each; 78 (28%) students claimed no denominational affiliation. Nearly a third (33%) of the students claimed to attend church weekly, 5% monthly, 19% several times a year, 19% once or twice a year and 25% never. Nearly a quarter (22%) of the students claimed to pray daily, 16% weekly, 33% sometimes, 7% once or twice a year and 22% never.

Questionnaire

The Images of Jesus Questionnaire included a modified form of the abbreviated revised Eysenck Personality Questionnaire (EPQ-RA) (Francis, Brown and Philipchalk, 1992). The EPQ-RA contains four sets of six items each, designed to measure extraversion, neuroticism, psychoticism and the lie scale. In the modified form the respondents were invited, 'Please answer for what you think about Jesus'. The 24 items were re-phrased in the third person singular. For example, the personality question 'Are you a talkative person?' was re-phrased as 'Is he a talkative person?' Each question was answered on the dichotomous scale 'Yes/No'.

Data analysis

The data were analysed by means of the SPSS statistical package (SPSS Inc., 1988).

Results

Table 14.1 presents the alpha reliability coefficients (Cronbach, 1951) for the four scales of extraversion, neuroticism, psychoticism and the lie scale and compares the mean scores on these four scales

Table 14.1
The personality scales

scales	alpha	A level mean	sd	control mean	sd	F	P<
extraversion	0.6934	4.2	1.7	3.7	1.8	6.0	.01
neuroticism	0.6606	2.9	1.5	2.3	1.8	8.0	.01
psychoticism	0.2744	2.8	1.0	3.1	1.1	7.0	.01
lie scale	0.7241	5.2	1.3	5.2	1.3	0.0	NS

recorded by the A level gospel study group and the control group. From these statistics it is clear that the extraversion, neuroticism and lie scales all achieve an alpha coefficient around 0.7 which is most satisfactory for scales of this length. The psychoticism scale does not reach a satisfactory level of internal reliability. This is consistent with the more general difficulties associated with operationalising this construct (Eysenck, Eysenck and Barrett, 1985). These statistics also make it clear that the students undertaking A level gospel study have a significantly different image of Jesus from those students who are not undertaking A level gospel study. The students undertaking A level gospel study locate Jesus higher on the extraversion scale, higher on the neuroticism scale and lower on the psychoticism scale.

In order to interpret these differences more fully, table 14.2 compares the proportions of the A level group and of the control group who respond in the affirmative to each of the 24 scale items. The items of the extraversion scale demonstrate that the A level gospel students see Jesus as being more socially active. Their Jesus is more likely to be a lively and talkative person who can bring life to a dull party. The items of the neuroticism scale demonstrate that the A level gospel students see Jesus as being more subject to human emotionality. Their Jesus is more likely to feel lonely and fed-up. He is more likely to experience mood swings and to worry about things. The items of the psychoticism scale demonstrate that the A level gospel students see Jesus as being more tender-minded and more constrained by his social context. Their Jesus is more likely to take matters seriously if there were mistakes in his

Table 14.2
Image of Jesus

	A level %	control %
extraversion		
Is he a talkative person?	77	63
Is he rather lively?	69	54
Can he easily get some life into a rather dull party?	77	69
Does he tend to keep in the background on social occasions?*	32	34
Is he mostly quiet when he is with other people?*	26	31
Do other people think of him as being very lively?	56	46
neuroticism		
Does his mood often go up and down?	67	55
Does he often feel 'fed-up'?	69	46
Would he call himself a nervous person?	10	19
Is he a worrier?	46	37
Does he suffer from 'nerves'?	28	23
Does he often feel lonely?	71	54
psychoticism		
Would being in debt worry him?*	33	27
Would he take drugs which may have strange or dangerous effects?	14	14
Does he prefer to go his own way rather than act by the rules?	78	90
Does he think marriage is old-fashioned and should be done away with?	3	11
Does it worry him if he knows there are mistakes in his work?*	69	59
Does he think it is better to follow society's rules than go his own way?*	17	17
lie scale		
Was he ever greedy by helping himself to more than his share of anything?*	8	7
Has he ever blamed someone for doing something he knew was really his fault?*	9	10
Has he ever taken anything (even a pin or button) that belonged to someone else?	17	19
Has he ever cheated at a game?	13	14
Has he ever taken advantage of someone?	18	18
Does he always practise what he preaches?	87	88

Note: * These items need to be reverse coded in order to compute the scale scores.

work or if he were to be in debt. He is less inclined to go his own way or to criticise a social institution like marriage. The lower reliability of this scale, however, is reflected in the way in which not all items co-vary so clearly with the distinction between A level gospel students and the control groups. The items of the lie scale confirm that there are no real differences in the responses of the A level gospel students and the control group to these questions.

Conclusion

These findings are consistent with the hypothesis that students undertaking A level gospel study tend to hold a low Christology informed more by a quest for the historical Jesus, rather than a high Christology informed more by a pietistic attachment to the Christ of faith. A level students who are studying the gospels are more likely to picture Jesus as a lively, talkative, psychologically volatile, anxious, depressed and lonely figure. This is a more human picture of Jesus. It lays greater stress on his fallibility and limitations. Such a Jesus has been brought more closely 'down to earth', in contrast to a perception that would still tend to envisage him as walking, talking and living 'a few feet above the ground'.

It is clear from this survey that an in-depth study of biblical texts, such as that offered by an A level course, can have an effect on the learner's own Christology, and thus that academic bible study can influence an individual's personal theological perspective. In other words, the study provides some evidence for the view that academic theological enquiry and personal religious belief are not as rigidly separated into discrete compartments as some educators may suggest.

References

Astley, J. (1992), Will the real Christianity please stand up? *British Journal of Religious Education*, 15, 4–12.

Bowden, J. (1988), *Jesus: the unanswered questions*, London, SCM.

Braaten, C.E. (1984), The person of Jesus Christ, in C.E. Braaten and R.W. Jenson (eds), *Christian Dogmatics, Vol. 1*, Philadelphia, Fortress.

Cronbach, L.J. (1951), Coefficient alpha and the internal structure of tests, *Psychometrika*, 16, 297–334.

Cullmann, O. (1963), *The Christology of the New Testament*, London, SCM.

Dunn, J.G.D. (1980), *Christology in the Making*, London, SCM.

Eysenck, S.B.G., Eysenck, H.J. and Barrett, P. (1985), A revised version of the psychoticism scale, *Personality and Individual Differences*, 6, 21–29.

Eysenck, H.J. and Eysenck, M.W. (1985), *Personality and Individual Differences: a natural science approach*, New York, Plenum Press.

Eysenck, H.J. and Eysenck S.B.G. (1975), *Manual of the Eysenck Personality Questionnaire*, London, Hodder and Stoughton.

Eysenck, H.J. and Eysenck, S.B.G. (1976), *Psychoticism as a Dimension of Personality*, London, Hodder and Stoughton.

Francis, L.J., Brown, L.B. and Philipchalk, R. (1992), The development of an abbreviated form of the Revised Eysenck Personality Questionnaire (EPQR-A): its use among students in England, Canada, the USA and Australia, *Personality and Individual Differences*, 13, 443–449.

Grillmeier, A. (1964), *Christ in Christian Tradition*, London, Mowbray.

Kelly, J.N.D. (1968), *Early Christian Doctrines*, London, A. and C. Black.

Lampe, G.W.H. (1978), Christian theology in the patristic period, in H. Cunliffe-Jones (ed.), *A History of Christian Doctrine*, Edinburgh, T. and T. Clark.

Lohse, B. (1966), *A Short History of Christian Doctrine*, Philadelphia, Fortress.

Macquarrie, J. (1990), *Jesus Christ in Modern Thought*, London, SCM.

McIntyre, J. (1966), *The Shape of Christology*, London, SCM.

Pelikan, J. (1971), *The Emergence of the Catholic Tradition (100–600)*, Chicago, Chicago University Press.

Robinson, J.A.T. (1973), *The Human Face of God*, London, SCM.

SPSS Inc. (1988), *SPSSX User's Guide*, New York, McGraw-Hill.

Turner, H.E.W. (1976), *Jesus the Christ*, London, Mowbrays.

15

Measuring Christian fundamentalist belief among adolescents in Scotland

Harry M. Gibson and Leslie J. Francis

Summary

A twelve item scale measuring Christian fundamentalist belief was developed among a sample of 866 adolescents between the ages of eleven and fifteen years attending non-denominational state maintained secondary schools in Scotland. The data support the reliability and construct validity of the scale among this age group.

Introduction

Fundamentalism is a rich and broadly based construct. Recent theoretical discussion of Protestant fundamentalism suggests that it may combine notions of biblical authority with conservatism in morality and politics, opposition to evolution, millenarianism, evangelicalism and personal assurance of salvation (Barr, 1977, 1980; Boone, 1990). There are two main problems associated with attempting to operationalise such a rich and broadly based construct. First, multidimensional constructs are notoriously difficult to capture in scaling instruments. A sensible strategy is to attempt to measure the theoretically distinct components of the construct. For this reason certain schools of attitude measurement are concerned to distinguish between measures of affect, belief and behavioural intention (Ajzen, 1988). Second, it is far from clear how well the components identified *theoretically* within the construct of fundamentalism actually cohere *empirically*. A sensible strategy is to test the theoretical coherence of the construct by first isolating the components empirically.

Most commentators agree that at the core of Protestant fundamentalism lies the firm conviction in the authority and inerrancy of the bible. Writing from inside the tradition, Ed Dobson and Ed Hindson in their contribution to Falwell (1981) state:

> The one unifying factor in all these movements, without a doubt, is their common adherence to the basic authority of scripture as the only dependable guide for faith and practice.

Writing from outside the tradition, using the tools of literary theory, Boone (1990) argues that:

> Only fundamentalists make a point of characterising themselves as bible believers. To believe the bible is to take it literally, to regard every word of it as inerrant and fully divine.

Likewise Peshkin (1986), using the tools of social anthropology, identifies the biblical inerrancy doctrine as the common trait by which all fundamentalists are identified.

For these reasons the objective of the present study is to develop a measure of Christian fundamentalist belief, appropriate for use among secondary school pupils. Such an instrument would properly stand alongside existing instruments concerned with other aspects of religiosity during adolescence, including attitude toward Christianity (Francis, 1989a) and rejection of Christianity (Greer and Francis, 1992). The use of this instrument in future research could then begin to establish the correlates of fundamentalist Christian belief during childhood and adolescence.

Method

A questionnaire containing 139 items concerned with Christianity and science was completed by 866 pupils attending two non-denominational state maintained schools in Scotland. A group of these items was designed to sample fundamentalist Christian belief. The pupils responded to these items on a five point Likert type scale, ranging from *agree strongly*, through *not certain* to *disagree strongly*. In addition to questions about age and sex, church attendance was assessed on a five point scale: nearly every week, at least once a month, sometimes, once or twice a year and never; bible reading and prayer were also both assessed on a five point scale:

nearly every day, at least once a week, at least once a month, occasionally and never.

The sample comprised 395 boys and 471 girls; 260 pupils in year seven, 226 in year eight, 172 pupils in year nine and 208 pupils in year ten. The data were analysed by means of the SPSS statistical package (SPSS Inc., 1988).

Results

Correlational analyses were employed to identify the items which correlated most highly with the three key markers of Christian fundamentalist belief included in the questionnaire: 'I believe that the bible is the word of God'; 'I believe that Jesus died to save me'; 'I believe that Jesus really rose from the dead'. Factor analysis and rest of test correlations were then used to identify from this pool the twelve items which cohered to produce the best homogeneous and unidimensional scale. These twelve items, together with the item rest of test correlation coefficients, are presented in table 15.1. The item rest of test correlation coefficients vary between

Table15.1
Item rest of test correlation coefficients
and percentage endorsements

item	r	agree %
I believe that God made the world in six days and rested on the seventh	0.6326	21
I believe that the bible is the word of God	0.6652	28
I believe that Jesus was born of a virgin	0.5217	28
I believe that Jesus will return to earth some day	0.6887	16
I believe in hell	0.3704	29
I believe that God judges what I do and say	0.6689	16
I believe that Jesus died to save me	0.7736	25
I believe that Jesus changed real water into real wine	0.7699	16
I believe that Jesus walked on water	0.7770	16
I believe that Jesus Christ is the Son of God	0.7193	39
I believe that God is controlling every bit of our lives	0.6342	11
I believe that Jesus really rose from the dead	0.7734	21
Alpha coefficient	0.9171	

0.37 and 0.78. The scale achieves the highly satisfactory alpha coefficient of 0.92 (Cronbach, 1951). This table also presents the proportions of pupils who express agreement with each of the individual items. In this case agreement is calculated as the product of those who check the 'agree' and the 'agree strongly' responses on the five point Likert scale.

While the reliability of an attitude scale is relatively straightforward to express in terms of an examination of the internal structure and covariance of the items (Livingston, 1988), the issue of testing and demonstrating validity is somewhat more complex (Orton, 1987). Table 15.2 explores the construct validity of the scale by examining its correlation with three indices of Christian practice.

Table 15.2
Correlations between Christian fundamentalism
and three indices of Christian behaviour

	r	P<
frequency of church attendance	+0.4446	.001
frequency of personal prayer	+0.4967	.001
frequency of personal bible reading	+0.4671	.001

While there is no direct nor simple relationship between attitude, belief and practice (Ajzen, 1988), it is reasonable to hypothesise that those who hold a Christian fundamentalist position are more likely to attend church, to pray and to read the bible. All of these hypothesised relationships are supported by the data.

After looking at reliability and validity, the third step in exploring the functional properties of the twelve item scale of Christian fundamentalist belief was to examine the differences of the scale scores between boys and girls and between the younger and older pupils. Table 15.3 presents the mean scale scores for boys and girls in year seven and year eight and year nine and year ten separately, while table 15.4 presents the summary analysis of variance statistics. These statistics demonstrate that girls display a higher level of Christian fundamentalist belief than boys and that year nine and year ten pupils display a higher level of Christian fundamentalist belief than year seven and eight pupils.

Table 15.3
Scale scores of Christian fundamentalism
by sex and school year

| | boys | | | girls | | |
	mean	sd	N	mean	sd	N
years 7 and 8	33.2	9.7	224	35.6	8.0	262
years 9 and 10	29.4	10.5	171	34.1	10.0	209

Table 15.4
Summary of analysis of variance

source	df	mean square	F	P<
main effects	2	1939.3	21.7	.001
sex	1	2549.0	28.6	.001
school year	1	1369.7	15.4	.001
two-way interaction	1	281.4	3.2	NS
explained	3	1386.6	15.6	.001
residual	862	89.2		
total	865	93.7		

Discussion

Six main conclusions emerge from these data.

First, the item rest of test correlations confirm that there is a clear pattern of beliefs which go hand in hand with the view that the bible is the word of God. These beliefs include acceptance of the virgin birth, the resurrection and the second coming of Jesus. They include the views that God is controlling every bit of our lives and that God judges what we do and say. They include the literal acceptance of the Genesis narrative of creation and of the Gospel account of miracles. The Jesus of the fundamentalist walked on water and turned water into wine. The fundamentalist believes in personal salvation through the death of Jesus and in hell as a real future for those who do not grasp the path to salvation.

Second, inclusion of belief in hell within the items found to cluster within the scale confirms Boone's (1990) view that the doctrine of hell arises specifically from the literal interpretation of an inerrant text. She argues that:

> Few if any fundamentalists take pleasure in the doctrine. But for its perceived foundation in the bible, it would not be believed.

Third, the proportions of pupils between the ages of eleven and fifteen years expressing agreement with the individual scale items indicates the extent to which pupils within the non-denominational state maintained schools in Scotland accept fundamentalist beliefs. One in four believe that the bible is the word of God, that Jesus was born of a virgin, and that Jesus died to save them. One in four also believe in hell. One in five believe that God made the world in six days and that Jesus really rose from the dead. One in six believe that Jesus will return to earth some day, that God judges what they do and say, and that Jesus walked on water and turned real water into real wine.

Fourth, the mean scale scores by sex demonstrate that girls score significantly higher than boys on the scale of Christian fundamentalist belief. This is consistent with the general finding that girls record higher levels of religiosity in terms of such dimensions as church attendance (Francis, 1984), prayer (Francis and Brown, 1991) and attitude toward Christianity (Gibson and Francis, 1989).

Fifth, the mean scale scores by school year demonstrate that pupils in year nine and year ten score significantly lower than pupils in year seven and year eight on the scale of Christian fundamentalist belief. This is consistent with the general finding regarding decline in religiosity during the early teenage years in terms of such dimensions as church attendance (Francis and Lankshear, 1991), prayer (Francis and Brown, 1991) and attitude toward Christianity (Francis, 1989b).

Sixth, the data presented on the reliability and validity of the scale clearly commend its further use in research concerned with exploring dimensions of religion during childhood and adolescence. In particular, further studies are now needed, employing this instrument, to tease out the relative significance of Christian fundamentalist belief in different geographical areas, for example, comparing Scotland with England, Wales and Northern Ireland.

Studies are also needed to explore the social and personal predeterminants of the development of Christian fundamentalist belief, and also the moral and political consequences of such belief.

References

Ajzen, I. (1988), *Attitudes, Personality and Behaviour*, Milton Keynes, Open University Press.

Barr, J. (1977), *Fundamentalism*, London, SCM.

Barr, J. (1980), The problem of fundamentalism, in *Exploration in Theology*, pp. 65–90, London, SCM.

Boone, K.C. (1990), *The Bible Tells Them So: the discourse of Protestant fundamentalism*, London, SCM.

Cronbach, L.J. (1951), Coefficient alpha and the internal structure of tests, *Psychometrika*, 16, 297–334.

Falwell, J. (ed.), *The Fundamentalist Phenomenon: the resurgence of conservative Christianity*, Garden City, Galilee-Doubleday.

Francis, L.J. (1984), *Teenagers and the Church: a profile of church-going youth in the 1980s*, London, Collins Liturgical Publications.

Francis, L.J. (1989a), Measuring attitude towards Christianity during childhood and adolescence, *Personality and Individual Differences*, 10, 695–698.

Francis, L.J. (1989b), Drift from the churches: secondary school pupils' attitudes towards Christianity, *British Journal of Religious Education*, 11, 76–86.

Francis, L.J. and Brown, L.B. (1991), The influence of home, church and school on prayer among sixteen year old adolescents in England, *Review of Religious Research*, 33, 112–122.

Francis, L.J. and Lankshear, D.W. (1991), *Continuing in the Way: children, young people and the church*, London, National Society.

Gibson, H.M. and Francis, L.J. (1989), Measuring attitudes towards Christianity among 11 to 16 year old pupils in Catholic schools in Scotland, *Educational Research*, 31, 65–69.

Greer, J.E. and Francis, L.J. (1992), Measuring 'rejection of Christianity' among 14–16 year old adolescents in Catholic and Protestant schools in Northern Ireland, *Personality and Individual Differences*, 13, 1345–1348.

Livingston, S.A. (1988), Reliability of test results, in J.P. Keeves (ed.), *Educational Research, Methodology and Measurement: an international handbook*, pp. 386–392, Oxford, Pergamon Press.

Orton, R.E. (1987), The foundations of construct validity: towards an update, *Journal of Research and Development in Education*, 21, 22–35.

Peshkin, A. (1986), *God's Choice: the total world of the fundamentalist Christian school*, Chicago, University of Chicago Press.

SPSS Inc. (1988), *SPSSX User's Guide*, New York, McGraw-Hill.

16

Science, creation and Christianity: a further look

Peter Fulljames

Summary

A sample of 3,427 pupils between the ages of eleven and fifteen years completed a questionnaire concerned with religious attitudes, beliefs and understanding. The present paper discusses the relationship between attitude toward Christianity, conflict between science and religion, creationist belief, and the view that Christianity necessarily involves creationism. The data demonstrate that the view that Christianity necessarily involves creationism has a detrimental influence on attitude toward Christianity among this age group, after taking personal belief in creationism into account. The implications of this finding for religious education are discussed.

Introduction

A recent report of the attitudes and opinions of pupils between the ages of twelve and sixteen years in England has highlighted the uncertainty of many young people about the relationship between science and religious belief (Francis, 1992). In response to the questionnaire item 'Science has disproved religion', while 16% agreed and 33% disagreed, 51% checked the 'not certain' category. Responses in other parts of the same questionnaire suggested that one focus of this uncertainty is the interpretation of the creation stories in Genesis. Interpretation of these stories is by no means the only issue in current debate about science and religion, yet it does seem that this issue needs to be given attention in the religious education curriculum, if young people are to develop an accurate understanding of what Christians believe and to clarify their own thinking about the relationship between science and religious belief.

An earlier investigation in this area was John Greer's study concerning the child's understanding of creation (Greer, 1972). Semi-structured interviews showed that many young people experienced difficulty in combining a religious understanding of the biblical stories of creation with what they knew of scientific accounts of the origins of the earth and humanity. Although some older pupils recognised symbolic meaning in the Genesis stories, Greer found that 'pupils all the way through the grammar school were struggling with problems raised by the literal interpretation of symbols' (p. 108). Greer's conclusion was that 'the importance of this kind of research for the future of religious education cannot be emphasised too greatly' (p. 109). His own subsequent research has been focused elsewhere, but fresh attention has been given to the issues he raised by recent studies in Kenya (Fulljames and Francis, 1987a; Fulljames and Francis, 1988) and in Scotland (Gibson, 1989; Francis, Gibson and Fulljames, 1990; Fulljames, Gibson and Francis, 1991; Francis, Fulljames and Gibson, 1992) as well as in the investigation in England referred to in the first paragraph above (Francis, 1992). The purpose of this chapter is to present new analysis of data from this investigation, but first a summary will be given of the results of the work in Kenya and Scotland.

The investigation in Kenya aimed to explore the relationships between particular views of science and of Christianity and attitude toward science and Christianity. A questionnaire was completed by 624 young people approaching the end of secondary school education in several parts of the country and included the Francis Scale of Attitude Toward Christianity, which was shown to be reliable in the Kenyan context (Fulljames and Francis, 1987b). New scales were developed for the measurement of attitude toward science, for one particular view of science (scientism) and for one particular view of Christianity (perception of Christianity as necessarily involving creationism). The concept of scientism may be represented by the item 'theories in science can be proved to be definitely true' and perception of Christianity as necessarily involving creationism by the item 'true Christians believe the universe was made in six days of 24 hours each'.

Multivariate analysis of the data showed that attitude toward Christianity was not influenced by the view that Christianity necessarily involves creationism, although there was a significant negative influence of scientism on attitude toward Christianity.

The view of Christianity as creationist was significant, however, in making it less likely that young people would combine a positive attitude toward science with a positive attitude toward Christianity. This result was interpreted by distinguishing between the view of Christianity as creationist and creationist belief. It was suggested that those who themselves believe in the literal truth of the biblical creation stories and view Christianity as necessarily creationist tend to have a positive attitude toward Christianity and a negative attitude toward science, while those who view Christianity as necessarily creationist but do not themselves have a creationist belief tend to have a negative attitude toward Christianity and a positive attitude toward science.

A similar methodology was used in the investigation in the secondary schools of a Scottish city. The Francis Scale of Attitude Toward Christianity was used together with modified versions of the other scales in a questionnaire completed by 6,653 pupils between the ages of eleven and sixteen years and 729 pupils between the ages of sixteen and eighteen years. As in the Kenyan study, it was found that those who view Christianity as creationist tend to be less likely to combine positive attitudes both toward Christianity and toward science. The data demonstrated a negative correlation between attitude toward Christianity and attitude toward science, but path analysis showed that this apparent negative relationship could be explained in terms of the influence of scientism and of the view of Christianity as creationist, implying that for those not holding these particular views there would not be any conflict between science and Christianity.

The relationship between attitude toward Christianity and the view of Christianity as creationist was found to depend upon age. There was a significant positive correlation among pupils between the ages of eleven and thirteen years ($r = +0.1670$) and pupils between the ages of fourteen and fifteen years ($r = +0.0673$) but a significant negative correlation among pupils between the ages of sixteen and seventeen years ($r = -0.1036$), and this change was interpreted in terms of Reich's theory of the development of complementarity in the thinking of young people (Francis, Fulljames and Gibson, 1992; Reich, 1989; Reich, 1991).

It is the relationship between attitude toward Christianity and the view of Christianity as creationist that is the focus of the further analysis of data from the investigation in England that is now to be presented. The sample of pupils between the ages of eleven and fifteen years was selected to correspond to the age range in which a positive relationship was observed in Scotland. A measure of creationist belief was included in the questionnaire used in England, so it is possible to consider the pattern of relationships between the three variables: creationist belief, view of Christianity as creationist and attitude toward Christianity.

Method

A self-completion questionnaire was administered by teachers in many parts of England to 3,427 pupils between the ages of eleven and fifteen years, 1709 males and 1718 females. The questionnaire was printed in the teacher's handbook for the *Words into Action* series produced by BBC Schools Television and teachers invited to send in the data that they collected (Lealman, 1988). Responses from those affiliated to faiths other than Christianity are not included in this analysis.

The questionnaire included 62 items related to religious attitudes, Christian belief and the biblical creation stories. The view of Christianity as creationist was assessed by response to the item 'Christians have to believe that God made the world in six days and rested on the seventh'. Creationist belief was assessed by response to the item 'God made the world in six days and rested on the seventh'. Conflict between science and religion was assessed by response to the item 'Science has disproved religion'. Attitude toward Christianity was assessed by responses to the 24 items of the Francis Scale of Attitude Toward Christianity ASC4B (Francis, 1989). Each item was assessed on a five point scale: agree strongly, agree, not certain, disagree and disagree strongly. Respondents were asked to indicate their sex and age.

The data were analysed by the SPSS statistical package, using the frequencies, correlation and multiple regression routines (SPSS Inc., 1988).

Results

The reliability of the Francis Scale of Attitude Toward Christianity was high, the alpha coefficient being measured as 0.9641.

Table 16.1 presents the responses to five representative items of the Francis Scale of Attitude Toward Christianity and five other items in the questionnaire. The pattern of responses is similar to that reported previously for a sample of pupils between the ages of twelve and sixteen years (Francis, 1992). Three-fifths of the respondents (60%) affirmed their belief in God, but only a third

(33%) regarded God as very real to them. More than twice as many (28%) were agnostic about belief in God than were atheist (12%).

Table 16.1
Frequency of responses

	agree %	not certain %	disagree %
I know that Jesus helps me	32	43	25
God is very real to me	33	38	29
I think church services are boring	49	23	28
I believe that God listens to prayers	49	32	19
I think the bible is out of date	21	32	47
I believe in God	60	28	12
I believe that Jesus really rose from the dead	42	39	19
Science has disproved religion	15	52	33
Christians have to believe that God made the world in six days and rested on the seventh	19	33	48
God made the world in six days and rested on the seventh	23	42	35

Just under a third (32%) were confident that Jesus helped them. Twice as many (42%) believed that Jesus rose from the dead than did not (19%). About a half of the respondents (49%) agreed that God listens to prayers, and about a half (49%) felt that church services are boring. Nearly a half (47%) did not accept that the bible is out of date.

More than a half of these pupils between the ages of eleven and fifteen years (52%) were uncertain whether science has disproved religion. About one in seven (15%) were clear that science has disproved religion, while more than twice as many (37%) were clear that it has not. About one-fifth (19%) thought that 'Christians have to believe that God made the world in six days and rested on the seventh'. This result may be contrasted with the 36% of pupils between the ages of eleven and fifteen years in a Scottish city who thought that 'true Christians believe the universe was made in six days of 24 hours each'. Just under a quarter (23%) affirmed their own belief that 'God made the world in six days and rested on the seventh', while about two-fifths (42%) were not certain about this item.

The correlation matrix in table 16.2 presents the relationships between the variables : sex, age, conflict between science and religion, view of Christianity as creationist, creationist belief, and attitude toward Christianity. From the correlation matrix it can be

Table 16.2
Correlation matrix

	attitude toward Christianity	creationist belief	view of Christianity as creationist	science has disproved religion	age
sex	+0.1957 .001	+0.1770 .001	−0.0033 NS	−0.0172 NS	+0.0325 NS
age	−0.1257 .001	−0.1172 .001	−0.1138 .001	−0.0344 .05	
science has disproved religion	−0.1683 .001	−0.0855 .001	+0.0638 .001		
view of Christianity as creationist	+0.1459 .001	+0.3238 .001			
creationist belief	+0.5818 .001				

seen that attitude toward Christianity is significantly more positive among females than among males and that attitude toward Christianity tends to decrease as young people grow through the teenage years, both of which are consistent with the results of other studies (Francis, 1984; Hyde, 1990). The distinction between creationist belief and the view of Christianity as creationist is clear from the contrasting relationships with the view that science has disproved religion. Those who themselves believe that God made the world in six days are more likely to think that science has not disproved religion than those who do not have a creationist belief, whereas those who view Christianity as creationist are more likely to think that science has disproved religion than those who do not hold this view of Christianity.

There is a significant positive relationship ($r = +0.1459$) between attitude toward Christianity and the view of Christianity as creationist, which is consistent with the results in Scotland for those in the same age range. There is an even stronger positive relationship between attitude toward Christianity and creationist belief ($r = +0.5818$). A positive relationship is also observed between creationist belief and the view of Christianity as creationist ($r = +0.3238$), and it is appropriate therefore to use multiple linear regression to identify the relationship between attitude toward Christianity and the view of Christianity as creationist when the influence of creationist belief has been taken into account.

Table 16.3 presents the multiple regression significance tests, allowing for the influence of sex, age and creationist belief, before examining the influence of the view of Christianity as creationist

Table 16.3
Multiple regression significance tests

predictor variables	R^2	change in R^2	F of change	P<	Beta	T	P<
sex	0.0383	0.0383	135.3	.001	+0.1957	+7.0	.001
age	0.0535	0.0152	54.5	.001	−0.1233	−4.3	.001
creationist belief	0.3508	0.2974	1556.5	.001	+0.5578	+39.5	.001
Christianity as creationist	0.3526	0.0018	9.3	.01	0.0447	−15.7	.01

on attitude toward Christianity. These results show that, when creationist belief has been taken into account, the influence of the view of Christianity as creationist on attitude toward Christianity is no longer positive but is indeed negative. In general, young people who have a view of Christianity as necessarily involving creationism tend to hold a less positive attitude toward Christianity than those who do not have this view of Christianity.

Conclusions

In the previous investigation in Scotland it was observed that there was a significant positive relationship between the view of Christianity as creationist and attitude toward Christianity among pupils between the ages of eleven and fifteen years and a significant negative relationship among pupils between the ages of sixteen and seventeen years. Among pupils between the ages of eleven and fifteen years in England a significant positive relationship has again been observed, but it has also been shown that, when the influence of creationist belief is taken into account, the relationship between the view of Christianity as creationist and attitude toward Christianity is negative. The observations in Scotland had suggested that there was a change in the direction of this influence during the teenage years, but this analysis of data from England leads to the conclusion that the influence is negative throughout the teenage years.

The previous investigations in Kenya and in Scotland led to recommendations that topics in science and religion should be included in the religious education curriculum, with aims that would include an understanding of the nature of science and an awareness of alternative interpretations of the biblical creation stories. Similar recommendations have been made by Poole (Poole, 1990; Poole, 1992) and relevant resources are now available. The above conclusion supports those recommendations, but also highlights the importance of alternative interpretations of creation stories being discussed earlier rather than later.

A second conclusion is that measurement of attitude toward Christianity can be of value in research in religious education. Its relevance has been questioned on the grounds that the development of a positive attitude toward Christianity is not an aim of religious education in schools (Levitt, 1994). Development in understanding of Christianity is, however, among the aims of religious education, and an aspect of this understanding is the appreciation of how particular beliefs and Christian commitment are related. It is intended that young people should be informed in ways that will give them the opportunity to decide for themselves whether or not to develop such commitment. Attention may appropriately be given in religious education to misunderstandings that may restrict the opportunity of young people to develop a positive attitude toward Christianity.

The series of investigations described in this chapter have explored the interaction between attitude and understanding, and have identified particular views of science (scientism) and Christianity (the view of Christianity as creationist) which tend to preclude the combination of positive attitudes both toward science and toward Christianity. The view of Christianity as creationist has been shown to make it less likely that young people will hold a positive attitude toward Christianity. If it is accepted that accurate understanding of Christianity includes an awareness that Christians have alternative interpretations of the creation stories and that people with different interpretations may each have a high level of Christian commitment, then the view of Christianity as creationist is a misunderstanding which the measurement of attitude toward Christianity has helped to identify as a topic needing attention in the curriculum.

A third conclusion repeats the plea of John Greer in 1972 for further research in this field. There are opportunities to go beyond the limited scope of the investigations described in this chapter. For example, measuring instruments need to be developed that will enable those affiliated to faiths other than Christianity to be included in analysis. It is possible to distinguish different elements in the concept of scientism and the influence of each could be explored. Several topics in current debate about science and religion involve concepts of divine presence and activity, and an investigation of how in the thinking of young people these concepts are related to other factors might be informed by Oser's stage theory of the development of religious judgement (Oser, 1992; Oser and Gmunder, 1991) and use both qualitative and quantitative methods of enquiry.

References

Francis, L.J. (1984), *Teenagers and the Church: a profile of churchgoing youth in the 1980s*, London, Collins.

Francis, L.J. (1989), Measuring attitude towards Christianity during childhood and adolescence, *Personality and Individual Differences*, 10, 695–698.

Francis, L.J. (1992), Christianity today: the teenage experience, in J. Astley and D. Day (eds), *The Contours of Christian Education*, pp. 340–368, Great Wakering, McCrimmons.

Francis, L.J., Fulljames, P. and Gibson, H.M. (1992), Does creationism commend the gospel? a developmental study among 11–17 year olds, *Religious Education*, 87, 19–27.

Francis, L.J., Gibson, H.M. and Fulljames, P. (1990), Attitude towards Christianity, creationism, scientism and interest in science among 11–15 year olds, *British Journal of Religious Education*, 13, 4–17.

Fulljames, P. and Francis, L.J. (1987a), Creationism and student attitudes towards science and Christianity, *Journal of Christian Education*, 90, 51–55.

Fulljames, P. and Francis, L.J. (1987b), The measurement of attitude towards Christianity among Kenyan secondary school students, *Journal of Social Psychology*, 127, 407–409.

Fulljames, P. and Francis, L.J. (1988), The influence of creationism and scientism on attitude towards Christianity among Kenyan secondary school students, *Educational Studies*, 14, 77–96.

Fulljames, P., Gibson, H.M. and Francis, L.J. (1991), Creationism, scientism, Christianity and science: a study in adolescent attitudes, *British Educational Research Journal*, 17, 171–190.

Gibson, H.M. (1989), Attitudes to religion and science among school children aged 11 to 16 years in a Scottish city, *Journal of Empirical Theology*, 2, 5–26.

Greer, J.E. (1972), The child's understanding of creation, *Educational Review*, 24, 99–110.

Hyde, K. (1990), *Religion in Childhood and Adolescence*, Birmingham, Alabama, Religious Education Press.

Lealman, B. (1988), *Words into Action*, London, Christian Education Movement.

Levitt, M. (1994), 'The church is very important to me': a consideration of the relevance of Francis's 'Attitude towards Christianity' scale to the aims of Church of England aided schools, *British Journal of Religious Education*, 17, 100–107.

Oser, F. (1992), Toward a logic of religious development, in J.W. Fowler, K.E. Nipkow and F. Schweitzer (eds) (1992), *Stages of Faith and Religious Development: implications for church, education and society*, pp. 37–64, London, SCM.

Oser, F. and Gmunder, P. (1991), *Religious Judgement*, Birmingham, Alabama, Religious Education Press.

Poole, M. (1990), Science and religion: a challenge for secondary education, *British Journal of Religious Education*, 13, 18–27.

Poole, M. (1992), Teaching about issues of science and religion, in B. Watson (ed.), *Priorities in Religious Education*, pp. 144–164, Lewes, Falmer Press.

Reich, K.H. (1989), Between religion and science: complementarity in the religious thinking of young people, *British Journal of Religious Education*, 11, 62–69.

Reich, K.H. (1991), The role of complementarity reasoning in religious development, in F.K. Oser, and W.G. Scarlett (eds), *Religious Development in Childhood and Adolescence: new directions for child development*, pp. 77–89, San Francisco, Jossey-Bass.

SPSS Inc. (1988), *SPSSX User's Guide*, New York, McGraw-Hill.

17

Religious education and assemblies: pupils' changing views

William K. Kay

Summary

In primary and secondary schools in England and Wales pupils are, subject to a conscience clause, required by law to receive religious education and to attend collective worship during school assembly. Data reported from two studies, conducted among 13,391 pupils in year nine and year ten and among 4,948 pupils in year six demonstrate that, while primary school pupils prefer school assembly to religious education, the reverse is true for secondary school pupils. This chapter suggests that the reversal is caused by the removal, at secondary level, of those features of assemblies which younger pupils most enjoy and by the tendency for older pupils to evaluate more positively those aspects of school which are related to public examinations and the job market.

Introduction

The religious element within the life of state maintained schools in England and Wales has, at least since 1944, been thought of as comprising two components: religious education and school assembly (or collective worship). These two components have been legally related. In the 1944 Education Act, under the heading 'Religious Education', a daily act of 'collective worship' is required by all pupils unless their parents, on grounds of conscience, withdraw them (sections 25 and 26), and the implication of the heading

267

is that 'collective worship' is considered to be part of religious education (Souper and Kay, 1982a).

Social, theological and educational changes altered the context in which education took place in the next four decades but, even at the time of the 1988 Education Reform Act, worship in school and religious education were legally connected in the same way as before. Reference to collective worship comes in Section 6 under the heading 'Religious Education'.

In circular 1/94 the Department for Education states that 'the Government also attaches great importance to the role of religious education and collective worship in helping to promote among pupils a clear set of personal values and beliefs. They have a role in promoting respect for and understanding of those with different beliefs and religious practices from their own, based on rigorous study of different faiths' (paragraph 9). A little later the circular continues, 'collective worship in schools should aim to present the opportunity for pupils to worship God, to consider moral and spiritual values and to explore their own beliefs . . .' (paragraph 50). The circular presents educational objectives or possibilities in this passage. Pupils may 'explore their own beliefs' and develop 'moral and spiritual values'.

Studies of school religion have almost completely ignored the connection between collective worship and religious education as it existed in the minds of the coalition Government of 1944, and as it existed in Mrs Thatcher's Conservative Government of 1988. The study by Souper and Kay (1982b) asked headteachers about the use to which daily assemblies were put and found that, in many instances, this use was broadly educational and, in some instances, specifically related to classroom teaching. Pupils themselves, as the studies reviewed below show, have tended to think of assemblies and religious education as distinct activities, a distinction under-lined by school timetables.

The main long-term finding of studies in this area since 1944 is that girls are more favourable than boys to both aspects of school religion. However, the evaluation system used in these studies has varied enormously so that it is usually not possible to make comparisons within a single study of pupils' views of religious education against their views of assembly. Nor is it possible to make accurate comparisons between pupils in one study and pupils in another. Furthermore, methodological rigour is less pronounced in studies dated before about 1960, and this means that it is difficult to know how much reliance to place in many of their conclusions or to know how adequately these conclusions may be applied to populations larger than the samples on which they are based.

Rixon (1959) found that less able pupils of both sexes thought religious education was more interesting and useful than did more able pupils. Varma (1959) found secondary modern pupils ranked religious education lowest in popularity after English, geography, science, mathematics and history, but also that religious education was not disliked as much as science and mathematics. Kesteven (1967) explored the views of young people aged between thirteen and twenty and, according to Hyde (1990), 'religious education was favoured by many, who claimed to have learnt much about God from it. Similarly, despite criticisms of it, most felt school assembly to have been worthwhile'. Jones (1969), in a study of twelve secondary schools, was also able to report, 'pupils in all types of (secondary) schools are in general favourably disposed to morning assembly' and, though he did find 'many pupils who are extremely unfavourably disposed to much that goes on under the name of worship in their schools', this view seemed to be related to the kinds of activities that made up assembly. Prayer was in general preferred to bible readings from the Old Testament. Such positive evaluations were contradicted by Russell (1978) who found, in the transition from the top of the primary school (age eleven) to the middle of the secondary school (age thirteen), school assembly came to be disliked for non-religious reasons. Taylor's (1970) results were dependent on the type of secondary school surveyed and the religious background of its pupils: about 66% of girls (aged sixteen) at Anglican schools approved of school worship, while about 80% of boys in county schools thought it was worthless. Brimer (1972), by contrast, found that ten year olds did not regard school worship as important, and Greer and Brown (1973) thought that newer and experimental syllabuses provoked more interest among primary aged children than traditional syllabuses. On the other hand, with a secondary aged group, Francis (1979) found less favourable attitudes toward Christianity were associated with newer syllabuses.

Two studies are examined in this chapter. The larger of the two, study 1, was reported by Francis and Kay (1995). The smaller, study 2, was reported by Francis (1987). Both databases were reanalysed to enable their data to relate more directly to each other.

Study 1

Method

A questionnaire was anonymously completed by 13,391 pupils, between the ages of thirteen and fifteen years, attending year nine and year ten classes in 65 schools in different parts of England and Wales. Eight of these schools were aided (two Church of England and six Roman Catholic) and the remaining 57 were not church related. The proportions of each type of school in the survey match the proportions of similar types in England and Wales as a whole (Francis and Kay, 1995). The sample comprised 49% males and 51% females. The questionnaire included the following two statements about religious education and school worship: 'Religious education should be taught in school' and 'Schools should hold a religious assembly every day'. Each pupil could respond to both statements on a five point scale: agree strongly, agree, uncertain, disagree and disagree strongly. The data were analysed by the SPSS statistical package, using the frequencies and t-test routine (SPSS Inc., 1988).

Results

Table 17.1 presents the proportions of pupils expressing agreement, uncertainty and disagreement with the two statements regarding religious education and daily religious assemblies. These figures

Table 17.1
Attitude toward religious education and religious assemblies among year nine and year ten pupils

	agree %	not certain %	disagree %
Religious education should be taught in school	33	36	31
Schools should hold a religious assembly every day	6	21	73

clearly show that there is more support among year nine and year ten pupils for religious education than for daily religious assemblies. Overall, pupils in this age group are fairly evenly divided over the provision of religious education. The largest percentage is uncertain, but there are slightly more pupils in favour of the continuance of religious education than those who are against it. We may put the figures another way by saying that less than a third of pupils would want religious education removed from the curriculum; it would be equally true to say, however, that only a third would wish to retain it. Overall, the vast majority of pupils (73%) are opposed to daily religious assemblies. Even if the pupils who are uncertain are combined with the pupils who would retain daily religious assemblies, clearly this figure only amounts to just over one pupil in four.

Closer analysis of these data reveal important differences between the responses of boys and girls and between the responses of year nine and year ten pupils concerning religious education. While 38% of the girls agree that religious education should be taught in schools, the proportion falls to 27% of the boys. While 37% of the year nine pupils agree that religious education should be taught in schools, the proportion falls to 28% of the year ten pupils. On the other hand, there are no significant age or sex differences concerning daily religious assemblies. Thus, 7% of the girls and 6% of the boys agree that schools should hold a religious assembly every day. Similarly, 7% of the year nine pupils and 6% of year ten pupils agree that schools should hold a religious assembly every day.

Study 2

Method

The second questionnaire was completed anonymously by 4,948 year six pupils attending Church of England, Roman Catholic and non-denominational state maintained schools within one local authority in the south of England. There were slightly more boys (51%) in the sample than girls (49%). The questionnaire included the semantic differential grid developed by Francis (1987), who demonstrated that this grid functioned reliably and unidimensionally among this age group. The seven adjective pairs in the grid are friendly–unfriendly, pleasant–unpleasant, bad–good, interesting–boring, nice–nasty, sad–happy and important–unimportant. These bi-polar adjectives were deliberately varied in order to offset response bias. The semantic differential space between the locations of the positive and negative adjectives allowed for a range of seven responses. The same grid was presented six times in respect of religious education, school assemblies and four other school subjects: English lessons, mathematics lessons, games lessons and music lessons.

Using the SPSS statistical package (SPSS Inc., 1988), the frequencies for each set of responses were computed and the distributions inspected for normality. After this t-tests were computed to see whether the mean score on each of the bi-polar pairs of adjectives was significantly different. Each of the five areas (English, mathematics, religious education, games and assemblies) was tested against every other area for boys and girls separately.

Results

Table 17.2 presents the mean scores recorded by boys and girls separably on the seven semantic differential grids for English lessons, mathematics lessons, music lessons, games lessons, religious education and assemblies. Table 17.3 presents the paired t-tests to inspect the relationship between attitudes toward religious education and both English lessons and mathematics lessons, the relationship between attitudes toward daily religious assemblies and both English lessons and mathematics lessons and the relationship between attitudes toward religious education and daily religious assemblies. All three calculations are performed separately for boys and for girls.

These tables show six things about assemblies: both sexes, at age eleven, rank assembly low in importance. Boys rank assembly sixth in importance and girls rank it fifth. Both sexes rank assembly as moderately pleasant. Both girls and boys rank it third. When t-tests are performed both sexes consider assembly to be more pleasant than English. Girls also find assembly more pleasant than mathematics, although the reverse is the case among boys.

Turning to religious education, table 17.3 shows that both sexes, at the age of eleven, think that religious education is significantly less important than either English or mathematics. Indeed the t-values in this column are the highest in the table. Boys compare religious education unfavourably with mathematics on all seven bi-polar pairs. Girls find religious education significantly less good, interesting, important or happy than mathematics. They rate it significantly less favourably than English on six bi-polar pairs.

When comparisons between religious education and assembly are made, both sexes rate religious education *lower* than assembly on each of the six bi-polar pairs of adjectives except importance–unimportance. Religious education is less friendly, less good, less

Table 17.2
Mean score on bi-polar adjectival pairs for boys and girls

	pleasant/ unpleasant	good/ bad	interesting/ uninteresting	nice/ nasty	happy/ sad	important/ unimportant	friendly/ unfriendly
boys							
English lessons	4.78	4.99	5.01	4.81	4.86	6.00	4.96
maths lessons	5.35	5.49	5.48	5.21	5.17	6.37	5.17
music lessons	4.89	4.86	4.57	4.84	5.10	4.60	5.03
religious education	4.90	4.92	4.88	4.81	4.78	5.44	5.03
assemblies	5.25	5.16	5.06	5.06	5.08	5.12	5.25
games lessons	6.72	6.62	6.51	6.45	6.36	6.07	6.29
girls							
English lessons	5.50	5.67	5.52	5.47	5.33	6.21	5.33
maths lessons	5.25	5.48	5.50	5.28	5.21	6.43	5.19
music lessons	6.07	5.95	5.71	5.82	5.84	5.53	5.72
religious education	5.29	5.36	5.33	5.23	5.07	5.79	5.40
assemblies	5.66	5.60	5.44	5.45	5.41	5.59	5.63
games lessons	6.64	6.52	6.42	6.37	6.31	6.06	6.25

Table 17.3: Paired t-tests

subject	pleasant	good	interesting	nice	happy	important	friendly
boys							
religious education maths	-8.73 .001	-11.58 .001	-11.38 .001	-8.63 .001	-8.98 .001	-21.70 .001	-3.37 .001
religious education English	2.82 .01	-1.37 NS	-2.35 .05	0.28 NS	-1.92 NS	-12.24 .001	1.76 NS
assembly maths	-2.16 .05	-7.06 .001	-8.29 .001	-3.22 .001	-2.28 .05	-27.57 .001	1.53 NS
assembly English	10.23 .001	3.73 .001	1.11 NS	6.35 .001	5.60 .001	-18.84 .001	7.05 .001
assembly religious education	7.42 .001	5.35 .001	3.45 .001	6.16 .001	7.46 .001	-7.82 .001	5.41 .001
girls							
religious education maths	0.24 NS	-2.73 .01	-2.52 .05	-1.22 NS	-3.24 .001	-16.29 .001	5.46 .001
religious education English	-4.87 .001	-7.75 .001	-4.25 .001	-5.98 .001	-6.50 .001	-10.45 .001	1.99 .05
assembly maths	8.29 .001	2.80 .01	-0.40 NS	4.18 .001	5.33 .001	-20.74 .001	11.52 .001
assembly English	3.82 .001	-2.06 .05	-2.07 .05	-0.43 NS	2.36 .05	-14.66 .001	8.41 .001
assembly religious education	9.06 .001	6.20 .001	2.46 .05	5.99 .001	8.98 .001	-4.80 .001	6.65 .001

Note: If the t value is positive the top subject of the pair has the higher mean. Thus girls find religious education more friendly than maths.

interesting, not as nice, less happy and less friendly than assembly. Table 17.3 shows that each of these differences between religious education and assembly is statistically significant.

Discussion

What these two studies show, therefore, is that school assembly is favoured more highly than religious education by pupils at the age of eleven, but that this position has been reversed by pupils in the middle of the secondary school age range.

Why should this be? The one place, even at the age of eleven, where assembly fails to register more highly in the opinions of pupils than religious education is in the important–unimportant adjectival pair. This perception of assembly as being relatively unimportant may be a clue to its widespread rejection in the older age group. It is unlikely that pupils approaching adolescence will alter their rating of assembly and consider it more important than other school subjects like English and mathematics which are examinable and have clear connections with higher education and the job market. Moreover, while religious education may have an intrinsic importance in the mind of pupils because of its subject matter, it is improbable that such importance will be transferred to assemblies since teachers normally make no attempt to connect assemblies with religious education.

An analysis of those features of assemblies which pupils aged eleven consider favourable suggests other reasons why assemblies are likely to drop in value. Year six pupils think of assemblies as relatively friendly and pleasant. Among year nine and year ten pupils, where the number of young people in attendance at each assembly may be counted in the hundreds and where discipline may need to be maintained or enforced, the friendly atmosphere is likely to dissipate. For this reason, assembly is likely to become a less pleasant occasion. Moreover, it may become physically more uncomfortable and the absence of music and singing, which are more common among assemblies for younger pupils, will reinforce this lessening of appeal. In essence, we may suggest that the positive evaluation of assembly in the primary school does not stem from a perception of the importance assigned to it by pupils. Rather it is the other features of assemblies (friendliness, pleasantness) which make it attractive to pupils. In the mid-secondary school these other features of assembly have been removed.

This interpretation of these two studies is in line with the findings of Brimer (1972) and Russell (1978) reported above. Before reaching a final verdict on pupil opinions about school assembly, however, a consideration of two other matters needs to be included. The first concerns the frequency of assembly. Souper and Kay (1982) found secondary school assemblies in Hampshire were less frequent than primary school assemblies. Most secondary school pupils did not attend assemblies daily. There is therefore a danger that the question asked in study 1 might have been seen by pupils as asking whether they wished to *increase* the number of assemblies they attended, not as whether they wished to abolish assemblies altogether. Such a possible reading of this item in the questionnaire does not invalidate the comparison made between study 1 and study 2 because, in primary schools, religious assemblies do take place on an almost daily basis. The relative popularity of assemblies in the primary school persists despite its higher frequency. The relative unpopularity of assemblies in the secondary school exists despite its lower frequency.

Secondly, there is evidence that pupils may come to value assemblies after they have left school. Rees (1967) found that 50% of his sample of university students 'did not disapprove of compulsory school prayers' and that many of the students 'pointed out that their attitude had changed since leaving school'. Commenting on the free contributions submitted by three out of four respondents Rees remarks, 'the combination of what seems to be genuinely religious *feeling* with a general distrust of churches and clergy . . . was a common theme' (p. 80).

If the present government's policy towards school assemblies is to succeed, it will have to ensure that pupils think more highly of the importance of assemblies and, at the same time, improve the physical conditions under which they are held. What should give the government some incentive to improve the implementation of its policy is that, until the age of eleven, pupils appear to prefer participating in religious worship than learning about it.

References

Brimer, J. (1972), School worship with juniors, *Learning for Living*, 11, 5, 6–12.

Department for Education (1994), Religious education and collective worship, *DFE Circular 1/94*.

Francis, L.J. (1979), School influence and pupil attitude toward religion, *British Journal of Educational Psychology*, 49, 107–123.

Francis, L.J. (1987), *Religion in the Primary School*, London, Collins Liturgical Publications.

Francis, L.J. and Kay, W.K. (1995), *Teenage Religion and Values*, Leominster, Gracewing.

Greer, J.E. and Brown, C.A. (1973), The effects of new approaches to religious education in the primary school, *Journal of Curriculum Studies*, 5, 73–78.

Hyde, K.E. (1990), *Religion in Childhood and Adolescence: a comprehensive review of the research*, Birmingham, Alabama, Religious Education Press.

Jones, C.M. (1969), *Worship in the Secondary School*, Oxford, Oxford University Press.

Kesteven, S.W. (1967), An enquiry into attitudes to religion of youth club members in Stafford and district, Unpublished M.Ed. dissertation, University of Birmingham.

Rees, R.J. (1967), *Background and Belief: a study of religion and religious education as seen by third-year students at Oxford, Cambridge and Bangor*, London, SCM Press.

Rixon, L.D. (1959), An experimental and critical study of the teaching of scripture in secondary school, Unpublished Ph.D. dissertation, University of London.

Russell, A. (1978), The attitude of primary school children to religious education, Unpublished M.Phil. dissertation, University of Nottingham.

Souper, P.C. and Kay, W.K. (1982a), *The School Assembly Debate: 1942–1982*, Southampton, University of Southampton.

Souper, P.C. and Kay, W.K. (1982b), *The School Assembly in Hampshire*, Southampton, University of Southampton.

SPSS Inc. (1988), *SPSSX User's Guide*, New York, McGraw-Hill.

Taylor, H.P. (1970), A comparative study of the religious attitudes, beliefs, and practices of sixth formers in Anglican, state, and Roman Catholic grammar schools, Unpublished M.Phil. dissertation, University of London.

Varma, C.K. (1959), A study of attitudes of school children towards six school subjects, Unpublished D.C.P. dissertation, University of Birmingham.

18

Measuring attitude toward Christianity through the medium of Welsh

Thomas E. Evans and Leslie J. Francis

Summary

The Francis Scale of Attitude Toward Christianity was translated into Welsh and back translated into English. The present study confirms the internal reliability and construct validity of the instrument among a sample of 258 year nine and year ten pupils attending Welsh-medium secondary schools in Dyfed.

Introduction

In parts of Wales the state maintained system of education provides parallel schools operating primarily through the medium of English or primarily through the medium of Welsh (Griffiths, 1986; Hopkin, 1987; Williams, 1988). The school examination system similarly makes provision for pupils to be assessed though the medium of their preferred language (Awdurdod Cwricwlwm ac Asesu Cymru, 1994). It is important, therefore, that educational research conducted within Wales should operate effectively through both languages. One way to ensure comparability between educational research conducted within Welsh-medium schools and studies conducted within the international English-speaking community is through the careful translation of well tested English language psychometric tools into Welsh.

Within the fields of religious education and Christian education the Francis Scale of Attitude Toward Christianity has gained considerable currency in recent years. This scale was developed originally by Francis (1976, 1978a) for use among the age range of between eight and sixteen years in England. Twenty-four items concerned with an affective response to God, Jesus, bible, prayer and church were selected by careful processes of item analysis from an original pool of 110 items. After comparing empirically the relative methods of the five techniques of attitude scaling proposed by Thurstone (1928), Likert (1932), Guttman (1944), Edwards (1957) and Osgood, Suci and Tannenbaum (1957), Francis chose the Likert method of scaling as most appropriate for use throughout the age range of between eight and sixteen years. Each item is assessed on a five point scale ranging from 'agree strongly' through 'uncertain' to 'disagree strongly'.

Since this foundation study, detailed reports have been published on the reliability and validity of this 24 item scale among school aged samples in England (Francis, 1987a, 1989a), Scotland (Gibson, 1989; Gibson and Francis, 1989), Ireland (Francis and Greer, 1990a; Greer and Francis, 1991), Kenya (Fulljames and Francis, 1987a) and Nigeria (Francis and McCarron, 1989). A short form of the scale has been tested among primary school pupils in England (Francis, 1992a) and among secondary school pupils in England, Scotland and Northern Ireland (Francis, Greer and Gibson, 1991). The scale has also been subjected to close scrutiny and criticism (Greer, 1983; Francis and Kay, 1984; Levitt, 1995; Francis, 1995a).

In a paper entitled 'Measurement reapplied' Francis (1978b) argued that it would be advantageous if other researchers concerned with monitoring or establishing the correlates of attitude toward Christianity during childhood and adolescence could agree on employing a common instrument to establish empirical comparability among different studies. Now more than eighty published studies, responding to this invitation, have begun to construct a cumulative picture of the correlates of attitude toward Christianity during the pre-adult years. These studies, summarised and synthesised by Kay and Francis (1995), can be most conveniently discussed in six main groups.

The first group of studies has used the scale to monitor changes in attitude toward Christianity both with age and over time. For example, Greer (1981, 1982) employed the scale to assess changes throughout the eight year period from primary year four to secondary year four. In a series of papers, Francis (1989b, 1989c, 1992b, 1996) monitored changes in pupil attitude at four yearly intervals between 1974 and 1994.

The second group of studies has concentrated on identifying the specific influence of denominational schools, at primary (Francis, 1986a, 1987b) and secondary level (Francis and Carter, 1980; Rhymer and Francis, 1985; Francis, 1986b). Boyle (1984) and Boyle and Francis (1986) explored the relative influence of Catholic middle and secondary schools among twelve year olds.

The third group of studies has focused specifically on the influence of home and parents. Gibson, Francis and Pearson (1990) and Francis, Pearson and Lankshear (1990) isolated the role of social class. Francis and Gibson (1993a) isolated the relative influence of mothers and fathers on sons and daughters at two different stages in development. Kay (1981a) explored the relationship between parental marital happiness and their children's attitude toward religion. Francis, Gibson and Lankshear (1991) charted the influence of Sunday school attendance.

The fourth group of studies has modelled the influence of personality on individual differences in religious development, including the function of neuroticism (Francis, Pearson, Carter and Kay, 1981a; Francis, Pearson and Kay 1983a; Francis and Pearson, 1991), extraversion (Francis, Pearson, Carter and Kay, 1981b; Francis, Pearson and Kay, 1983b; Francis and Pearson, 1985a) and psychoticism (Kay, 1981b; Francis and Pearson, 1985b; Francis, 1992c). Francis, Pearson and Kay (1983c, 1988) and Pearson and Francis (1989) explored the relationship between religiosity and lie scale scores or truthfulness. Other studies concerned with the relationship between Eysenck's dimensional model of personality and individual differences in religiosity during childhood and adolescence include Francis, Pearson and Stubbs (1985), Francis, Lankshear and Pearson (1989), Francis and Montgomery (1992) and Robbins, Francis and Gibbs (1995). Francis and Pearson (1987) charted the role of religion in the development of empathy during adolescence. Pearson, Francis and Lightbown (1986) modelled the relationship between religion and impulsivity and venturesomeness during adolescence. Jones and Francis (1996) modelled the relationship between religion and self-esteem among samples of primary and secondary school pupils.

The fifth group of studies has explored the relationship between attitude toward Christianity and attitude toward science, giving particular attention to the ideas of scientism and creationism (Fulljames and Francis, 1987b, 1988; Francis, Gibson and Fulljames, 1990; Fulljames, Gibson and Francis, 1991; Francis, Fulljames and Gibson, 1992).

The sixth group of studies has employed the attitude scale to explore issues like the religious significance of denominational identity (Francis, 1990), the impact of popular religious television (Francis and Gibson, 1992), the influence of pop culture (Francis and Gibson, 1993b), the contribution of conversion experiences (Kay, 1981c) or religious experience (Greer and Francis, 1992; Francis and Greer, 1993), the relationship between religion and prejudice (Greer, 1985), the impact of teaching world religions on adolescent attitude toward Christianity (Kay, 1981d), the relationship between religion and subject preferences (Kay, 1981e), the relationship between religion and moral values (Francis and Greer, 1990b).

Alongside the form of the scale developed for use among the age range between eight and sixteen years, Francis and Stubbs (1987) developed an adult form of the scale of attitude toward Christianity to extend the earlier research into the post-adolescent years and to test whether relationships found among school pupils held true in later life. Subsequent studies have confirmed the reliability and validity of the scale among samples of adults in England (Francis, 1992d), the Republic of Ireland (Maltby, 1994), the United States of America (Lewis and Maltby, 1995a) and the United Kingdom, United States of America, Australia and Canada (Francis, Lewis, Philipchalk, Brown and Lester, 1995). This adult form is also being increasingly used in a range of studies, including examinations of the relationship between religiosity and pre-oedipal fixation (Lewis and Maltby, 1992), aspects of obsessionality (Lewis, 1994; Lewis and Joseph, 1994a, 1994b; Lewis and Maltby, 1994, 1995b; Maltby, McCollam and Millar, 1994), Eysenck's dimensional model of personality (Francis, 1991, 1992e, 1993; Francis and Bennett, 1992; Lewis and Maltby, 1995c; Maltby, Talley, Cooper and Leslie, 1995; Francis, Lewis, Brown, Philipchalk and Lester, 1995; Carter, Kay and Francis, 1995) and suicidal ideation (Lester and Francis, 1993). Other studies have employed the scale to monitor religious changes during residence in a rehabilitation centre for female drug misusers (Bennett and Rigby, 1991), to isolate the mediating influence of religion on the effectiveness of television advertisements (Al Mossawi, 1992) and to compare the religious profile of Catholics and Protestants (Maltby, 1995).

The aim of the present study is to develop and to test the psychometric properties of a Welsh language edition of the Francis Scale of Attitude Toward Christianity suitable for use among secondary school pupils.

Method

The 24 items of the Francis Scale of Attitude Toward Christianity were translated into Welsh and back translated into English in order to check the translation. The translation was then independently checked by five bilingual Welsh/English speakers with academic and professional training in theology and religion. The Welsh translation of the scale, presented in appendix 1, was completed by 258 adolescents attending year nine and year ten classes of Welsh-medium secondary schools in Dyfed. The sample comprised 149 year nine pupils and 109 year ten pupils, 122 boys and 136 girls.

The respondents also provided information regarding proficiency in the Welsh language, church attendance and personal prayer. Proficiency in the Welsh language was assessed on a five point scale: none, a little, learner, moderate and fluent. Church attendance was assessed on a five point scale: never, once or twice a year, sometimes, at least once a month, nearly every week. Personal prayer was assessed on a five point scale: never, occasionally, at least once a month, at least once a week, nearly every day.

The data were analysed by the SPSS statistical package, using the reliability and correlation routines (SPSS Inc., 1988).

Results

Table 18.1 presents the item rest of test correlation coefficients in respect of all 24 scale items, together with the alpha coefficient, and the loadings on the first factor of the unrotated solution proposed by principal component analysis, together with the percentage of variance explained by this factor. Both sets of statistics support the conclusion that the Welsh translation of the Francis Scale of Attitude Toward Christianity is characterised by homogeneity, unidimensionality and internal consistency among year nine and year ten pupils.

While the formal statistics of reliability are relatively easy to calculate for an attitude scale (Livingston, 1988), the question of assessing validity is more problematic (Zeller, 1988). Steps towards establishing the construct validity of this scale can be made by assessing the extent to which certain predictions about the theoretical variations in attitude scores are reflected empirically (Orton, 1987). While attitudes alone may not be simple or direct predictors of behaviour (Ajzen, 1988), substantial evidence exists to suggest a fairly close relationship between attitude toward

Table 18.1
Item rest of test correlations and factor loadings

Scale item	item rest of test correlations	factor loadings
I find it boring to listen to the bible*	0.5571	0.5754
I know that Jesus helps me	0.6883	0.7345
Saying my prayers helps me a lot	0.7279	0.7716
The church is very important to me	0.7108	0.7449
I think going to church is a waste of my time*	0.6503	0.6502
I want to love Jesus	0.6564	0.6943
I think church services are boring*	0.4093	0.4220
I think people who pray are stupid*	0.3619	0.3700
God helps me to lead a better life	0.7953	0.8274
I like to learn about God very much	0.7606	0.7856
God means a lot to me	0.8600	0.8884
I believe that God helps people	0.7901	0.8212
Prayer helps me a lot	0.8181	0.8517
I know that Jesus is very close to me	0.8150	0.8502
I think praying is a good thing	0.7334	0.7663
I think the bible is out of date*	0.3221	0.3196
I believe that God listens to prayers	0.7309	0.7749
Jesus doesn't mean anything to me*	0.6997	0.7188
God is very real to me	0.7626	0.8002
I think saying prayers does no good*	0.4445	0.4628
The idea of God means much to me	0.8194	0.8484
I believe that Jesus still helps people	0.7850	0.8166
I know that God helps me	0.8020	0.8430
I find it hard to believe in God*	0.5433	0.5623
alpha coefficient / % of variance	0.9566	52.2%

Note: * These negative items were reverse scored.

Christianity and both public and personal religious behaviour among young people in Britain (Francis, 1989a). For this reason the questionnaire included two measures of religious behaviour, namely personal prayer and public church attendance. The correlation with church attendance was +0.4650; the correlation with personal prayer was +0.2483. These statistics demonstrate similar relationships between scores of attitude toward Christianity and public and personal religious behaviour using the Welsh-medium instrument as previously established using the original English medium instrument. Consequently they support the stability of the construct validity of the scale.

Conclusion

The data provide some evidence for the unidimensionality, internal consistency reliability and construct validity of the Welsh language edition of the Francis Scale of Attitude Toward Christianity among year nine and year ten pupils attending Welsh-medium secondary schools in Dyfed. Further research is now needed to establish the generalisability of these findings among younger pupils in South Wales. Also, given linguistic variations between North and South Wales, it is to be recommended that the instrument should be tested in the North as well as in the South.

References

Ajzen, I. (1988), *Attitudes, Personality and Behaviour*, Milton Keynes, Open University Press.

Al Mossawi, M. (1992), Factors mediating the effectiveness of TV advertisements, Unpublished Ph.D. dissertation, University of Manchester.

Awdurdod Cwricwlwm ac Asesu Cymru (1994), *Cymraeg yn y Cwricwlwm Cenedlaethol*, Caerdydd, Awdurdod Cwricwlwm ac Asesu Cymru.

Bennett, G. and Rigby, K. (1991), Psychological change during residence in a rehabilitation centre for female drug misusers, *Drug and Alcohol Dependence*, 27, 149–157.

Boyle, J.J. (1984), Catholic children's attitudes towards Christianity, unpublished M.Sc. dissertation, University of Bradford.

Boyle, J.J. and Francis, L.J. (1986), The influence of differing church aided school systems on pupil attitude towards religion, *Research in Education*, 35, 7–12.

Carter, M., Kay, W.K. and Francis, L.J. (1995), Personality and attitude toward Christianity among committed adult Christians, *Personality and Individual Differences*, in press.

Edwards, A.L. (1957), *Techniques of Attitude Scale Construction*, New York, Appleton-Century-Crofts.

Francis, L.J. (1976), An enquiry into the concept 'Readiness for Religion', unpublished Ph.D dissertation, University of Cambridge.

Francis, L.J. (1978a), Attitude and longitude: a study in measurement, *Character Potential*, 8, 119–130.

Francis, L.J. (1978b), Measurement reapplied: research into the child's attitude towards religion, *British Journal of Religious Education*, 1, 45–51.

Francis, L.J. (1986a), Denominational schools and pupil attitudes towards Christianity, *British Educational Research Journal*, 12, 145–152.

Francis, L.J. (1986b), Roman Catholic secondary schools: falling rolls and pupil attitudes, *Educational Studies*, 12, 119–127.

Francis, L.J. (1987a), Measuring attitudes towards Christianity among 12–18 year old pupils in Catholic schools, *Educational Research*, 29, 230–233.

Francis, L.J. (1987b), *Religion in the Primary School*, London, Collins Liturgical Publications.

Francis, L.J. (1989a), Monitoring changing attitudes towards Christianity among secondary school pupils between 1974 and 1986, *British Journal of Educational Psychology*, 59, 86–91.

Francis, L.J. (1989b), Drift from the churches: secondary school pupils' attitudes towards Christianity, *British Journal of Religious Education*, 11, 76–86.

Francis, L.J. (1989c), Measuring attitude towards Christianity during childhood and adolescence, *Personality and Individual Differences*, 10, 695–698.

Francis, L.J. (1990), The religious significance of denominational identity among eleven year old children in England, *Journal of Christian Education*, 97, 23–28.

Francis, L.J. (1991), Personality and attitude towards religion among adult churchgoers in England, *Psychological Reports*, 69, 791–794.

Francis, L.J. (1992a), Reliability and validity of a short measure of attitude towards Christianity among nine to eleven year old pupils in England, *Collected Original Resources in Education*, 16, 1, fiche 3, A02.

Francis, L.J. (1992b), Monitoring attitude towards Christianity: the 1990 study, *British Journal of Religious Education*, 14, 178–182.

Francis, L.J. (1992c), Is psychoticism really the dimension of personality fundamental to religiosity? *Personality and Individual Differences*, 13, 645–652.

Francis, L.J. (1992d), Reliability and validity of the Francis Scale of Attitude Toward Christianity (adult), *Panorama: international journal of comparative religious education and values*, 4, 1, 17–19.

Francis, L.J. (1992e), Neuroticism and intensity of religious attitudes among clergy in England, *Journal of Social Psychology*, 132, 577–580.

Francis, L.J. (1993), Personality and religion among college students in the UK, *Personality and Individual Differences*, 14, 619–622.

Francis, L.J. (1995a), Church schools and pupils attitudes towards Christianity: a response to Mairi Levitt, *British Journal of Religious Education*, 17, 133–139.

Francis, L.J. (1996), Monitoring attitudes toward Christianity between 1974 and 1994 among secondary school pupils in England, in M. Bar-Lev and W. Shaffir (eds), *Leaving Religion and Religious Life: patterns and dynamics*, Greenwich, JAI Press, in press.

Francis, L.J. and Bennett, G.A. (1992), Personality and religion among female drug misusers, *Drug and Alcohol Dependence*, 30, 27–31.

Francis, L.J. and Carter, M. (1980), Church aided secondary schools, religious education as an examination subject and pupil attitude towards religion, *British Journal of Educational Psychology*, 50, 297–300.

Francis, L.J., Fulljames, P. and Gibson, H.M. (1992), Does creationism commend the gospel? a developmental study among 11–17 year olds, *Religious Education*, 87, 19–27.

Francis, L.J. and Gibson, H.M. (1992), Popular religious television and adolescent attitudes towards Christianity, in J. Astley and D.V. Day (eds), *The Contours of Christian Education*, pp. 369–381, Great Wakering, McCrimmons.

Francis, L.J. and Gibson, H.M. (1993a), Parental influence and adolescent religiosity: a study of church attendance and attitude towards Christianity among 11–12 and 15–16 year olds, *International Journal for the Psychology of Religion*, 3, 241–253.

Francis, L.J. and Gibson, H.M. (1993b), Television, pop culture and the drift from Christianity during adolescence, *British Journal of Religious Education*, 15, 31–37.

Francis, L.J., Gibson, H.M. and Fulljames, P. (1990), Attitude towards Christianity, creationism, scientism and interest in science, *British Journal of Religious Education*, 13, 4–17.

Francis, L.J., Gibson, H.M. and Lankshear, D.W. (1991), The influence of Protestant Sunday Schools on attitudes towards Christianity among 11–15 year olds in Scotland, *British Journal of Religious Education*, 14, 35–42.

Francis, L.J. and Greer, J.E. (1990a), Measuring attitudes towards Christianity among pupils in Protestant secondary schools in Northern Ireland, *Personality and Individual Differences*, 11, 853–856.

Francis, L.J. and Greer, J.E. (1990b), Catholic schools and adolescent religiosity in Northern Ireland: shaping moral values, *Irish Journal of Education*, 24, 40–47.

Francis, L.J. and Greer, J.E. (1993), The contribution of religious experience to Christian development: a study among fourth, fifth and sixth year pupils in Northern Ireland, *British Journal of Religious Education*, 15, 38–43.

Francis, L.J., Greer, J.E. and Gibson, H.M. (1991), Reliability and validity of a short measure of attitude towards Christianity among secondary school pupils in England, Scotland and Northern Ireland, *Collected Original Resources in Education*, 15, 3, fiche 2, G09.

Francis, L.J. and Kay, W.K. (1984), Attitude towards religion: definition, measurement and evaluation, *British Journal of Educational Studies*, 32, 45–50.

Francis, L.J., Lankshear, D.W. and Pearson, P.R. (1989), The relationship between religiosity and the short form JEPQ (JEPQ-S) indices of E, N, L and P among eleven year olds, *Personality and Individual Differences*, 10, 763–769.

Francis, L.J., Lewis, J.M., Brown, L.B., Philipchalk, R. and Lester, D. (1995), Personality and religion among undergraduate students in the United Kingdom, United States, Australia and Canada, *Journal of Psychology and Christianity*, 14, 250–262.

Francis, L.J., Lewis, J.M., Philipchalk, R., Brown, L.B., and Lester, D. (1995), The internal consistency reliability and construct validity of the Francis Scale of Attitude Toward Christianity (adult) among undergraduate students in the UK, USA, Australia and Canada, *Personality and Individual Differences*, 19, 949–953.

Francis, L.J. and McCarron, M.M. (1989), The measurement of attitudes towards Christianity among Nigerian secondary school students, *Journal of Social Psychology*, 129, 569–571.

Francis, L.J. and Montgomery, A. (1992), Personality and attitudes towards Christianity among eleven to sixteen year old girls in a single sex Catholic school, *British Journal of Religious Education*, 14, 114–119.

Francis, L.J. and Pearson, P.R. (1985a), Extraversion and religiosity, *Journal of Social Psychology*, 125, 269–270.

Francis, L.J. and Pearson, P.R. (1985b), Psychoticism and religiosity among 15 year olds, *Personality and Individual Differences*, 6, 397–398.

Francis, L.J. and Pearson, P.R. (1987), Empathic development during adolescence: religiosity, the missing link? *Personality and Individual Differences*, 8, 145–148.

Francis, L.J., and Pearson, P.R. (1991), Religiosity, gender and the two faces of neuroticism, *Irish Journal of Psychology*, 12, 60–68.

Francis, L.J., Pearson, P.R., Carter, M. and Kay, W.K. (1981a), The relationship between neuroticism and religiosity among English 15–16 year olds, *Journal of Social Psychology*, 114, 99–102.

Francis, L.J., Pearson, P.R., Carter, M. and Kay, W.K. (1981b), Are introverts more religious? *British Journal of Social Psychology*, 20, 101–104.

Francis, L.J., Pearson, P.R. and Kay, W.K. (1983a), Neuroticism and religiosity among English school children, *Journal of Social Psychology*, 121, 149–150.

Francis, L.J., Pearson, P.R. and Kay, W.K. (1983b), Are introverts still more religious? *Personality and Individual Differences*, 4, 211–212.

Francis, L.J., Pearson, P.R. and Kay, W.K. (1983c), Are religious children bigger liars? *Psychological Reports*, 52, 551–554.

Francis, L.J., Pearson, P.R. and Kay, W.K. (1988), Religiosity and lie scores: a question of interpretation, *Social Behaviour and Personality*, 16, 91–95.

Francis, L.J., Pearson, P.R. and Lankshear, D.W. (1990), The relationship between social class and attitude towards Christianity among ten and eleven year old children, *Personality and Individual Differences*, 11, 1019–1027.

Francis, L.J., Pearson, P.R. and Stubbs, M.T. (1985), Personality and religion among low ability children in residential special schools, *British Journal of Mental Subnormality*, 31, 41–45.

Francis, L.J. and Stubbs, M.T. (1987), Measuring attitudes towards Christianity: from childhood to adulthood, *Personality and Individual Differences*, 8, 741–743.

Fulljames, P. and Francis, L.J. (1987a), The measurement of attitudes towards Christianity among Kenyan secondary school students, *Journal of Social Psychology*, 127, 407–409.

Fulljames, P. and Francis, L.J. (1987b), Creationism and student attitudes towards science and Christianity, *Journal of Christian Education*, 90, 51–55.

Fulljames, P. and Francis, L.J. (1988), The influence of creationism and scientism on attitudes towards Christianity among Kenyan secondary school students, *Educational Studies*, 14, 77–96.

Fulljames, P., Gibson, H.M. and Francis, L.J. (1991), Creationism, scientism, Christianity and science: a study in adolescent attitudes, *British Educational Research Journal*, 17, 171–190.

Gibson, H.M. (1989), Measuring attitudes towards Christianity among 11–16 year old pupils in non-denominational schools in Scotland, *Educational Research*, 31, 221–227.

Gibson, H.M. and Francis, L.J. (1989), Measuring attitudes towards Christianity among 11-to 16- year old pupils in Catholic schools in Scotland, *Educational Research*, 31, 65–69.

Gibson, H.M., Francis, L.J. and Pearson, P.R. (1990), The relationship between social class and attitude towards Christianity among fourteen and fifteen year old adolescents, *Personality and Individual Differences*, 11, 631–635.

Greer, J.E. (1981), Religious attitudes and thinking in Belfast pupils, *Educational Research*, 23, 177–189.

Greer, J.E. (1982), Growing up in Belfast: a study of religious development, *Collected Original Resources in Education*, 6, 1, fiche 1, A14.

Greer, J.E. (1983), Attitude to religion reconsidered, *British Journal of Educational Studies*, 31, 18–28.

Greer, J.E. (1985), Viewing 'the other side' in Northern Ireland: openness and attitudes to religion among Catholic and Protestant adolescents, *Journal for the Scientific Study of Religion*, 24, 275–292.

Greer, J.E. and Francis, L.J. (1991), Measuring attitudes towards Christianity among pupils in Catholic Secondary schools in Northern Ireland, *Educational Research*, 33, 70–73.

Greer, J.E. and Francis, L.J. (1992), Religious experience and attitude towards Christianity among secondary school children in Northern Ireland, *Journal of Social Psychology*, 132, 277–279.

Griffiths, P.H. (1986), *O'r Fesen, Derwen a Dyf: hanes ysgol Gymraeg Caerfyrddin 1955–1985*, Llandysul, Gomer.

Guttman, L. (1944), A basis for scaling qualitative data, *American Sociological Review*, 9, 139–150.

Hopkin, D. (1987), *Ysgol Gymraeg Dewi Sant Llanelli 1947–1987: y blynyddoedd cynnar*, Llanelli, Cyngor Bwrdeistref Llanelli.

Jones, S.H. and Francis, L. J. (1996), Religiosity and self-esteem during childhood and adolescence, in L.J. Francis, W.K. Kay and W.S. Campbell (eds), *Research in Religious Education*, Leominster, Gracewing.

Kay, W.K. (1981a), Marital happiness and children's attitudes to religion, *British Journal of Religious Education*, 3, 102–105.

Kay, W.K. (1981b), Psychoticism and attitude to religion, *Personality and Individual Differences*, 2, 249–252.

Kay, W.K. (1981c), Conversion among 11–15 year olds, *Spectrum*, 13, 2, 26–33.

Kay, W.K. (1981d), Syllabuses and attitudes to Christianity, *The Irish Catechist*, 5, 2, 16–21.

Kay, W.K. (1981e), Subject preference and attitude to religion in secondary schools, *Educational Review*, 33, 47–51.

Kay, W.K. and Francis, L.J. (1995), *Drift from the Churches: attitude toward Christianity during childhood and adolescence*, Cardiff, University of Wales Press.

Lester, D. and Francis, L.J. (1993), Is religiosity related to suicidal ideation after personality and mood are taken into account? *Personality and Individual Differences*, 15, 591–592.

Levitt, M. (1995), 'The church is very important to me.' A consideration of the relevance of Francis' attitude towards Christianity scale to the aims of Church of England aided schools, *British Journal of Religious Education*, 17, 100–107.

Lewis, C.A. (1994), Religiosity and obsessionality: the relationship between Freud's 'religious practices', *Journal of Psychology*, 128, 189–196.

Lewis, C.A. and Joseph, S. (1994a), Religiosity: psychoticism and obsessionality in Northern Irish university students, *Personality and Individual Differences*, 17, 685–687.

Lewis, C.A. and Joseph, S. (1994b), Obsessive actions and religious practices, *Journal of Psychology*, 128, 699–700.

Lewis, C.A. and Maltby, J. (1992), Religiosity and preoedipal fixation: a refinement, *Journal of Psychology*, 126, 687–688.

Lewis, C.A. and Maltby, J. (1994), Religious attitudes and obsessional personality traits among UK adults, *Psychological Reports*, 75, 353–354.

Lewis, C.A. and Maltby, J. (1995a), The reliability and validity of the Francis Scale of Attitude Toward Christianity among US adults, *Psychological Reports*, 76, 1243–1247.

Lewis, C.A. and Maltby, J. (1995b), Religious attitude and practice: the relationship with obsessionality, *Personality and Individual Differences*, 19, 105–108.

Lewis, C.A. and Maltby, J. (1995c), Religiosity and personality among US adults, *Personality and Individual Differences*, 18, 293–295.

Likert, R. (1932), A technique for the measurement of attitudes, *Archives of Psychology*, 140, 1–55.

Livingston, S.A. (1988), Reliability of test results, in J.P. Keeves (ed.), *Educational Research, Methodology and Measurement: an international handbook*, pp. 386–392, Oxford, Pergamon Press.

Maltby, J. (1994), The reliability and validity of the Francis Scale of Attitude Toward Christianity among Republic of Ireland adults, *Irish Journal of Psychology*, 15, 595–598.

Maltby, J. (1995), Is there a denominational difference in scores on the Francis Scale of Attitude Toward Christianity among Northern Irish adults? *Psychological Reports*, 76, 88–90.

Maltby, J., McCollam, P. and Millar, D. (1994), Religiosity and obsessionality: a refinement, *Journal of Psychology*, 128, 609–611.

Maltby, J., Talley, M., Cooper, C. and Leslie, J.C. (1995), Personality effects in personal and public orientations toward religion, *Personality and Individual Differences*, 19, 157–163.

Orton, R.E. (1987), The foundations of construct validity: towards an update, *Journal of Research and Development in Education*, 21, 22–35.

Osgood, C.E., Suci, G.J. and Tannenbaum, P.H. (1957), *The Measurement of Meaning*, Urbana, University of Illinois Press.

Pearson, P.R. and Francis, L.J. (1989), The dual nature of the Eysenckian lie scales: are religious adolescents more truthful? *Personality and Individual Differences*, 10, 1041–1048.

Pearson, P.R., Francis, L.J. and Lightbown, T.J. (1986), Impulsivity and religiosity, *Personality and Individual Differences*, 7, 89–94.

Rhymer, J. and Francis, L.J. (1985), Roman Catholic secondary schools in Scotland and pupil attitude towards religion, *Lumen Vitae*, 40, 103–110.

Robbins, M., Francis, L.J. and Gibbs, D. (1995), Personality and religion: a study among 8–11 year olds, *Journal of Beliefs and Values*, 16, 1, 1–6.

SPSS Inc. (1988), *SPSSX User's Guide*, New York, McGraw-Hill.

Thurstone, L.L. (1928), Attitudes can be measured, *American Journal of Sociology*, 33, 529–554.

Williams, C. (1988), *Addysg Ddwyieithog yng Nghymru ynteu Addysg ar gyfer Cymru Ddwyieithog?* Bangor, Canolfan Astudiaethau Iaith.

Zeller, R.A. (1988), Validity, in J.P. Keeves (ed.), *Educational Research, Methodology, and Measurement: an international handbook*, pp. 322–330, Oxford, Pergamon Press.

Appendix 1

CYFARWYDDIADAU
Darllenwch y frawddeg yn ofalus a meddwl, 'Ydw i'n cytuno?'

Os ydych chi'n *Cytuno'n Gryf*, rhowch gylch o amgylch . CG C DS A AG

Os ydych chi'n *Cytuno*, rhowch gylch o amgylch . . . . . CG C DS A AG

Os ydych chi *Ddim yn Siwr*, rhowch gylch o amgylch . . CG C DS A AG

Os ydych chi'n *Anghytuno*, rhowch gylch o amgylch . . . CG C DS A AG

Os ydych chi'n *Anghytuno'n Gryf*, rhowch gylch o amgylch CG C DS A AG

82	Rwy'n ei chael yn ddiflas gwrando ar y beibl . .	CG C DS A AG
83	Rwy'n gwybod bod Iesu yn fy helpu	CG C DS A AG
84	Mae dweud fy ngweddïau yn gymorth mawr i fi	CG C DS A AG
85	Mae'r eglwys/capel yn bwysig iawn i mi	CG C DS A AG
86	Rwy'n meddwl bod mynd i'r eglwys/capel yn wastraff amser	CG C DS A AG
87	Rydw i eisiau caru Iesu	CG C DS A AG
88	Rwy'n meddwl bod gwasanaethau eglwys/capel yn ddiflas	CG C DS A AG
89	Rwy'n meddwl fod pobl sy'n gweddïo yn dwp .	CG C DS A AG
90	Mae Duw yn fy helpu i fyw bywyd gwell	CG C DS A AG
91	Rwy'n hoffi dysgu am Dduw yn fawr iawn . . .	CG C DS A AG
92	Mae Duw yn golygu llawer i fi	CG C DS A AG
93	Rwy'n credu fod Duw yn helpu pobl	CG C DS A AG
94	Mae gweddïo yn gymorth mawr i fi	CG C DS A AG
95	Rwy'n gwybod bod Iesu'n agos iawn ataf i . . .	CG C DS A AG
96	Rwy'n meddwl fod gweddïo'n beth da	CG C DS A AG
97	Rwy'n meddwl bod y beibl yn hen ffasiwn . . .	CG C DS A AG
98	Rwy'n credu fod Duw yn gwrando ar weddïau .	CG C DS A AG
99	Nid yw Iesu'n golygu dim i fi	CG C DS A AG
100	Mae Duw yn real iawn i fi	CG C DS A AG
101	Rwy'n meddwl nad yw dweud gweddïau'n gwneud unrhyw les o gwbl	CG C DS A AG

102 Mae'r syniad o Dduw yn golygu llawer i fi . . . CG C DS A AG

103 Rwy'n credu fod Iesu'n parhau i helpu pobl . . CG C DS A AG

104 Rwy'n gwybod bod Duw yn fy helpu . . . . . . CG C DS A AG

105 Rwy'n ei chael yn anodd credu yn Nuw . . . . . CG C DS A AG

19

Christian children at school: their religious beliefs and practices

Bernadette O'Keeffe

Summary

This chapter discusses the development of the independent Christian schools movement in Britain. First, a brief overview is provided of the character of these schools from the author's study of fifteen primary and secondary schools. Then more detailed information is presented on the religious attitudes, beliefs and practices of 439 pupils between the ages of eight and seventeen years.

Introduction

During the last two decades there has been a new Christian initiative in education. Acting separately, many independent churches and Christian groups have established their own schools, without state funding. These schools are non-denominational in character. The house church movement has played a significant part in their steady growth and many of the members of the movement are disillusioned with denominational religion.[1]

There are approximately eighty such schools throughout England, Wales and Scotland. My own recent research on fifteen primary and secondary schools has begun to construct a detailed profile of these schools (O'Keeffe, 1992). These are all day schools. Two-thirds provide continuing education through primary and secondary level. They usually open with small numbers of pupils. A few of these schools charge set fees which are substantially lower than the per capita costs of state maintained schools, some rely entirely on donations from parents and church members, whilst others adopt ability-to-pay schemes. Some of these schools, a minority, cater only for children of the sponsoring churches, but most accept children from other Christian denominations and other faiths.

In many cases the founders of the new Christian schools were dissatisfied with the spiritual approach of their local state maintained schools. Reflecting this concern Cooling and Oliver (1989, p. 6) observe that pupils 'are given fewer and fewer points of spiritual contact and possibilities of Christian understanding at school'. Furthermore, they express the view that increasingly schools, especially secondary schools 'do not even offer the possibility of serious encounter with the ideas and beliefs of Christianity as a vigorous, modern and relevant world-view' (p. 6).

Supporters of this new independent Christian schools movement readily acknowledge that traditional Christian values and beliefs may be found in existing church schools. However, they point to the encroaching secularisation which is taking place and draw attention to the increasing number of non-Christian teachers in church schools.

Like all institutions and communities, Christian schools in the study vary considerably in their approaches to achieving shared aims and objectives. Looking across them, however, the observer can identify a unity of purpose, insofar as all schools seek to provide an education that is simultaneously this-worldly and other-wordly. These schools are perceived as educational institutions where God is recognised, and where 'gospel values' and the teachings of Christ are reflected in their policies, practices, structures and relationships. The focus and direction of schools are a return to an education which promotes the view that the bible has relevance for our time and context. In other words, the bible is pivotal in the educational enterprise. In preparing pupils to take their place as responsible citizens, schools reflect an awareness that Christianity has demands to make on every area of life. Teachers in the study constantly stressed their role in helping pupils to mature in their faith and to come to the realisation that Christ is 'the way, the truth and the life' (John 14: 6).

Supporters of these new Christian schools assert unequivocally that education of the child is primarily the responsibility of parents and they, not the state, have the prior right to determine an appropriate education for the children according to their 'deepest religious and philosophical beliefs' (Deakin, 1989). Parents are offered an education for their children based on Christian principles, Christian approach to the curriculum, and a climate where pupils can develop a Christian world-view and a unified way of looking at the world. A central aim of schools in the study is the education of the whole person, to integrate the spiritual, academic, moral, social and physical aspects of learning. This approach is highlighted in the following extract from a school prospectus in which the objectives are said to be summed up by Jesus' commandment to:

> Love the Lord your God with
> all your heart (spiritual)
> and with all your soul (emotional)
> and with all your strength (physical)
> and with all your mind (intellectual)
> and, love your neighbour as yourself (social) (Luke 10: 27).

Concern for an holistic approach to education is an essential background to any portrait of Christian schools in the study.

Teachers constantly emphasised that in 'witnessing to their faith' they were making an important contribution to the Christian growth of pupils. This position is outlined by a head teacher in the following way:

> We do not use our school to indoctrinate our children but rather it is an environment of faith where many will come to a personal knowledge of Jesus for themselves. We hope not only to inform them about the Word of God but to immerse them in the Word of God.

To this end, pupils are inducted into the beliefs and practices of their religious communities. The orientation is 'education in faith'. A context is thus provided which enables teachers in the study to be involved in nurture without many of the complexities which teachers in county schools, and in certain instances, in church schools, are grappling with in classrooms exhibiting a multiplicity of belief systems (O'Keeffe, 1986). In short, there is a marked convergence of the personal commitment of the teachers with the lesson content and teaching aims in schools. Clearly, there is no existing tension between the religious commitments of teachers and their role as teachers (Hull, 1984, p. 177).

Glock and Stark (1968) have identified five dimensions which provide a framework for studying religion and assessing religiosity. These dimensions may be conceptualised as consisting of five analytically discrete though interrelated dimensions: the *ideological* dimension encompasses the religious beliefs held by adherents;

the *ritualistic* dimension involves the specific practices and religious rites, for example, prayer, worship and the sacraments; the *experiential* dimension concerns the subjective religious experience and emotions; the *intellectual* dimension is closely related to the ideological dimension and involves an understanding and knowledge of the basic doctrines of faith; and the *consequential* dimension includes the effects of religious belief, practice, experience and knowledge upon the individual's behaviour. Included in this dimension 'are all those religious prescriptions which specify what people ought to do and the attitudes they hold to as a consequence of their religion'.

The religious climate and the teaching of religion in schools encompasses the same ideological, ritualistic, experiential, intellectual and consequential elements above. What seems evident from the research is that the religious influence *within* the schools, as far as religious socialisation of pupils is concerned, is the task of all teachers. On the practical level, schools in the study enable their pupils to come into contact with teachers who are committed to Christ and to living a Christian way of life. Schools staffed by Christian teachers seek to help their pupils to grow in their knowledge and love of God.

The above is admittedly a brief and simplified account of the research undertaken in Christian schools and omits many of the refinements. However, for our purposes it conveys an essential characteristic of schools in their different endeavours, namely that they are seeking to provide a learning environment akin to an 'absorbing ambition' of Thomas Arnold where education is not based on religion, but is itself religious (quoted in Patterson, 1946, p. 87). In other words, the purpose of Christian schools is not simply to add a religious dimension of education. Schools set out to influence the religious development of their pupils.

What patterns of religious behaviour do pupils exhibit? What are their attitudes toward Jesus, God, the bible and personal prayer? In line with Glock and Stark's multi-dimensional model I now turn to look at the empirical reality concerning pupils' attitude toward Christianity.

Method

This information was gathered using a questionnaire and the research methodology developed by Francis for use in county schools and in Church of England and Roman Catholic state maintained schools (1986, 1987). The questionnaire employed a Likert scaling technique for measuring attitudes and contained 24 unambiguous sentences which were indicative of the attitudinal areas under review. The usefulness of the Francis attitude scale is that it can be readily employed in new situations. The attitude scale covers items which relate to pupils' attitude toward God, Jesus, personal prayer, the bible and the church. The frequency of pupils' and their parents' attendances at church is measured on a four point scale ranging from weekly attendance to non-attendance. A question is also included on parental occupations. Other variables cover pupils' ages, their sex and their parents' religious involvement. The questionnaires were administered to 439 pupils in my study between the ages of eight and seventeen years. In order to ensure confidentiality, pupils were asked not to put their names on the questionnaires.

Results

We shall begin our examination of the attitudes of pupils toward Jesus and God. Table 19.1 brings together a number of sentences to which pupils were asked to respond by indicating whether they 'agreed strongly', 'agreed', were 'not certain', 'disagreed' or

Table 19.1
Pupils' religious beliefs and values

	positive response %	negative response %	not certain %
I know that Jesus helps me	92	3	3
I want to love Jesus	93	3	4
God helps me to lead a better life	89	4	6
I know that Jesus is very close to me	87	5	8
God is very real to me	88	5	7
I know God helps me	92	3	5

Note: Not all columns add up to 100%, since percentages have been rounded to nearest whole numbers. Also in a few cases pupils did not register their responses.

'disagreed strongly' with their content. The religious values expressed in the table 19.1 include aspects of the experiential dimension of Glock and Stark's model.

The responses to the statements in table 19.1 provide clear evidence that the majority of pupils see the role of Jesus in terms of personal relationships. The majority (88%) of pupils indicate positively that Jesus is a real person to them in their daily lives. An even higher percentage (93%) indicate that they wanted to love Jesus. Their responses to the two statements on God highlight the important distinction between *knowing* and *knowing about* God. Replies indicate a trusting relationship with God for 92% of pupils.

Reliance is usually placed on church membership and the frequency of church attendance as indicators of religiosity within the ritualistic dimension. In the context of my study two aspects of religious practice were explored among pupils. The first concerned the participation of pupils in their worshipping community through church attendance, and the second concerned personal prayer. Religious practice, which is an external expression of religion, corresponds to the ritualistic dimension of the Glock and Stark model.

Research findings show that regular attendance at church is extremely high among pupils. Eighty-two per cent of pupils in the study attend church once a week. Another 4% attend church at least once a month. For 11% of pupils, attendance at church is irregular while the remaining 3% never attend church. Overall, 97% of all pupils have some experience of participating as a member of a believing community.

Studies on attitudes of young people toward church attendance indicate that churchgoing for many adolescents ceases to be a meaningful experience and is considered boring. A recent study dealing with young people between the ages of sixteen and twenty years found that 47% of Roman Catholics were more likely to complain that Sunday worship was boring, compared with 31% of Anglicans and 16% of young people who attend Free Churches (Francis, 1984, p. 53). In order to uncover the attitudes of pupils toward their churches a number of statements were included to tap this dimension. The responses of pupils are provided in table 19.2.

For the majority of pupils church attendance is not regarded as a waste of their time. Nevertheless, while 73% indicated that the church is important to them, 20% found the actual experience of church services boring. This group's responses raise an all too familiar question — what can be done to make church involvement a more meaningful experience?

Table 19.2
Pupils' attitudes to church involvement

	positive response %	negative response %	not certain %
The church is very important to me	73	8	18
I think going to church is a waste of my time	80	9	10
I think church services are boring	61	19	20

In addition, the majority of pupils (87%) go to Sunday school or young people's church groups. Just over half (56%) of pupils are involved on a weekly basis; another 9% attend on a regular monthly basis. For the remaining pupils their contact with Sunday school or church groups for young people is far less frequent.

A number of studies on religious development point to a strong correlation between parental church attendance and child church attendance (Flynn, 1978; Hornsby-Smith, 1978; Francis and Gibson, 1993). An item was included in the questionnaire on parents' church attendance to ascertain the extent to which the families of pupils support them in their religious development. The majority of pupils (88%) come from homes where at least one parent attends church on a weekly basis. Churchgoing on a weekly basis is more frequent among pupils' mothers. Whereas 85% of mothers attend church weekly, the corresponding statistic drops to 73% for fathers.

The data show that parental church attendance has a very strong influence on the pattern of church attendance for their children. To illustrate this finding, 82% of the pupils whose mothers attend church weekly also go to church once a week. A similar picture emerges with the corresponding statistic for fathers. Seventy-two per cent of pupils whose fathers attend church weekly also attend on a weekly basis.

Educational literature has increasingly confirmed the importance of the home in the formation and development of religious beliefs, values and practice. Argyle (1958), for example, comments that there 'can be no doubt that the attitudes of parents are among the most important factors in the formation of religious attitudes'. So strong is the influence of the home, that what the Christian school can achieve is significantly determined by the existing religious and cultural patterns of the home (Greeley and Rossi, 1966, p. 223). Flynn (1975), in a sociological study of sixth form students in 21 Catholic boys' high schools in Australia, also supports this view. He found that Catholic schools were most successful in achieving their religious goals when the school and the home 'mutually reinforce each other' (p. 179). In addition, Flynn makes the important observation that the Catholic school acts as a powerful 'multiplier' 'by reinforcing the religious values of the home'. However, 'the school acts as a "modifier" of the religious values of the home if this climate is weak or non-existent' (p. 287).

There is also a close relationship between church attendance and the religious attitudes of pupils. Children who are regular churchgoers are more likely to indicate positive attitudes toward Jesus, God, prayer and the bible in comparison to children who attend church less frequently.

While church attendance and involvement is frequently used as an index of religious commitment, the frequency of church attendance is itself unsatisfactory as a measure of religious commitment. Berger and Luckman (1966) have argued that in concentrating on institutional forms of religion, which are bound up with the institutional churches, only a partial picture of religious commitment is provided. It is necessary to 'get behind' religion as it manifests itself in institutional forms, to arrive at the basic 'underlay of factors which give rise to religiosity'. Table 19.3 brings together a number of sentences to which pupils were asked to respond. The sentences were intended to tap the dimension of free, personal commitment. Their responses on personal prayer provide an indication of the place of private religion in their lives in contrast to the public place of religion which finds expression in church attendance.

The statistics in table 19.3 illustrate the overall positive responses of pupils in respect of the value of personal prayer. In addition, they provide a glimpse of the meaning of prayer for pupils who engage in prayer. Ninety-two per cent of pupils agree that prayer is a good thing and 94% believe that God listens to their prayers. While the majority of pupils confirm the general importance and value of personal prayer, 13% are less certain whether prayer helps them individually.

Table 19.3
Personal prayer

	positive response %	negative response %	not certain %
Saying my prayers helps me a lot	79	6	19
I think prayer is a good thing	92	2	6
I believe that God listens to my prayers	94	3	2
I think people who pray are stupid	3	83	5

In respect of pupils' patterns of prayer, over half (59%) of the pupils say daily prayers at home. Another 10% pray at least once a week and another 3% pray at least once a month. For a further 22% of the pupils, praying at home is irregular. Only a small percentage (6%) said they never prayed at home. When pupils responded to the statement 'I think saying prayers in schools does no good', only a small percentage (6%) agreed with the statement. Clearly, the overwhelming majority of pupils hold very positive attitudes toward both public and personal prayer.

In order to tap pupils' attitude toward the bible, two statements were included in the questionnaire: 'I think the bible is old fashioned and out of date' and 'I find it boring to listen to the bible'. The responses of pupils show that a high percentage of pupils hold a positive attitude toward the bible. While 86% of the pupils reject the suggestion that the bible is out of date, only 6% hold a negative attitude toward the bible and a slightly higher number of pupils (8%) are uncertain. There is, however, less enthusiasm among pupils when it comes to listening to the bible being read to them. While 73% of the pupils enjoy listening to the bible, 15% are uncertain, and the rest found such an activity boring. This response highlights the need for some schools to review how the bible is presented and to explore ways of making this area of activity more meaningful.

The research carried out by Goldman (1964, 1965), using the insights of Piaget and directed at the intellectual aspects of children's religious understanding, had a major formative influence on

the place of the bible in religious education when the new generation of Agreed Syllabuses began to appear in the late 1960s and
early 1970s. Goldman maintained that young people in the
Piagetian concrete thinking stage, misunderstood religious language. Consequently, he maintained, they arrive at a literalist view
of symbolic religious statements of what religion is saying. He
contended that this caused confusion for many of them in early
adolescence. On the basis of his research, Goldman concludes that
the bible is not suitable for children as traditionally taught and
consequently it should no longer hold a central place in religious
education. The case put forward is that very little of the bible is
suitable before adolescence. It is often regarded by children as
remote, irrelevant and boring. Howkins, in a critique of the research and conclusions of Goldman, observes that Goldman 'may
have shown the inadequacy of the teaching but he has not shown
the unsuitability of the bible' (1968, p. 13). Based on research on
children's religious thinking, Slee (1986) also challenges the
Piagetian-style analysis applied by Goldman to religious education.

Although Goldman found that children who were members of
'Gospel Sects', and who regularly attended classes where bible
teaching was central, scored higher on aspects of religious development and understanding than one would have expected for their
age, he dismisses the significance of this finding. However, in
taking Goldman to task, Howkins suggests that the evidence
presented points to the fact that 'if children are taught the bible
from an early age (and taught properly) they do show better
religious development, even on Dr Goldman's own rather narrow
definition of "religious understanding" ' (p. 14).

My research shows that from an early age children are socialised
within a world-view where religion is the guiding force. Their
everyday experiences are linked to bible stories and pupils are
encouraged to see the relevance of the bible in their own lives.
Religious education continues to be bible-centred and yet there is
no evidence of adverse effects identified by Goldman. Goldman
has not proved his case as far as my research is concerned. By
ignoring the findings relating to children from what Goldman
labels as a 'fundamentalist background', he fails to pay due attention to the significant variables of church and family in the child's
religious understanding and development. The home, school and
religious community each play their part and make their own
distinctive contribution to the religious development of the child.
Children learn about the Christian faith first and foremost through

participation in primary groups such as the Christian family and secondary groups such as Sunday schools and the church. The Christian school has grasped the unique opportunity of bringing together the family, the church and the school in an endeavour to nurture their pupils in the Christian faith.

My research among pupils in Christian schools also challenges some of the empirical research which points to the importance of social class in determining the child's religious behaviour. For example, Francis (1987) found that in his study of fourth year junior pupils, in county schools and both Anglican and Roman Catholic church schools, children from professional homes are much more likely to have parents who attend church regularly, and this is also mirrored in their children's church attendance. In Francis' study, 36% of children from class one homes attend church every Sunday, compared with 25% in class two, 21% in class three (non-manual), 14% in class three (manual), 13% in class four and 6% in class five (1987, p. 177). The comparable statistics for my study are significantly higher for all social classes. The proportion of fathers in social class one who attend church weekly is 82%. A similar pattern of church attendance also emerges for the remaining classes: 90% in class two, 90% in class three, 75% in class four and 58% in class five. In my study it is not the children from professional homes who have a higher percentage of parents who attend church weekly, but pupils whose parents are in social classes two and three.

A range of studies report higher levels of religiosity among girls than among boys (Argyle and Beit-Hallahmi, 1975; Francis, 1979). The research carried out by Francis (1987) with pupils in church and county schools mentioned above, found that girls have more positive religious attitudes than boys (p. 173). He found that girls record more favourable attitudes toward Christianity and attend church more frequently. By analysing pupils' answers to the individual items of the Likert scale used by Francis, I compared my research findings with the research carried out by Francis. The main conclusion to be drawn from the comparison is that pupils in my study are exceptions to the trend identified by Francis. Although variations in attitudes between boys and girls are evident in some of their responses, there is little evidence to suggest strong sex differences in religious behaviour and attitude toward religion. In Francis' study, a third of boys found it hard to believe in God, compared with a quarter of girls. While under a half (47%) of boys thought Jesus was close to them, the corresponding statistic is 57% for girls. While 48% of boys believe that God helps them, the corresponding figure is much higher at 61% for girls. Whereas 54% of boys believe that God listens to prayer, the proportion increases to 64% for girls.

Turning to look at the corresponding areas in relation to my sample of pupils, a higher percentage of boys find it hard to believe in God (38%), whereas the corresponding figure for girls is significantly lower at 27%, a picture similar to that of the Francis study. However, there is a smaller percentage difference in their responses to the question 'God means a lot to me'. Eighty-nine per cent of boys and 92% of girls affirmed the importance of God for them. It is interesting to note the marked difference in pupils' replies to these two questions. While a higher percentage of boys and girls affirm God means a lot to them, a much smaller number of pupils find it hard to believe in God. Further research needs to be undertaken to explore more fully the significance of this finding. One explanation for the marked differences in responses to these two questions is the possibility that the former question may well have presented a conceptual problem for younger pupils. The second statement, however, is very much linked to the experiential component of religion and subjective religious experiences of children.

While 90% of girls in my study say Jesus is close to them, the figure for boys is just 4% less. Similarly, 90% of boys believe that God helps them, compared with 93% of girls. The percentage difference between boys (93%) and girls (94%) who believe that God listens to their prayers is marginal. On the other hand, a slightly higher percentage of boys (94%) say Jesus helps them, compared with 92% of girls. However, a small proportion of boys (76%) find prayer helpful, compared with 82% of girls. A slightly higher percentage of girls (60%) pray daily, compared with 58% of boys.

The replies of pupils in my study show that not only do they demonstrate a significantly more positive attitude toward Christianity, compared with pupils in county schools, Church of England and Roman Catholic schools, but they also score significantly higher on the ritual dimensions involving religious practice, both on the institutional level of church involvement and on the personal level of prayer.

My research found that the religious commitment of teenagers did not differ significantly from the younger pupils in the study. This is an important research finding since it is frequently suggested and backed by empirical research that as pupils move towards adulthood they frequently discard childhood forms of faith. For example, data reported by Francis (1989a) shows that there is a steady decline in attitude toward Christianity from the first year in junior school to the fourth year in secondary school. The increasing alienation of young people from Christianity 'is greatly accelerated between the ages of fifteen and sixteen' (p. 6). When Francis (1989b) replicated the study in 1978 and again in 1982 not only were the trends identified in the first study confirmed but alienation of young pupils from Christianity was occurring at an earlier age. Although age variations in responses to a number of statements are apparent among my sample of pupils there is no persistent statistical curve to confirm the findings in the study undertaken by Francis which show that attitude toward Christianity becomes progressively less favourable from the age of eight to fifteen years.

Conclusion

To sum up at this point, the responses of pupils demonstrate that the majority hold very positive attitudes toward God, Jesus, the bible, their churches and personal prayer. It is clear that the overwhelming majority of pupils have a high regard for personal religion. In addition, the majority of pupils receive parental religious support, in terms of church attendance. It would appear that the house churches are able to maintain the active involvement and interests of the majority of their young members to a far greater extent than would appear to be the case for the mainstream churches. In addition, there are strong indications that schools in the study are effective in achieving their religious goals.

The research findings represent a snapshot at one point in time. They provide a contemporary picture of the attitude toward Christianity and the religious practice of pupils attending newly established independent Christian schools. In order to provide a more detailed picture of the religious development of pupils and the impact of schools over a period of time this type of study needs to be replicated, beginning with pupils in primary schools. Such a study could follow the religious development of a representative group of pupils through their adolescent years until they reach early adulthood. It would lead not only to deeper insights into the religious development of pupils but it would also illuminate the significance of the roles of the family, schools and churches and their impact.

As an alternative to state maintained schools, Christian schools in the study engage in religious nurture and offer a form of schooling which provides a context of relative stability of beliefs and practices. In many schools pupils are not confronted with the ambiguities and challenges which arise from competing values, beliefs and alternative life styles. When pupils leave school, they will be continually exposed to every variety of moral and theological options, stances for living and competing world-views. A longitudinal study involving school-leavers would provide valuable insights into the continuing religious commitment of pupils when they leave the secure environment of the school and go out into the world to put their faith into action in their lives. Such a study would provide insights into their ability to respond critically to conflicting world-views which contrast starkly their experiences in the school, home and Christian community and their experience in a society which is becoming increasingly inhospitable to a religious *Weltanschauung*.

Notes

1. The term House Church Movement is used to describe a variety of Christian fellowships and independent groups which exist outside the mainstream denominations. The charismatic renewal played a significant part in the formation of the movement. The House Church Movement contains several hundred house churches. The English Church Census indicates that independent Christian churches have increased their adult members by 43% between 1975 and 1989 and that child attendance has risen by 30%.

References

Argyle, M. (1958), *Religious Behaviour*, London, Routledge and Kegan Paul.

Argyle, M. and Beit-Hallahmi, B. (1975), *The Social Psychology of Religion*, London, Routledge and Kegan Paul.

Batson, C.D. and Ventis, W.L. (1982), *The Religious Experience*, New York, Oxford University Press.

Berger, P.L. and Luckman, T. (1966), Sociology of religion and sociology of knowledge, *Sociology and Social Research*, 47, 417–427.

Cooling, T. and Oliver, G. (1989), *Church and School: the contemporary challenge*, Bramcote, Grove Books.

Deakin, R. (1989), *New Christian Schools: the case for public funding*, Bristol, Regius.

Flynn, M. (1975), *Some Catholic Schools in Action*, Sydney, Catholic Education Office.

Francis, L.J. (1979), The child's attitude toward religion and religious education: a review of research, *Educational Research*, 21, 103–108.

Francis, L.J. (1984), *Teenagers and the Church: a profile of churchgoing youth in the 1980s*, London, Collins Liturgical Publications.

Francis, L.J. (1986), Denominational schools and pupil attitude toward Christianity, *British Educational Research Journal*, 12, 145–152.

Francis, L.J. (1987), *Religion in Primary School*, London, Collins Liturgical Publications.

Francis, L.J. (1989a), Measuring attitude towards Christianity during childhood and adolescence, *Personality and Individual Differences*, 10, 695–698.

Francis, L.J. (1989b), Monitoring changing attitudes toward Christianity among secondary school pupils between 1974 and 1986, *British Journal of Educational Psychology*, 59, 86–91.

Francis, L.J. and Gibson, H.M. (1993), Parental influence and adolescent religiosity: a study of church attendance and attitude toward Christianity among 11–12 and 15–16 year olds, *International Journal for the Psychology of Religion*, 3, 241–253.

Glock, G.Y. and Stark, R.N. (1965), *Religion and Society in Tension*, Chicago, Rand McNally.

Goldman, R. (1964), *Religious Thinking from Childhood to Adolescence*, London, Routledge and Kegan Paul.

Goldman, R. (1965), *Readiness for Religion*, London, Routledge and Kegan Paul.

Greeley, A.M. and Rossi, P.H. (1966), *The Education of Catholic Americans*, Chicago, Aldine.

Hornsby-Smith, M.P. (1978), *Catholic Education: the unobtrusive partner*, London, Sheed Ward.

Howkins, K.G. (1968), *Religious Thinking and Religious Education*, London, Tyndale Press.

Hull, J. (1984), *Studies in Religion and Education*, Lewes, Falmer Press.

O'Keeffe, B. (1986), *Faith Culture and the Dual System: a comparative study of church and county schools*, Lewes, Falmer Press.

O'Keeffe, B. (1992), A look at the Christian schools movement, in B. Watson (ed.), *Priorities in Religious Education*, pp. 92–112, Lewes, Falmer Press.

Patterson, H. (ed.) (1946), *Great Teachers*, New Brunswick, Rutgers University Press.

Slee, N. (1986), Goldman yet again: an overview and critique of his contribution to research, *British Journal of Religious Education*, 8, 84–93.

20

Church of England schools and teacher attitudes: personal commitment or professional judgement?

Carolyn Wilcox and Leslie J. Francis

Summary

A detailed questionnaire, containing three Likert attitude scales originally designed by Francis (1986a) to assess teachers' attitudes toward the church school system, toward the distinctiveness of church schools, and toward traditional teaching methods, was completed by 145 of the 229 teachers employed within Church of England voluntary schools in the Diocese of Newcastle. The findings indicated that age and personal commitment to the church are significant predictors of the individual teacher's attitude toward church schools. Older teachers and teachers who attend church hold a more positive attitude toward church schools and are more likely to wish to emphasise the distinctiveness of church schools. These findings have implications both for the claims which the Church of England makes regarding the contemporary distinctiveness of church schools and for future changes in the character of church schools.

Introduction

Through the founding of the National Society in 1811 (Burgess, 1958) the Church of England played a crucial role in the establishment of a national network of schools in England and Wales (Cruickshank, 1963; Murphy, 1971) long before the 1870 Education

311

Act established the machinery for building non-denominational schools (Murphy, 1972). As a direct consequence of this historical initiative, the Anglican church in England and Wales continues to have the privilege and responsibility of providing around 12% of all school places within the state maintained sector. The Anglican presence is considerably stronger in the primary sector than in the secondary sector, and considerably stronger in England than in Wales. According to figures provided by the Department for Education, at January 1994 Church of England schools provided 12.24% of all full time places within the state maintained sector, or 17.76% of places deemed primary and 4.81% of places deemed secondary. According to figures provided by the Welsh Office, at January 1994 Church in Wales schools provided 5.12% of all full time places within the state maintained sector, or 6.84% of places deemed primary and 2.5% of places deemed secondary. In his analysis of the size of Anglican primary schools, Gay (1985) draws attention to the fact that the church's main investment is in the small schools, while Francis' (1986a) analysis of the geographical distribution of church schools points to their concentration in the more rural shire counties.

The 1944 Education Act safeguarded the partnership between church and state in the provision of a national network of schools and proposed a system of voluntary aided and voluntary controlled status (Dent, 1947). According to the 1944 Education Act, voluntary controlled status absolved the church from ongoing financial responsibility for maintenance of the school, although the church retained the right to appoint a minority of governors, provide denominational worship throughout the school, offer denominational religious education on parental request, and in schools of more than two teachers appoint 'reserved teachers' competent to give denominational religious instruction. Voluntary aided status gave the churches additional rights, including the appointment of the majority of governors and the provision of denominational instruction as well as worship throughout the school, but also involved them in continued financial liability for certain capital expenditures (Brooksbank, Revell, Ackstine and Bailey, 1982). The 1944 Education Act, therefore, clearly envisaged the denominational distinctiveness of church schools.

Historically the denominational distinctiveness of church schools was, in some places, a source of bitter controversy, especially in single school areas where the Church of England owned the only school. According to Cruickshank (1963) 'perhaps nothing in the educational controversies of the nineteenth century did more to influence denominational bitterness than the Anglican refusal to concede rights of conscience'. During the twentieth century the Church of England became increasingly sensitive to the responsibilities and constraints of operating church schools in single school areas and in an increasingly secular and pluralist society. The key statement on the Anglican philosophy of church schools, *The Fourth R* (Ramsey, 1970), sharpens the distinction between the Church of England's *domestic* and *general* functions in education. The domestic function characterises the inward-looking concern to 'equip the children of the church to take their place in the Christian community', while the general function characterises the outward-looking concern 'to serve the nation through its children'. This report recognises that while historically the two roles were 'indistinguishable, for nation and church were, theoretically, one, and the domestic task was seen as including the general', in today's environment 'no one would pretend to claim that nation and church are coextensive'. In the light of this observation *The Fourth R* recommends that the church should see its church schools 'principally as a way of expressing its concern for the general education of all children', that 'religious education, even in a church aided school, should be seen in domestic terms' and that especially in single school areas church schools should be 'looked on as a service provided by the church, rather than something provided for the church'.

The green paper, *A Future in Partnership* (Waddington, 1984), reaffirmed that the *voluntary* aspects of Church of England schools should be stressed in preference to their denominationalism. In three important essays on the future of Church of England schools within the state maintained sector, Geoffrey Duncan, while deputy secretary and schools officer of the National Society and schools secretary of the General Synod Board of Education, developed the case further for the role of 'church schools in service to the community' (Duncan, 1986, 1988, 1990). More recently, however, Geoffrey Duncan's successor as schools officer, David Lankshear, has emphasised wider aspects of the potential religious distinctiveness of church schools in a series of seminal publications (Lankshear, 1992a, 1992b, 1993; Brown and Lankshear, 1995).

The Church of England has also needed to be conscious of the criticisms levelled against denominational schools by a number of secular sources. The British Humanist Association (1967) argues that the state should not be involved in financing and recognising denominational teaching and accuses the churches of abusing their privileged position by indoctrination. The Socialist Education Association (1981, 1986) suggests that denominational schools frustrate true equality of opportunity in education. Professor Paul Hirst (1972, 1981) argues that Christian belief and educational principles are logically incompatible; the logic of education precludes the churches from influencing the educational curriculum and from operating distinctive educational institutions. Dummett and McNeal's (1981) study on race and church schools argues that the Christian reference of church schools can hamper the development of multi-racial institutions in some areas. The Swann Report, *Education for All* (1985), in its majority recommendation, advises against the extension of voluntary aided status to other faith communities and on this basis seriously calls into question 'the role of the churches in the provision of education'. In his analysis of the implications of the Swann report for religious education, Cole (1988) argues that 'denominational schools become increasingly anachronistic and less desirable'.

Church schools are likely, therefore, to be conscious of needing to steer a careful path between remaining loyal to the full intentions of their original trust deed, listening attentively to current Anglican statements on the nature of church schools, utilising the full legal rights enshrined in the 1944 and 1988 Education Acts and listening to secular criticisms of the church school system. Given both the politically sensitive nature of these issues and the size of the contribution which Anglican schools make to the state maintained sector of education, it is not surprising that a growing body of educational research has begun to explore the contemporary distinctiveness and effectiveness of Anglican schools. Five main strands of research emerge from the literature.

The first strand of research has focused on the pupils who attend Church of England schools. Four separate studies have employed attitude scaling techniques and multiple regression to assess the comparative influence of Church of England schools on their pupils' religiosity. Francis (1986b) reports on three studies conducted in East Anglia in 1974, 1978 and 1982 to assess the comparative influence of Church of England, Roman Catholic and county schools on the religious attitudes of their year five and year six pupils. All three studies point to the positive influence of Catholic schools and the negative influence of Anglican schools on pupil attitudes, after using path analysis to control for other influences, like sex, age, church and home. Francis (1987) examined the religious attitudes of year six pupils in Roman Catholic, Church of England and county schools in Gloucestershire. This study, too, pointed to the positive influence of Roman Catholic primary schools on pupils' attitudes toward Christianity. In this study Church of England voluntary aided primary schools exerted neither a positive nor a negative influence, while Church of England voluntary controlled schools were found to exert a negative influence. At the secondary level, Francis and Carter (1980) examined the religious attitudes of pupils in year eleven attending Church of England voluntary aided, Roman Catholic voluntary aided and county schools. These findings provided no support for the notion that church voluntary aided secondary schools exert a positive influence on their pupils' attitudes toward religion. A second study by Francis and Jewell (1992) among year ten pupils attending the four county and the one Church of England voluntary secondary schools serving the area around the same town also found that the Church of England school exerted neither a positive nor a negative influence on its pupils' religious practice, belief or attitude.

A fifth study by Levitt (1993) undertook a longitudinal case study among 38 families in Cornwall from Penvollard county junior school, the Church of England voluntary aided school and a neighbouring voluntary aided village school. The author concludes that this study 'points to the possibility that Anglican schools are popular because they are seen as "good" schools which do not affect children's religiosity unduly'.

The second strand of research has focused on the parishes which support church schools. Francis and Lankshear (1990, 1991) report two studies conducted in rural and urban areas to assess the impact of Church of England primary schools on quantitative indicators of local church life. Both studies point to the positive impact of church schools on church life, after using path analysis to control for other influences, like the size of the parish, the church electoral roll and the age of the priest. For example, in rural areas the presence of a church school is shown to augment slightly the village church's usual Sunday contact with children between the ages of six and nine years and with adults. The presence of a church school is also shown to have a small positive influence on the number of infant baptisms, the number of children between the ages of six and thirteen years in the village church choir and the number of young confirmands under the age of fourteen years.

The third strand of research has focused on whether in practice Church of England voluntary aided and voluntary controlled primary schools display a different religious ethos and character from county schools. In a detailed study of the primary schools in Gloucestershire Francis (1987) found that, although the church schools were serving specific local neighbourhoods in the same way as county schools, they continued to express more signs of church-relatedness than county schools. Church of England schools in Gloucestershire encouraged more contact with the clergy and with the church. They held more explicitly Christian assemblies and gave more emphasis to the church-related aspects of religious education.

O'Keeffe (1986) conducted research in 102 county secondary and Church of England secondary and primary schools in London, the North West and the West Midlands with a special concern to explore the role of church schools in multi-racial and multi-faith Britain. She concludes that:

> For the most part church schools do not admit 'other faith' expressions within the area of school activity and in addition tend towards a policy of selectivity in their admission of other than Christian pupils and staff. Culture often seen as Christian, for many schools, means belonging to the historic British or European tradition.

The fourth strand of research has focused on the governors of church schools. Gay, Kay, Newdick and Perry (1991) compared the views provided by 99 heads of Church of England primary schools and 100 chairs of governors in the Diocese of London. This study revealed that 82% of the chairs of governors thought that the headteachers should be practising Christians; 61% thought that senior members of the teaching staff should be practising Christians; 34% thought that the teachers should be practising members of a Christian church. This study is not, however, able to explore the extent to which the views of the chairs of governors reflect the views of the governing body as a whole. Kay, Piper and Gay (1988) analysed the views of 843 governors from the 81 Church of England voluntary aided primary schools in the Diocese of Oxford. This study found that the foundation governors were markedly more committed to preserving the religious ethos of the school than the other members of the governing bodies. The authors conclude that 'in contrast parents of children in the school tend to value the Christian ethos of the school less. Since this is a group that we can expect to see increasing in numbers and influence, this is potentially a worrying situation for those who value the distinctiveness of the church school'. These findings are confirmed in a study among 486 governors from the 55 Church of England voluntary aided schools in the Diocese of Chichester conducted by Francis and Stone (1995). The findings from this study indicate that governors' attitudes toward the religious ethos of Church of England voluntary aided primary schools are closely related to their age, personal religious commitment and role on the governing body. More positive attitudes are held by older, churchgoing and foundation governors.

The fifth strand of research has focused on the teachers who work in Church of England schools. This strand of research may be of particular importance in understanding the dynamics which determine the distinctiveness and effectiveness of church schools on the grounds that it is the teachers themselves who implement the policy of the school and communicate that policy to the pupils. Francis (1986a) analysed the views of 338 teachers employed in the 20 Church of England voluntary aided and 91 voluntary controlled first, primary and middle schools within the Diocese of St Edmundsbury and Ipswich. This study demonstrated considerably more goodwill towards the church school system than antipathy against it and more support for the distinctiveness of church schools than rejection of this potential for distinctiveness. At the same time, this study also noted that there is considerable variation in the attitudes of teachers in both voluntary aided and voluntary controlled church schools.

In order to understand this variation in attitudes from one teacher to another, Francis (1986a) identified three main attitudinal clusters and constructed an attitude scale to measure each of these areas. Then he employed path analysis to model the major influences on the scores recorded on each of these scales.

The first attitude scale sets out to identify the issues which are best able to distinguish between those teachers who are *in favour of the church school system* and those who are not in favour of it. The statistical procedures of item analysis selected the 16 items which cohered most satisfactorily to assess this dimension, producing an alpha coefficient of 0.85. These 16 items demonstrate that those who are most in favour of the church school system tend to say things like 'I applied for my present post specifically because it was in a Church of England school', 'Anglican parents should be encouraged to send their children to a Church of England school', and 'the Church of England should develop more secondary/middle/upper schools'. Those who are most hostile to the church school system say things like, 'the Church of England school system has outlived its usefulness', 'Church of England schools should be given over to the state', and 'the Church of England has too many schools'. Closely associated with the individual teachers' stand on these polarising issues are their views on the relationship between church and school and the relationship between religion and education. Those in favour of church schools tend to believe that the school system should teach about the church and encourage pupils to accept and practise the Christian faith, while those against church schools tend to believe that the task of Christian education should rest with the churches and with parents rather than with the school system and that it is inappropriate for schools to ask pupils to participate in signs of religious commitment like worship and prayer.

The construct validity of this scale was checked against the preferences expressed by individual teachers for working in different types of schools. Teachers who stated their preference as working in a Church of England aided school scored 65.4 points on the scale; those who opted for a Church of England controlled school scored 57.6 points; those who opted for a county school scored 49.5 points. Those who said that they had no real preference between a church and county school scored 53.8 points, a score higher than those who opted for a county school, but lower than those who opted for a controlled school.

The second attitude scale sets out to identify the characteristics of church schools which are most likely to be emphasised by those who wish to assert *the distinctiveness of the church school*. Again, the statistical procedures of item analysis selected the 16 items which most satisfactorily distinguish between those teachers who say that church schools are or should be different from county schools and those who say that church schools and county schools should be doing exactly the same sort of job, with the same kind of priorities. This scale produced an alpha coefficient of 0.94.

These 16 items demonstrate that those who wish to emphasise the distinctiveness of church schools tend to talk in terms of the specifically religious characteristics of the school. Right at the top of their list they tend to place the ideas of providing a regular Christian assembly and teaching about Christianity, God and Jesus. They also consider it important to teach about the bible and the church. They feel that church schools should have committed Christians on the staff and develop close contacts with the local clergy. They believe that prayer has a place in the classroom. They argue that the church school should be a place for putting Christian values into practice and for providing an atmosphere of Christian community.

The construct validity of this scale was also checked against the preferences expressed by individual teachers for working in different kinds of schools. Teachers who stated their preference as teaching in a Church of England aided school scored 73.8 points on the scale; those who opted for Church of England controlled schools scored 66.3 points; those who opted for a county school scored 52.7 points. Those who said that they had no real preference between a church school and a county school scored 63.9 points, a score higher than those who opted for a county school, but lower than those who opted for a controlled school.

The third attitude scale sets out to identify the teaching preferences of those who would characterise themselves as *favouring traditional teaching methods*, rather than progressive teaching methods. Again, the statistical procedures of item analysis selected the 16 items which most satisfactorily distinguished between those in favour of traditional teaching methods and those in favour of progressive teaching methods, producing an alpha coefficient of 0.88.

These 16 items demonstrate that those who value traditional teaching methods place a high priority on teaching children to know their multiplication tables by heart, giving regular maths tests and giving regular spelling tests. They believe in training children in hard work, teaching children to be tidy and adopting firm discipline. They like to follow a regular timetable for different lessons. They emphasise the importance of bringing the best out of bright pupils and of rewarding good work by giving stars and other credit marks. They expect children to seek permission before leaving the classroom, and they expect children to be punished for persistent disruptive behaviour.

Two key findings emerged from the path analysis conducted on these attitude scales. The first finding was that preference for traditional teaching methods was independent of the individual teacher's age or religious commitment. Decisions about teaching styles appear to be thoroughly professional matters uninfluenced by more personal issues. The second finding was that views about church schools were clearly not independent of the individual teacher's age or religious commitment. Decisions about the distinctiveness of church schools and whether or not church schools are viewed favourably are influenced by more personal issues.

The scale of attitude toward the church school system demonstrated that, while many teachers who find themselves working in the church school system still show considerable goodwill towards that system, their goodwill towards church schools is also clearly associated with their goodwill towards the church in general. The statistical model suggests that the younger teachers are less likely to be churchgoers and that the teachers who are not churchgoers are less likely to be favourably disposed towards the church school system. This model could imply that the next generation of teachers in church schools is likely to be less favourably disposed towards the church school system than the present generation.

The scale of attitude toward the distinctiveness of church schools demonstrated that, while many teachers who find themselves working in the church school system still argue in favour of the distinctiveness of church schools, this notion of distinctiveness is not only related to the individual teachers' attitudes toward the church, but also to their age.

In the case of their attitude toward the church school system, younger churchgoing teachers are just as likely to be favourably disposed to the church's involvement in education as older churchgoing teachers. It is simply the case that fewer young teachers go to church. In the case of their attitude toward the distinctiveness of church schools, younger churchgoing teachers are less likely to support the Christian distinctiveness of church schools than older churchgoing teachers. This model could imply that the belief among teachers in church schools that church schools should be different is likely to disappear more rapidly, as the next generation of church school teachers emerges, than their general goodwill towards the church's continued involvement in education.

These potentially controversial findings were based on the results of a single study conducted among the Church of England voluntary schools in one diocese in East Anglia in 1982. The aim of the present study is to replicate this research a decade later in 1992 in a different geographical area by selecting one diocese in the North East.

Method

Sample

A detailed questionnaire was sent to every full-time and part-time teacher (with the exception of supply teachers) employed in Church of England voluntary schools within the Diocese of Newcastle in March 1992. This involved a total of 43 schools in three Local Education Authorities: North Tyneside, Newcastle and

Northumberland. Of the 229 questionnaires sent out, 145 were returned completed, making a response rate of 63%.

Questionnaire

The *Church Schools Survey* questionnaire was a modified version of the one employed by Francis (1986a) in his survey of teacher attitudes in church schools within the Diocese of St Edmundsbury and Ipswich. The questionnaire contained four main parts.

Part one of the questionnaire employed multiple choice questions to gather information regarding characteristics of the respondents and of the school. Key variables for the present analysis, in addition to sex, were as follows. Age was assessed on a five point scale: 20–29 years, 30–39 years, 40–49 years, 50–59 years and 60–69 years. Teaching post was assessed on a four point scale: standard scale, incentive allowance post, deputy headteacher and headteacher. Church attendance was assessed on a five point scale: never, at least once a year, major festivals only, at least once a month and most weeks.

Part two of the questionnaire contained 71 questions to assess a range of views regarding the church school system, including the 16 item scale of attitude toward the church school system developed by Francis (1986a). These items are presented in table 20.1. Each item was assessed on a five point scale: disagree strongly, disagree, not certain, agree and agree strongly.

Part three of the questionnaire contained 73 questions to assess educational priorities within the church school, including both the 16 item scale of attitude toward the distinctiveness of church schools and the 16 item scale of attitude toward traditional teaching methods developed by Francis (1986a). These items are presented in table 20.2 and table 20.3. Each item was assessed on a five point scale: not appropriate, very unimportant, quite unimportant, quite important and very important.

Part four of the questionnaire re-presented the same 73 questions employed in part three to assess how much attention church schools should give to these priorities *compared* with county schools. This time each item was assessed on a five point scale: much less, little less, same, little more and much more.

Respondents

The respondents included 21 men and 124 women. Half the respondents (73) were in their forties, seven were in their twenties, 36 were in their thirties, 28 were in their fifties and one was aged sixty or over. Half the respondents (74) held standard scale posts, 24 held incentive allowance posts, thirteen held deputy headships and 33 held headships. Almost half the respondents (68) attended Sunday church services most weeks, 19 attended at least once a month, 31 attended major festivals only, thirteen attended at least once a year and twelve never attended Sunday church services. The majority of the respondents (129) held full-time posts, while 16 held part-time posts. The majority of the respondents (112) were employed in the voluntary aided sector, 18 were employed in the voluntary controlled sector and thirteen were employed in the special agreement sector. Three-fifths of the respondents (89) were employed in first schools, three were employed in infant schools, 40 were employed in primary schools, twelve were employed in middle schools and one was employed in a junior school. The majority of the respondents (127) regarded their schools as operating an admissions policy best characterised as exclusively or mainly neighbourhood, with only nine regarding their schools as operating an admissions policy best characterised as exclusively or mainly selective.

Data analysis

The data were analysed by the SPSS computer package (SPSS Inc., 1988), using especially the reliability and regression routines.

Results

Table 20.1 displays the items which compose the scale of attitude toward the church school system, together with the item rest of test correlations and the percentage of teachers who agree with each statement. The item rest of test correlations confirm that each individual item contributes toward the overall scale score. The internal reliability of the scale is supported by an alpha coefficient of 0.86 (Cronbach, 1951).

The individual items demonstrate four main features about the overall attitude of teachers toward the church school system. The first point is that the majority of the teachers did not specifically seek to work within the church school sector. Just one in four (25%) of the teachers applied for their present post specifically because it was in a Church of England school. The second point is that, once employed in a church school, the majority of teachers are supportive of the church school system. Only one in twenty (5%) of the teachers believe that Church of England schools should be

Table 20.1
Scale of attitude toward the church school system

scale item	agree %	item rest of test r
I applied for my present post specifically because it was in a Church of England school	26	0.3989
The Church of England has too many schools*	2	0.5663
There is no such thing as a specifically Christian view of education*	22	0.3486
The Church of England should develop more secondary/ middle/upper schools	49	0.6405
Church of England schools should teach their pupils about the communion service	60	0.4613
The Church of England school system has outlived its usefulness*	3	0.6990
Christian education is the job of parents and the church, not schools*	10	0.5553
It is not the task of Church of England schools to initiate children into a religious faith*	36	0.6291
Church of England schools should be given over to the state*	5	0.6023
Church of England schools should encourage pupils to accept the Christian faith	69	0.4733
The diocese should foster links between Church of England schools and local churches	93	0.3463
It is educationally unsound for Church of England schools to try to teach the Christian faith*	15	0.5559
Church of England schools are racially divisive*	2	0.4357
The idea of 'worshipping' God in school assembly should be abandoned*	3	0.6138
Anglican parents should be encouraged to send their children to a Church of England school	53	0.4700
The Church of England spends too much money on church schools*	0	0.3210

Note: * These items have been reverse scored to compute the item rest of test correlations.

given over to the state. The third point is that many of the teachers actually wish to see the church school system developed. As many as 93% want the diocese to foster links between Church of England schools and local churches. Half the teachers (53%) argue that Anglican parents should be encouraged to send their children to a Church of England school. Half the teachers (49%) argue that the Church of England should develop more secondary, middle or upper schools. The fourth point is that the majority of the teachers see the Church of England school as working in partnership with the church. For example, two-thirds (69%) of the teachers argue that Church of England schools should encourage pupils to accept the Christian faith.

Table 20.2 displays the items which compose the scale of attitude toward the distinctiveness of church schools, together with the item rest of test correlations and the percentage of teachers

Table 20.2
Scale of attitude toward the distinctiveness
of church schools

scale item	agree %	item rest of test r
teaching about Jesus	99	0.6067
putting into practice Christian values	99	0.5306
having RE taught by a committed Christian	74	0.5709
providing an atmosphere of Christian community	95	0.6298
saying classroom prayers	81	0.5339
developing close contacts with clergy	94	0.5346
integrating religious and secular studies	90	0.3479
teaching about God	98	0.7398
teaching about Christianity	98	0.7165
encouraging regular visits from clergy	92	0.5265
providing a daily Christian assembly	94	0.6607
teaching about the bible	97	0.6551
providing a regular Christian assembly	95	0.6621
having committed Christians on the staff	71	0.6021
teaching RE	99	0.5014
teaching about the church	91	0.5951

who agree with each statement. The item rest of test correlations confirm that each individual item contributes toward the overall scale score. The internal reliability of the scale is supported by an alpha coefficient of 0.90.

The individual items clearly demonstrate that the majority of the teachers envisage the Church of England school operating as a community committed to the Christian faith. Nineteen out of every twenty of the teachers argue that church schools should put into practice Christian values, provide an atmosphere of Christian community and provide a regular Christian assembly. Eighteen out of every twenty of the teachers argue that church schools should develop close contacts with clergy, encourage regular visits from the clergy and teach about the church. As many as 81% of the teachers favour saying classroom prayers, while 74% believe that religious education should be taught by committed Christians.

Table 20.3 displays the items which compose the scale of attitude toward traditional teaching methods, together with the item rest of test correlations and the percentage of teachers who agree

Table 20.3
Scale of attitude toward traditional teaching methods

scale item	agree %	item rest of test r
promoting a high level of academic attainment	99	0.3082
giving stars or credits for good work	78	0.4102
punishing children for persistent disruptive behaviour	82	0.4979
training children in hard work	94	0.5887
giving regular maths tests	46	0.4861
bringing the best out of bright pupils	100	0.2417
teaching children to read	100	0.1716
teaching children to know their multiplication tables by heart	81	0.5379
teaching children to be tidy	94	0.5238
teaching children to write clearly	99	0.4074
adopting strict discipline	79	0.5625
correcting most spelling and grammatical errors	78	0.3814
giving regular spelling tests	73	0.3613
expecting children to seek permission before leaving the classroom	86	0.3617
adopting firm discipline	97	0.5999

with each statement. Once again the item rest of test correlations confirm that each individual item contributes toward the overall scale score. The internal reliability of the scale is supported by an alpha coefficient of 0.81.

The individual items demonstrate a considerable commitment to many of the features of a traditional approach to teaching. For

Table 20.4

dependent variables	predictor variables	R^2	change in R^2
teaching grade	sex	0.0612	0.0612
	age	0.1019	0.0407
church attendance	sex	0.0004	0.0004
	age	0.0161	0.0157
attitude toward the church school system	sex	0.0001	0.0001
	age	0.0503	0.0503
	church attendance	0.3064	0.2560
	teaching grade	0.3097	0.0033
	controlled school	0.3322	0.0225
	middle school	0.3322	0.0000
	selective admissions policy	0.3455	0.0133
attitude toward the distinctiveness of church schools	sex	0.0003	0.0003
	age	0.0810	0.0807
	church attendance	0.2293	0.1483
	teaching grade	0.2335	0.0043
	controlled school	0.2464	0.0129
	middle school	0.2513	0.0049
	selective admissions policy	0.2533	0.0020
attitude toward traditional teaching methods	sex	0.0127	0.0127
	age	0.0880	0.0753
	church attendance	0.1070	0.0191
	teaching grade	0.1080	0.0009
	controlled school	0.1080	0.0000
	middle school	0.1190	0.0111
	selective admissions policy	0.1276	0.0086

Multiple regression significance tests

F of change	P<	Beta	T	P<
7.1	.01	−0.2823	−3.1	.01
4.9	.05	+0.2047	+2.2	.05
0.0	NS	−0.0020	−0.0	NS
1.7	NS	+0.1271	+1.3	NS
0.0	NS	−0.0177	−0.2	NS
5.7	.05	+0.1742	+2.1	.05
39.5	.001	+0.5045	+5.7	.001
0.5	NS	−0.0541	−0.6	NS
3.5	NS	−0.1423	−1.7	NS
0.0	NS	+0.0102	+0.1	NS
2.1	NS	+0.1169	+1.4	NS
0.3	NS	−0.0144	−0.2	NS
9.5	.01	+0.2323	+2.6	.01
20.6	.001	+0.3284	+3.5	.001
0.6	NS	+0.0729	+0.8	NS
1.8	NS	−0.1175	−1.3	NS
0.7	NS	−0.0750	−0.8	NS
0.3	NS	+0.0454	+0.5	NS
1.4	NS	−0.1860	−1.8	NS
8.8	.01	+0.2851	+2.9	.01
2.3	NS	−0.1786	−1.7	NS
0.1	NS	+0.0209	+0.2	NS
0.0	NS	+0.0009	+0.0	NS
1.3	NS	−0.1092	−1.1	NS
1.0	NS	+0.0941	+1.0	NS

example, around four out of every five of the teachers are in favour of giving stars or credits for good work, teaching children to know their multiplication tables by heart, correcting most spelling and grammatical errors and adopting strict discipline. Regular spelling tests are favoured by 73% of the teachers although the proportion falls to 46% who favour giving regular maths tests.

Having demonstrated the internal reliability of all three scales of attitude toward the church school system, attitude toward the distinctiveness of church schools, and attitude toward traditional teaching methods, it is now legitimate to employ multiple regression analysis to explore the extent to which the scores of individual teachers on these three scales can be predicted from knowledge regarding their personal characteristics or regarding the school in which they are employed. Table 20.4 presents the findings from five regression equations. The first two equations explore the influence of sex and age on teaching grade and church attendance. The other three equations explore the influence of sex, age, church attendance, teaching grade and type of school on each of the attitude scales. Five main features emerge from these regression equations.

The first regression equation demonstrates that both age and sex are significant predictors of teaching grade. It is not surprising that the senior posts tend to be occupied by older teachers. The senior posts are also more likely to be occupied by male teachers. While only 21 of the 145 teachers in the sample were men, these men were more likely to be found holding senior posts. This is consistent with the findings of Francis (1986a) in the church schools in the Diocese of St Edmunsbury and Ipswich.

The second regression equation demonstrates that neither age nor sex is a significant predictor of church attendance. While in society as a whole women are more likely to attend church than men (Argyle and Beit-Hallahmi, 1975), the present data confirm the findings of Francis (1986a) that this is not the case among teachers in church schools. The male teachers in church schools are no less likely to be churchgoers than the female teachers. While Francis' (1986a) study in the Diocese of St Edmundsbury and Ipswich found that the younger teachers were less likely to be churchgoers than the older teachers, this finding was not replicated in the present study.

The third regression equation demonstrates that male and female teachers hold comparable attitudes toward the church school system. At the same time, there is no significant difference between those working in voluntary aided and in voluntary controlled schools, between those working in middle schools and in other types of school, or between those working in schools which emphasise a selective admissions policy and in schools which emphasise a neighbourhood admissions policy. The two main predictors of differences in teachers' attitude toward the church school system are the teachers' ages and personal church attendance. Older teachers hold a more positive attitude toward the church school system than younger teachers. Churchgoing teachers hold a more positive attitude toward the church school system than teachers who do not attend church. After taking age and church attendance into account, teaching grade is not a significant predictor of attitude toward the church school system.

The fourth regression equation demonstrates that attitude toward the distinctiveness of church schools follows a very similar path to attitude toward the church school system. Once again, male and female teachers hold comparable attitudes toward the distinctiveness of church schools. Once again, there is no significant difference between those working in voluntary aided and in voluntary controlled schools, between those working in middle schools and in other types of school, or between those working in schools which emphasise a selective admissions policy and those which emphasise a neighbourhood admissions policy. The two main predictors of differences in teachers' attitude toward the distinctiveness of church schools are the teachers' ages and personal church attendance. Older teachers hold a more positive attitude toward the distinctiveness of church schools than younger teachers. Churchgoing teachers hold a more positive attitude toward the distinctiveness of church schools than teachers who do not attend church. After taking age and church attendance into account, teaching grade is not a significant predictor of attitude toward the distinctiveness of church schools.

The fifth regression equation demonstrates that, unlike attitude toward the church school system and attitude toward the distinctiveness of church schools, attitude toward traditional teaching methods is unrelated to the individual teacher's personal church attendance. Only one of the independent variables in this equation is a significant predictor of attitude toward traditional teaching methods. The older teachers are more likely to advocate traditional teaching methods than the younger teachers.

Conclusion

This new study among teachers in Church of England voluntary schools within the Diocese of Newcastle confirms the three main conclusions of Francis' (1986a) earlier study among teachers in Church of England voluntary schools within the Diocese of St Edmundsbury and Ipswich.

The first conclusion is that there are many more teachers who are supportive of the church school system than critical of it. While only one in four of the teachers currently working in Church of England schools within the Diocese of Newcastle applied for their present post specifically because it was a church school, once employed within the system the majority of teachers clearly support the continuing role of church schools and wish to emphasise the Christian distinctiveness of church schools. This finding may be good news for many concerned with promoting and developing the Church of England's involvement within the state maintained system of education.

The second conclusion is that there is a close relationship between teachers' personal religious commitment and their views on the church school system. Churchgoing teachers are inclined both to hold a more positive attitude toward the church school system and to wish to assert the distinctiveness of church schools. This finding underlines the clear interrelationship between personal commitment and professional judgement and calls into question the view that educational decisions are professional matters uninfluenced by personal beliefs. This finding needs to be taken seriously both by those responsible for appointing teaching staff to church schools and by those responsible for the in-service professional development of teachers.

The third conclusion is that the older teachers hold a more positive attitude toward the church school system than the younger teachers. The older teachers are also more concerned to promote the distinctiveness of church schools than the younger teachers. This finding may have clear implications for the future development of the church school system. As the older teachers are slowly replaced by a younger generation of teachers, it seems likely that there may be a decline in general support for the church school system among the teaching staff. There may also be a decline in commitment to promoting the distinctiveness of church schools. This finding may not be such good news for many concerned with promoting and developing the Church of England's involvement within the state maintained system of education.

These conclusions are based on two studies conducted in 1982 and 1992 within two dioceses in different parts of England. Proper monitoring of the ethos of church schools would benefit from the regular replication of similar studies over a wider range of dioceses.

References

Argyle, M. and Beit-Hallahmi, B. (1975), *The Social Psychology of Religion*, London, Routledge and Kegan Paul.

British Humanist Association (1967), *Religion in Schools*, London, British Humanist Association.

Brooksbank, K., Revell, J., Ackstine, E. and Bailey, K. (1982), *County and Voluntary Schools*, Harlow, Longman.

Brown, A. and Lankshear, D.W. (1995), *Inspection Handbook: for section thirteen inspections in schools of the Church of England and the Church in Wales*, London, National Society.

Burgess, H.J. (1958), *Enterprise in Education*, London, National Society and SPCK.

Cole, W. (1988), Religious education after Swann, in B. O'Keeffe (ed.) *Schools for Tomorrow*, pp. 125–144, Barcombe, Falmer Press.

Cronbach, L.J. (1951), Coefficient alpha and the internal structure of tests, *Psychometrika*, 16, 297–334.

Cruickshank, M. (1963), *Church and State in English Education*, London, Macmillan.

Dent, H.J. (1947), *The Education Act 1944: provisions, possibilities and some problems* (third edition), London, University of London Press.

Dummett, A. and McNeal, J. (1981), *Race and Church Schools*, London, Runnymede Trust.

Duncan, G. (1986), Church schools: present and future, in G. Leonard (ed.) *Faith for the Future*, pp. 67–78, London, National Society and Church House Publishing.

Duncan, G. (1988), Church schools in service to the community, in B. O'Keeffe (ed.) *Schools for Tomorrow*, pp. 145–161, Barcombe, Falmer Press.

Duncan, G. (1990), *The Church School*, London, National Society.

Francis, L.J. (1986a), *Partnership in Rural Education*, London, Collins Liturgical Publications.

Francis, L.J. (1986b), Denominational schools and pupil attitudes towards Christianity, *British Educational Research Journal*, 12, 145–152.

Francis, L.J. (1987), *Religion in the Primary School*, London, Collins Liturgical Publications.

Francis, L.J. and Carter, M. (1980), Church aided secondary schools, religious education as an examination subject and pupil attitudes towards religion, *British Journal of Educational Psychology*, 50, 297–300.

Francis, L.J. and Jewell, A. (1992), Shaping adolescent attitude towards the church: comparison between Church of England and county secondary schools, *Evaluation and Research in Education*, 6, 13–21.

Francis, L.J. and Lankshear, D.W. (1990), The impact of church schools on village church life, *Educational Studies*, 16, 117–129.

Francis, L.J. and Lankshear, D.W. (1991), The impact of church schools on urban church life, *School Effectiveness and School Improvement*, 2, 324–335.

Francis, L.J. and Stone, E.A. (1995), The attitudes of school governors towards the religious ethos of Church of England voluntary aided primary schools, *Educational Management and Administration*, 23, 176–187.

Gay, J. (1985), *The Size of Anglican Primary Schools*, Abingdon, Culham College Institute Occasional Paper 7.

Gay, J., Kay, B., Newdick, H. and Perry, G. (1991), *A Role for the Future: Anglican primary schools in the London diocese*, Abingdon, Culham College Institute.

Hirst, P.H. (1972), Christian education: a contradiction in terms? *Learning for Living*, 11, 4, 6–11.

Hirst, P.H. (1981), Education, catechesis and the church school, *British Journal of Religious Education*, 3, 85–93.

Kay, B.W., Piper, H.S. and Gay, J.D. (1988), *Managing the Church Schools: a study of the governing bodies of Church of England aided primary schools in the Oxford diocese*, Abingdon, Culham College Institute Occasional Paper 10.

Lankshear, D.W. (1992a), *Looking for Quality in a Church School*, London, National Society.

Lankshear, D.W. (1992b), *A Shared Vision: education in church schools*, London, National Society and Church House Publishing.

Lankshear, D.W. (1993), *Preparing for Inspection in a Church School*, London, National Society.

Levitt, M. (1993), The influence of a church primary school on children's religious beliefs and practices: a Cornish study, unpublished Ph.D. dissertation, University of Exeter.

Murphy, J. (1971), *Church, State and Schools in Britain 1800–1970*, London, Routledge and Kegan Paul.

Murphy, J. (1972), *The Education Act 1870*, Newton Abbot, David and Charles.

O'Keeffe, B. (1986), *Faith, Culture and the Dual System: a comparative study of church and county schools*, Barcombe, Falmer Press.

Ramsey, I. (1970), *The Fourth R: the report of the commission on religious education in schools*, London, National Society and SPCK.

Socialist Education Association (1981), *The Dual System of Voluntary and County Schools*, London, Socialist Education Association.

Socialist Education Association (1986), *All Faiths in All Schools*, London, Socialist Education Association.

SPSS Inc. (1988), *SPSSX User's Guide*, New York, McGraw-Hill.

Swann Report (1985), *Education for All*, London, Her Majesty's Stationery Office.

Waddington, R. (1984), *A Future in Partnership*, London, National Society.

21

'Catechesis' and 'religious education' in Catholic theory and practice

James Arthur and Simon Gaine

Summary

This chapter is concerned to trace the history of the distinction between catechesis and religious education, with particular reference to its more recent application to primary schools, the publication of Weaving the Web *having been followed in 1992 by the arrival of the National Project's programme for pupils aged three to eleven,* Here I Am. *This chapter also offers some provisional findings of research into how far a distinction between catechesis and religious education has been appropriated by primary school teachers themselves. Data from 47 teachers in Kent indicate that a strong separation between catechesis and religious education has not yet been greatly influential at primary level.*

Introduction

The most controversial event in the history of Catholic religious education in England and Wales during recent years must surely be the adoption of *Weaving the Web* as the framework for the religious education in Catholic schools of children between the ages of eleven and fourteen. Two dioceses (Birmingham and Salford) went so far as to discourage the use of this programme. *Weaving the Web* grew out of the work of the National Project of Catechesis and Religious Education, the initiation of which was endorsed by the Bishops' Conference of England and Wales. It was published by

the Project during 1987–88 as a framework for the development of
school curricula, and has been widely criticised for its alleged lack
of doctrinal content and presentation of all religions as being of
equal value. One possible response to these criticisms appears to
have been that its critics mistook the programme for 'catechesis',
whereas it is in fact 'religious education'. And in the *Teachers' Book*
it is stated that 'religious education should be non-exclusive'
(Lohan and McClure, 1988). Thus religious education is aimed
equally at all pupils of whatever religious conviction or none; faith
is presupposed neither in teacher nor in pupil. Religious education
is geared towards learning about and from various religions; though
it is admitted that pupils may be challenged to deepen their own
faith-commitments (whatever they might be), religious education
is not primarily concerned with developing Christian (or any other)
faith. The principles of the programme are those of the National
Project, and are drawn from its *Guidelines*. Here, Fr J. Gallagher,
SDB, then Assistant National Adviser for Religious Education,
maintains this distinction between catechesis and religious education. He appeals to church documents such as *Catechesis in Our Time*
to define catechesis as a 'process of education in faith'. Religious
education is, however, about coming to a 'knowledge and understanding of the beliefs and practices of religious traditions' (Gallagher, 1986). While it is both recognised that catechesis is a
life-long process and that catechesis, religious education and evangelisation are not entirely mutually exclusive, the illustrations
present catechesis as more suitable for a voluntary group of adults
and religious education as more suitable for the classroom. *Weaving
the Web* is intended to play a role in religious education rather than
in catechesis, and hence it offers a framework which can be used
within schools of any religious commitment or none. What then is
the authority for a distinction between catechesis and religious
education? Gallagher gave references to official church documents
for his definitions of catechesis and evangelisation, but not for that
of religious education. All he says is, 'Recent documents which deal
with catechesis and religious education distinguish these activities' (Gallagher, 1986). However, these terms had traditionally
been used interchangeably.

Catechetical Movement

A distinction between religious education and catechesis was first
made against the background of the twentieth-century expansion

of the notion of catechesis by what has come to be known as the 'Catechetical Movement' (see Marthaler, 1978). Due to the influence of this movement, 'catechesis' was understood to encompass the total development of the faith of a Christian over the whole period of his or her life in all its aspects, and not simply the bare transmission of the content of the Christian faith to children. Particularly influential in the development of this 'Catechetical Movement' were the six International Study Weeks on Catechetics held between 1959 and 1968 at Nijmegen in 1959, Eichstätt in 1960, Bangkok in 1962, Katigondo in 1964, Manila in 1967 and Medellín in 1968 (see Erdozain, 1970). Thus the Catechetical Movement underwent a number of phases, bringing new concerns into the expanding concept of 'catechesis': liturgical (the role of corporate worship in catechesis), kerygmatic (the proclamation of salvation-history), anthropological (concern with the cultural context of those being catechised) and political (motivation for social action).

The general period of the Catechetical Movement coincided with the history of the church's *General Catechetical Directory*, first suggested in the late 1950s and finally published in 1971. The Second Vatican Council (1962–65) approved a proposal for a *Directory* for the use of bishops, episcopal conferences and those responsible for catechesis. After much international consultation, the *Directory* was produced as a set of guidelines for regional and national directories, which would in turn serve as guidelines for catechetical materials. As such, it provides principles of pastoral theology rather than teaching theory, and so stands clearly in the tradition of the Catechetical Movement. While the *Directory* cites mainly Vatican II and the teaching of Pope Paul VI, the influence of the Study Weeks and various national directories is not difficult to trace. Thus, the *Directory* shared with the Catechetical Movement a broad understanding of catechesis as aimed at 'maturity of faith'. Moreover, like the Study Weeks and previous official church documents, it made no distinction between catechesis and religious education. In summary, the language of catechesis had now flowed into the centre of the church's life, together with a concentration on the whole span of human life rather than just on the school years.

This change of emphasis can be well illustrated by the Pastoral Letters and National Meetings of the Bishops of the United States of America. What we might call their catechetical concerns had mainly been with the religious instruction of children by their parents and schools. 'Religious Instruction' was the term most commonly used, while forms of the term 'catechesis' occurred very rarely. However, from the middle of the 1960s, pastorals slowly began to betray the influence of the Catechetical Movement. Following the publication of the *General Catechetical Directory* and the holding of an International Catechetical Congress in Rome the same year, the Administrative Board of the United States Catholic Conference requested the Bishops' Committee on Education to plan the development of a national directory. In 1972, the Bishops finally devoted an entire pastoral letter to the whole issue of catechesis or religious education, using the two terms interchangeably and broadening the concept with the ideas developed within the Catechetical Movement. After wide consultation throughout the dioceses, a draft was sent by the Bishops for approval to the Sacred Congregation of the Clergy in Rome. After some reworking, the *National Catechetical Directory*, entitled *Sharing the Light of Faith*, was published in 1979 (see Bryce, 1973, 1979). Once more ideas of the Catechetical Movement were endorsed, and in the later drafts a preference had developed for the language of catechesis. However, no distinction was clearly made between catechesis and religious education, although it was hinted that religious instruction should be seen as part of catechesis along with the sharing of faith-experiences, liturgy and service.

Since catechesis and religious education had not yet been distinguished, the expansion of the notion of catechesis raised the expectations laid on classroom religious education in America and elsewhere. Hence, classroom methods attempted to keep pace with those tendencies which prevailed in catechetical theory. Thus, from the kerygmatic phase to the political, the trends of the Catechetical Movement were also to be found in classroom religious education. However, as the old question-and-answer catechism had had its difficulties, so now the new approaches were also found to be problematic. Expectation for religious experience and enthusiasm in the classroom proved too often to be artificial. However, rather than deduce that these new catechetical approaches were bad in themselves, one important response was to suggest a clear differentiation between the methods of classroom religious education and more general catechesis. This response was most clearly given by the Australian Christian Brother, Graham Rossiter, who has held, among other appointments, the post of Project Officer for Religious Education at the federal Curriculum Development Centre (Rossiter, 1982, 1986, 1988).

Rossiter's 'creative divorce'

Rossiter's response is linked with a wider tendency in the 1970s to seek for a conceptual distinction between catechesis and religious education, despite the fact that official church documents still used the terms interchangeably. For example, in 1973, a tentative distinction was drawn by Fr Berard Marthaler, OFM, Conv., a consultant to the American directory committee who later wrote the 'official' commentary on *Sharing the Light of Faith*. In *Catechetics in Context*, he writes that 'religious education is primarily an academic enterprise'. On the other hand, catechesis 'includes the kerygma, preparation for the sacraments, as well as more advanced instruction to nourish and sustain a living faith in the community and its individual members' (Marthaler, 1973). Applied to the problems experienced in the classroom in the wake of the Catechetical Movement, this would imply that less could be expected of religious education; the classroom would be the context for intellectual exercise, not for religious experience. A similar distinction was then made six years later by Fr William Paradis, the director of the project which produced *Sharing the Light of Faith*. He writes how this *National Catechetical Directory* had approved the catechetical developments of the previous twenty years. He hoped that the document's impact would result in the disappearance of the term 'religious education', which would simply signify the transmission of information, while 'catechesis' would refer to all activities which enriched faith (Paradis, 1979). He devotes the remainder of this article largely to adult and family catechesis. Despite the fact that he writes of religious education in a negative tone, he clearly distinguishes it, as does Marthaler, as being concerned with knowledge. A more positive estimation of religious education had been given shortly before by Fr Kevin Nichols, the first National Adviser to the Bishops of England and Wales for religious education. Writing under the auspices of his Bishops' Conference, he recognised that secular theorists had developed a form of religious education which did not involve religious commitment, which he styled 'education in religion' (Nichols, 1978). However, Catholic religious education would instead be a particular 'mode or style' of catechesis aimed at the pupils developing an understanding of their faith. That some such distinction was not only made but also favoured is demonstrated by the fact that in 1981, Pope John Paul II himself indicated that catechesis and religious instruction were both distinct and complementary (John Paul II, 1981).

In his article of 1982, 'The need for a "creative divorce" between catechesis and religious education in Catholic schools', Rossiter noted how religious education theory had depended heavily on catechetical theory, as though all that applied to one naturally applied to the other. He also noted the shift in focus in catechetical theory from the school towards pastoral ministry with adults, such that catechesis was no longer dependent on the 'schooling-paradigm'. Thus, the fact that both teachers and official church documents had continued to use 'religious education' and 'catechesis' inter-changeably had proved problematic. Rossiter recognised that church documents do this since they are written from the perspective of the faith-community, so that religious education is an instrument of catechesis for the socialisation of its members into faith. However, he asserts that there had been a failure in transposing the catechetical aims and ideas of these documents into the context of the school. Catechetical methods suited to a pastoral, voluntary, adult-orientated, faith-sharing context were being uncritically applied to compulsory classroom lessons. Due to such uncritical application, catechesis as it had developed now seemed unsuitable for the classroom. Rossiter notes that while teachers had strongly subscribed to the new understandings of catechesis as a paradigm for religious education, some had also rejected a 'schooling/instructional' paradigm. These teachers thought that religious education should not be presented as an academic subject with emphasis on content, written work and assessment. They wanted pupils to perceive religious education as different from other subjects — it should be more personal and pastoral, without competition and examinations, and with the emphasis on dialogue and faith-sharing. Since it was found to be difficult for this approach to be fitted to the classroom, teachers had even attempted to create alternative, more informal environments.

This, however, is not Rossiter's solution. He wants not to modify the school situation to fit catechetical requirements, but to qualify what might be expected of catechesis in the schooling or instructional context. Although he allows that there is value in innovation in the structures for religious education, he refuses to hold that this entails rejection of the schooling or educational paradigm. He blames neither the broad understanding of catechesis nor the nature of the school, but the way in which principles had been transferred from one to the other. His solution, therefore, is to call for a reformulation of a theory of Catholic religious education. This would involve a 'creative divorce' between catechesis and religious education. After 'divorce proceedings', religious education would not be so much a catechetical as an educational enterprise, and so catechesis and religious education would be more independent of each other. This would not at all be to exclude catechesis from the school, but would be to determine the possibilities and limitations of faith-sharing less uncritically.

Rossiter turns then for the development of the classroom curriculum to the educational paradigm. Moreover, he hopes to make use of the paradigm of religious education as it is taught in secular state schools in the United Kingdom and in Australia as a source for Catholic religious education. That is, he wishes to bring 'education in religion' to the service of 'education in faith'. While 'education in faith' denotes the transmission of a particular faith-tradition, 'education in religion' denotes a study of religion justified solely on educational grounds, independently of catechetical concerns or the specific assumptions of a faith-community. This secular approach, he says, has advocates and theorists in England, Germany, France and the United States of America. By a critical appropriation of its methods, Rossiter suggests that Catholic religious education may be reconceptualised. Thus the content of the formal curriculum is highlighted, and the potential of the classroom context to communicate and develop personal faith is not overestimated.

One important qualification must be added here: Rossiter is not suggesting the simple substitution of education in faith by education in religion. Although the academically-orientated religious education has been distinguished from catechetical faith-sharing, religious education has not been removed from the domain of faith. Religious education continues to relate to faith, but through an impartation of a knowledge and understanding of the pupils' faith-tradition; it is a faith seeking understanding, a faith being given intellectual expression. Thus, in terms of immediate aims and methods, catechesis and religious education are distinct, but they nevertheless share the broader aim of nurturing faith in their own distinct ways. Rossiter, therefore, stands not too far from Nichols' notion of religious education as a special form of catechesis.

Moran's 'ecumenical education'

When Rossiter recommended his agenda, he was aware that he was drawing out some ideas implicit in some of the writings of the American Christian Brother, Gabriel Moran. By the late 1960s,

Moran was the chief influence in American catechetics. However, from this time on, his thought underwent a striking development. At the beginning of this development, his main concern was for a more positive theological basis for catechetics. Thus catechesis was firmly founded in principles drawn from his theology of revelation. Moreover, taking his stand against the background of the then pervasive kerygmatic approach and the reaction against the old catechism method, Moran did not wish to see the intellectual and academic excluded. He feared that the Catechetical Movement was in danger of trivialisation, and maintained that catechesis was just as doctrinal as theology, while theology was as concerned with the kerygma as was catechesis. Moran therefore believed that catechetics was facing a crisis: a little scripture and liturgy was not proving enough; understanding and knowledge were also required. Thus, even before the advent of the methods of the 1970s, Moran (1967) was anticipating something of the later criticisms made by Rossiter. However, his immediate response was not to develop a distinction between catechesis and religious education. Next, Moran moved his attention away from the school to catechesis as a lifelong process. It was a natural result of his theology of revelation that he should focus on the adult rather than the child, and he emphasised that Catholic education was a wider concern than Catholic schools. As far as children were concerned, he hoped for some alternative to the classroom. Although he denied that he wanted to make an all-out attack on schools, he was quite prepared to suggest that if some Catholic schools stood in the way of Catholic education, they should be scrapped rather than improved (Moran, 1968).

By 1968, Moran had been wondering not what the future of catechetics was, but whether it had a future at all. However, within a few years he felt able to write an article which received the title, 'Catechetics, RIP'. Catechetical change had proved a disaster and a waste of effort. There had been a crisis in religious education, but now the crisis was religious education itself. His concern for the 1970s was not to revivify a dead catechetics, but to create a new discipline which he called 'ecumenical education'. Thus, he did not make a distinction between catechesis and religious education, but wished to replace the kind of religious education which was being created by the Catechetical Movement with a new 'ecumenical' kind. The term 'religious education' would thus die to be reborn with a new meaning. This suggestion was in part Moran's attempt to demonstrate that he was in favour of some kind of religious education for children. The word 'ecumenical' was used to cover Christianity's encounter with other religions and non-religious realities. The use of the term in connection with religious education did not only mean the teaching of other religions, it also meant the teaching of Christianity in a wholly new way. While the church should try to raise the educational level of the wider community, religion should be taught free of church structures. Thus, the kerygmatic preaching model was deemed unsuitable for the teacher, and teaching was centred on a nuanced understanding of experience as the final norm of truth. Although ecumenical education was seen as co-extensive with the whole of life, what was appropriate for an adult would not be appropriate for a child. While catechesis or theology may be suited to an adult who had made a free and intelligent choice, children should not be catechised at all. Moran denies that Christianity can be taught to children — their religious education should merely be the ecumenical study of religion. The importance of comparing different religions is stressed, although this should be done impartially and without the intention to convert. Thus, not only catechesis, but also evangelisation is excluded from this kind of religious education, which does not have a faith-context. Among the implications of this view is the fact that Catholic schools can no longer be justified on the religious content of their curricula. Moreover, on such a view, religious education would not only be something other than catechesis, it would be removed from the context of faith altogether. In the work of Moran, the influence is evident not only of the Catechetical Movement, but also of the growth of secularism and pluralism (Moran, 1970). Two broad approaches may then be discerned in the distinguishing of catechesis and religious education. One separates them to a greater degree such that its understanding of religious education is much influenced by pluralism (Moran), and the other separates them to a lesser degree and treats religious education as a certain type of catechetical activity (Rossiter, Nichols).

Purnell and the National Project

In view of the complexity of the history of the Catechetical Movement, it is not surprising that much confusion arose as to what catechesis and religious education were supposed to be and what the relationship was between them. In England and Wales, Fr Nichols had maintained that catechesis was the broader concept of the two. It was aimed at maturity of faith, and religious education was a particular educational form of catechesis. However, Nichols clearly differentiated *Christian* religious education from the 'education in religion' which would take place in a pluralist rather than a faith-context. However, due to the fact that Christian theorists such as Moran had been promoting a secular religious education in Catholic schools, the possibility was open for the current distinction between catechesis and religious education to be reformulated by Catholics in England, such that religious education would be kept quite separate from the catechetical domain of faith.

The fact that the National Pastoral Congress of 1980 had continued to treat religious education as a catechetical activity (as had Nichols) was to come under attack from more radical elements in the mould of Moran in the pages of *The Tablet*. In the issue dated 30 August 1980, a religious education teacher at Trinity School, Leamington Spa, Geoffrey Turner, took as his starting-point an understanding of catechesis as by definition offered to those who had made a free decision to be Christians and had freely sought instruction in their faith. Secondary school pupils, however, could be not counted as such, since their religious education was compulsory. Since there was a wide range of religious commitments or none amongst pupils, the Catholic school could not be called a 'Christian community' without qualification, such that religious education (Turner calls it 'theological education') had to be 'flexible', without any core content, with everything questioned, beginning with and expressing the pupils' interests. The aim of religious education was to make pupils aware of the 'religious dimension' of life and the fact that there are important religious questions, so that they could make their own judgements about them. Catechesis was for voluntary groups only, and it and evangelisation were to be excluded from the classroom.

Similar lines were pursued in the issue dated 22 November 1980 by David Jackson, the head of religious education at Cardinal Heenan High School, Leeds. Catholic schools (and not just secondary ones, though they were especially the case) contained pupils of a variety of levels of commitment. Since catechesis was properly for adults who had made a free commitment, the classroom was therefore not an appropriate place for catechesis. The values of the Gospel must pervade the whole school, but in religious education pupils are only asked to make sense of religious belonging, concepts, feelings and actions, so that they can judge the truth-claims made by religious traditions. Pupils without a faith-background are not asked to commit themselves to anything but a general appreciation of the 'religious dimension'. In other words, evangelisation is excluded. The possibility of development of the religious faith of a pupil by religious education must be left to the Holy Spirit, while nothing catechetical is to be intended by the teacher. Both these articles not only exclude evangelisation, but make a strong separation between catechesis and religious education. The basic reason for the strong distinction made comes nearer to Moran's than had previous theorists in England; this reason was the growth of pluralism. With the creation of a National Project of Catechesis and Religious Education in England and Wales and the appointment of Fr Patrick Purnell, SJ, as Nichols' successor as National Adviser, the way lay open for this more extreme distinction between catechesis and religious education to make its way into official circles.

By the early 1980s, dissatisfaction in England and Wales with religious education syllabuses used in Catholic schools was evident. In particular, the widely-used Irish catechetical programme for primary schools, *Children of God*, was seen as culturally inappropriate. The Bishops were advised by The National Board of Religious Inspectors and Advisers either to revise the programme or to produce something new and more suited to the national context. The response of the Bishops at their Low Week meeting in 1982 was positive. After all, *The General Catechetical Directory* of over ten years before had recommended that each region have its own catechetical materials. The Bishops' Department for Catholic Education and Formation endorsed a new programme which was initiated by The National Board of Religious Inspectors and Advisers. The programme was named 'PREP: The Primary Religious Education Programme'. A contract was drawn up between the Bishops and Collins Publishers, such that this project would be financed as a co-operative partnership between these two parties. Thanks to the influence of the catechetical developments in the wider church and to the National Pastoral Congress, the task of this particular venture soon expanded beyond mere primary school education: not only secondary education but the whole life-long process of the development of faith was included in its agenda. Thus PREP was transformed into 'Living and Sharing Our Faith: A National Project of Catechesis and Religious Education'. The National Project promised not only a vision, but a process for making this vision a reality by means of a community effort throughout the dioceses. It aimed to produce resources for home, parish and school. It is important to note that both the terms catechesis and religious education are included in the full title of the Project, implying a distinction between the two as of the very essence of the Project. However, what precisely was the distinction being made by the Project as it planned and produced resources during the 1980s? As the Project developed, it was guided by the new National Adviser of Religious Education, Patrick Purnell. It was his book, *Our Faith Story* (Purnell, 1985), which furnished the principles of the National Project. Among these was a theory of the distinction between catechesis and religious education which can itself be distinguished from those theories which had been developed and which were still being developed elsewhere.

Following in the tradition of the Catechetical Movement, Purnell affirms catechesis as a lifelong process of nurturing and maturing faith within the faith-community. Evangelisation, on the other hand, is aimed outside this community to challenge, transform and convert. Nevertheless, catechesis and evangelisation are not mutually exclusive. Most frequently, catechesis is an 'evangelising catechesis' since the members of the faith-community are themselves in need of constant conversion. In defining religious education, Purnell's first concern seems to be for the protection of the 'dignity and freedom' of the individual child. This means a very strict differentiation of religious education from catechesis and evangelisation. Telling pupils what to believe is explicitly ruled out. Instead the pupils must simply be told about different religious beliefs and their skills developed so that they may gain a 'sympathetic understanding' of various religions. Therefore, evangelisation is ruled out of the classroom altogether, except that it is hoped that the values of the Gospel will pervade classroom activity. It is not for the teacher to attempt to influence the beliefs or values of the pupils deliberately. If some pupils are challenged, this would seem to take place only as a side-effect. Not only is evangelisation excluded, but the classroom is not the normal setting for catechesis, since the latter presupposes *faith* as evangelisation seeks to evoke it. Religious education is not concerned with the maturation of faith and the handing-on of various aspects of a religious tradition, but with the imparting of those skills necessary to ask the fundamental questions of human existence. Religious education should lead pupils to the point where they might be able to make a mature commitment to or thoughtful rejection of a faith-tradition. If believing children happen to receive religious education as catechesis and non-believing ones as evangelisation, this is seen as a kind of by-product. Such responses are neither the purpose of religious education nor the intention of the teacher. This view seems to have much in common with Turner, Jackson, and Moran's ecumenical education. Indeed, Purnell acknowledges Moran as an important influence on him. However, it should be pointed out that Purnell differs entirely from Moran in his general estimate of catechesis.

What then are Purnell's reasons for these distinctions? Evidently, Purnell does not seem to think the methods of catechesis inappropriate to the classroom for the same reasons as does Rossiter. While Rossiter saw such methods as unsuitable, he both maintained the faith context of religious education and desired to give it more academic and intellectual content in opposition to current opinion. These concerns are not characteristic of Purnell. He emphasises that education is not ultimately about learning facts or skills: it concerns not only the intellectual but also emotions, actions and relations. Moreover, he rejects catechesis in the classroom on the grounds that the class would contain a range of religious commitment. He recognises that the school had been part of the local faith-community in the past, but sees this as now no longer being the case: faith (Christian or otherwise) cannot be presumed in either pupils or parents. Consequently, some other place should be found in the school for the voluntary catechesis of the committed. It seems then that Purnell is giving a pragmatic response to the pluralism which can now be found in Catholic schools. In fact, he tends to embrace a pluralist model of the school (Arthur, 1992).

The fact of pluralism then is what led Purnell and the National Project to make their distinction the way they did. In the foreword to the *Teachers' Book* for the *Weaving the Web* series, the authors write that the previous syllabus 'was based on assumptions that were no longer tenable, and did not enable teachers and pupils to respond to a changed and changing situation with new demands' (Lohan and McClure, 1988). These assumptions seem to be that pupils and teachers previously shared a common faith, while the new situation is that of pluralism. Again, Gallagher notes in *Guidelines* that 'The pupils in both our primary and secondary schools come from a variety of religious backgrounds' (Gallagher, 1986). He then points to the distinctions made between catechesis, evangelisation and religious education as 'important and relevant' in this respect. Gallagher is here clearly following Purnell in no longer treating Catholic schools as faith-communities. The National Project differed then in two main ways from what had been previously accepted in England: religious education was not (as Nichols had thought) a catechetical activity, and evangelisation was excluded (while Nichols [1978] had only recognised its difficulty at secondary level and not absolutely excluded it).

Later developments

In 1988, the Congregation for Catholic Education issued some guidelines entitled *The Religious Dimension of Education in a Catholic School*. For the first time, a distinction between 'catechesis' and 'religious instruction' (the term here preferred to religious education) was clearly made in an official church document. While the National Project had presented religious education as a broader concept than catechesis, this document chose to make catechesis the broader one. Catechesis was seen as the manifold handing-on of the Gospel to be received as a 'salvific reality'. Religious instruction, however, has the goal of knowledge, and is clearly treated as an academic discipline. While religious instruction is limited by time and space to the school, catechesis takes place in the wider faith-community over a whole lifetime. The National Project soon included references to this document's distinction in its own literature to lend weight to its own distinction. Indeed, it might appear superficially that the same distinction was being made by both parties. However, there would appear to be a crucial difference: the Congregation has not removed religious instruction from the context of faith. In continuity with previous official church documents, the Congregation also sticks resolutely to the 'holistic' model of the school rather than embrace a pluralist model. The 'holistic' view involves a critical integration of culture and religion, with the school firmly inserted into the evangelising mission of the church. Evangelisation is consequently not excluded at all, but is positively encouraged. Like the National Project, the document is aware that there are non-Catholics in the schools, but this is an opportunity for the proclamation of the Gospel, which is said to be quite different from forcibly imposing it.

There is then not only a distinction between catechesis and religious instruction, but also a 'close connection' between them. On the one hand, catechesis will involve the transmission of knowledge, and on the other, religious instruction will involve growth in faith on the part of believers as well as the evangelisation of unbelievers. This is not seen, as it is by the National Project, as a kind of unintended, accidental by-product, but is of the very essence of religious instruction. A glance at the course suggested *in lieu* of the 'Universal Catechism' confirms that religious instruction takes place with the concerns of faith. The teacher should intend to bring children closer to the mystery of the Trinity, encourage a devotion to the church and a valuing of the sacraments, and help pupils to open their hearts in prayer. Moreover, religious instruction should be integrated into the wider catechetical activities of school and parish.

The distinction made by the Congregation differs fundamentally from the one made by the National Project, in that it is made not primarily in response to pluralism, but is an attempt to integrate the impartation of knowledge firmly within the wider work of catechesis. That is not to say, however, that the issue of pluralism and the presence of non-Catholics in the schools has been ignored. In fact, the principles of the Congregation and the National Project encapsulate two divergent responses to this issue. While the National Project responded with a secular religious education, the Congregation responds with evangelisation. With two such differing trends current in Catholic thought, it was not long before not only *Weaving the Web* was challenged, but also the concept of religious education on which it was based. Such challenges came from within England itself and not simply from Rome. Inspired more by the Congregation's kind of vision than the National Project's, critics proposed a specifically Catholic religious education in place of the *Web*. Fr John Redford of Maryvale, the Archdiocese of Birmingham's institute for religious education, argued in *The Tablet* of 22 February 1992 that there should be a specifically Catholic religious education aimed at developing the faith of the pupils. These challenges to the National Project pointed to a much closer relationship between religious education and catechesis.

Most significant in this connection was Pope John Paul II's *Ad Limina* Address given to the Bishops of the Liverpool Province in March 1992. Here the Pope affirmed that religious education was indeed broader than catechesis. Now this contention had been maintained by the National Project, while the 1988 document from the Congregation had set forth catechesis as the broader of the two. It must be concluded that the official Vatican line is that there is a sense in which catechesis is broader than religious education, but also a sense in which the converse is true. In other words, neither catechesis nor religious education would entirely contain the other, but the two activities would quite properly overlap. However, the

Pope is clearly in continuity with previous official teaching when he goes on to assert that religious education 'must also include catechesis, since a principal goal of the Catholic school must be to hand on the faith'. He encouraged the Bishops to 'review religious education materials in order to see that they are based on principles of sound catechesis' (reported in *Briefing*, 1992). This would appear to be an expression of dissatisfaction with the principles and work of the National Project. Not that the *Web* itself would be rejected or revised — the Congregation of the Clergy had approved it a role within curriculum planning. However, Catholic theorists in England and Wales were now pointed towards a much closer relationship between catechesis and religious education than they had advocated in the 1980s.

It was during this period of intense debate over the *Web* in the early 1990s that *Here I Am*, the National Project's programme for religious education in primary schools, was introduced. As with *Weaving the Web*, its contents were the object of criticism which led as far as a pamphlet being published in its defence in 1994 (White, 1992). What though of the notion of religious education which underlay the programme? First, the programme recognises the diversity of religious backgrounds in the classroom and that religious education is aimed at them all, to promote their innate capacity for the 'spiritual', to provide them with the language of religious experience. However, while it is affirmed that the context of England and Wales requires appropriate material on religions other than Christianity, Christianity occupies the central place in *Here I Am* which it had not in *Weaving the Web*. It is now stated that a religious education programme will give a 'systematic presentation' of Christianity in a way appropriate to the age and stage of development of the child. This is the language of official church documents, such as the Congregation for Catholic Education's 1988 document, and the content of this presentation was subsequently underlined in 1994 (*What are we to teach?*) in a booklet issued by the Bishops' Conference and based on the Universal Catechism which had been published in 1992. *Here I Am* does not go so far as to say that this presentation of Christianity will be evangelistic with regard to pupils who do not share the Christian faith, but it is the nearest the National Project has come to inserting the school fully into the church's evangelistic mission in the manner of the Congregation. Although the relationship between evangelisation and religious education is not explicitly treated here, the relationship between catechesis and religious education is.

This relationship is presented as a much closer one than had been the case in previous National Project material. The notion that religious education is primarily about teaching about religions and not about the catechetical concerns of faith is absent. Religious education is said to be 'complementary' to catechesis's 'educating to and in faith'. Religious education is not identical with catechesis, but 'in the case of many children it will deepen and enrich their understanding and living of their Catholic faith'. That this is seemingly not a mere by-product but part-and-parcel of the very nature of religious education is reinforced by the statements that much of what is said of catechesis applies to religious education so that church documents on catechesis are referred to in *Here I Am*, that the programme has 'underlying theological as well as educational principles', and that religious education provides opportunity for 'celebration, prayer and reflection'. In summary, it is the aim of *Here I Am* to explore the 'religious dimension of questions about life, dignity and purpose within the Catholic tradition'. Children from committed backgrounds will have their faith developed, but the intention towards non-Catholics is made no clearer. So much for the theoretical developments of the relationship between catechesis and religious education as applied to primary schools: what of the opinions of the primary school teachers themselves?

Method

It was decided to conduct a survey by questionnaire of a small opportunity sample of Catholic primary school teachers in Kent. This research was undertaken in November 1994 and completed in January 1995. The sampling strategy was to select a number of Catholic primary schools with a total staff composition of 100 teachers. Nine schools were selected at random from the Kent local education authority directory and the exact number of staff was subsequently obtained for each school in consultation with the headteacher or school secretary. All nine headteachers were sent a letter and received a follow-up telephone call to seek their co-operation in distributing the questionnaire to their staff, and all agreed to this in principle. Each questionnaire was individually addressed; each was accompanied by a covering letter asking for assistance by completing the questionnaire and guaranteeing confidentiality, together with an addressed envelope for its return. The questionnaire was printed on four pages, as a short and simple questionnaire often attracts a greater rate of response.

The aim of the questionnaire was to discover whether or not Catholic primary teachers perceived there to be a difference between catechesis and religious education. A particular concern was how teachers viewed the role of the Catholic school in the religious education of Catholic children. With this in mind the questionnaire was drawn up in five parts, based on the questionnaire used by Francis (1986) in his study of teachers in Anglican schools. Part one of the questionnaire sought some basic information on the respondent and his or her school, such as his or her age, position in the school, religious affiliation, and the school's admissions policy. Part two of the questionnaire asked for responses to a series of questions about the respondents' personal views on the general purpose of Catholic education in their schools. An example question reads, 'Catholic schools should encourage pupils to live and practise the Catholic faith'. Part three of the questionnaire asked for information on what ideas had influenced their views of religious education and catechesis and the sources of these ideas. Parts four and five of the questionnaire explored the respondents' perceptions of the roles of religious education and catechesis by inviting them to assess the contributions made to these two areas by sixteen specific components, like teaching children about church services and preparing children for mass. By this method it was possible to measure or indicate the main differences in staff perceptions of religious education and catechesis.

A total of 100 questionnaires were sent for distribution to the nine Kent Catholic primary schools, and by the middle of December a total of 38 questionnaires had been returned. In contacting the schools and asking staff to be reminded to complete and return the questionnaires, it was discovered that one headteacher had not distributed the questionnaire on the sole ground that members of staff were particularly busy and would not have time to respond. Consequently, 14 members of staff had not been given the opportunity to read, complete and return the questionnaire. This reduced the number of possible respondents to 86. By January 1995 a further ten questionnaires were received, making a total of 48 responses, one of which was spoiled. Since the following results represent only a small opportunity sample, it is not to be expected that the results would be exactly replicated throughout England and

Wales, but only that the same broad outline of teacher-perceptions may be revealed by further research.

Results

All the respondents indicated that their schools contained a majority of Catholic pupils on roll. Three respondents described themselves as non-Catholic. This figure would be consistent with national statistics on the number of non-Catholics teaching in Catholic primary schools. What is of interest, however, is that these three teachers were teaching religious education in Catholic schools. The age-range of the respondents included ten between the ages of twenty and twenty-six years, 18 between the ages of twenty-seven and thirty-nine years, and 20 between the ages of forty and sixty-nine years, and this spread of respondents revealed no specific correlations between the opinions and the ages of the respondents. Only six named any specific influence on them, but none of these influences included National Project theorists, documents or programmes. The overwhelming majority of the sample considered the traditional Catholic elements of catechesis and religious education to be either important or very important. The only elements that were generally if at all considered less important were preparation for the sacraments (which was almost certainly dealt with in the parish in these cases) and teaching on other denominations and religions, which was considered only marginally more important in religious education than in catechesis. This suggests that whatever is to be revealed by the survey on the opinions of respondents on the theoretical relationship between religious education and catechesis, the practice of these activities appears to be largely similar and traditional. A central position for Catholicism and less emphasis on other religious traditions also points more to the Congregation's and *Here I Am's* understanding of religious education than *Weaving the Web's*. The fact that a majority (25) favoured evangelisation, while only eight rejected it, points to a greater tendency towards the Congregation's view on this issue than the National Project's.

On the question of the relationship between catechesis and religious education, four groups may be identified. The first group, made up of five respondents comprising two non-Catholics (one 'Church of England' and one 'Christian'), thought that religious education and catechesis should be separate from one another in a Catholic school. Of the three Catholics, one rejected any role for evangelisation in education and two were unsure. In contrast with two of the Catholics, the two non-Catholics and the remaining Catholic (not the one who rejected evangelisation) did not feel they had applied to their schools specifically because they were Catholic. The Anglican respondent in particular provided conflicting answers in the questionnaire. While this teacher excluded catechesis from religious education, he or she gave support to evangelisation in a school which he or she claimed anyway was exclusively Catholic (this teacher was the only respondent to make such a claim). The Christian disagreed strongly that there was any such thing as specifically Catholic education and strongly rejected evangelisation in education. In contrast to the Catholics who specifically wanted to teach in a Catholic school, the two non-Catholics and the remaining Catholic were stronger on the importance of teaching about other religions and denominations in catechesis and religious education.

The second group comprised 31 respondents who agreed that catechesis and religious education were part of each other, with eleven of them leaving open the possibility that they might be the same within the context of a Catholic school. Only five disagreed that they had applied to their school because it was Catholic. Of this group, 19 accepted evangelisation, six rejected it, and six were unsure. The tendency to admit evangelisation was in fact stronger (14 out of 19) amongst those who were certain that catechesis and religious education were distinct though closely related. As a general observation, teaching about other denominations and religions was considered by this group as only fairly important if not fairly unimportant in both catechesis and religious education.

A third group comprising eight respondents indicated that catechesis and religious education were the same thing in a Catholic school. Whilst none of this group opposed evangelisation in education, three were actively in favour. Most of this group agreed strongly that they had applied for their present posts specifically because the school was Catholic. On closer examination of their responses on the content of catechesis and religious education, it was found that most thought that teaching about other denominations and religions was not appropriate.

A fourth group comprising four respondents said that they were uncertain as to whether or not catechesis and religious education were in any way linked with each other. Two of the respondents had applied to their schools specifically because they were Catholic and both accepted the role of evangelisation in education. The other two had not applied to their schools because they were Catholic and both were unsure on the evangelisation issue. There was a general tendency to count traditional Catholic content as important in both catechesis and religious education, with other denominations and religions being counted slightly less important by two of the group (one of these respondents being one of those who favoured evangelisation).

In conclusion, only a small minority of five respondents (the first group) wished to keep catechesis and religious education separate. While it might be tempting to identify them with the ideas of Moran, Purnell, the National Project and the *Web*, they do not name any of these as influences and in fact occasionally diverge from them on issues such as the role of evangelisation which not all of them reject. A larger group of eight respondents (the third group) absolutely identified catechesis and religious education, the view generally held before the modern developments in catechetical theory and now officially rejected by both the Congregation and the National Project, but a view nearer the Congregation's than the Project's. It might be speculated therefore that these respondents might accept the Congregation's distinction were they made aware of the nature of it. If this speculation is valid, the third group could be assimilated to the second group, so that the overwhelming majority (39) accepts that catechesis and religious education are closely related, as do the Congregation and the more recent manifestation of the National Project, *Here I Am*. Since 22 of this combined group also support evangelisation and only six reject it, a considerable proportion leans more to the Congregation's view than the Project's. A similar speculation might be made of the group of four respondents (the fourth group), who, though unsure on the theoretical link between religious education and catechesis, betrayed a practical understanding of both similar to that of the Congregation and *Here I Am*, with two of them taking up the Congregation's view on evangelisation and none of them the Project's view. If these respondents were combined together with groups two and three, this would give a total of 42 respondents treating catechesis and religious education in practice as closely related, with 24 endorsing the Congregation's acceptance of evangelisation and only six endorsing the Project's rejection of it.

Conclusion

Two broad theoretical approaches to how catechesis and religious education should be distinguished have been identified. One separates them to a greater degree, removing catechesis from the domain of faith in response to pluralism; the other relates them more closely, treating religious education as a catechetical enterprise. The first is represented in England and Wales by the National Project and its *Weaving the Web*; the second is represented by Rome's Congregation for Catholic Education and can also be discerned in the more recent product of the National Project, *Here I Am*. The findings of the survey of primary school teachers outlined above indicate that the Project's strong separation of catechesis and religious education has not been greatly influential at primary level. The vast majority of respondents supported a closer link between the two, in line with the Congregation and *Here I Am*. Moreover, a significant number came closer to the Congregation than to the Project by endorsing evangelisation in education. However, while this may well be the case among primary school teachers, the question must be asked how the closer link made between catechesis and religious education in *Here I Am* will influence the situation in secondary schools, for which the Project had previously provided *Weaving the Web* with its stronger separation between the two. Further research is required both to monitor what the theorists will say on this matter and how secondary school teachers will appropriate possible developments.

References

Arthur, J. (1992), Communicating the faith in Catholic schools, *The Allen Review*, 8, 20–26.

Bryce, M.C. (1973), Religious education in the pastoral letters and national meetings of the U.S. hierarchy, *The Living Light*, 10, 249–263.

Bryce, M.C. (1979), Sharing the light of faith: catechetical threshold for the U.S. church, *Lumen Vitae*, 34, 393–407.

Erdozain, L. (1970), The evolution of catechetics: a survey of six international study weeks in catechesis, *Lumen Vitae*, 25, 7–13.

Francis, L.J. (1986), *Partnership in Rural Education*, London, Collins Liturgical Publications.

Gallagher, J. (1986), *Guidelines*, London, Collins.

Lohan, R. and McClure, M. (1988), *Weaving the Web*, London, Collins.

John Paul II (1981), Address to the priests of the diocese of Rome, *Insegnamenti*, 4, 629f.

Marthaler, B. (1973), *Catechetics in Context*, Huntington, Indiana, Our Sunday Visitor.

Marthaler, B. (1978), The modern catechetical movement in Roman Catholicism: issues and personalities, *Religious Education*, 73, 77–91.

Moran, G. (1967), *God Still Speaks*, London, Burns and Oates.

Moran, G. (1968), *Vision and Tactics: towards an adult church*, London, Burns and Oates.

Moran, G. (1970), Catechetics R.I.P., *Commonweal*, 18 December, 299–302.

Nichols, K. (1978), *Guidelines for Religious Education: 1 Cornerstone*, Slough, St Paul.

Paradis, W.H. (1979), Catechesis in the Catholic community, *Religious Education*, 74, 46–62.

Purnell, P. (1985), *Our Faith Story: its telling and its sharing*, London, Collins.

Rossiter, G. (1982), The need for a 'creative divorce' between catechesis and religious education in Catholic schools, *Religious Education*, 77, 21–40.

Rossiter, G. (1986), The place for faith in religious education in Catholic schools, *The Living Light*, 26, 7–16.

Rossiter, G. (1988), Perspectives on change in Catholic religious education since the Second Vatican Council, *Religious Education*, 83, 264–276.

White, A. (1994), *Appreciating Here I Am*, London, Catholic Truth Society.

22

Growing up Catholic today:
the teenage experience

Linda Burton and Leslie J. Francis

Summary

This paper illustrates the usefulness of techniques developed within social psychology for promoting research into adolescent religiosity. The religious identity of young people who claim affiliation to the Roman Catholic Church is constructed from a database provided by 673 twelve to sixteen year olds, and this identity is compared with the religious profile of 2,112 young people who have no religious affiliations. A further distinction is made between three groups of young Catholics: regular Catholics who attend church most weeks; occasional Catholics who attend church from time to time; and lapsed Catholics who never attend church. The findings illuminate the experience of growing up Catholic in England today.

Introduction

The study of religious development during childhood and adolescence, so well documented by Hyde (1990), is a proper subject of enquiry for branches of practical and empirical theology, as demonstrated by the contents of the newly conceived *Journal of Empirical Theology* and exampled by studies like Gibson (1989), Greer and Francis (1990) and Francis and Brown (1990). Nevertheless, when undertaking such enquiry, practical theology of necessity draws upon theories and methods proposed by the discipline of psychology. Like theology, psychology embraces a number of diverse perspectives.

During the 1960s the dominant influence within empirical research into religion during childhood and adolescence in the

359

United Kingdom derived from developmental psychology, as exampled by Ronald Goldman's (1964) classic study, *Religious Thinking from Childhood to Adolescence*, and by those who built on Goldman's approach, like Whitehouse (1972). During the late 1970s the dominant influence in the United Kingdom noticeably moved from developmental psychology to social psychology (Francis, 1979; Kay and Francis, 1983). This change involved shifts in the type of questions raised about religion during childhood and adolescence, in the psychological hypotheses regarding the nature and significance of religion, in the methods of investigations employed, and in the criteria for establishing true and rejecting false hypotheses.

The introduction of the techniques of social psychology to this field of enquiry is characterised by a dominant concern with measurement, with large samples, with sophisticated statistical methods of model building and significance testing, and with the identification of social and contextual causative influences.

In a paper entitled 'Measurement reapplied', Francis (1978) argued that a cumulative picture of religious development during childhood and adolescence could be most conveniently constructed, from the perspective of social psychology, if a number of researchers agreed upon employing common measuring instruments in a series of inter-related studies. Given the particular strength of social psychology in the area of attitude measurement, Francis proposed a 24 item Likert scale of attitude toward Christianity, known at that stage to function reliably and validly between the ages of eight and sixteen years, as a key component in this programme (Francis, 1989). The usefulness of this scale has been subsequently extended into adulthood by Francis and Stubbs (1987) and incorporated within over a hundred published studies (Francis, 1993a). It has been employed, for example, to establish the relationship between attitude toward religion and factors like personality (Francis, Lankshear and Pearson, 1989), social class (Gibson, Francis and Pearson, 1990) and attendance at denominational schools (Francis, 1986).

Data collected by means of carefully constructed attitude scales can be utilised in a number of different ways. At one level, the mathematical properties of attitude scaling techniques permit complex multivariate statistical methods to explore intricate causal analysis. At another level, the simple items from which the scales are constructed permit straightforward descriptive narrative. A major strength of the method is that both presentations can emerge from the same set of data. The present paper illustrates a straightforward descriptive use of this kind of data by posing a question about the distinctive characteristics of teenagers who identify themselves as Roman Catholics. The question is answered by the re-analysis of a set of data collected in association with BBC Schools Television.

Comparatively little is known about the significance of claiming denominational identity among young people in England today (Francis, 1990). What is clear is that the tendency for people who have no real contact with any church to claim the identity of 'Church of England' is being replaced, especially among young people, by a willingness to claim 'no religious affiliation' in response to survey questions. This trend is a natural correlate of secularisation (Gilbert, 1980), and one which may have been accelerated by current Anglican baptismal policy (Francis and Lankshear, 1993). What is less clear, however, is the current significance attached to claiming membership of the Roman Catholic church in England. The present paper sets out to illuminate this issue by distinguishing between three groups of young Catholics. The first group is the lapsed Catholics, those young people who claim denominational affiliation but who never attend church. The second group is the occasional Catholics, those young people who claim denominational affiliation and attend church from time to time. The third group is the regular Catholics, those young people who claim denominational affiliation and attend church most weeks. These three groups are contrasted with the young people who clearly identify themselves as having *no* religious affiliation.

Method

When BBC Schools Television prepared its five programme series, *Words into Action*, in 1988, schools were invited to undertake their own research into the religious attitudes of their pupils. The questionnaire published in the companion teachers' handbook (Lealman, 1988) included the Francis Scale of Attitude Toward Christianity, alongside a set of other similar questions, producing a total of 62 items, each of which was assessed on a five point scale: agree strongly, agree, not certain, disagree and disagree strongly. Multiple choice questions were also included to record factors like sex, age and denominational identity. Church attendance was assessed on a five point scale: nearly every week, at least once a month, sometimes, once or twice a year and never.

Overall, the questionnaire allows a detailed picture to be constructed of the respondents' attitude toward the following areas: God, Jesus, prayer, church, Christians, science and religious education, science and the bible, and personal wellbeing. The handbook suggested ways in which teachers could generate their own feedback from the questionnaire. Teachers were then invited to send the completed questionnaires to Leslie Francis in order to build up a central database.

The initial aim was to prepare around 4,000 of the returned questionnaires for computer analysis. The basic description of the original group of 3,863 pupils, together with a discussion of sex differences, age trends and the influence of church attendance on shaping attitudes, has been made available in a recent collection of essays published by the North of England Institute for Christian Education (Francis, 1992). A second analysis has utilised the same database to profile the identity of young Anglicans (Francis, 1993b).

Since those original analyses, further questionnaires have been added to the database. This extended database has become available to address other specific questions about religious characteristics and trends during the teenage years. The present analysis is based on the responses of 5,038 pupils from all over England who either claimed allegiance to one of the Christian denominations or who denied any religious affiliation. In view of the project's main aim to explore the role of Christianity in the lives of young people, additional questionnaires submitted by adherents to other world faiths were deliberately excluded from the database. The sample included 2,377 males and 2,661 females; 1,143 twelve year olds, 1,144 thirteen year olds, 1,185 fourteen year olds, 1,098 fifteen year olds and 468 sixteen year olds.

From this group of 5,038 pupils, 2,112 identified themselves as having no religious affiliation (42%) and 673 identified themselves as Roman Catholics (13%). Of the Roman Catholics, 314 attended church most weeks (47%), 278 attended church from time to time but less often than weekly (41%) and 81 never attended church (12%). The following discussion is based on the comparisons between these four groups.

The data were analysed by the SPSS statistical package, using the cross-tabulation and breakdown routines (SPSS Inc., 1988).

Results

The questionnaire enabled the young people's responses to be profiled in relationship to eight themes, namely attitude toward God, Jesus, prayer, church, Christians, science and religious education, science and the bible, and personal wellbeing. Data relevant to each of these themes will be presented in tabular form and then discussed. Two kinds of information are included in each table. First, the tables display the percentages of unchurched young people, lapsed Catholics, occasional Catholics and regular Catholics who agree with each item. This percentage is the product of those who *agree* or *agree strongly* with the item on the five point Likert scale. Second, two tests of statistical significance are reported. These are calculated on the mean values attributed by the four groups to individual items on the five point scale. The first statistical test assesses whether the responses of the four groups are significantly different. The second statistical test assesses whether the scores from the unchurched, through lapsed Catholics and occasional Catholics, to regular Catholics progress in a linear fashion.

Attitude toward God

In some ways lapsed Catholics adopt a similar attitude toward God to that adopted by the unchurched. For example, 10% of both groups feel that their lives are being guided by God; 11% of lapsed Catholics and 13% of unchurched young people say that they are sometimes aware of God's presence; 43% of lapsed Catholics and 44% of unchurched young people say that they find it hard to believe in God. In other ways, however, lapsed Catholics clearly hold a more positive attitude toward God than the unchurched. Half the lapsed Catholics (49%) claim belief in God, compared with less than two-fifths of the unchurched (37%). A quarter of the lapsed Catholics (25%) feel that God is very real to them, compared with less than one-fifth of the unchurched (17%). The lapsed Catholics are also more likely to feel that they are surrounded by people who believe in God. Thus 31% of lapsed Catholics feel that most of their best friends believe in God, compared with 20% of the unchurched. It seems, therefore, that young people who feel themselves to be Catholic, even when they do not practise the faith, are more inclined to keep faith in God than young people who grow up without denominational identity.

Table 22.1
Attitude toward God

	unchurched %	lapsed %	occasional %	regular %	between groups F	P<	non linearity F	P<
I believe in God	37	49	77	89	189.0	.001	0.8	NS
Most of my friends believe in God	20	31	48	54	88.0	.001	2.6	NS
I know that God helps me	17	14	44	65	151.5	.001	2.3	NS
God is very real to me	17	25	46	65	170.4	.001	0.4	NS
I feel that my life is being guided by God	10	10	25	42	121.6	.001	4.5	NS
Sometimes I am aware of God's presence	13	11	28	43	106.2	.001	2.0	NS
I find it hard to believe in God	44	43	25	18	66.7	.001	0.6	NS

Young Catholics who attend church most weeks are relatively sure of their faith in God. For example, 89% of regular Catholics are confident of their belief in God; 65% feel that God is very real to them and 65% know that God helps them. Regular Catholics are much more likely than other groups to be aware of God's presence (43%) and to feel that their lives are being guided by God (42%). Regular Catholics are more likely to feel that most of their best friends believe in God (54%). On the other hand, as many as one in five regular Catholics (18%) let it be known that they find it hard to believe in God.

Occasional Catholics stand clearly midway between regular Catholics and lapsed Catholics. Occasional Catholics are less likely to believe in God than regular Catholics. Occasional Catholics are more likely to find it hard to believe in God than regular Catholics. Occasional Catholics are less likely to be supported by friends who believe in God than regular Catholics. Occasional Catholics are less likely than regular Catholics to feel awareness of God's presence or to feel that their lives are being guided by God.

Attitude toward Jesus

Overall lapsed Catholics hold a more positive attitude toward Jesus than young people who have grown up outside the churches. Three-fifths of the lapsed Catholics (58%) accept the traditional Christological statement that Jesus is the Son of God, compared with two-fifths of the unchurched (41%). A third of the lapsed Catholics believe that Jesus really rose from the dead (33%), compared with a quarter of the unchurched (24%). A quarter of the lapsed Catholics (24%) profess that they want to love Jesus, compared with less than a fifth of the unchurched (18%).

The majority of the regular Catholics are confident that Jesus is the Son of God. The proportion falls, however, to 72% of the regular Catholics who are confident that Jesus really rose from the dead. Between six and seven regular Catholics out of every ten assert that they want to love Jesus (70%), that they know that Jesus helps them (66%) and that they know that Jesus is close to them (61%).

Again the occasional Catholics stand clearly midway between regular Catholics and lapsed Catholics. Occasional Catholics are less likely to confess that Jesus is the Son of God or to believe that Jesus really rose from the dead in comparison with regular Catholics. Occasional Catholics are less likely than regular Catholics to feel that Jesus helps them or to feel that Jesus is close to them.

Table 22.2
Attitude toward Jesus

	unchurched %	lapsed %	occasional %	regular %	between groups F	P<	non linearity F	P<
I believe that Jesus is the Son of God	41	58	74	88	125.4	.001	0.2	NS
I believe that Jesus really rose from the dead	24	33	55	72	152.5	.001	2.3	NS
I know that Jesus helps me	16	19	42	66	150.7	.001	3.7	.05
I know that Jesus is close to me	13	11	39	61	183.4	.001	4.0	.05
I want to love Jesus	18	24	51	70	188.4	.001	1.5	NS
Jesus doesn't mean anything to me	27	22	6	5	138.8	.001	1.4	NS

Occasional Catholics are less likely than regular Catholics to assert that they want to love Jesus.

Attitude toward prayer

While lapsed Catholics are more likely than the unchurched to believe that God listens to prayer, they are no more likely than the unchurched to feel that they derive personal benefit from prayer. Thus, four out of every ten lapsed Catholics (41%) believe that God listens to prayers, compared with three out of every ten unchurched young people (29%). On the other hand, similar proportions of the unchurched and lapsed Catholics (around 17%) feel that prayer helps them a lot. Similar proportions of the unchurched (40%) and lapsed Catholics (37%) think that saying prayers in school does no good.

Regular Catholics are somewhat less confident in the value of prayer than in the existence of God or in the divinity of Jesus. While 89% of regular Catholics believe in God and 88% believe that Jesus is the Son of God, the proportion drops a little to 80% who believe that God listens to prayers. While 65% of regular Catholics believe that God helps them and 66% believe that Jesus helps them, the proportion drops a little to 56% who believe that prayer helps them a lot. While 54% of regular Catholics consider that most of their best friends believe in God, the proportion falls to 31% who consider that most of their best friends believe in prayer. Just 12% of the regular Catholics think that saying prayers in school does no good.

The occasional Catholics remain balanced midway between the lapsed Catholics and the regular Catholics. Occasional Catholics are less likely than regular Catholics to believe that God listens to prayer, that most of their best friends believe in prayer, or that prayer helps them a lot. Occasional Catholics are more likely than regular Catholics to think that saying prayers in school does no good.

Attitude toward church

Lapsed Catholics adopt a more hostile attitude toward the church than the young people who have grown up without denominational affiliation. Thus, 67% of lapsed Catholics feel that church services are boring, compared with 59% of unchurched young people. Similarly, two-fifths of lapsed Catholics (40%) consider going to church a waste of time, compared with one-third of unchurched young people (34%). In spite of this greater antipathy toward the church, lapsed Catholics show a higher intention than unchurched

Table 22.3
Attitude toward prayer

	unchurched %	lapsed %	occasional %	regular %	between groups F	between groups P<	non linearity F	non linearity P<
I believe that God listens to prayers	29	41	62	80	159.9	.001	1.1	NS
Most of my best friends believe in prayers	9	14	24	31	71.2	.001	2.7	NS
Saying my prayers helps me a lot	17	18	41	58	131.5	.001	5.2	.01
Prayer helps me a lot	17	16	36	56	133.8	.001	6.1	.01
I think saying prayers in school does no good	40	37	19	12	73.3	.001	0.7	NS
I think people who pray are stupid	9	4	4	3	51.3	.001	0.4	NS

Table 22.4
Attitude toward church

	unchurched %	lapsed %	occasional %	regular %	between groups F	P<	non linearity F	P<
The church is very important to me	9	6	27	60	234.5	.001	16.9	.001
Most of my best friends go to church	10	21	28	48	124.9	.001	0.4	NS
I think going to church is a waste of my time	34	40	21	9	79.9	.001	9.6	.001
I think church services are boring	59	67	59	42	29.7	.001	12.6	.001
People who go to church are hypocrites	10	9	7	4	19.4	.001	1.8	NS
I want to get married in church	74	80	85	87	16.3	.001	0.3	NS
I want my children to be baptised in church	47	68	81	89	113.2	.001	1.1	NS

young people to turn to the church for the major rites of passage. Thus, 80% of lapsed Catholics say that they want to get married in church, compared with 74% of unchurched young people. Similarly, two-thirds of the lapsed Catholics (68%) say that they want their children to be baptised in church, compared with half of the unchurched (47%). Although they are not attending church themselves, lapsed Catholics are more likely than unchurched young people to count churchgoers among their close friends. Thus, 21% of lapsed Catholics feel that most of their best friends go to church, compared with 10% of the unchurched.

Regular Catholics show a great deal of loyalty to their church. Nine out of ten regular Catholics say that they want to get married in church (87%) or that they want their children to be baptised in church (89%). They seem keen to keep the denominational identity alive into the next generation. As many as three-fifths (60%) of regular Catholics affirm that the church is very important to them. As many as half (48%) of regular Catholics consider that most of their best friends go to church. In this sense, regular Catholics tend to be supported by like-minded friends. While very few regular Catholics (9%) consider that their practice of church attendance is a waste of their time, two out of every five regular churchgoers (42%) find the services which they attend boring.

Occasional Catholics are much less likely than regular Catholics to feel that the majority of their best friends go to church. In other words, occasional churchgoers are more likely than regular churchgoers to select their close friends outside the believing community. This in turn may reinforce their detachment from the church. In other ways occasional Catholics occupy the midway position between lapsed Catholics and regular Catholics. Occasional Catholics are more likely than regular Catholics to consider that going to church is a waste of their time, and that church services are boring. Occasional Catholics are less likely than regular Catholics to consider that the church is very important to them. While occasional Catholics are not really less likely than regular Catholics to turn to the church when they want to get married, occasional Catholics are less likely than regular Catholics to want their children to be baptised in church.

Attitude toward Christians

Lapsed Catholics hold a more honest or a more cynical view about Christians than the view held by the unchurched. A small but significant group of unchurched young people hold the view that

Table 22.5
Attitude toward Christians

	unchurched %	lapsed %	occasional %	regular %	between groups F	P<	non linearity F	P<
People who believe in Christ are more honest	29	27	31	25	2.5	NS	2.7	NS
People who believe in Christ are kinder to others	28	21	31	31	3.6	.05	2.3	NS
People who believe in Christ live happier lives	18	17	30	38	38.1	.001	2.5	NS
Christians do not smoke	8	0	3	3	30.5	.001	4.7	.01
Christians do not drink	7	1	2	1	41.5	.001	5.6	.01
Christians do not swear	12	1	5	5	22.6	.001	7.1	.001

Christians do not smoke, drink or swear. Lapsed Catholics may be much more likely to assert that they know Christians who do all these things. Between a quarter and a third of unchurched young people (28%) hold the view that people who believe in Christ are kinder to others. The proportion falls to a fifth (21%) among lapsed Catholics. Similar proportions of lapsed Catholics and unchurched young people hold the views that people who believe in Christ are more honest (27% and 29%) and that people who believe in Christ live happier lives (17% and 18%).

In many ways regular Catholics and occasional Catholics hold similar views on what it means to be a Christian. Only very small proportions of regular Catholics and occasional Catholics hold the view that Christians do not smoke, drink or swear. Indeed they are less likely to think of Christians abstaining from such behaviours than is the case among unchurched young people. Overall, there is relatively little variation in the ways in which regular Catholics, occasional Catholics and unchurched young people evaluate the honesty or kindliness of Christians. For example, between 28% and 31% of all three groups consider that people who believe in Christ are kinder to others. On the other hand, young Catholics who live closer to the church are more inclined to consider that people who believe in Christ live happier lives. Thus, while 17% of lapsed Catholics and 18% of unchurched young people consider that people who believe in Christ live happier lives, the proportions rise to 30% among occasional Catholics and to 38% among regular Catholics.

Attitude toward science and religious education

Lapsed Catholics show no more interest in religion in general than unchurched young people. For example, 18% of lapsed Catholics say that they like finding out about Christianity, compared with 17% of the unchurched; 26% of lapsed Catholics say that they like finding out about world religions, compared with 27% of the unchurched. In spite of these close similarities, lapsed Catholics are more likely than unchurched young people to like religious education lessons in school (32% compared with 23%). Lapsed Catholics are less likely than unchurched young people to be interested in science, to like finding out about science, or to like science lessons in school.

Regular Catholics reveal quite a healthy attitude toward religious education. It is also clear from the statistics that their interest in religion extends beyond Christianity to the wider canvas of world

Table 22.6
Attitude toward science and religious education

	unchurched %	lapsed %	occasional %	regular %	between groups F	between groups P<	non linearity F	non linearity P<
I am interested in religion	17	19	52	67	204.6	.001	2.3	NS
I like finding out about Christianity	17	18	35	53	111.3	.001	3.5	.05
I like finding out about world religions	27	26	47	55	58.8	.001	3.2	.05
I like religious education lessons in school	23	32	51	58	80.2	.001	2.9	NS
I am interested in science	63	57	55	60	4.1	.01	2.2	NS
I like finding out about science	59	47	54	58	1.8	NS	1.7	NS
I like science lessons in school	64	56	54	58	5.7	.001	2.2	NS

faiths. Thus, between one-half and two-thirds of regular Catholics say that they like finding out about Christianity (53%), that they like finding out about world religions, that they like religious education lessons in school (58%), and that they are interested in religion (67%). Generally the regular Catholics hold a slightly more positive attitude toward science than lapsed Catholics, but a slightly less positive attitude than the unchurched. This interpretation is supported by the fact that 58% of regular Catholics claim to like finding out about science, compared with 47% of lapsed Catholics, while 64% of unchurched young people claim to like science lessons in school, compared with 58% of regular Catholics.

Occasional Catholics reveal a much greater interest in religion than lapsed Catholics, but less interest than regular Catholics. For example, 52% of occasional Catholics say that they are interested in religion, compared with 67% of regular Catholics and 19% of lapsed Catholics. Similarly, 51% of occasional Catholics say that they like religious education lessons in school, compared with 58% of regular Catholics and 32% of lapsed Catholics.

Attitude toward science and the bible

Lapsed Catholics are better informed than unchurched young people regarding what it is Christians really believe about the bible. While as many as one in five unchurched young people (22%) reckon that Christians have to believe that every word of the bible is true, the proportion falls to 11% among lapsed Catholics. While one in five unchurched young people (21%) reckon that Christians have to believe that God made the world in six days, the proportion falls to 15% among lapsed Catholics. On the other hand, lapsed Catholics are just as likely as unchurched young people to consider that there is a conflict between science and religion. For example, between 29% and 31% of both groups believe science disproved the bible account of creation. About one in four of both groups (24%) believe scientific laws make miracles impossible. Between 17% and 18% of both groups believe science has disproved religion. Finally, lapsed Catholics hold a slightly more hostile attitude toward the bible than unchurched young people. Thus, 35% of lapsed Catholics think the bible is out of date, compared with 30% of unchurched young people.

As many as one in five regular Catholics believe that Christians have to hold a fundamentalist view of scripture. Thus, 17% of regular Catholics reckon that Christians have to believe that every word of the bible is true; 20% reckon that Christians have to believe

Table 22.7
Attitude toward science and the bible

	unchurched %	lapsed %	occasional %	regular %	between groups F	between groups P<	non linearity F	non linearity P<
Science has disproved religion	18	17	15	12	6.4	.001	0.2	NS
Science disproved the bible account of creation	31	29	31	27	0.9	NS	0.2	NS
Scientific laws make miracles impossible	24	24	16	14	9.3	.001	0.8	NS
I think the bible is out of date	30	35	20	17	26.4	.001	1.7	NS
Christians have to believe that every word of the bible is true	22	11	15	17	5.8	.001	2.3	NS
Christians have to believe that Jesus walked on water	15	11	15	21	3.2	.05	4.6	.01
Christians have to believe that God made the world in six days	21	15	19	20	3.9	.01	2.4	NS

that God made the world in six days; 21% reckon that Christians have to believe that Jesus walked on water. As many as one in eight regular Catholics believe that science has disproved religion (12%) or that scientific laws make miracles impossible (14%). Nearly one in five regular Catholics (17%) feel that the bible is out of date.

Occasional Catholics are slightly more inclined than regular Catholics to believe that science has disproved religion (15% compared with 12%). Occasional Catholics are slightly more inclined than regular Catholics to feel that the bible is out of date (20% compared with 17%). Occasional Catholics are less inclined than regular Catholics to reckon that Christians have to believe that Jesus walked on water (15% compared with 21%).

Personal wellbeing

Lapsed Catholics enjoy a considerably higher level of personal wellbeing than unchurched young people. For example, nearly three-quarters of lapsed Catholics (72%) find life really worth living, compared with nearly two-thirds (64%) of unchurched young people. Similarly 51% of lapsed Catholics feel their lives have a sense of purpose, compared with 44% of unchurched young people. At the same time lapsed Catholics are more likely to feel depressed than unchurched young people (64% compared with 48%).

Among Catholic young people there is a clear positive correlation between church attendance and purpose in life and an equally clear negative correlation between church attendance and depression. Thus, while 51% of lapsed Catholics feel their lives have a sense of purpose, the proportions rise to 57% among occasional Catholics and to 68% among regular Catholics. Similarly while 64% of lapsed Catholics often feel depressed, the proportions fall to 57% among occasional Catholics and to 49% among regular Catholics.

Conclusion

This study set out to explore the religious significance of growing up Catholic today by profiling four groups of young people between the ages of twelve and sixteen years. Five main conclusions emerge from these findings.

First, from a methodological perspective, it is clear that the two simple multiple choice questions inviting young people to indicate their denominational identity and frequency of church attendance are accurate predictors of individual differences in young people's

Table 22.8
Personal wellbeing

	unchurched %	lapsed %	occasional %	regular %	between groups F	P<	non linearity F	P<
I find life really worth living	64	72	72	78	7.9	.001	1.0	NS
I often feel depressed	48	64	57	49	4.3	.01	4.8	.01
	44	51	57	68	29.7	.001	1.0	NS

responses to a range of religious issues. The clarity with which these differences emerge in the preceding tables is itself evidence of the construct validity of the multiple choice questions.

Second, the category of *lapsed Catholic*, operationally defined in the project as a young person who claims denominational identity without having any current contact with a church, has been shown to generate a profile quite distinct from the profile of unchurched young people. Lapsed Catholics are more likely than unchurched young people to believe in God, to accept faith in Jesus and to want to celebrate the major rites of passage within the context of the church. Although these young people are not practising the faith in which they have been baptised, they are by no means lost to the church. They are different from totally secular young people growing up outside the churches. At the same time, they hold a slightly more hostile attitude toward the church than unchurched young people.

While the survey itself provides no information about the home background of the young people who completed the questionnaire, it is reasonable to suppose that many of the lapsed Catholics came from homes in which at least one parent is a non-practising Catholic but where the residual faith remained sufficiently strong for the child to be baptised as a Catholic. Indeed, the majority of the young lapsed Catholics indicate that very same intention to have their own children baptised. What the data do suggest is that such non-practising homes continue to communicate not only the sense of being Catholic, but also a more fundamental set of religious beliefs and values. In these homes young people may be more likely to grow up sharing the basic assumption that they are living in God's world. Such young people are also quite likely to attend Catholic schools. Indeed, 64% of the lapsed Catholics in the present sample were within Catholic voluntary secondary schools. Attendance at such schools also contributes toward socialisation within the Catholic tradition.

Third, the category of *regular Catholics*, operationally defined in the project as young Catholics who attend church most weeks, highlights the religious needs of the young people over whom the Catholic church has the greatest opportunity for influence. While the majority of these young people appear, at least superficially, secure in their faith, there are within the data also significant pointers for the local churches' concern. For example, one in every ten young people who attend mass most Sundays has lost faith in God. Practice is sometimes easier to maintain during adolescence than belief. Two in every ten young people who attend mass most Sundays come away with the idea that Christians have to believe that Jesus walked on water and that God made the world in six days. The content and images of scripture are easier to communicate than informed theological reflection on the nature of scripture. Three in every ten young people who attend mass most Sundays are not clear that their lives have a sense of purpose, while five in every ten say that they often feel depressed. Although regular Catholics enjoy a higher level of personal wellbeing than young people who have less contact with the church, local churches need to remain aware of their *pastoral* as well as of their *liturgical* and *educational* commitment to the regular Catholics.

Fourth, the category of *occasional Catholics*, operationally defined in the project as young Catholics who attend church at least once a year but not on a weekly basis, reveals that there is a group of young people almost as numerous as the regular Catholics who stand more lightly in relationship to their faith. Throughout the religious issues raised by the survey these occasional Catholics occupy a position midway between lapsed Catholics and regular Catholics. Because occasional Catholics have some contact with the local churches these young people constitute the group over whom the liturgy may exert the greatest influence. On the one hand, such influence may be positive, drawing these young people into more regular practice and deepening their faith. On the other hand, such influence may be negative, encouraging these young people to drift further from practice and eroding their faith. It is from observing the changing level of practice among the occasional Catholics that local Catholic churches may best be able to gauge the effectiveness of their ministry among young people.

Fifth, the study offers helpful pointers for further research. In particular two developments would be helpful. The present study has demonstrated the usefulness of the three-fold classification of young Catholics over a relatively restricted range of attitudinal areas. Further research should extend this range of issues. The present study has included a wide range of young people within the category of occasional Catholics, from those who attend church only once a year to those who attend at least once a month but not most Sundays. The total number of young Catholics in the present database was insufficient to enable secure generalisations to be made regarding subdivisions of this group. Further research should look for a larger sample of young Catholics.

References

Francis, L.J. (1978), Measurement reapplied: research into the child's attitude towards religion, *British Journal of Religious Education*, 1, 45–51.

Francis, L.J. (1979), The psychology of religion: beyond revival, *Bulletin of the British Psychological Society*, 32, 141–142.

Francis, L.J. (1986), Denominational schools and pupil attitude towards Christianity, *British Educational Research Journal*, 12, 145–152.

Francis, L.J. (1989), Measuring attitude towards Christianity during childhood and adolescence, *Personality and Individual Differences*, 10, 695–698.

Francis, L.J. (1990), The religious significance of denominational identity among eleven year old children in England, *Journal of Christian Education*, 97, 23–28.

Francis, L.J. (1992), Christianity today: the teenage experience, in J. Astley and D.V. Day (eds), *The Contours of Christian Education*, pp. 340–368, Great Wakering, McCrimmons.

Francis, L.J. (1993a), Attitudes towards Christianity during childhood and adolescence: assembling the jigsaw, *The Journal of Beliefs and Values*, 14, 2, 4–6.

Francis, L.J. (1993b), The identity of Anglicanism: the teenage experience, *Collegium*, 2, 1, 4–12.

Francis, L.J. and Brown, L.B. (1990), The predisposition to pray: a study of the social influence on the predisposition to pray among eleven year old children in England, *Journal of Empirical Theology*, 3, 2, 23–34.

Francis, L.J. and Lankshear, D.W. (1993), Asking about baptism: straw polls and fenced fonts, *Modern Churchman*, 34, 5, 88–92.

Francis, L.J., Lankshear, D.W. and Pearson, P.R. (1989), The relationship between religiosity and the short form JEPQ (JEPQ-S) indices of E, N, L and P among eleven year olds, *Personality and Individual Differences*, 10, 763–769.

Francis, L.J. and Stubbs, M.T. (1987), Measuring attitudes towards Christianity: from childhood to adulthood, *Personality and Individual Differences*, 8, 741–743.

Gibson, H.M. (1989), Attitudes to religion and science among school children aged 11 to 16 years in a Scottish city, *Journal of Empirical Theology*, 2, 5–26.

Gibson, H.M., Francis, L.J. and Pearson, P.R. (1990), The relationship between social class and attitude towards Christianity among fourteen- and fifteen-year-old adolescents, *Personality and Individual Differences*, 11, 631–635.

Gilbert, A.D. (1980), *The Making of Post-Christian Britain*, London, Longman.

Goldman, R.J. (1964), *Religious Thinking from Childhood to Adolescence*, London, Routledge and Kegan Paul.

Greer, J.E. and Francis, L.J. (1990), The religious profile of pupils in Northern Ireland: a comparative study of pupils attending Catholic and Protestant secondary schools, *Journal of Empirical Theology*, 3, 2, 35–50.

Hyde, K.E. (1990), *Religion in Childhood and Adolescence: a comprehensive review of the research*, Birmingham, Alabama, Religious Education Press.

Kay, W.K. and Francis, L.J. (1983), Progress in the psychology of religious development, *Lumen Vitae*, 38, 342–346.

Lealman, B. (1988), *Words into Action*, London, Christian Education Movement.

SPSS Inc. (1988), *SPSSX User's Guide*, New York, McGraw-Hill.

Whitehouse, E. (1972), Children's reactions to the Zacchaeus story, *Learning for Living*, 11, 4, 19–24.

23

Measuring 'Catholic identity' among pupils in Catholic secondary schools

Michael Curran and Leslie J. Francis

Summary

A twelve item scale measuring Catholic identity was developed among a sample of 526 eleven to twelve year old pupils attending Catholic state maintained schools in England. The data support the reliability and construct validity of the scale among this age group.

Introduction

Following the 1944 Education Act the Catholic church in England and Wales invested heavily in developing a national network of secondary schools within the state maintained sector (Hornsby-Smith, 1978). The proportion of state maintained secondary places within Catholic schools rose steadily from 2.9% in 1949 to 4.4% in 1959, 7.9% in 1969 and 8.8% in 1979 (Francis, 1987a). According to figures provided by the Department for Education and the Welsh Office, in January 1992 Catholic schools provided 9.5% of the secondary places within the state maintained system. In spite of the considerable cost to the Catholic community, comparatively little empirical research has been undertaken to monitor the effectiveness of these schools in terms of their contribution to promoting the religious development and orientation of their pupils.

Such studies as have investigated pupil religiosity within Catholic schools in England and Wales have been limited by the measures of religiosity employed. Three main strands emerge from the current literature.

First, several studies have employed the Francis Scale of Attitude Toward Christianity (Francis, 1978, 1989). For example, Francis (1986a) explored the comparative influence of Anglican, Catholic and non-denominational primary schools on attitude toward Christianity among eleven year olds. Boyle (1984) and Boyle and Francis (1986) explored the comparative influence of Catholic secondary and Catholic middle schools on the attitude toward Christianity of twelve to thirteen year olds. Francis (1986b) explored the relationship between Catholic home background and attitude toward Christianity among pupils attending Catholic secondary schools. Montgomery (1990) profiled the attitude toward Christianity of girls attending a single sex Catholic secondary school. The same instrument has also been employed in studies of Catholic schools in Scotland (Rhymer, 1983; Rhymer and Francis, 1985; Gibson and Francis, 1989) and Northern Ireland (Greer, 1985; Greer and Francis, 1990, 1991).

Second, Egan (1985, 1988) and Egan and Francis (1986) developed a set of three instruments to assess attitude toward attending Catholic schools. The scales measured 'attitude toward the traditional view of the Catholic school system', 'attitude toward religious education in the Catholic school' and 'attitude toward attending the Catholic school'. The original studies explored the differences between practising Catholic, non-practising Catholic and non-Catholic pupils in the Catholic secondary schools in Wales. Subsequent studies employed the same instruments to replicate the findings in Catholic schools in Australia (Francis and Egan, 1987) and the United States of America (Francis and Egan, 1990).

Third, Hornbsby-Smith and Petit (1975) employed a set of 16 items concerned with a range of social, moral and religious attitudes. Their factor analyses identified as many as six factors within this group of items, with most factors being defined by only two items each. The items were used to discuss the differences between pupils attending Catholic and county schools, as well as to profile the attitudes of pupils within the Catholic school sector.

Studies in the wider international literature have also included the following indices of religiosity in order to discuss the distinctiveness and effectiveness of Catholic schools: religious orthodoxy (De Vaus, 1981), regular church attendance (Anderson, 1971), belief in God (Anderson and Western, 1972), 'experience of being somehow in the presence of God' (Mol, 1968), vocational interest

(Fahy, 1982) and traditional Christian moral values (Francis and Greer, 1990). Fahy (1976) employed an inventory found to tap eleven factors, including home climate, school climate, satisfaction with principal and staff, acceptance of religious values, liking for religious education classes, parental religious expectations, vocational interest, apostolic action, drugs and alcohol, religious practice and personal prayer. Fahy (1978) extended the range of factors to twenty, which he described as home background, religious beliefs, religious practice, influence of peer group, self-esteem, apostolic action, racial attitudes, openness to drugs and alcohol, home religious climate, vocational interest, social-sexual concerns, push for liberal education, actual liberal education, push for social education, actual social education, push for religious education, actual religious education, altruism-selfishness, liking for religious education and liking for principals and staff. Fahy (1980) proposed a further re-grouping of these factors. Little attention, however, seems to have been given to measuring 'Catholic identity' among pupils attending Catholic schools. The intention of the present study, therefore is to develop an instrument capable of measuring Catholic identity among secondary school pupils, to report on the reliability and validity of this instrument, and to suggest how it may be employed in further studies.

Method

A questionnaire containing 22 negatively and positively phrased items reflecting attitudinal responses to a number of features thought to characterise early adolescent perception of the practice of the Catholic faith was administered to the first year pupils on two successive years throughout one co-educational and one boys Catholic state maintained secondary school. The questionnaire also included the Francis Scale of Attitude Toward Christianity (Francis, 1989), which is known to function reliably and validly among pupils of this age in Catholic secondary schools in England (Francis, 1987b) and seven other key questions relating to religious background. Personal baptismal status was assessed on a two point scale: baptised Catholic and not baptised Catholic. Parental baptismal status was assessed on a three point scale: both parents, one parent and neither parent baptised Catholic. Primary school education was assessed on a two point scale: Catholic primary school and non-Catholic primary school. Frequency of personal prayer was assessed on a five point scale: daily, weekly, at least once a month, sometimes, never. Frequency of personal church attendance, father's church attendance and mother's church attendance were assessed on a five point scale: weekly, at least once a month, sometimes, once or twice a year, never. The sample comprised 429 boys and 97 girls. The data were analysed by means of the SPSS statistical package (SPSS Inc., 1988).

Results

Exploratory factor analyses and item analyses identified twelve of the original pool of 22 items as cohering to produce a homogeneous and unidimensional scale, achieving a highly satisfactory alpha coefficient of 0.8723 (Cronbach, 1951). These twelve items, together with the item rest of test correlation coefficients are

Table 23.1
Item rest of test correlation coefficients
and percentage endorsement

item	r	agree %
Going to mass is important to me	0.7068	44
Going to confession is very helpful	0.5892	63
I do not enjoy listening to the lives of the saints*	0.4722	18
I sometimes pray to a saint	0.4789	39
I sometimes pray to Our Lady	0.4686	68
I do not like priests*	0.4422	7
I think that religious sisters are good people	0.4540	70
Going to confession is very important to me	0.6593	50
Going to mass is very helpful	0.6962	50
I would like to know more about the Catholic faith	0.6462	50
I think that going to confession is a silly idea*	0.6149	12
I think that we should have fewer masses in school*	0.5149	20

Note: * Negative items have been reverse coded to compute the item rest of test correlation coefficients, not to produce the percentage endorsement.

presented in table 23.1. The item rest of test correlation coefficients vary between 0.4422 and 0.7068. This table also presents the proportions of pupils who express agreement with each of the individual items. In this case agreement is calculated as the product of those who check the 'agree' and the 'agree strongly' responses on the five point Likert scale.

While the reliability of an attitude scale is relatively straightforward to express in terms of an examination of the internal structure and covariance of the items (Livingston, 1988), the issue of testing and demonstrating validity is somewhat more complex (Orton, 1987). Table 23.2 explores the construct validity of the scale by exploring its correlation with a range of other indices of Catholicity in particular and Christianity in general. These correlations demonstrate that higher scores on the scale of Catholic identity are clearly associated with being baptised Catholic, with having one or both parents baptised Catholic, with attending a Catholic primary school, with frequency of paternal and maternal church attendance, with frequency of personal prayer and personal church attendance and with a positive attitude toward Christianity. All of these relationships are highly consistent with the construct of 'Catholic identity'.

After exploring the reliability and validity of the scale of Catholic identity, table 23.3 presents the mean scale scores for the boys and

Table 23.2
Correlations between scores on the scale of Catholic
identity and other indices of religiosity

	r	P<
personal baptismal status	0.2259	.001
parental baptismal status	0.2052	.001
attendance at Catholic primary school	0.1311	.01
frequency of personal prayer	0.3921	.001
frequency of church attendance	0.3939	.001
attitude toward Christianity	0.8147	.001
frequency of father's church attendance	0.2372	.001
frequency of mother's church attendance	0.3357	.001

girls in the sample separately. There is no significant difference between the mean scores of boys and girls in this sample.

Table 23.3
Mean scores on the scale of Catholic identity by sex

boys			girls				
mean	sd	N	mean	sd	N	F	P<
42.70	8.62	429	43.85	7.45	97	1.47	NS

Discussion

Four main conclusions emerge from these data.

First, the highest item rest of test correlation coefficients are concerned with the importance and helpfulness of mass attendance. High correlations are also associated with the importance and helpfulness of confession. The other issues clearly associated with Catholic identity concern the saints, Our Lady, priests and religious sisters.

Second, the proportions of pupils expressing agreement with the individual scale items indicate a basically positive view of being a Catholic. Half (50%) the pupils report that they find going to mass *very* helpful and nearly two-thirds (63%) report that they find going to confession *very* helpful. Over two-thirds (68%) sometimes pray to Our Lady.

Third, the correlations with other indices of religiosity indicate the importance of a Catholic background, a Catholic home and church involvement in promoting Catholic identity, in addition to attendance at a Catholic secondary school. Young people who are baptised Catholic, whose parents are baptised Catholic and who attended a Catholic primary school hold a more positive view of Catholic identity.

Fourth, the data presented on the reliability and validity of this scale clearly commend its further use in research concerned with exploring the religious ethos of the Catholic school and with monitoring the religious development of young Catholics. In particular further studies employing this instrument should be able to tease out the relative significance of home, church and school in shaping Catholic identity and so contribute significantly to the debate concerning the practical value of maintaining Catholic secondary schools within the state maintained educational system in England and Wales.

References

Anderson, D.S. (1971), Do Catholic schools cause people to go to church? *Australian and New Zealand Journal of Sociology*, 7, 65–67.

Anderson, D.S. and Western, J.S. (1972), Denominational schooling and religious behaviour, *Australian and New Zealand Journal of Sociology*, 8, 19–31.

Boyle, J.J. (1984), Catholic children's attitudes towards Christianity, Unpublished M.Sc. dissertation, University of Bradford.

Boyle, J.J. and Francis, L.J. (1986), The influence of differing church aided school systems on pupil attitude towards religion, *Research in Education*, 35, 7–12.

Cronbach, L.J. (1951), Coefficient alpha and the internal structure of tests, *Psychometrika*, 16, 297–334.

De Vaus, D.A. (1981), The impact of Catholic schools on the religious orientation of boys and girls, *Journal of Christian Education*, 71, 44–51.

Egan, J. (1985), An evaluation of the implementation of the principles of Catholic education in the Catholic comprehensive schools in Wales, Unpublished Ph.D. dissertation, University of Wales (Cardiff).

Egan, J. (1988), *Opting Out: Catholic schools today*, Leominster, Fowler Wright.

Egan, J. and Francis, L.J. (1986), School ethos in Wales: the impact of non-practising Catholic and non-Catholic pupils on Catholic secondary schools, *Lumen Vitae*, 41, 159–173.

Fahy, P.S. (1976), School and home perceptions of Australian adolescent males attending Catholic schools, *Our Apostolate*, 24, 167–188.

Fahy, P.S. (1978), Religious beliefs of 15,900 youths: attending Australian Catholic schools, years 12, 10, 8, 1975–1977, *Word in Life*, 26, 66–72.

Fahy, P.S. (1980), The religious effectiveness of some Australian Catholic high schools, *Word in Life*, 28, 86–98.

Fahy, P.S. (1982), Predictors of religious vocational interest among 3,431 Australian Catholic adolescents, *Word in Life*, 30, 149–160.

Francis, L.J. (1978), Attitude and longitude: a study in measurement, *Character Potential*, 8, 119–130.

Francis, L.J. (1986a), Denominational schools and pupil attitudes towards Christianity, *British Educational Research Journal*, 12, 145–152.

Francis, L.J. (1986b), Roman Catholic secondary schools: falling rolls and pupil attitudes, *Educational Studies*, 12, 119–127.

Francis, L.J. (1987a), *Religion in the Primary School: partnership between church and state?* London, Collins Liturgical Publications.

Francis, L.J. (1987b), Measuring attitudes towards Christianity among 12 to 18 year old pupils in Catholic schools, *Educational Research*, 29, 230–233.

Francis, L.J. (1989), Measuring attitude towards Christianity during childhood and adolescence, *Personality and Individual Differences*, 10, 695–698.

Francis, L.J. and Egan, J. (1987), Catholic schools and the communication of faith, *Catholic School Studies*, 60, 2, 27–34.

Francis, L.J. and Egan, J. (1990), The Catholic school as 'faith community': an empirical enquiry, *Religious Education*, 85, 588–603.

Francis, L.J. and Greer, J.E. (1990), Catholic schools and adolescent religiosity in Northern Ireland: shaping moral values, *Irish Journal of Education*, 24, 2, 40–47.

Gibson, H.M. and Francis, L.J. (1989), Measuring attitudes towards Christianity among 11 to 16 year old pupils in Catholic schools in Scotland, *Educational Research*, 31, 65–69.

Greer, J.E. (1985), Viewing 'the other side' in Northern Ireland: openness and attitude to religion among Catholic and Protestant Adolescents, *Journal for the Scientific Study of Religion*, 24, 275–292.

Greer, J.E. and Francis, L.J. (1990), The religious profile of pupils in Northern Ireland: a comparative study of pupils attending Catholic and Protestant secondary schools, *Journal of Empirical Theology*, 3, 2, 35–50.

Greer, J.E. and Francis, L.J. (1991), Measuring attitudes towards Christianity among pupils in Catholic secondary schools in Northern Ireland, *Educational Research*, 33, 100–103.

Hornsby-Smith, M.P. (1978), *Catholic Education: the unobtrusive partner*, London, Sheed and Ward.

Hornsby-Smith, M. and Petit, M. (1975), Social, moral and religious attitudes of secondary school students, *Journal of Moral Education*, 4, 261–272.

Livingston, S.A. (1988), Reliability of test results, in J.P. Keeves (ed.), *Educational Research, Methodology and Measurement: an international handbook*, pp. 386–392, Oxford, Pergamon Press.

Mol, J.J. (1968), The effects of denominational schools in Australia, *Australian and New Zealand Journal of Sociology*, 4, 1, 18–35.

Montgomery, A. (1990), Change in attitudes towards religion and religious education, Unpublished M.Ed. dissertation, the Polytechnic of North East London.

Orton, R.E. (1987), The foundations of construct validity: towards an update, *Journal of Research and Development in Education*, 21, 22–35.

Rhymer, J. (1983), Religious attitudes of Roman Catholic secondary school pupils in Strathclyde region, Unpublished Ph.D. dissertation, University of Edinburgh.

Rhymer, J. and Francis, L.J. (1985), Roman Catholic secondary schools in Scotland and pupil attitude towards religion, *Lumen Vitae*, 40, 103–110.

SPSS Inc. (1988), *SPSSX User's Guide*, New York, McGraw-Hill.

24

Attitudes toward assembly and religious education among Roman Catholic girls

Alice Montgomery and William K. Kay

Summary

A sample of 588 girls at a voluntary aided Roman Catholic comprehensive school in England completed an Osgood semantic differential questionnaire which assessed their attitudes toward games, English lessons, maths lessons, school itself, music/singing lessons, religious education/lessons about religion and school assemblies. The analysis shows how attitudes toward all these areas, except English lessons, decline in an age-related way. However, attitude toward assemblies declines non-linearly and attitude toward religious education/lessons about religion declines linearly. The theoretical implications of these findings are discussed both with regard to attitude toward Christianity and with regard to Piagetian psychology.

Introduction

Attitudes have been recognised as an important part of the attempt by social psychologists to understand social activity (Tajfel and Fraser, 1978; Eiser, 1979). In an educational context, attitudes have long been recognised not only as an outcome of the learning process but also as an aid or impediment to learning (Evans, 1965; Hyde, 1965; Schools Council, 1981; Hills, 1982). For these reasons, considerable effort has been allocated to devising methods by which attitudes might best be measured. Three basic approaches have been put forward. Thurstone (1928), Likert (1932) and Guttman

(1944) have each proposed methods that use self-completed questionnaires to produce valid and reliable attitude scales.

Francis (1987) was able to show how widely these different methods have been used in respect of different areas of the school curriculum. For instance, the Thurstone method has been used to assess attitude toward English (Whitehead, 1954), history (Musgrove, 1963), homework (Jones, 1974), mathematics (Gopal Rao, 1973), school (Slee, 1968), science (Billeh and Zakharides, 1975) and Welsh (Sharp, Thomas, Price, Francis and Davies, 1973). The Likert method has been used to discover the attitude of pupils toward computers (Moore, 1985), French (Roger, Bull and Fletcher, 1981), geography (Barlett, 1940), Latin (Winter, 1950), mathematics (Adwere-Boamah, Muller and Kahn, 1986), moral education (Edwards, 1964), music (Edwards and Edwards, 1971; Crowther and Durkin, 1982), physical education (Stensaasen,1975), reading (Kennedy and Halinski, 1975; Parker and Paradis, 1986), school (Dowling, 1980), science (Kempa and McGough, 1977; Doherty and Dawe, 1985) and social studies (Steiner and Barnhart, 1972). Finally, the Guttman method has been used to assess attitude toward mathematics (Anttonen, 1969) and school (Kniveton, 1969).

One of the most prolonged and systematic attempts to explore the functioning of a particular attitude among young people has been carried out by Francis and others in a series of studies stretching over 25 years. These studies used a common attitude scale (Francis, 1976) and have been summarised by Kay and Francis (1996). They show, among other things, that there is a persistent and consistent decline in *attitude toward Christianity* in pupils aged between eight and sixteen years and that this finding applies to both sexes and occurs within a wide variety of school types and cultural situations. The attitude scale used in these studies includes specific reference to school religion, that is, religious education lessons and prayers within school.

Although the finding that attitude toward Christianity declines consistently and persistently has been replicated many times and in many circumstances, and although it fits comfortably within the general and wider set of findings relating to religion (Argyle and Beit-Hallahmi, 1975; Wulff, 1991), Francis (1987) decided to test his results still further by means of a parallel study. He wished to eliminate two possibilities in connection with the results he and others had obtained. The first possibility was that the observed decline was an artifact of the measuring instrument he employed and of the scaling process he had used. Second, it was possible that the decline in attitude toward Christianity which he had discovered was part of a larger set of declining attitudes within the adolescent world-view. In other words, it was possible that pupils were demonstrating not so much a growing antipathy toward Christianity and school religion but rather a growing disregard for orthodox social values and adult-structured institutions.

Consequently, Francis made use of a technique for measuring attitudes based on the semantic differential and pioneered by Osgood, Suci and Tannenbaum (1957). The particular feature of this technique is that it allows measurements of attitude toward a variety of areas to be made using exactly the same set of adjectival opposites. The seven pairs Francis developed were: friendly-unfriendly, pleasant-unpleasant, bad-good, interesting-boring, nasty-nice, sad-happy and important-unimportant. Pupils were asked to rate English lessons, maths lessons, school, lessons about religion, music lessons, lessons about history and games lessons on each of the seven pairs. Pupils could place each lesson on a range of seven points (3,2,1,0,1,2,3) between each adjective and its opposite. This meant that an area could gain a maximum of 49 points if a pupil scored it as three in a positive direction on each of the pairs. Thus, if maths lessons were scored as three in the direction of friendly, pleasant, good, interesting, nice, happy and important, a total of 49 would be reached.

The 1987 study (which did not cover school assemblies) showed that, though there was a general age-related decline in attitude toward all of the subject areas that were assessed, the decline was most marked with respect to lessons about music and lessons about religion. The decline in attitude toward lessons on religion was linear. In other words, if a graph of decline had been plotted, the best-fitting line would have been straight. This decline took place between the first year of the junior school (year two) and the fourth year of the secondary school (year ten).

The results of this study lent no support to the possibility that the Likert-style scale of attitude toward Christianity, which Francis had employed in other studies, was showing a decline in attitude toward Christianity as a result of an artifact. The semantic differential scales, constructed according to a different theory and by a different technique, produced results showing a comparable decline. Attitude toward Christianity, then, clearly *does* decline among the majority of pupils within the years of compulsory schooling. The second possibility, that attitude toward Christianity should be understood as part of a set of other declining attitudes registering growing disaffection with the adult world, also received no support. The attitudes toward English, maths, history and school fluctuated during the period under review, and they did not appear to tail off sharply. Such declines as were observed in these areas were non-linear. Attitude toward Christianity and toward school religion are distinct from attitudes toward other school subjects. They are also distinct from attitude toward school itself.

A later study by Kay, Francis and Gibson (1995) explored a different facet of the decline in attitude toward Christianity. Piaget's monumental researches have charted mental development from infancy to adolescence (Piaget, 1972; Inhelder and Piaget, 1958; Flavell, 1963; Modgil and Modgil, 1976; Modgil, Modgil and Brown, 1983). The picture of mental development drawn by these researches is of a series of stages, each emerging from the previous one, by which knowledge and information gained at a lower stage is transformed and re-understood at a higher stage. The transition from the stage most common in the junior school, that of concrete operational thinking, to the stage associated with secondary school, that of formal operational thinking, takes place some time between the ages of twelve and sixteen years. However, there is evidence that the transition to formal operational thinking correlates with mental ability. Shayer, Kuchemann and Wylam (1976), in a survey of over 10,000 young people in Britain aged between nine and fourteen, found that formal operational thinking was far more prevalent among pupils at selective schools than among pupils at non-selective schools.

Goldman, who used Piaget's research as the basis for his own work, thought that 'about the age of thirteen represents a marked watershed in religious thinking' though he considered 'fully formal operational thinking does not occur until a little later' (Goldman, 1964, p. 239). He expressed this idea equally strongly in a second book by saying 'about the age of thirteen marks a sudden change in religion as in other school subjects' (Goldman, 1965, p. 162). This watershed in religious thinking was, according to Goldman, accompanied by a change in attitude toward religion, and specifically toward Christianity, since this was the particular subject of his study.

Kay, Francis and Gibson (1995) examined the linearity of the decline in attitude toward Christianity among pupils at selective and non-selective schools. They concluded that the onset of formal operational thinking has no impact on attitude toward Christianity.

Pupils who might be expected to experience a transition from concrete operational to formal operational thinking showed a steady and linear decline in attitude toward Christianity. The same steady and linear decline was shown by pupils who might be expected to remain at the level of concrete operational thinking.

The study reported in this chapter engages with both the issues addressed by Francis (1987) and by Kay, Francis and Gibson (1995). It simultaneously replicates and extends Francis' 1987 study. The 1987 study was carried out on pupils at a maintained comprehensive secondary school and its feeder primary schools. The current study was carried out at a single sex voluntary aided Roman Catholic comprehensive school. It therefore replicates the 1987 study by using the same instrumentation, and it extends it by applying this instrumentation to a sample of girls drawn from a school with strong religious connections covering the whole compulsory secondary age range. The 1995 study focused on the issue of linearity, and the present study (though without bringing to bear comparisons between different kinds of schools) likewise examines this issue.

Method

Sample

The study was carried out in a Roman Catholic voluntary aided single sex school for girls. The questionnaire was completed by 588 pupils distributed reasonably evenly between year seven and year eleven.

Measures

The seven pairs of adjectival opposites had been developed and tested in preparation for the 1987 study. The semantic differential space between the adjectives allowed for a range of seven responses. The directionality of the adjectival pairs was deliberately varied to offset response bias. That is to say, positive adjectives were alternately on the left and right hand side of the grid. Negative adjectives were interleaved between the positive ones, and also varied on either side of the grid. The scale was presented seven times for each of these concepts: English lessons, maths lessons, school, religious education/lessons about religion, singing/music lessons, school assemblies, physical education/games lessons.

Procedure and data analysis

The questionnaires were administered by staff during normal lesson time. The data were analysed by means of SPSS statistical package, using the reliability and breakdown routines (SPSS Inc., 1988).

Results

Table 24.1 displays the reliability of the semantic differential scales in terms of the alpha coefficient (Cronbach, 1951) for each concept area separately. The alpha coefficients vary between 0.81 and 0.91. This shows that the scales are internally consistent and that they all work well. The logic of comparing the different concept areas with each other is therefore strong.

Table 24.1
Reliability of the semantic differential scales

scale	alpha	mean	sd
games	0.9126	37.92	10.00
English	0.8142	39.47	6.60
maths	0.8588	37.48	8.45
school	0.8442	38.21	8.08
music	0.9059	31.03	11.01
religion	0.8546	37.39	7.83
assemblies	0.8928	30.33	10.33

Table 24.1 also displays the means and standard deviations for the whole sample for each concept area. It can be seen that the most popular curriculum subject is English (39.47), followed by games (37.92), maths (37.48), religion (37.39), music (31.03) and assemblies (30.33). School itself is rated highly (38.21).

Table 24.2 presents the means and standard deviations for each of the five age groups separately, together with information about the statistical significance of differences in the mean scale scores according to age. The table also shows the extent to which the age-related scores for each concept area significantly diverge from the linear trend. In each concept area, apart from English lessons, there is a significant age-related decline in attitude. This age-related decline is greatest for music lessons and assemblies. A linear

Table 24.2
Mean attitude scores by age

	games		English		maths		school		music		religion		assemblies	
	mean	sd	mean	sd	mean	sd	mean	sd	mean	sd	mean	sd	mean	sd
year 7	41.8	8.4	40.1	7.2	40.1	7.6	42.0	7.3	37.3	10.5	40.1	7.9	36.5	9.5
year 8	38.9	9.9	38.3	7.4	37.9	8.5	39.1	7.2	35.6	9.2	39.5	6.9	34.9	9.4
year 9	35.5	10.6	38.9	6.6	36.2	8.6	36.1	9.2	28.5	11.5	36.3	7.3	27.3	10.0
year 10	38.0	9.6	40.0	5.7	37.1	8.7	37.8	7.9	28.8	9.5	37.2	7.4	27.7	9.9
year 11	36.8	10.0	40.3	6.0	36.9	8.2	37.2	7.4	26.7	10.6	34.6	8.4	27.7	9.2
between groups	$F=5.4$ $P<.001$		$F=2.1$ NS		$F=3.2$ $P<.05$		$F=8.0$ $P<.001$		$F=22.2$ $P<.001$		$F=9.9$ $P<.001$		$F=22.4$ $P<.001$	
non linearity	$F=4.2$ $P<.01$		$F=2.2$ NS		$F=2.2$ NS		$F=5.3$ $P<.01$		$F=4.5$ $P<.01$		$F=2.3$ NS		$F=8.7$ $P<.001$	

decline is observable in respect of maths lessons and lessons about religion. The other concept areas, games, school itself, music lessons and assemblies demonstrate a non-linear decline.

Discussion

The findings presented here support the view that the linear decline in attitude toward Christianity found in many other studies (Kay and Francis, 1995) cannot be adequately interpreted as an artifact of the Likert scale construction procedure or by reference to the supposed more general alienation of teenagers from adult-structured institutions and orthodox social values. The present study shows that, while attitudes toward some school subjects show a decline, at least one other (English) does not. The variability in decline is conclusive evidence that decline is due to other factors than the method of scale construction or a generalised teenage alienation.

The findings presented here also show that many of the general trends applicable to an ordinary country comprehensive school are closely matched by those found in a Roman Catholic voluntary aided comprehensive school. For example, in both types of school, there is an age-related decline in attitude toward school, maths, games, lessons about religion, assemblies and music. But there are two differences to which future research may give attention. In the Roman Catholic school there is no age-related decline in attitude toward English and in the Roman Catholic school the age-related decline in attitude toward lessons about religion is much less sharp.

When the linear trends in the present study are examined in more detail, it is clear that pupil attitudes toward lessons about religion and toward assemblies are different. They both decline with age, but attitude toward lessons about religion declines in a linear fashion, while attitude toward assemblies does not. The figures in table 24.2 show that attitude toward lessons about religion drifts downwards at a steady rate year by year, while attitude toward assemblies drops sharply between year eight and year nine, and remains at this low level thereafter. How is this to be related to Piagetian psychology and to the work of Goldman?

Goldman believed, on the basis of Piagetian psychology, that there was a sudden change in religious thinking and in pupils' reaction to the school subject of religion at about the age of thirteen (year eight and year nine). The figures relating to school assemblies would appear to support Goldman's contention, while the figures relating to lessons about religion do not. In order to interpret these contradictory indications, it is necessary to consider any other features of the data presented here. The most obvious feature is that assemblies and music/singing are very closely parallel. They both decline in almost exactly the same way. The drop of seven points between year eight and year nine observed with assemblies is matched by a similar decline observed with music/singing. Neither subject recovers after this sudden drop and music/singing actually declines slightly more in the final year.

One interpretation, therefore, would be that the decline in attitude toward assemblies is linked with the singing they involve. What this interpretation suggests is that the sudden emergence of a negative attitude toward assemblies is not brought about by the transition to formal operational thinking, but simply by a dislike of compulsory group singing, which pupils may find increasingly embarrassing as they progress into adolescence.

Such an interpretation of the falling popularity of assemblies is compatible with the analysis of pupil attitudes given by Kay elsewhere in this book. The falling popularity of assemblies is linked with its deteriorating importance in the eyes of pupils; factors drawn from Piagetian psychology do not apply.

If this general interpretation is correct, then it leaves the way open for a consideration of the linear decline in attitude toward lessons about religion. Here, on the basis of Goldman's conclusions, we would anticipate a non-linear decline in attitude. Some caveat, it is true, might be placed on this supposition on the basis of the school type used in this study. Nevertheless, a comprehensive school would be expected to include a substantial percentage of pupils making the transition from concrete to formal operations. The linear decline in attitude toward lessons about religion suggests that there is no sudden psychological change responsible for the observed trend.

This conclusion is strengthened by a consideration of the scores in relation to attitude toward maths. Attitude toward maths declines in a linear fashion. We would anticipate that the transition to formal operation thinking would be *more* decisive in maths than it would be in religious education. This is because Piagetian psychology has found in maths, physics and logic the best paradigms for the transition process between concrete and formal operational thinking. The understanding of balance, refraction of light and ratios is much more central to the expression of formal operational thinking than is the understanding of theological concepts.

In summary, then, we may explain the non-linear decline in attitude toward assemblies by reference to the embarrassment caused by singing and the linear decline in attitude toward religion lesson by factors other than the transition to formal operational thinking.

What might these factors be? Kay and Francis (1995) have suggested that an age-related linear decline is most likely to be associated with a socialisation model of attitude change. The advantage of this model is that socialisation takes place at a steady pace in step with increasing age. The decline in attitude toward lessons about religion would then be explained by a gradual induction by the socialisation process into the adult world of indifference to religion. As pupils pass from childhood into the upper end of the secondary school, they become more aware of adult attitudes toward religion, or of the attitudes of young adults who have left school, and begin to adopt these attitudes for themselves. Since British society generally holds a neutral or indifferent attitude toward religion, pupils leave the positive attitude of childhood behind and adopt the attitude of the prevailing culture. There are no sudden drops or shifts but simply a drift into a new evaluation of religion.

Finally, this study reveals a sharp distinction between the way pupils evaluate assemblies and the way they evaluate lessons about religion. Such a distinction is amply supported by the large survey reported on by Francis and Kay (1995). Instead of helping religious education, as the legislators of the 1944 Education Act had hoped (a hope which even the legislators of the 1988 Education Reform Act had broadly supported), assembly appears, even in the sympathetic environment of a church-related school, to offer a negative experience, as Hull (1975) had, on different grounds, warned.

References

Argyle, M. and Beit-Hallahmi, B. (1975), *The Social Psychology of Religion*, London, Routledge and Kegan Paul.

Adwere-Boamah, J., Muller, D. and Kahn, H. (1986), Factorial validity of the Aiken-Dreger mathematics attitude scale for urban school students, *Educational and Psychological Measurement*, 46, 233–236.

Anttonen, R.G. (1969), A longitudinal study in mathematic attitudes, *Journal of Educational Research*, 62, 467–471.

Bartlett, D.B. (1940), An investigation into the attitudes of boys and girls towards the content of, and the methods of teaching geography in grammar schools, Unpublished MA dissertation, University of London.

Billeh, V.Y. and Zakharides, G.A. (1975), The development and application of a scale for measuring scientific attitudes, *Science Education*, 59, 155–165.

Cronbach, L.J. (1951), Coefficient-alpha and the internal structure of tests, *Psychometrika*, 16, 297–334.

Crowther, R.D. and Durkin, K. (1982), Sex- and age-related differences in the musical behaviour, interests and attitudes towards music of 232 secondary school students, *Educational Studies*, 8, 131–139.

Doherty, J. and Dawe, J. (1985), The relationship between development maturity and attitude to school science: an exploratory study, *Educational Studies*, 11, 93–107.

Dowling, J.R. (1980), Adjustment from primary to secondary school: a one year follow-up, *British Journal of Educational Psychology*, 50, 26–32.

Edwards, J.B. (1964), Some moral attitudes of boys in a secondary modern school, *Educational Review*, 17, 234–244.

Edwards, J.S. and Edwards, M.C. (1971), A scale to measure attitudes towards music, *Journal of Research in Music Education*, 19, 228–233.

Eiser, J.R. (1979), Attitudes, in K. Connolly (ed.), *Psychology Survey No. 2*, London, George Allen and Unwin.

Evans, K.M. (1965), *Attitudes and Interests in Education*, London, Routledge and Kegan Paul.

Flavell, J.H. (1963), *The Developmental Psychology of Jean Piaget*, London, D. Van Nostrand.

Francis, L.J. (1976), An enquiry into the concept 'Readiness for Religion', Unpublished Ph.D. dissertation, University of Cambridge.

Francis, L.J. (1987), The decline in attitudes towards religion among 8–15 year olds, *Educational Studies*, 13, 125–134.

Francis, L.J. and Kay, W.K. (1995), *Teenage Religion and Values*, Leominster, Gracewing.

Goldman, R.J. (1964), *Religious Thinking from Childhood to Adolescence*, London, Routledge and Kegan Paul.

Goldman, R.J. (1965), *Readiness for Religion*, London, Routledge and Kegan Paul.

Gopal Rao, C.S.R. (1973), A study of the attitudes towards mathematics of junior and secondary school pupils in a new town, and of factors relating to them, Unpublished Ph.D. dissertation, University of London.

Guttman, L. (1944), A basis for scaling qualitative data, *American Sociological Review*, 9, 139–150.

Hills, P.J. (1982), *A Dictionary of Education*, London, Routledge and Kegan Paul.

Hull, J.M. (1975), *School Worship: an obituary*, London, SCM.

Hyde, K.E. (1965), *Religious Learning in Adolescence* (University of Birmingham, Institute of Education, Monograph 7), London, Oliver and Boyd.

Inhelder, B. and Piaget, J. (1958), *The Growth of Logical Thinking*, London, Routledge and Kegan Paul.

Jones, K.W. (1974), Children's attitudes towards homework, Unpublished M.Ed. dissertation, University of Nottingham.

Kay, W.K. and Francis, L.J. (1996), *Drift from the Churches*, Cardiff, University of Wales Press.

Kay, W.K., Francis, L.J. and Gibson, H.M. (1995), Attitude toward Christianity and the transition to formal operational thinking, in press.

Kempa, R.F. and McGough J.M. (1977), A study of attitudes towards mathematics in relation to selected student characteristics, *British Journal of Educational Psychology*, 47, 296–304.

Kennedy, L.D. and Halinski, R.S. (1975), Measuring attitudes: an extra dimension, *Journal of Reading*, 18, 518–522.

Kniveton, B.H. (1969), An investigation of the attitudes of adolescents to aspects of their schooling, *British Journal of Educational Psychology*, 39, 78–81.

Likert, R. (1932), A technique for the measurement of attitudes, *Archives of Psychology*, 140, 1–55.

Modgil, S. and Modgil, C. (1976), *Piagetian Research: compilation and commentary*, Windsor, NFER Publishing Company.

Modgil, S., Modgil, C. and Brown, G. (1983), *Jean Piaget: an interdisciplinary critique*, London, Routledge and Kegan Paul.

Moore, J.L. (1985), Development of a questionnaire to measure secondary school pupils' attitudes to computers and robots, *Educational Studies*, 11, 33–40.

Musgrove, F. (1963), Five scales of attitude to history, *Studies in Education*, 3, 423–439.

Osgood, C.E., Suci, G.J. and Tannenbaum, P.H. (1957), *The Measurement of Meaning*, Urbana, University of Illinois Press.

Parker, A. and Paradis, E. (1986), Attitude development toward reading in grades one through six, *Journal of Educational Research*, 79, 313–315.

Piaget, J. (1972), Intellectual evolution from adolescence to adulthood, *Human Development*, 15, 1–12.

Roger, D., Bull P. and Fletcher, R. (1981), The construction and validation of a questionnaire for measuring attitudes towards learning foreign languages, *Educational Review*, 33, 223–230.

Schools Council (1981), *The Practical Curriculum: schools council working paper 70*, London, Methuen Educational.

Sharp, D., Thomas, B., Price, E., Francis, G. and Davies, I. (1973), *Attitudes to Welsh and English in the Schools of Wales*, Basingstoke, Macmillan/University of Wales Press.

Shayer, M., Kuchemann, D.E. and Wylam, H. (1976), The distribution of Piagetian stages of thinking in British middle and secondary school children, *British Journal of Educational Psychology*, 46, 164–173.

Slee, F.W. (1968), The feminine image factor in girls' attitudes to school subjects, *British Journal of Educational Psychology*, 38, 212–214.

SPSS Inc. (1988), *SPSSX User's Guide*, New York, McGraw Hill.

Steiner, R.L. and Barnhart, R.B. (1972), The development of an instrument to assess environmental attitudes utilizing factor analytic techniques, *Science Education*, 56, 427–432.

Stensaasen, S. (1975), Pupils' liking for physical education as a school subject, *Scandinavian Journal of Educational Research*, 19, 111–129.

Tajfel, H. and Fraser, C. (eds) (1978), *Introducing Social Psychology*, Harmondsworth, Penguin.

Thurstone, L.L. (1928), Attitudes can be measured, *American Journal of Sociology*, 33, 529–554.

Whitehead, F.S. (1954), An investigation into the attitudes of grammar school boys and girls aged 11–16 towards some works of English prose fiction commonly read in school, Unpublished MA dissertation, University of London.

Winter, P.E. (1950), An investigation into the attitude towards Latin of girls at secondary grammar school at the end of two years' study of Latin, Unpublished MA dissertation, University of London.

Wulff, D.M. (1991), *Psychology of Religion: classic and contemporary views*, New York, John Wiley and Sons.

25

Religiosity, personality and tertiary educational choice

Yaacov J. Katz

Summary

The present chapter compares the religiosity and personality traits of 99 female Jewish students who studied at the Bar-Ilan University School of Education and 77 comparable students who attended the Jerusalem College for Women. Both Bar-Ilan University and the Jerusalem College for Women are religious institutions, but whereas the university is open to secular students, the college only accepts students who are religious in their outlook and observance. The subjects responded to the Eysenck Personality Questionnaire, the Wilson Conservatism Scale, the Democracy Questionnaire and the Student Religiosity Questionnaire. The data indicate that, despite similarity between the research groups on the religious practices and religious principles variables, the college sub-group was characterised by significantly higher levels of religion-puritanism, anti-hedonism, anti-feminism, anti-artism and neuroticism, and by lower levels of democracy, thus intimating a more conservative personality tendency, in comparison with the university sub-group. In light of the results of the study, it was postulated that the students' differential tertiary educational choice was related to their particular placement on the conservative-liberal personality continuum.

State religious education in Israel

State religious education in Israel is, by definition, comprehensive and flexible in its outlook (Ministry of Education and Culture, 1989). Thus state religious education, as initiated by the Education Act of 1953, perceives itself as being responsible for expressing the different outlooks and behaviours of the religious community.

407

The state religious educational system legitimises 'limited pluralism' (Ron, 1973), so that pupils from diverse religious backgrounds (such as hassidic families belonging to the Lubavich sect, families where the parents are graduates of theological academies, liberal orthodox families, and traditional families where the parents attended high schools in the state religious and state secular systems) are all able to feel at home within the system. The common denominator of all pupils and teachers (and their families) belonging to the state religious educational system is a Jewish orthodox way of life in one of its multifarious forms. This pluralism is limited to the orthodox life style and excludes conservative and reform Jews, as well as those who do not accept traditional Jewish law.

The educational efforts of the religious educational system mirror the need to bridge the gap between the holy and secular worlds. The system maintains an applied ideology, meaning that study of the torah and other religious topics such as Jewish law and philosophy, should lead to religious belief and observance. Religious education is designed to promote an identification with Jewish law and the sages who developed the law on the one hand, and involvement in all walks of life on the other. This philosophy of study is not limited to formal frameworks only, but permeates life in the home, and lasts long after formal studies have been completed. Goldschmidt (1984) stated that the emerging character and developing personality of the Jew or Jewess will include the necessity to perform Jewish precepts as a pupil, a soldier, a businessman or woman, a husband or wife, and a father or mother. Religious education is not just another detail in the life of the observant Jew, but is the vehicle which elevates the Jew to a better life in the present and future.

Torah (*Yeshiva* and *Michlala*) education and teacher training

One of the streams within the state religious educational system is the torah stream represented at the secondary level by the yeshiva high school for boys and the comparable ulpana high school for girls. At the tertiary torah level, males study in the yeshiva and females attend the michlala. A central theme of Jewish torah education is the inculcation of religious observance and beliefs. Alon (1957) stated that the Lithuanian torah academies, which remain to this day the ideal prototype of the typical modern yeshiva, advocated learning torah, and morals and ethics. Alon pointed out that modern-day Jewish humanism developed from the religious concept of ethics, which basically means the understanding of others' needs. Bialoblotzky (1971) added that the typical Lithuanian yeshiva student was an upright, proud and independent individual who was subservient to God alone. He was educated towards love of the torah and love of the people. Moral education was employed in order to improve interpersonal behaviour and religiosity.

Volbe (1986) stated that the aim of modern yeshiva education is not only to inculcate the student with knowledge of Jewish law, but also to purify his ideas and heart and to promote public responsibility and sensitivity to the needs of the individual. Urbach (1986) added that the study of the torah should emphasise the centrality of moral and ethical education. Yogel (1971) wrote that yeshiva education should impress upon the student the importance of desirable moral, ethical and social conduct as well as religiosity. The aim of torah education is worldliness, namely, the preparation of the yeshiva student to contribute to the world at large, as an upright religious individual.

Bar-Lev (1985) described yeshiva (or michlala) type education as promoting the fulfilment of religious life as well as moral, national and civic responsibilities. The clear-cut educational mode of promoting a new type of ethical and religious citizen who participates in all walks of life characterises the yeshiva and the michlala. The goals of the curricula for Biblical Studies, Talmud and Oral Law, Jewish Philosophy in the yeshiva include the issue of moral, ethical and values education (Ministry of Education and Culture, 1973; Ministry of Education and Culture, 1985; Ministry of Education and Culture, 1986). The curricula suggest that focus be placed on the internalisation of ethics, morals and values that appear in biblical, talmudic and philosophical texts in order to promote religiosity. In addition, students are expected to identify with the values inherent in Jewish religious literature.

Lichtenstein (1983) proposed that the typical modern hesder yeshiva (a yeshiva where the student combines torah study and military service) student should be rooted in a pre-eminently torah climate, this being important for both his spiritual development and for the future of the nation, at present in critical need of broadly based spiritual commitment and moral leadership. Thus, the hesder yeshiva and the michlala seek to instil profound loyalty to the state, as well as to inculcate spiritual perspectives as well as ethical and moral values which are to serve as the basis for a radical critique of the secularly oriented state and society. Lichtenstein added that modern nationalistically oriented torah education is designed to reconcile the conflicting claims of spirituality and security, of personal growth and public service.

In a landmark empirical study which Levi and Guttman (1976) conducted on a representative sample of religious and non-religious Israeli youth, the researchers found that religious hesder yeshiva and michlala students are more intensively value oriented, nationalistically oriented and zionistically oriented than non-religious youth. The researchers inferred from these results that religious educational institutions, such as the yeshiva and the michlala, especially emphasise morals and values, nationalism and zionism in addition to the academic aspects of their curriculum, as opposed to secular educational institutions which almost exclusively promote academic excellence.

In recent years the hesder yeshiva and the michlala have opened teacher training programmes designed to provide specialist teachers of Jewish religious subjects, such as bible, Mishna, Talmud, Jewish Philosophy, for the Israeli educational system in general and the state religious system in particular. In addition to the subject matter, the hesder yeshiva and the michlala have incorporated the issue of morality and contribution to the public at large into their teacher training curriculum. Their basic educational philosophy emphasises a direct approach in which students are imbued with a will to assist society in general and those who are less fortunate in particular. Teacher training within the framework of the hesder yeshiva and the michlala, similarly accentuates the need to embrace the ideals of community service. Teacher trainees are made aware of the major issues facing society and are trained to broach the issues in the classroom. Teaching, therefore, is perceived as a mission in which students are not only taught subject matter for examination purposes, but also are subjected to discussions on the issues of the day and have value oriented solutions to these issues laid before them. Thus the yeshiva or michlala teacher training department, in addition to formal professional teacher training, adheres to a clearly defined religiously oriented ideology and ethos which emphasises religious and societal goals and missions.

University education and teacher training

Universities, traditionally, have had an educational philosophy totally divorced from ideological values. Altbach (1979) and Ben-

David (1977) intimated that one of the most important characteristics of higher education throughout the ages up till modern
times has been academic freedom and autonomy. Clarke and Edwards (1980) stated that, by their very autonomy and freedom,
universities managed to preserve the positive heritage of society.
Pedley (1977) said, after reviewing policy statements made by
higher education policy formers, that universities are identified
with learning for its own sake as well as with autonomy and
privileges which are not congruent with the immediate needs of
society. Wolff (1970) described the university as an ivory tower with
scholarly life removed from the immediate affairs of the social
order. The scholar is concerned with the textual world and not with
the world about which the text speaks. However, Chitoran and
Pombejr (1984) showed that in recent years, government, public
and press have accused universities of aloofness, antiquated practices and overall wastefulness. As a result, universities are now
being asked to account for their academic and financial activities
in order to improve their efficiency and to enhance their contribution to society but thus far no attempt has been made to persuade
universities to promote ideological education.

Rushton (1976) outlined all the official goals of teacher education in general and in the United Kingdom in particular. Nowhere
are moral, ethical or value goals of teacher training at university
level mentioned. The main issue is that of transferring knowledge
in the best possible way so as to bring about superior student
achievement. The contribution of teachers to society is perceived,
almost solely, in terms of academic achievement. Katz (1985)
demonstrated that in Israel universities are perceived as contributing to society mainly in the field of science and technology. In
the realm of morals and values, Israeli universities are perceived
not to be fulfilling their public role, thereby diminishing the will
of the public to agree to continued funding in time of economic
crisis. Katz indicated that the disappointment with Israeli universities is particularly obvious in the field of education and teacher
training.

In Israel, university teacher training departments concentrate
solely on pedagogy and methodology. Teacher trainees are expected to meet the laid down standards of excellence which will
ensure their performance in the teaching of formal subject matter.
The major aim of the university teacher training department is to
turn out teachers who are capable of successfully assisting their
students to fulfil all obligations in the realm of subject matter. No

emphasis is placed on matters that are not part and parcel of the formal curriculum at the university teacher training departments. No time is spent on issues affecting Israeli society and the teacher trainee is not made aware of the major problems facing Israeli society. Thus the university teacher training departments have no specific ideological goals apart from that of the formal and professional training of teachers.

Personality traits and profiles

Numerous research and theoretical studies have indicated the existence of two distinct personality trait profiles, the conservative and the liberal. For example, Baer and Mosele (1970), Bhushan and Sinha (1975), De Fronzo (1972), Josefowitz and Marjoribanks (1978), Thomas (1975) and Weller, Levinbok, Maimon and Shaham (1975) examined the relationship between conservatism and a range of social orientations in different ethnic and societal samples and confirmed the existence of a significant relationship between conservatism and religious belief. Wilson (1973) noted that conservatism reflects a dimension of personality loading on fascism, authoritarianism, dogmatism and rigidity. Kerlinger (1984) emphasised that conservatism is a set of social orientations characterised by a tendency to maintain the status quo, social stability, religiosity, natural inequality of men, social regimes that tend to be undemocratic, and anti-modernism. On the other hand, studies have confirmed the existence of a positive relationship between the liberal personality trait profile and typical social orientations, such as democratic tendencies and racial tolerance (Bahr and Chadwick, 1974), risk-taking and upward social mobility (Ray and Wilson, 1976), progressive- and tender-mindedness (Eysenck, 1975), and novelty and change (Kish, Netterberg and Leahy, 1973; Larr and Zea, 1977).

In studies which examined the conservatism-liberalism personality model and led to the development of the Conservatism Scale, Wilson and Patterson (1970) found that in several European societies, namely Britain, the Netherlands, New Zealand and West Germany, a number of common major components cohered to produce a factor of general conservatism. These major components were, in each society, intercorrelated in a fairly even degree. Wilson and Schutte (1973) found a factor pattern for the Conservatism Scale in a white South African sample, as did Katz and Ronen (1986) in an adult Israeli population. Wilson and Lee (1974), after conducting a study of a South Korean sample, concluded that social attitudinal patterns and their relationships to demographic variables show a great deal of consistency across widely different societies because they reflect basic personality dynamics. Bagley (1972), after reviewing several cross-cultural studies on general conservatism, came to a similar conclusion.

Katz (1984) summarised the conservative and liberal personality trait profiles. On the one hand, the conservative is characterised by traits such as religiosity, authoritarianism, dogmatism, ethnocentrism and racism, rejection of change, rigidity, fear of ambiguity, and cognitive simplicity. On the other, the liberal is characterised by secularism, the promotion of equality and democracy, flexibility, cognitive sophistication, the will to progress and change, and the ability to cope with uncertain and ambiguous situations.

Another comprehensive model of personality which has been shown to be an effective predictor of individual differences is provided by Eysenck and Eysenck (1985). This model argues that personality can be most adequately summarised in terms of three major dimensions of extraversion, neuroticism and psychoticism, as well as by a fourth dimension indicated by lie scale responses.

Eysenck's extraversion scale measures sociability and impulsivity. The opposite of extraversion is introversion. Eysenck and Gudjonsson (1989) characterise the high scorer as sociable, lively, active, assertive, sensation-seeking, carefree, dominant, surgent and venturesome. The low scorer on this dimension is characterised by the opposite set of traits. Eysenck's neuroticism scale measures emotional lability and over-reactivity. The opposite of neuroticism is emotional stability. Eysenck and Gudjonsson (1989) characterise the high scorer as anxious, depressed, tense, irrational, shy, moody, emotional, suffering from guilt feelings and low self-esteem. The low scorer on this dimension is characterised by the absence of these traits.

Eysenck's psychoticism scale identifies the underlying personality traits which at one extreme define psychotic mental disorders. The opposite of psychotic is normal personality. Eysenck and Eysenck (1976) characterise the high scorers as cold, impersonal, hostile, lacking in sympathy, unfriendly, untrustful, odd, unemotional, unhelpful, lacking in insight, strange and with paranoid ideas that people are against them. In addition, high scorers are impulsive, stimulus-seeking, sensation-seeking, risk-taking individuals who often crave for change. The low scorers are empathic, unselfish, altruistic, warm, peaceful and generally more pleasant, although possibly less socially decisive individuals.

Eysenck's lie scale characterises the personality trait usually described as social desirability. A high score on the lie scale indicates a need for conformity, a measure of dependence on social acceptance and approval, as well as a rather weak character. A low score on this scale typifies the independent, self-confident and strong-charactered individual.

Against this background, the aim of the present study was twofold. The first aim was to examine whether religious female teacher trainees, coming from similar family backgrounds and with similar personal histories, who chose to study either at a university teacher training department or at a torah teacher training college, can be successfully and significantly characterised and differentiated on the basis of personality traits. The second aim was to examine whether tertiary educational choices of the students can be attributed to the possible existence of differential personality trait profiles between students attending university or college teacher training departments.

Method

Sample

The research sample consisted of 176 female first-year teacher trainees of whom 99 attended the Bar-Ilan University School of Education and 77 studied at the Jerusalem College for Women (Michlala). All subjects were high school graduates who successfully passed the national university entrance psychometric examination and were eligible for studies at any Israeli university or teacher training college. All subjects came from zionistically oriented national-religious middle-class Jewish families and received their education in the state religious educational system from kindergarten level through elementary school and ulpana type secondary school. All subjects were graduates of the national-religious Bnei Akiva youth movement and all underwent two years of voluntary national service during which period the subjects served as assistants to teachers in infant classes in state religious elementary schools. The fathers of all subjects were university graduates and all mothers were graduates of state religious teacher training seminaries (the seminary is the forerunner of the academic teacher training college).

Instruments

The Eysenck Personality Questionnaire (Eysenck and Eysenck, 1975), in the Hebrew translation compiled by Eysenck and Yannai (1985), consists of 90 items intended to assess four major personality factors, namely extraversion (alpha = 0.74), neuroticism (alpha = 0.81), psychoticism (alpha = 0.52) and a lie scale (alpha = 0.76).

The Conservatism Scale (Wilson and Patterson, 1968) consists of 50 items, each dealing with a different component of general conservatism. Katz and Ronen (1986) translated and validated the Hebrew version of the Conservatism Scale which, in the present study, yielded four significant factors, namely religion-puritanism (alpha = 0.84), anti-hedonism (alpha = 0.80), anti-feminism (alpha = 0.79) and anti-artism (alpha = 0.83).

The Democracy Questionnaire consists of ten items and was specially compiled for this study to assess one significant factor labelled General Democracy (alpha = 0.87). The items included issues concerned with civil rights, equality of minority groups, women's rights and religious freedom.

The Students' Religiosity Questionnaire, consisting of 20 items, was compiled and validated by Katz and Schmida (1992) to tap the religiosity level of the respondents. The questionnaire consisted of two significant factors. The first factor, labelled Jewish practices (alpha = 0.76), included items tapping religious practices such as sabbath observance, inter-sex socialising, dietary laws observance at home, observance of fast days, sabbath termination prayers and tabernacles festival observance. The second factor, labelled Jewish principles (alpha = 0.89), included items loading on religious belief such as biblical miracles, rabbinical authority, reward and punishment, resurrection of the dead, creation ex nihilo, messianic era and divine law.

Procedure

The four instruments were administered to the subjects after they had been given a general explanation of the purpose of the research. The subjects were asked to carefully consider the items in all four questionnaires and to respond as accurately as possible. The subjects were told that all responses would be held in strict confidence and that full anonymity would be maintained.

Results

Table 25.1 presents the mean scores recorded by the two groups of students attending the university school of education and the college teacher training department on the indices of extraversion, neuroticism, psychoticism, lie scale, general democracy, religion-puritanism, anti-hedonism, anti-feminism, anti-artism, religious practices and religious principles. Table 25.1 also presents the significance of the differences between the mean scores recorded by the two groups of students according to multivariate analysis of variance. These data demonstrate that the subjects attending the michlala teacher training department scored significantly higher

Table 25.1
Descriptive statistics and F (MANOVA) values
for subjects attending university and theological
college teacher training departments

variable	university mean	sd	college mean	sd	F	P<
extraversion	13.75	4.04	14.98	3.58	3.80	NS
neuroticism	9.92	4.39	11.56	4.00	6.93	.01
psychoticism	3.86	2.46	4.46	2.50	2.78	NS
lie scale	8.10	3.16	9.37	4.00	5.25	.05
democracy	38.22	7.28	33.68	5.96	23.07	.001
religion-puritanism	18.20	5.85	23.19	1.67	52.14	.001
anti-hedonism	9.97	2.47	11.20	1.29	15.22	.001
anti-feminism	4.10	1.57	6.55	1.25	126.56	.001
anti-artism	4.35	1.74	5.58	1.76	20.36	.001
religious practices	43.31	4.27	44.45	3.98	1.13	NS
religious principles	40.95	6.02	41.06	5.83	1.27	NS

on the neuroticism, lie scale, religion-puritanism, anti-hedonism, anti-feminism and anti-artism factors than the subjects studying teacher training at the university. On the other hand, subjects studying at the university teacher training department achieved significantly higher scores on the general democracy factor than their michlala counterparts. No significant inter-group differences were indicated for Jewish practices and Jewish principles.

Thereafter a discriminant function analysis computed for the independent variables confirmed the inter-group differences ascertained in the multivariate analysis of variance. The discriminant function indicated a significant Wilks Lamda coefficient of 0.51, a significant canonical correlation coefficient of 0.69, and successfully classified 84.7% of the research sample according to correct group membership (university or michlala teacher training department).

Discussion

The trait profile characterising the michlala students confirms the findings of Baer and Mosele (1970), Bhushan and Sinha (1975), De Fronzo (1972), Josefowitz and Marjoribanks (1978), Thomas (1975) and Weller, Levinbok, Maimom and Shaham (1975) who indicated a significant relationship between religiosity and conservatism. The fact that the personality traits and profiles of the students attending the michlala were orientated towards religion-puritanism, anti-hedonism, anti-feminism and anti-artism is understandable, bearing in mind the religiously conservative atmosphere pervading the michlala ideology and campus. In addition, the tendency towards neuroticism, which includes, among other traits, anxiety, tension, a measure of irrationality, shyness and emotionality, is also understandable in view of the relationship known to exist between conservatism and the components of neuroticism as indicated by Cattell (1971) and Sidanius (1977).

The michlala students were also typified by significantly higher lie scale scores, indicating a tendency towards social desirability and conformity, a logical phenomenon in light of empirical findings reported by Loubser (1968), Orpen (1970) and Morse and Orpen (1975) who indicated that social desirability and conformity are intrinsically related to general conservatism. Thus, the fact that these more religious-puritan, conservative and socially conforming students chose the michlala as their preferred institution of higher education, indicates that they felt that their personality needs would be best actualised in the more overtly religious and socially closed college which promotes an unambiguously religious and moral atmosphere which closely correlated with their own ideologies and beliefs.

The significantly higher scores of the university teacher training students on the democracy factor and their correspondingly lower scores on the conservatism oriented independent variables are also understandable. The university students were less religiously-puritan and less conservative in their traits and personality profiles, indicating that despite their family, educational, and socioeconomic backgrounds, which closely matched those of the michlala students, their tertiary educational choice served as an outlet for their less conservative personality needs. Even at the religiously oriented Bar-Ilan University, the pervading atmosphere is one of openness and flexibility, thus drawing religious but more liberally oriented and flexible students to an institution typified by a pluralistic academic and social ethos. The lower scores on the religion-puritan and conservative factors also indicate that the university students had the inner personality strength and will to cope with dilemmas posed by open university society without feeling anxiety or threat to their personalities or the need to attend a tertiary educational institution characterised by clear-cut religiously and conservatively oriented goals and ideologies.

The results of the research do not call into question the religiosity of the university teacher training students. Their mean scores on the Students' Religiosity Questionnaire, on both religious practices and religious principles, do not significantly differ from those of the michlala students. Thus, it seems clear that the different aspects of conservatism, neuroticism, social conformity and democracy, rather than the religious practices and religious principles factors, were the salient variables which led to the differential choices of the university and michlala teacher trainees.

In conclusion it appears that despite their similar religious observance and belief levels, the teacher trainees attending university and michlala were differentiated by their personality traits and profiles which appear to be closely connected to their choice of institution of higher education. Both university and michlala students chose the institution which satisfied their inner personality needs, seemingly indicating that psychological self-actualisation, rather than religious observance or belief, led to their tertiary educational choices.

Acknowledgement

The research study described in this chapter was sponsored by the Institute for Community Education and Research, School of Education, Bar-Ilan University.

References

Alon, G. (1957), *Studies in Jewish History*, Tel Aviv, Hakibbutz Hameuchad. (Hebrew)

Altbach, P.G. (1979), *Comparative Higher Education*, London, Mansell.

Baer, D.J. and Mosele, V.F. (1970), Political and religious beliefs of Catholics and attitudes towards lay dress of sisters, *Journal of Psychology*, 74, 77–83.

Bagley, C.R. (1972), *The Dutch Plural Society: a comparative study of race relations*, London, Oxford University Press.

Bahr, H.M. and Chadwick, B.A. (1974), Conservatism, racial intolerance and attitudes towards racial assimilation among whites and American Indians, *Journal of Social Psychology*, 94, 45–56.

Bar-Lev, M. (1985), Yeshiva educational institutions in Israel, in W. Ackerman, A. Carmon and D. Zucker (eds), *Education in an Evolving Society*, Tel Aviv, Hakibbutz Hameuchad and the Van Leer Institute. (Hebrew)

Ben-David, J. (1977), *Centres of Learning*, New York, McGraw-Hill.

Bhushan, L.I. and Sinha, N.P. (1975), Politico-economic conservatism and ethnic prejudice in religious and non-religious caste Hindus, *Journal of Psychological Researches*, 20, 2, 60–64.

Bialoblotzky, S. (1971), *The Matter of Tradition*, Ramat Gan, Bar-Ilan University Press. (Hebrew)

Cattell, R.B. (1971), *Abilities: their structure, growth and action*, Boston, Houghton Mifflin Company.

Chitoran, D. and Pombejr, V.na. (1984), The role of higher education in international understanding, cooperation, peace and human rights, *Higher Education in Europe*, 9, 2, 5–9.

Clarke, A.M. and Edwards, L.M. (1980), The Williams committee of inquiry into education and training in Australia: recommendations for universities, *Higher Education*, 9, 5, 495–528.

De Fronzo, J. (1972), Religion and humanitarianism in Eysenck's T-dimension and left-right political orientation, *Journal of Personality and Social Psychology*, 21, 3, 265–269.

Eysenck, H.J. (1975), The structure of social attitudes, *British Journal of Social and Clinical Psychology*, 14, 323–331.

Eysenck, H.J. and Eysenck, S.B.G. (1975), *Manual of the Eysenck Personality Questionnaire*, London, Hodder and Stoughton.

Eysenck, H.J. and Eysenck, S.B.G. (1976), *Psychoticism as a Dimension of Personality*, London, Hodder and Stoughton.

Eysenck, H.J. and Eysenck, M.W. (1985), *Personality and Individual Differences: a natural science approach*, New York, Plenum Press.

Eysenck, H.J. and Gudjonsson, G. (1989), *Causes and Cures of Criminality*, New York, Plenum Press.

Eysenck, S.B.G. and Yannai, O. (1985), A cross-cultural study of personality: Israel and England, *Psychological Reports*, 57, 111–116.

Goldschmidt, J. (1984), State religious education in Israel, in A. Wasserteil (ed.), *Philosophy and Education: letters of Joseph Goldschmidt*, Jerusalem, Ministry of Education and Culture. (Hebrew)

Josefowitz, N. and Marjoribanks, K. (1978), Religious affiliation, church attendance and social attitudes, *Psychological Reports*, 42, 1097–1098.

Katz, Y.J. (1984), The influence of some attitudes on intelligence, Unpublished Ph.D. dissertation, University of Witwatersrand.

Katz, Y.J. (1985), The image of Israeli universities as perceived by professional journalists, Paper presented at the Annual Meeting of Israeli University Public Relations Departments. (Hebrew)

Katz, Y.J. and Ronen, M. (1986), A cross-cultural validation of the Conservatism Scale in a multi-ethnic society: the case of Israel, *Journal of Social Psychology*, 126, 555–557.

Katz, Y.J. and Schmida, M. (1991), Religiosity of students in the Israeli national-religious comprehensive high school, *British Journal of Religious Education*, 13, 2, 109–113.

Katz, Y.J. and Schmida, M. (1992), Validation of the Student Religiosity Questionnaire, *Educational and Psychological Measurement*, 52, 2, 353–356.

Kerlinger, F.N. (1984), *Liberalism and Conservatism: the nature and structure of social attitudes*, Hillsdale, New Jersey, Lawrence Erlbaum and Associates.

Kish, G.B., Netterberg, E.E. and Leahy, L. (1973), Stimulus-seeking and conservatism, *Journal of Clinical Psychology*, 29, 17–20.

Larr, M. and Zea, R.L. (1977), Moral judgement and liberal-conservative attitudes, *Psychological Reports*, 40, 627–629.

Levi, S. and Guttman, A. (1976), *Values and Attitudes of Israeli Youth*, Jerusalem, Institute for Applied Social Research. (Hebrew)

Lichtenstein, A. (1983), The ideology of hesder, *Alon Shevut*, 100, 9–22. (Hebrew)

Loubser, J.J. (1968), Calvinism, equality and inclusion: the case of Afrikaner Calvinism, in S. Eisenstadt (ed.), *The Protestant Ethic and Modernisation: a comparative view*, pp. 367–383, New York, Basic Books.

Ministry of Education and Culture (1973), *Curriculum for Talmud and Oral Law*, Jerusalem, Religious Education Authority. (Hebrew)

Ministry of Education and Culture (1985), *High School Biblical Studies Curriculum*, Jerusalem, Ma'alot Publishing Company. (Hebrew)

Ministry of Education and Culture (1986), *Jewish Philosophy for High Schools: an elective curriculum*, Jerusalem, Religious Education Authority. (Hebrew)

Ministry of Education and Culture (1989), *Principles of Policy for State Religious Education*, Jerusalem, Religious Education Authority. (Hebrew)

Morse, S.J. and Orpen, C. (1975), *Contemporary South Africa: social-psychological perspectives*, Johannesburg, Juta and Company.

Orpen, C. (1970), Authoritarianism in an 'authoritarian' culture: the case of Afrikaans speaking South Africa, *Journal of Social Psychology*, 81, 119–120.

Pedley, R. (1977), *Towards the Comprehensive University*, London, Macmillan Press.

Ray, J.J. and Wilson, R.S. (1976), Social conservatism in Australia, *Australian and New Zealand Journal of Sociology*, 12, 3, 254–257.

Ron, A. (1973), Philosophical principles of state religious education, in H. Ormian (ed.), *Education in Israel*, Jerusalem, Ministry of Education and Culture. (Hebrew)

Rushton, J. (1976), The education of the teacher, in J.D. Turner and J. Rushton (eds), *Education for the Professions*, Manchester, Manchester University Press.

Sidanius, J. (1977), Cognitive functioning and socio-politico ideology revisited, *Report of the Department of Psychology*, University of Stockholm.

Thomas, D.R. (1975), Conservatism and premarital sexual experience, *British Journal of Social and Clinical Psychology*, 14, 2, 195–196.

Urbach, E.E. (1986), On Judaism and education, in M. Bar-lev (ed.), *Religious Education in Israeli Society*, Jerusalem, Hebrew University. (Hebrew)

Volbe, S. (1986), The modern theological academy (yeshiva), in M. Bar-Lev (ed.), *Religious Education in Israeli Society*, Jerusalem, Hebrew University. (Hebrew)

Weller, L., Levinbok, S., Maimon, R. and Shaham, A. (1975), Religiosity and authoritarianism, *Journal of Social Psychology*, 95, 1, 11–18.

Wilson, G.D. (1973), The factor structure of the C-Scale, in G.D. Wilson (ed.), *The Psychology of Conservatism*, pp. 71–92, New York, Academic Press.

Wilson, G.D. and Lee, H.S. (1974), Social attitude patterns in Korea, *Journal of Social Psychology*, 94, 1, 27–30.

Wilson, G.D. and Patterson, J.R. (1968), A new measure of conservatism, *British Journal of Social and Clinical Psychology*, 8, 264–269.

Wilson, G.D. and Patterson, J.R. (1970), *The Conservatism Scale*, Windsor, NFER Publishing Co.

Wilson, G.D. and Schutte, P. (1973), The structure of social attitudes in South Africa, *Journal of Social Psychology*, 90, 323–324.

Wolff, R.P. (1972), *The Ideal of the University*, Boston, Beacon Press.

Yogel, Y. (1971), The way of the Midrashia, *Niv Hamidrashia*, 137–146. (Hebrew)

26

The relationship between religious education and values

Avraham Leslau and Mordechai Bar-Lev

Summary

Two samples of final year students in Israel, one from state religious schools and the other from state non-religious schools, completed Schwartz' values questionnaire, rating 56 specific values on a nine point scale. After controlling for individual differences in the students' self-reported levels of religiosity, the data demonstrate that students educated in religious schools place greater emphasis on the values of tradition and universalism, while students educated in non-religious schools place greater emphasis on values of hedonism, achievement, self-direction and security.

Introduction

Every religious community attempts to transmit its heritage to the younger generation, including faith, rituals, and the community's world view, life style and values. Educators, philosophers and social scientists have long debated whether schools can or should transmit values. But this issue is not controversial in religious education, where the aim extends beyond merely communicating knowledge about religion, to the socialisation of pupils in terms of commitment to faith, acceptance of religious rules of behaviour, and adoption of the world view of their religion. This kind of religious education may play an important role in the transmission of the religious ethos (Greer, 1983).

The purpose of this study is to reveal the relationship between Jewish religious education in Israel and its pupils' value systems. The relationship between values and religiosity has been investigated by a number of scholars, including Rokeach (1973), Batson and Ventis (1982), Levy (1986), Sohlberg (1986) and Schwartz and Huismans (1996). Our study comprises two unique features: it emphasises the relationship between religious education (not religiosity) and an entire system of values (rather than a single value). Religious educational institutions serve pupils with varying degrees of religious commitment. We are particularly interested in whether the influence of religious education on pupils' value systems is dependent upon their level of commitment. Thus, we studied the value systems of pupils educated in religious and non-religious educational institutions while controlling for their religiosity.

Values and value systems

Before examining the relationship between value systems and religious education, we must be clear about what we intend by the terms 'values' and 'value systems'. Following the conceptual framework of Rokeach (1973) and Schwartz (1992), we define values as concepts and beliefs pertaining to desirable end states or behaviours, which transcend specific situations, guide the selection or evaluation of behaviour and events, and are ordered by relative importance within each individual. This hierarchical ordering transforms individual values into a value system connecting them together. Schwartz's topology of values is universally understood because these values represent 'three universal requirements of human existence to which all individuals and societies must be responsive: needs of individuals as biological organisms, requisites of coordinate social interaction, and survival and welfare needs of groups' (Schwartz, 1992). Single values are categorised according to ten value types, each of which is characterised by unique motivational goals.

For *self-direction*, the motivational goals are independent thought and action, and the need for control and mastery. For *stimulation*, the motivational goals are excitement, novelty and challenge. *Hedonism* is motivated by pleasure or sensuous gratification. For *achievement*, the motivational goal is personal success through the demonstration of competence as judged by social standards. *Power* is motivated by the attainment of social status and prestige, and the control and domination of people and resources. People who value *security* are motivated by safety, harmony, and stability in society, in relationships, and within themselves. *Conformity* demands the restraining of actions, inclinations and impulses likely to upset or harm others and violate social expectations or norms. For *tradition*, the motivating goal is acceptance of religious and cultural customs and ideas. *Benevolence* is motivated by concern for the welfare of familiar and frequently-encountered individuals. Finally, *universalism* is motivated by understanding, appreciation, tolerance and protection for the welfare of all people and for nature.

The value type *self-direction* includes the single values of creativity, freedom, independence, curiosity, choosing own goals, and self-respect. The value type *stimulation* includes the single values of daring, a varied life, and an exciting life. The value type *hedonism* includes the single values of pleasure, and enjoying life. The value type *achievement* includes the single values of success, ability, and ambition. The value type *power* includes the single values of social power, authority, wealth, preserving my public image, and social recognition. The value type *security* includes the single values of national security, family security, social order, health, cleanness, sense of belonging, and reciprocation of favours. The value type *conformity* includes obedience, politeness, and honouring parents and elders. The value type *tradition* includes the single values of respect for tradition, devoutness, accepting my portion in life, humility, and moderation. The value type *benevolence* includes the single values of helpfulness, responsibility, forgiveness, and honesty. The value type *universalism* includes the single values of broad-mindedness, wisdom, social justice, equality, a world at peace, a world of beauty, unity with nature, and protecting the environment.

Beyond simply grouping the values around ten motivational types, Schwartz devised a dynamic structure of value relationships, calculating the compatibility and conflict of values and their motivational types. To formulate this structure, Schwartz constructed two hypotheses, namely that certain value types could be grouped into pairs, the simultaneous pursuit of which was mutually compatible, and that actions taken in pursuit of each pair would be in conflict with the pursuit of any other pair.

Then Schwartz proceeded to examine his empirical results to determine which value types were compatible with one another, and which pairs were in conflict. Schwartz' results can be summarised in a structure composed of four higher-order value types forming two basic, bi-polar conceptual dimensions. In the first dimension, stimulation and self-direction stand opposite security, conformity and tradition. Schwartz superimposed the label 'openness to change versus conservatism' on this dimension. The second dimension positions power, achievement and hedonism opposite universalism and benevolence; this dimension Schwartz labels 'self-transcendence versus self-enhancement'.

Thus, we begin our study with a list of value types, which are aligned in opposing groups of self-transcendence versus self-enhancement, and openness to change versus conservatism. Our aim is to assess the impact of religious education on pupils' values based on specific value types, and also in light of Schwartz' two-dimensional structure.

Religious education and values

An important goal of Jewish religious education is to transmit the value system of Jewish religious heritage to the new generation. The term 'Jewish religious heritage' is itself problematic, because different groups do not agree on its scope or contents. However, there is sufficient consensus as to some common denominator differentiating between religious and non-religious Jews. We derive our working notion of Jewish religious heritage from what is known as the Modern Orthodox stream, a group controlling the religious state educational system which supervises about 20% of the state-sponsored Jewish secondary education in Israel. Its schools are religious in nature: the education staff is religious as is the content of the curriculum and the inherent values and life-style presented.

Within the religious division of the public schools, it is taken for granted that Jewish religious values should be taught. In our analysis of what pupils are absorbing from religious instruction, we encountered a basic definitional problem. Not all of the values taught can be categorised easily within Schwartz' value system, largely because the system comprises values with very specific and detailed content. Values are transmitted both directly and indirectly within the framework of formal religious education. We can analyse the written curriculum, and the value content of the educational or religious rules of the schools; but without empirical studies we cannot measure the influence on the value system of pupils, of their educational activity as a whole. In our discussion we therefore combine theoretical and empirical considerations in predicting the principal trends.

We hypothesise that, in general, modern Orthodoxy would emphasise the values which form the dimensions of self-transcendence and conservatism, and we would expect self-enhancement and openness toward change to receive little emphasis. According to Schwartz, self-transcendence comprehends the value types of universalism and benevolence, and conservatism comprehends security, conformity and tradition. We base our hypothesis on the following considerations, which we present under the heading of each value type.

First, we consider *tradition*. Jewish Orthodoxy is committed to the tradition of the bible and the commandments derived therefrom and from the Talmud. Practices are based on traditional interpretations of these texts, with changes occurring very slowly, and new interpretations strictly anchored in traditional writings. It is true that the Modern Orthodox movement aims to integrate modernity into the traditional Jewish world, but the scope of this integration is limited to those aspects of the modern world which can be legitimised by the Jewish tradition. We may thus safely hypothesise that pupils in religious schools will place tradition higher in their system of values than would their counterparts in the non-religious schools.

Second, we consider *conformity, hedonism and stimulation*. Traditional Judaism prescribes a number of rituals which a person must perform, on a daily, weekly or yearly basis. Quotidian prescriptions also include restrictions on the performance of a range of activities, from the most intimate and personal, to family and group activities. This socialisation into a very disciplined lifestyle seems compatible with conformity, and in conflict with hedonism and stimulation. Sohlberg (1986) concludes that non-religious students attach more importance to materialistic values than their religious counterparts. Levy and Guttman (1976) and Maslovaty and Dor-Shav (1989) found that non-religious pupils place more importance on enjoying 'the good life' and excitement than do religious pupils. Gombo and Schwartz (1989) conclude that religious female students place greater importance on the values of restriction and conformity than do their non-religious counterparts, whereas enjoyment and a comfortable life were more important to the latter.

Third, we consider *benevolence and universalism*. Benevolence involves concern for the welfare of one's closed group; by contrast, universalism addresses the welfare of all people and nature. The Jewish 'commandments between man and man' demand that one be helpful, honest, forgiving, loyal and responsible, which are all values belonging to the motivational type of benevolence. Although these values also appertain to the socialist ideology which once dominated the non-religious educational system in Israel, they seem to be less emphasised in these schools. Insofar as universalism is concerned, there is some lack of consensus on this issue. However, it is fair to say that in general, Orthodox Jews in Israel do not consider the welfare of Jews and non-Jews to be of equal importance (Liebman and Cohen, 1990), and this attitude is perpetuated in religious schools. Gombo and Schwartz (1989) found that religious students valued forgiveness, helpfulness and honesty, but were less concerned about equality and world peace. Similar results were found by Maslovaty and Dor-Shav (1989), by Sohlberg (1986) and by Zuckerman-Bareli (1975).

Fourth, we consider *self-direction*. The Modern Orthodox stream is highly dogmatic in its world view, allowing some degree of independent thought, choice of activity, creativity and exploration, but restricting these qualities within the boundaries of religious tradition. Self-direction is thus of limited depth and ambivalent importance.

Fifth, we consider *achievement*. This value type has two facets, one tending toward material achievement, the other toward intellectual achievement. Research shows that pupils in religious schools value learning for intellectual reasons more highly than do pupils from non-religious schools; however, no differences were found between the two educational groups with regard to occupational and economic achievement (Zuckerman-Bareli, 1975; Maslovaty and Dor-Shav, 1993). Gombo and Schwartz (1989) found that religious female students place more importance on a 'feeling of accomplishment' than non-religious female students, and place less emphasis on the instrumental values 'ambitious' and 'capable' than their non-religious counterparts. Our analysis of this motivational goal relies on the more materialistic, competitive definition of achievement. We would expect, despite the somewhat ambivalent empirical results described, that religious education would not encourage achievement to the extent this is fostered by non-religious education.

Sixth, we consider *security and power*. The theory of the structure of value types allows us to hypothesise that since security is associated more with conservatism, and power is connected more closely with self enhancement, security will be more favoured in religious schools than power. Some empirical studies confirm these assumptions. The values 'family security' and 'national security' were found to be more important among religious than among non-religious youths (Sohlberg, 1986; Herman, 1970; Gombo and Schwartz, 1989).

All the results presented above are based on studies which compare religious and non-religious youths, or pupils attending religious and non-religious schools; but they are not intended to evaluate the effects of religious schooling *per se*. To assess the overall influence of formal religious education, we posit three hypotheses that predict the value type preferences of pupils educated in religious schools, as compared with those who receive a non-religious education, while controlling for religiosity. First, we suggest that tradition and conformity will be higher priorities for pupils of religious schools than for pupils of non-religious schools. The reverse should be true for hedonism and stimulation. Second, we suggest that benevolence will receive somewhat higher priority among religious school pupils than among pupils of non-religious schools. The reverse will be true with regard to self-direction, power and achievement. Third, we suggest that no significant differences will be found between religious and non-religious school groups with regard to universalism and security.

Method

To test these hypotheses, we surveyed two groups of students, one completing the final year in the modern religious secondary school system, the other completing the same year in non-religious institutions. As the basis of our questionnaire, we presented these pupils with Schwartz' nine-point scale for rating 56 specific values as 'a guiding principle' in the life of the respondent. Schwartz' nine possible responses range from 'of supreme importance' (score 7) to 'very important' (6), 'important' (3), 'not important' (0) and 'opposed to my values' (−1).

In order to distinguish between the effect of religiosity and that of religious education, we tested the level of religiosity of the pupils by asking them to assess their religiosity on a six point scale: very religious, religious, fairly religious, not so religious, not religious and entirely non-religious. We could not obtain results for all levels of religiosity in both samples, since practically no 'very religious' or 'religious' pupils attend non-religious schools, and very few 'entirely non-religious' pupils attend religious secondary schools. Our endeavour to control for religiosity is based, therefore, on 1,442 out of 3,521 pupils in religious schools, and 1,177 out of 1,658 pupils in non-religious schools. The 3,521 represent the entire final year religious school population, while the 1,658 from the non-religious schools are a representative sample from within the state school system.

In addition to controlling for religiosity, we controlled for ethnicity (either Oriental or Ashkenazi origin). This was necessary because some scholars have suggested that Oriental Jews in Israel are generally more traditional than Ashkenazi Jews. Thus, by comparing Oriental-origin youths only with other Oriental-origin youths, and Ashkenazi with Ashkenazi, we eliminate ethnicity as a possible misleading factor. We also controlled for sex.

Results

First, we tested that the specific values were appropriately grouped into the ten theoretical value types by calculating the alpha coefficient for each type. The following results were obtained, supporting the reliability of each measure: power (0.64), achievement (0.66), hedonism (0.67), stimulation (0.65), self-direction (0.57), universalism (0.67), benevolence (0.66), tradition (0.64), conformity (0.60) and security (0.63). Then we calculated the score for each value type by averaging the scores for all of the specific values comprehended by them. In order to control for differences in individual valuation styles, we calculated a standardised score for each respondent by subtracting from each value type score the mean score for all of that individual's specific values. The results are based on this score.

Our research shows that without controlling for religiosity, some similarities and some differences exist between the value type priorities selected by religious and non-religious school pupils. Both groups value achievement and security very highly (ranks 1, 2 and 3), with differences only in the magnitude of the value type scores. Self-direction and universalism receive lower priority (ranks 4, 5 and 6), and both groups rank stimulation and power lowest (ranks 7, 8 and 9). We found significant differences where benevolence was concerned: religious school pupils hold this to be the most important value type (rank 1) while non-religious pupils place it on the middle of their priority scale (rank 5). A similar disparity exists in terms of conformity and tradition, where religious school pupils attribute moderate priority levels (ranks 4 and 7), and non-religious school pupils rank these values close to the bottom of the scale (8 and 10). The most extreme difference is found with regard to hedonism. Non-religious school pupils rank this highly (rank 3), and religious school pupils give it the lowest priority (rank 10).

It should be noted that, although a certain value type may be ranked similar by the two groups of pupils, its absolute scores may differ quite substantially. For example, if we do the rating according to the scores given by both groups of pupils, power ends up in the ninth rank; however, absolute scores show that religious school pupils assign much less importance to power than their non-relig-ious counterparts. In the following analysis, we present results based on absolute scores, not on ranked-order ones.

To compare value preferences between religious school pupils and pupils educated in non-religious schools, we subtracted the non-religious school pupils' standardised score from that of the religious school pupils. This subtraction was performed separately for each pair of corresponding groups, controlling for sex, ethnicity and religiosity, while investigating the net effects of religious education. The scores presented in tables 26.1 and 26.2 are the differences between the value type standardised scores of the religious school pupils and those of the non-religious school pupils. Whenever a value type received the same evaluation by both groups, the score in tables 26.1 and 26.2 is zero. If a given value type takes higher priority for religious school pupils than for non-religious school students, the score is positive; if a value type has lower priority for the religious school pupils than for the non-relig-ious school students, then the score is negative.

When we do not control for religiosity (see total in tables 26.1 and 26.2), then for eight out of the ten value types there are substantial differences in the priority rankings of religious school and non-religious school pupils. The highest positive difference is found in tradition, then conformity, then benevolence. The high-est negative difference is found in hedonism, then in stimulation, power, self-direction and achievement. Security and universalism present no substantial differences. We note that the fact that tradition shows the highest positive difference between the two groups does not necessarily mean that pupils from religious schools value tradition more highly than all other value types. (As a matter of fact they rate it very close to average.) What these absolute scores mean is that religious school pupils place greater importance on this value in comparison with the preference score given by the pupils from non-religious schools. Since, in general, the pupils of religious schools in Israel are more religious than those that are educated in non-religious schools, the results are quite compatible

Table 26.1
Religious school pupils' scores minus non-religious pupils'
scores, by ethnicity, and religiosity (males)

value types	not religious	not so religious	fairly religious	total
Orientals				
tradition	+0.38*	+0.27*	+0.34*	+0.91*
conformity	+0.10	+0.14	+0.40*	+0.41*
benevolence	+0.21*	+0.18	+0.44*	+0.36*
universalism	+0.29*	+0.33*	+0.26*	+0.23*
achievement	−0.24*	−0.24*	−0.38*	−0.27*
security	−0.39*	−0.27*	−0.03	−0.20*
power	−0.22*	−0.22*	−0.11	−0.48*
self-direction	−0.26*	−0.20*	−0.54*	−0.40*
stimulation	+0.17	+0.05	−0.11	−0.41*
hedonism	−0.28	−0.34*	−0.61*	−1.19*
Ashkenazis				
tradition	+0.52*	+0.20	+0.17	+1.57*
conformity	+0.23	+0.30	−0.36	+0.48*
benevolence	+0.21	+0.47*	+0.05	+0.60*
universalism	+0.26*	+0.16	+0.22	−0.02
achievement	−0.27*	−0.06	−0.08	−0.21*
security	−0.35*	−0.13	−0.09	−0.13*
power	−0.20	−0.44*	−0.28	−0.61*
self-direction	−0.22*	−0.21*	+0.01	−0.48*
stimulation	+0.06	−0.28	+0.19	−0.75*
hedonism	+0.21	−0.23	−0.47	−1.73*

Note: * $p < 0.05$

Table 26.2
Religious school pupils' scores minus non-religious pupils' scores, by ethnicity, and religiosity (females)

value types	not religious	not so religious	fairly religious	total
Orientals				
tradition	+0.28*	+0.24*	+0.17	+0.97*
conformity	+0.22*	−0.01	+0.15	+0.40*
benevolence	+0.05	−0.03	−0.03	+0.27*
universalism	−0.03*	+0.04*	+0.08	−0.01
achievement	−0.10	−0.06	−0.37*	−0.26*
security	−0.10	−0.18*	+0.02	−0.08*
power	+0.08	+0.00	+0.08	−0.26*
self-direction	−0.22*	−0.05	−0.12	−0.29*
stimulation	+0.25*	+0.23*	+0.06	−0.36*
hedonism	−0.15	−0.22	−0.88*	−1.07*
Ashkenazis				
tradition	+0.43*	+0.74*	+0.15	+1.62*
conformity	−0.09	−0.07	−0.13	+0.32*
benevolence	−0.03	−0.24	+0.25	+0.41*
universalism	−0.09	+0.29*	+0.21	−0.10*
achievement	+0.12	−0.50*	−0.61*	−0.31*
security	−0.19	−0.04	+0.35*	−0.04
power	+0.11	−0.34	+0.08	−0.47*
self-direction	+0.00	−0.10	−0.29	−0.42*
stimulation	+0.34	+0.10	+0.13	−0.57*
hedonism	−0.22	−0.70*	−0.31	−1.55*

Note: * $p < 0.05$

with what was found about the relationship between religiosity and value preferences (Schwartz and Huismans, 1996).

The primary concern of the present study, however, is to measure the effect of religious education while controlling for religiosity. For this purpose, we present in tables 26.1 and 26.2 the score differential between religious and non-religious school students for each level of religiosity separately. Although we present in the table t-test results for statistical significance, we give more weight to the consistency of the trends revealed by the scores. The table shows that for each level of religiosity, pupils from religious schools place higher priority on tradition and universalism, and less on hedonism, achievement, self-direction and security, than pupils in non-religious schools. Among male pupils in religious schools, higher priority is given to conformity and benevolence, while the same group gives less priority to power than their non-religious school counterparts. The results for stimulation are ambivalent, but there does seem to be a trend toward religious school pupils, especially females, giving higher priority to this value type than pupils from non-religious schools.

The overall results for the population we studied are fully compatible with our predictions. However, we encounter some discrepancies when we control for religiosity. First, pupils from religious schools value conformity and benevolence less than expected, and place higher priority on universalism than we anticipated. Second, we predicted that religious school pupils would place relatively low priority on stimulation, and our results show that, to the contrary, most rank this value even higher than pupils from non-religious schools.

Discussion

In general, we may say that studying in state religious schools in Israel has an effect on the value preferences of the pupils, even when we control for religiosity. Comparing even the less religious pupils (those who define themselves as 'not religious', 'not so religious', and 'fairly religious'), we see that pupils educated in religious schools place higher priority on tradition and universalism, and non-religious school pupils place greater emphasis on hedonism, achievement, self-direction and security.

Some of these results deserve further elaboration. Stimulation is the most striking example of the failure of religious education to bear influence: it is clearly contrary to the aim of the religious school system, and yet religious school pupils place much greater emphasis on this than do non-religious school pupils. By contrast, religious education does seem to have an effect with regard to hedonism. We find an explanation for the uneven influence of religious education, when we examine more closely the groups affected by the disparity. Stimulation is preferred largely by the least religious among religious school pupils, that is to say youths who, at least in part, reject the influence of their education. They tend to be more daring and sensation-seeking than their counterparts from the non-religious schools, where the majority belongs to the secular mainstream. Hedonism, however, is so strongly opposed by religious education that its repression is evidenced even in the least religious pupils.

Now let us examine the value types we anticipated would have highest priority among religious school pupils. Where conformity is concerned, males in religious schools placed slightly more emphasis on this than their male counterparts in non-religious schools, but among female groups there was no significant difference. At first glance, this difference is less dramatic than we might have expected. Upon reflection, however, we explain the near-parity by the fact that the religious school groups which have parallels in the non-religious school system tend to be the least religious of their religious school peers. They have thus already expressed strong non-conformist tendencies, and the fact that conformity is not much more important for them than for students in non-religious institutions is not surprising.

Benevolence is the most perplexing value type. It is highly valued among religious school students generally, and given a somewhat lower priority by pupils in non-religious schools. But our results show that religious education has significant influence only on male pupils' rating of benevolence. These results may be partially explained by the fact that females from non-religious schools place higher priority on benevolence than do males, whereas among the pupils from religious schools this kind of sex differential is not found. Thus, the difference between the two male groups is significant, while the one between the female groups is equivocal.

Universalism also produced unexpected results. We predicted that no differences would be found between pupils of religious and non-religious schools, and this prediction was confirmed for the entire investigated population. However, the least religious pupils in the religious schools value universalism more highly than their counterparts in non-religious schools. Firm conclusions may be drawn only upon further, comprehensive investigation; we may speculate, meanwhile, that some of the less religious pupils have developed a less parochial world-view, which leads them to be more open to universal issues.

It was surprising to find that religious education generally has no influence on priority ranking of security. This was unexpected, since security is composed of values such as 'national security', 'family security' and 'social order', bringing it close to a traditional conformist world-view. Had we encountered similar priority in all groups, this finding would be compatible with the preoccupation about national security problems which plagues all Israelis, and the centrality of family life characteristic of even the most modern sector (Peres and Katz, 1991). But we cannot explain why pupils in non-religious schools place higher priority on this value type than their religious school counterparts.

In summary, we may state that our results were largely as expected. Even the less religious pupils educated in religious schools prefer self-transcendence over self-enhancement, and conservatism over openness to change. Whether this value system will persist throughout their adulthood is a matter for further investigation. Moreover, this study was done within a particular community, Jews living in Israel. Schwartz and Huismans (1996) demonstrated that religious people belonging to different religions within the Judeo-Christian culture share similar value system preferences. It might be interesting to investigate the influence of religious schooling on the value system of pupils in other Jewish communities, and among other Judeo-Christian cultures.

Acknowledgement

This research was supported in part by the Schnitzer Foundation for Research on the Israeli Economy and Society.

References

Batson, C.D. and Ventis, W.L. (1982), *The Religious Experience: a social psychological perspective*, New York, Oxford University Press.

Gombo, R. and Schwartz, S. (1989), Value system of young ultra-orthodox females in comparative perspective, *Megamot*, 32, 332–360. (Hebrew)

Greer, J.E. (1983), Religious and moral education: an exploration of some relevant issues, *Journal of Moral Education*, 12, 92–99.

Herman, S. (1970), *Israelis and Jews: the continuity of an identity*, New York, Random House.

Levy, S. (1986), *The Structure of Social Values*, Jerusalem, The Israel Institute of Applied Social Research.

Levy, S. and Guttman, L. (1976), *Values and Attitudes of Israel High School Youth, Second Research Project*, Jerusalem, The Israel Institute of Applied Social Research. (Hebrew)

Liebman, C.S. and Cohen, S.M. (1990), *Two Worlds of Judaism*, New Haven, Yale University Press.

Maslovaty, N. and Dor-Shav, Z. (1989), The relationship between religiosity and value system among high school youth, *B'sde Hemed*, 32, 90–96. (Hebrew)

Maslovaty, N. and Dor-Shav, Z. (1993), Differences in values as guiding principle among pupils from religious and non-religious comprehensive schools, *B'sde Hemed*, 36, 51–65. (Hebrew)

Rokeach, M. (1973), *The Nature of Human Values*, New York, Free Press.

Peres, Y. and Katz, R. (1991), The family in Israel: change and continuity, in L. Shamgar-Handelman and R. Bar-Yosef (eds), *Families in Israel*, pp. 9–32, Jerusalem, Academon.

Schwartz, S.H. (1992), Universals in the content and structure of values: theoretical and empirical tests in 20 countries, in M. Zanna (ed.), *Advances in Experimental Social Psychology*, vol. 25, pp. 1–65, Orlando, Florida, Academic Press.

Schwartz, S.H. and Huismans, S. (1996), Value priorities and religiosity in four western religions, *Social Psychology Quarterly*, in press.

Sohlberg, S.C. (1986), Similarity and dissimilarity in value patterns of Israel kibbutz and city adolescents, *International Journal of Psychology*, 21, 189–202.

Zuckerman-Bareli, C. (1975), Religion and its connection to consensus and polarisation of opinions among Israeli youth, *Megamot*, 22, 62–80. (Hebrew)

27

Religious schooling and secularisation in Israel

Mordechai Bar-Lev and Avraham Leslau

Summary

In this article, we will present research findings regarding factors for leaving religion, as were gathered in 1990 and 1991 from male and female youths (eighteen years of age) and young adults (thirty years of age) from state-religious Jewish educational institutions in all geographical regions and in all types of high schools (secondary/grammar, vocational/technical, yeshiva, kibbutz and boarding schools) in Israel. The data were collected via structured questionnaires filled out by 5,345 grade twelve graduates (2,406 males and 2,939 females) and a national sample of 1,344 thirty year olds who had studied in state-religious educational institutions (626 males and 718 females).

Introduction

Collective secularisation has been defined as a pattern of:

> disengagement of society from religion. Society separates itself
> from the religious understanding which has previously informed it,
> in order to constitute itself an autonomous reality and consequently
> to limit religion to the sphere of private life. The culmination of
> this kind of secularisation would be a religion of a purely inward
> character, influencing neither institutions nor corporate action, and
> a society in which religion made no appearance outside the sphere
> of the religious group (Shiner, 1967, p. 212).

In addition to collective secularisation, there is also the concept
of individual secularisation, which may be defined as a person's
departure from commitments and loyalties to religious behavioural

patterns, religious beliefs, religious values and legitimate religious institutions.

Individual leaving of the Jewish religion is unique, as compared with the leaving of other religions. The departure is, on the one hand, not necessarily the departure from Judaism and Jewish links altogether. Yet, on the other hand, it is possible to find, among those members who remain loyal and committed to the Jewish religion, internal signs of leaving, even if there are no external signs of departure whatsoever. Indeed, the religious community takes notice of the internal secularity of a religious person and pushes him or her out to external secularity, whether by sanctions or via social stigma (Brinkerhoff and Burk, 1980).

This article does not deal with the process of departure, nor the passage of the leaver to the secular world, but rather focuses entirely on the causes for leaving. To be more specific, this article deals with the different factors in individuals' external departure from the Jewish religion, as reflected among youth and young Jews in Israel in the modern era.

In the theoretical literature, factors for leaving religion have been addressed for approximately 25 years. However, until recently, only two researchers have attempted to suggest a typological framework of factors. The first researcher was Mauss (1969), who developed three clusters of factors: intellectual, interpersonal and emotional. The second researcher was Roozen (1980), who attempted to concentrate the principle factors into five categories: arrival at maturation, personal and contextual, disagreements within the church, religious rituals without relevance, and other reasons. Both researchers suggested universal or Christian typologies for factors regarding the departure from religion.

Recently, a third typological framework that is both universal and particular to Judaism has been developed in Israel (Bar-Lev, Leslau and Neeman, 1996). In this framework, there are six clusters of factors for leaving: intellectual and cognitive, emotional, social and cultural, familial, pedagogical and educational, material and hedonistic.

Method

During 1990 and 1991 structured questionnaires were completed by two samples. The first sample comprised 5,345 twelfth grade graduates (2,406 males and 2,939 females) from state-religious[1] Jewish educational institutions in all geographical regions and in all types of high schools (secondary/grammar, vocational/technical, yeshiva, kibbutz and boarding schools) in Israel. The second sample comprised 1,344 thirty year olds who had studied in state-religious educational institutions (626 males and 718 females).

In the questionnaire each respondent was asked to assess thirteen factors for leaving religion from two perspectives. The first perspective invited all the respondents to think generally, that is, why they think people stop observing ritual practices. The second perspective invited the respondents who defined themselves as not religious to think personally, that is, why they stopped observing ritual practices. Respondents were asked to rate each of the thirteen factors according to its importance (from very much to very little on a five point scale) and then to list the three most important factors from the list of all of the thirteen factors. We will present the question here as it was presented to the respondents.

> There are young people who received a religious education, but have ceased to lead a religious way of life. Listed below are a number of reasons which explain such behaviour. Specify the degree of influence of the following reasons which, in your opinion, contribute to young people giving up a religious way of life.
>
> •   social contacts with secular friends
> •   secular spouse/girlfriend/boyfriend
> •   the negative image of religious people
> •   'since it is difficult to observe all the religious commandments, we will observe none'
> •   sexual restrictions
> •   limited leisure activities
> •   doubts about the existence of God
> •   doubts about the divine origin of the bible
> •   religious law is incompatible with the developments of the modern world
> •   temptation to give up religious practices for career advancement or social status
> •   rebellion against the traditions and values of the home
> •   reasons of convenience
> •   'it is sufficient to feel religious, and there is no need for ritual practices'

Results

Though the main focus of this article deals with factors for leaving religion, we wish first to present the subjective definitions of the respondents' religiosity. In table 27.1, the self-defined religiosity of all respondents is presented, according to age and sex. According to the table, we can determine that the largest group is that which defines itself as religious. Those defining themselves as non-religious are a minority, between one fifth (22%) of the adult males to less than one tenth (8%) among the young females. In addition, there is also a fairly large group (39% of the young males and 26% of the adult males) who, while they do not define themselves as loyal to religion, clearly do not define themselves as non-religious. Focusing on the two sexes, we learn that the females usually define themselves as more religious than the males.

Table 27.1
Religiosity of respondents according to age and sex

sex/age	very religious %	religious %	fairly religious %	not so religious %	not religious %	very non-religious %
male youths	8	41	21	18	9	3
female youths	8	50	19	16	7	1
male adults	15	37	11	15	18	4
female adults	9	41	17	17	13	3

From this point on, we will deal with the respondent's assessment of the thirteen factors for leaving religion. Table 27.2 presents the mean values ascribed to each of the thirteen factors for leaving religion by the adult and youth samples separately. From these mean values, we learn that the social factors are perceived of (generally) as the most influential, both among adults and among youths. As such, the convenience factor is perceived by both the youths and adults as the most influential one, immediately after the social factors. Factors such as sexual restrictions and limited leisure activities were seen as much less influential. On the other hand, the intellectual-theological factors were perceived of as having a lesser influence, and an intellectual factor such as 'perception of the religious law as being incompatible with the developments of the modern world' was ranked below average by the adult graduates (also by the young graduates, where it appears in seventh place out of thirteen factors).

Table 27.2
Evaluation of the thirteen factors for leaving religion
by adults and youths

factors for leaving religion	adults		youths	
	mean	sd	mean	sd
secular partners	4.03	1.07	3.91	1.07
convenience	3.72	1.06	3.76	1.12
secular contacts	3.69	1.13	3.90	1.05
sexual restrictions	3.16	1.16	3.53	1.18
leisure activities	3.09	1.14	3.38	1.18
ritual practices	3.05	1.19	3.18	1.24
law outdated	2.95	1.21	3.17	1.23
career	2.68	1.18	3.16	1.19
all or nothing	2.64	1.16	3.07	1.22
rebellious behaviour	2.62	1.19	3.07	1.24
convenience	2.31	1.13	2.77	1.19
divine law	2.27	1.26	2.91	1.38
existence of God	2.24	1.29	2.93	1.44

It is interesting to note that 'the negative image of religious people' appears as a factor with very little influence among youths and adults (among youths it appears last in the ranking, although from a practical perspective, its relative value among adults is much lower). In addition, factors such as career advancement or rebellion against values and traditions in the parents' house rank low in terms of their influence, especially among the adults.

Table 27.3 examines the proportions of male adults who assess each of the thirteen factors as the *most important reason* for young people leaving religion, according to the respondents' personal level of religiosity. Table 27.4 examines the proportions of adult males defining themselves as not religious who assess each of the thirteen factors as the *most important reason* for leaving religion themselves, according to the respondents' personal level of religiosity.

Table 27.3
Percentages of adult males assessing each factor as the most important reason for young people leaving religion, by level of religiosity

factors for leaving religion	very religious %	religious %	fairly religious %	not so religious %	not religious %	very non-religious %
secular contacts	26	16	14	16	18	9
secular partners	15	21	18	16	10	14
religious image	0	1	2	0	6	4
all or nothing	4	2	2	1	3	0
sexual restrictions	10	3	5	1	2	0
leisure activities	3	2	5	1	0	0
existence of God	6	7	3	3	11	27
divine law	4	5	2	4	6	0
law outdated	3	5	10	16	8	18
career	1	4	2	1	2	0
rebellious behaviour	1	2	0	3	4	9
convenience	21	26	29	27	20	9
ritual practices	4	4	10	12	8	9
N	89	209	62	77	96	22

From tables 27.3 and 27.4, three principal trends are clear. First, for certain factors there is no influence or a very marginal influence. There is no influence at all for the 'sexual' and 'leisure' factors, and perhaps this reflects internal and external secular expression of

Table 27.4
Percentages of adult males who define themselves
as not religious assessing each factor as the most
important reason for leaving religion themselves,
by level of religiosity

factors for leaving religion	not so religious %	not religious %	very non-religious %
secular contacts	20	13	9
secular partners	7	10	9
religious image	3	3	0
all or nothing	5	10	0
sexual restrictions	3	0	0
leisure activities	2	1	0
existence of God	7	13	32
divine law	7	9	0
law outdated	7	9	18
career	0	0	0
rebellious behaviour	2	2	9
convenience	25	27	14
ritual practices	12	3	9
N	59	92	22

these areas. Perhaps this also expresses their compartmentalisation
as seemingly legitimate, permitted areas. Similarly, there is no
influence whatsoever of the 'career' factor. It appears that in the
modern religious community, no conflict is seen between the
integration of a career or social status with religious commitment.
This expresses an almost revolutionary social change as compared
with the current situation in traditional, religious Israeli society
and as compared with the situation in previous modern religious
generations. This trend also does not change regarding responses
to the second or third factors in terms of the importance of their
influence.

The 'negative image' factor also has a very marginal influence, particularly for those who are loyal to the religious way of life, but also for those who have abandoned it. This marginal influence of the 'image' factor can be attributed to the prominent change in the collective and personal self-assurance of the modern religious community. This appears to be a result of the increasing integration in the army, in higher education, in occupations and Israeli culture. The factor 'rebellion against traditions and values in the parents' home' was perceived also as a factor with marginal influence, except to a certain degree among the adults who defined themselves as very non-religious. Perhaps it is possible to attribute this to the new type of relationship among the generations, characterised by tolerance and openness to differences in life-style and views, even in the religious realm.

Second, other factors have a considerable effect or even a very considerable one. The most prominent factor, above all others in its influence (including the responses regarding the second and third factors in level of importance) is the 'convenience' factor. Another factor that is prominent in its influence is the social factor, that of 'partner or boyfriend/girlfriend who is not religious' and especially the factor 'contact with friends who do not perform ritual practices'.

Third, there are considerable differences in the perception of the influence of factors between religious and non-religious respondents. This is true also between the non-religious respondents — those who define themselves as 'very non-religious' and those who call themselves 'not-religious' — and all other defined groups. These differences are considerable for two types of factors: the intellectual factor and the convenience factor. Among the very non-religious, the intellectual factors of 'doubts regarding the existence of God' and of 'the perception of religious law as being incompatible with the developments of the modern world' are very prominent as influencing factors (also as responses to the second or third factor in terms of importance of influence). In the responses of the religious respondents, this factor becomes secondary or even marginal in its influence. To a lesser degree, we can point to the convenience factor as a factor that is prominent in its influence more for religious and intermediate groups than for the non-religious.

These differences are even more prominent among those who define themselves as 'very non-religious' and all the rest of the respondents, in both their higher ranking in the influence of the intellectual factor (and the factor 'rebellion against the traditions and values in the parents' home') and in the significantly lower ranking of the convenience factor or the influence of the social factor. Perhaps there is a desire, or at least a hidden desire, of those who define themselves as loyal to the religious way of life, to call those who have left this way of life 'people who are looking for convenience' or 'people influenced by a secular society'. On the other hand, there appears to be a desire of the leavers to perceive themselves, or perhaps present themselves, as motivated by factors and dilemmas in the spiritual-intellectual realm.

Table 27.5 examines the proportions of female adults who assess each of the thirteen factors as the *most important reason* for young people leaving religion. Table 27.6 examines the proportions of adult females defining themselves as not religious who assess each of the thirteen factors as the *most important reason* for leaving religion themselves.

The most prominent feature here is the similarity between the responses of the females and those of the males, in both directions and general trends, as well as on most of the items. No substantial differences were found in the perceptions of the influence of factors such as career or leisure, and not even on factors such as 'difficulty with self-restraint in male-female relationships'.

Despite this, certain differences were found between females and males, as the females, more than the males, perceive the social factor of 'partner or boy/girlfriend who is not religious' as an influential factor. As such, the females perceive, more so than the males, 'rebellion against traditions and values of the parents' home' as a more influential cause for not keeping the ritual practices. On the other hand, the females perceive the convenience factor as a much less influential factor than do the males.

At any rate, it appears to us that the dominant trend is the similarity rather than the differences between the responses of the male and female respondents. This similarity testifies, it appears, to similarity in religious socialisation processes of males and females, and perhaps even to significant internalisation of the value of equality, in the religious realm, between males and females.

Table 27.7 examines the proportions of male youths who assess each of the thirteen factors as the *most important reason* for young people leaving religion. Table 27.8 examines the proportions of male youths defining themselves as not religious who assess each of the thirteen factors as the *most important reason* for leaving religion themselves.

Table 27.5
Percentages of adult females assessing each factor as the
most important reason for young people leaving religion,
by level of religiosity

factors for leaving religion	very religious %	religious %	fairly religious %	not so religious %	not religious %	very non-religious %
secular contacts	29	19	13	16	10	6
secular partners	20	29	30	28	24	11
religious image	0	2	2	2	1	0
all or nothing	0	3	3	3	5	0
sexual restrictions	2	2	5	1	0	0
leisure activities	2	1	1	4	4	0
existence of God	7	7	8	7	11	28
divine law	0	0	1	1	3	6
law outdated	5	9	8	7	10	17
career	4	3	1	1	3	0
rebellious behaviour	12	4	5	2	0	17
convenience	14	14	12	17	15	6
ritual practices	5	4	10	10	13	11
N	56	244	94	94	78	18

Also among the young males, the social factor and the convenience factor stand out as the factors most influential to not performing the ritual practices. Similarly, among the young males there are differences between the religious respondents and the non-religious respondents, though these differences are smaller.

Table 27.6
Percentages of adult females who define themselves
as not religious assessing each factor as the most
important reason for leaving religion themselves,
by level of religiosity

factors for leaving religion	not so religious %	not religious %	very non-religious %
secular contacts	16	11	17
secular partners	43	29	6
religious image	1	1	0
all or nothing	5	6	6
sexual restrictions	0	1	0
leisure activities	3	1	0
existence of God	0	9	22
divine law	1	2	11
law outdated	7	9	17
career	0	0	0
rebellious behaviour	1	6	11
convenience	16	15	6
ritual practices	5	9	6
N	74	80	18

Nevertheless, something of a generation gap of twelve years between the adults and the youths can be found in the responses, especially in the change in emphases and their degrees regarding the different factors. A brief explanation is in order, regarding why the young respondents answered, as opposed to the older respondents, that 'difficulty with self-restraint in male-female relationships', 'since it is difficult to observe all the religious commandments, we will observe none' and 'contact and recreation with friends who do not perform ritual practices' are more influential factors. This appears to be due to the sexual impulses, and the romantic approach of the youth and their tendency towards intensive social activities.

Table 27.7
Percentages of male youths assessing each factor as the
most important reason for young people leaving religion,
by level of religiosity

factors for leaving religion	very religious %	religious %	fairly religious %	not so religious %	not religious %	very non-religious %
secular contacts	21	19	21	23	19	12
secular partners	11	11	8	9	11	9
religious image	1	2	3	5	2	5
all or nothing	12	6	7	7	8	12
sexual restrictions	5	8	8	5	5	5
leisure activities	2	4	4	6	4	5
existence of God	7	10	6	6	11	16
divine law	1	2	3	1	4	5
law outdated	6	4	6	4	3	5
career	2	3	4	2	1	5
rebellious behaviour	1	2	4	3	6	5
convenience	23	20	16	17	17	14
ritual practices	4	3	5	6	4	5
N	153	757	365	279	151	43

On the other hand, changes in internal secularisation, the increasing self-assurance of the religious community and its involvement in fields of science and technology, and an increase in the Israeli standard of living (including among the religious sector), have apparently brought about changes in trends in the opposite

Table 27.8
Percentages of male youths who define themselves
as not religious assessing each factor as the most
important reason for leaving religion themselves,
by level of religiosity

factors for leaving religion	not so religious %	not religious %	very non-religious %
secular contacts	23	17	19
secular partners	6	5	6
religious image	7	4	6
all or nothing	9	9	6
sexual restrictions	5	3	3
leisure activities	7	9	6
existence of God	7	12	17
divine law	1	8	11
law outdated	3	4	6
career	3	2	3
rebellious behaviour	4	3	6
convenience	17	17	14
ritual practices	7	3	0
N	195	148	36

direction. These changes have also brought about the fact that factors such as 'partner or boy/girlfriend who is not religious' are perceived by religious youths as a much less influential factor as compared with their adult cohorts, and that a factor such as 'the perception of religious law as being incompatible with the developments of the modern world' is not as relevant and, accordingly, is perceived by them as a less influential factor. The increase in standard of living and in the comfort level of the religious community have apparently led to a relative decrease in the perception of influence of the convenience factor.

Table 27.9
Percentages of female youths assessing each factor as the
most important reason for young people leaving religion,
by level of religiosity

factors for leaving religion	very religious %	religious %	fairly religious %	not so religious %	not religious %	very non-religious %
secular contacts	27	21	21	24	25	17
secular partners	19	12	9	12	9	8
religious image	1	2	2	2	2	0
all or nothing	3	4	6	4	7	4
sexual restrictions	4	4	6	4	3	0
leisure activities	1	2	3	3	6	0
existence of God	10	15	15	10	9	29
divine law	5	4	3	3	6	0
law outdated	7	6	4	4	5	8
career	3	2	3	4	0	4
rebellious behaviour	4	4	3	5	5	12
convenience	14	16	15	13	18	12
ritual practices	3	4	5	5	5	0
N	188	1081	371	295	148	23

Table 27.9 examines the proportions of female youths who assess
each of the thirteen factors as the *most important reason* for young people
leaving religion. Table 27.10 examines the proportions of female youths
defining themselves as not religious who assess each of the thirteen
factors as the *most important reason* for leaving religion themselves.

Table 27.10
Percentages of female youths who define themselves
as not religious assessing each factor as the most
important reason for leaving religion themselves,
by level of religiosity

factors for leaving religion	not so religious %	not religious %	very non-religious %
secular contacts	24	28	23
secular partners	11	9	11
religious image	5	3	0
all or nothing	5	7	4
sexual restrictions	2	4	0
leisure activities	7	2	4
existence of God	5	10	31
divine law	3	3	4
law outdated	3	4	0
career	3	0	0
rebellious behaviour	3	4	8
convenience	23	21	15
ritual practices	5	2	0
N	188	133	26

One particularly prominent finding among the female youths is the influence of the factor 'doubts regarding the existence of God' on not performing the ritual practices, and the gap (regarding this factor) between those who define themselves as very non-religious and all other groups. This finding fits in with the data on this factor among the adult females.

Also among the female youths, the social factor and particularly the factor of 'contact and recreation with friends who do not perform ritual practices' are prominent. In the factor 'rebellion against traditions and values of the parents' home', there is a considerable difference between those who define themselves as 'very non-religious' and all others. The 'rebellion' factor appears as a more influential factor among the female youths who define themselves as 'very non-religious' as compared with the male youths who define themselves thus. Young religious females are usually less rebellious than the males and are less inclined to abandon the religious way of life. However, among the female youths who define themselves as 'very non-religious', the rate of those who perceive this factor as influential is much greater and we should continue to investigate the motives behind this factor on the non-performance of ritual practices.

Attention must be paid to the marginality of the influence, especially on the personal level, of factors such as: 'it is sufficient to feel religious, and there is no need for ritual practices', 'the temptation to give up religious practices in favour of career/occupational advancement or social status', 'the perception of religious law as being incompatible with the developments of the modern world', 'difficulty with self-restraint in male-female relationships' and 'the negative image of the religious'.

Conclusion

Individual, external departure from the Jewish religion occurs in one quarter to one third of all graduates of state-religious education in Israel. These graduates participated in our study as self-defined groups of: very non-religious, not religious and not so religious.

In an overview of the empirical findings of adults and youth, both male and female, we find that there are two factors, according to the respondents themselves, which have a strong influence on their leaving: the social factor and the convenience factor.

On the other hand, for almost all of the other factors there is a very weak or marginal influence. This is true both for the intellectual factors (especially for males) and for factors such as career, negative image of religious people, rebellion against traditions and values of the parents' home, difficulty with sexual self-restraint and restricted leisure opportunities. This was found to be true on both a general level and a personal level.

In light of our empirical findings regarding the relative decrease in the perception of the influence of the convenience factor among youth, we must focus on social factors, in general, and in particular on the factor 'contact and recreation with friends who do not perform ritual practices'. The combined coping with all socialisation agents (family, school, peer group and religious institutions) along with the social factor, can influence the scope and depth of the external secularisation among state-religious graduates in Israel. The religious boarding schools (such as the Hesder Yeshiva, Yeshiva high-schools and Ulpanas) have been successful in creating a social environment that is meaningful to their students both during the period when they are studying and during short and long vacations. In addition, their success in combining activities for students simultaneously in informal religious educational agencies such as religious youth movements (Bar-Lev, 1991) reflects their lower rates of secularisation as compared with all other state-religious educational institutions (Leslau and Bar-Lev, 1994).

This success hints at concealed educational potential to religious educators in Israel and the world at large, for effective coping with the social causes for secularisation.

Notes

1. In Israel, more than one fifth of the student population studies in state-religious schools. Close to one tenth of the population studies in religious schools that do not officially belong to the state (independent education, Shas education) or are totally private institutions (yeshiva and 'exemption' institutions). See Bar-Lev (1991) pp. 101–111.

References

Bar-Lev, M. (1991), Tradition and innovation in Jewish religious education in Israel, in Z. Sobel and B. Beit-Hallahmi (eds), *Tradition, Innovation, Conflict: Jewishness and Judaism in contemporary Israel*, pp. 101–131, Albany, State University of New York Press.

Bar-Lev, M., Leslau, A. and Neieman, N. (1996), Particular factors of leaving religion in the Jewish Israeli society, in M. Bar-Lev and W. Shaffir (eds), *Leaving Religion and Religious Life: patterns and dynamics*, Greenwich, JAI Press, in press.

Brinkerhoff, M.B. and Burk, K.L. (1980), Disaffiliation: some notes on 'falling from the faith', *Sociological Analysis*, 41, 1, 41–54.

Leslau, A. and Bar-Lev, M. (1994), Religiosity among oriental youth in Israel, *Sociological Papers*, 3, 5, 1–57.

Mauss, A.L. (1969), Dimensions of religious defection, *Review of Religious Research*, 10, 128–135.

Roozen, D.A. (1980), Church dropouts: changing patterns of disengagement and re-entry, *Review of Religious Research*, 21, 427–450.

Shiner, L. (1967), The concept of secularisation in empirical research, *Journal for the Scientific Study of Religion*, 6, 207–220.

Contributors

The Revd Dr Jeff Astley is Director of the North of England Institute for Christian Education, Durham, and Honorary Lecturer in the Department of Theology and School of Education, University of Durham, England.

Dr James Arthur is Senior Lecturer in Education at Canterbury Christ Church College, Canterbury, England.

Professor Motti Bar-Lev is Professor at the School of Education, Bar-Ilan University, Israel.

Ms Linda Burton is Lecturer in religious education at the School of Education, University of Durham, England.

Dr William S. Campbell is Reader in Religious and Theological Studies and Director of the Centre for Beliefs and Values at Westhill College, Selly Oak, Birmingham, England.

Brother Michael Curran is school chaplain and Director of the De La Salle Community, Liverpool, England.

The Revd Thomas E. Evans is Senior Lecturer in Theology and Religious Studies at Trinity College, Carmarthen, Wales.

Dr Gabriel Faust-Siehl is Professor of Elementary Education at the University of Frankfurt/Main, Germany.

The Revd Professor Leslie J. Francis is D. J. James Professor of Pastoral Theology at Trinity College, Carmarthen, and University of Wales, Lampeter, and Director of the Centre for Theology and Education at Trinity College, Carmarthen, Wales.

The Revd Dr Peter Fulljames is Tutor at Crowther Hall, Selly Oak Colleges and Honorary Research Fellow at the School of Education, University of Birmingham, England.

Dr Simon Gaine studied theology at Worcester College and St John's College, Oxford, England.

The Revd Dr Harry M. Gibson is Parish Minister at The High Kirk, Dundee, Scotland, and Research Fellow in the Centre for Theology and Education at Trinity College, Carmarthen, Wales.

Dr David Hay is Director of the Children's Spirituality Project and Senior Lecturer in the Centre for the Study of Human Relations at the School of Education, University of Nottingham, England.

Professor Robert Jackson is Director of the Warwick Religions and Education Research Unit, in the Institute of Education, University of Warwick, England.

The Revd Susan H. Jones is Chaplain at the University of Wales, Swansea, and Research Fellow in the Centre for Theology and Education at Trinity College, Carmarthen, Wales.

Dr Yaacov J. Katz is Deputy Director and Head of Educational Studies, as well as Director of the Institute for Community Education and Research, at the School of Education, Bar-Ilan University, Israel.

The Revd Dr William K. Kay is Senior Research Fellow in the Centre for Theology and Education at Trinity College, Carmarthen, Wales.

Mr Bernd Krupka is Research Assistant in Religious Education at the Faculty of Protestant Theology, Department of Practical Theology, at the University of Tübingen, Germany.

Dr Avraham Leslau is Lecturer at the School of Education and Department of Criminology, Bar-Ilan University, Israel.

Mr Christopher A. Lewis is Lecturer in the Department of Psychology at the University of Ulster Magee College, Londonderry, Northern Ireland.

The Revd John M. Lewis is Head of Theology and Religious Studies at Trinity College, Carmarthen, Wales.

Dr Andrew G. McGrady is Lecturer in the Educational Department at Mater Dei Institute of Education, Dublin, Republic of Ireland.

Sister Alice Montgomery is Headteacher at the Ursuline College, Westgate-on-Sea, England, and Research Fellow in the Centre for Theology and Education at Trinity College, Carmarthen, Wales.

Professor Roger Murphy is Dean of the Faculty of Education, University of Nottingham, England.

Professor Karl Ernst Nipkow is Professor of Religious Education, emeritus, in the Faculty of Evangelical Theology, Department of Practical Theology, and a member of the Faculty of Social and Behavioural Sciences, at the University of Tübingen, Germany.

Ms Rebecca Nye is Research Assistant to the Children's Spirituality Project at the School of Education, University of Nottingham, England.

Dr Bernadette O'Keeffe is a Fellow of St Edmund's College, and Assistant Director of the Von Hugel Institute of St Edmund's College, Cambridge, England.

Dr -Ing. K. Helmut Reich is Research Fellow at the Pädagogisches Institut, University of Fribourg, Switzerland and Senior Professor at the School of Religious Studies and Sacred Traditions, (non residential) Senior University, Evanston, Wyoming, United States of America and Richmond, British Columbia, Canada.

Ms Mandy Robbins is Junior Research Fellow in the Centre for Theology and Education at Trinity College, Carmarthen, Wales.

Professor Friedrich Schweitzer is Professor of Practical Theology and Religious Education in the Faculty of Protestant Theology, Department of Practical Theology, at the University of Tübingen, Germany.

Ms Nicola Slee is Director of Studies at Aston Training Scheme, Birmingham, England.

Professor Kalevi Tamminen is Professor of Religious Education, emeritus, Department of Practical Theology, University of Helsinki, Finland.

Mrs Carolyn Wilcox is Research Fellow at the North of England Institute for Christian Education, Durham, England, and Research Fellow in the Centre for Theology and Education at Trinity College, Carmarthen, Wales.

Index of Names